MINOR LEAGUE BASEBALL STARS

Volume II

Career Records of Players and Managers

Compiled By

The Society for American Baseball Research

Minor League Baseball Stars
Volume II

In 1978 the Society for American Baseball Research (SABR) published the first volume of *Minor League Baseball Stars*. In addition to 20 pages of narrative and charts about the best season and career records, the book contained the lifetime playing records of about 175 of the leading minor league players of the past 100 years. That book has been updated and reprinted and is available for $5.00.

This second volume of *Minor League Baseball Stars* is similar in that it includes career playing records of about 175 additional minor league players. It also carries a section on the top 15 all-time minor league players selected by SABR, and a section on the greatest minor league managers.

The Society's Minor League Committee, headed by John F. Pardon of Crugers, NY, is the primary sponsor of this research compilation. L. Robert Davids, 4424 Chesapeake St. NW, Washington, DC 20016, is the editor. Robert C. McConnell of Wilmington, Delaware, and Robert C. Hoie of San Marino, California, assisted.

This volume can be obtained through the mail for $5.00 from SABR, P.O. Box 1010, Cooperstown, NY 13326. Information about the Society and its various activities and publications also may be obtained from that office.

Copyright 1985 Society for American Baseball Research
Typography and Printing by Ag Press, Manhattan, Kansas

Table of Contents

Introduction

About four months after *Minor League Baseball Stars* was published by the Society in July 1978, all the excess copies (beyond the 640 membership of SABR at that time) were sold out. Obviously, the "grass roots" interest in this modest compilation of minor league records was not anticipated. The book was immediately reprinted and the Society's Minor League Committee soon began consideration of a second volume. But who do you include in a follow-up publication when you have already taken the cream off the top?

Some readers felt all the cream was not included in the first volume — what about Zeke Bonura, Count Campau, Luke Easter, Wilbur Good, Bill Hart, Bill Norman, Prince Oana, Eddie Onslow, Lance Richbourg, Ben Tincup, Rube Vickers, and many others?

An ad hoc committee was established to draw up criteria for selection. Included would be all ten-year players with a .333 career batting average, 300 home runs, or 2500 hits (2000 if they played prior to 1900). For hurlers it was 250 wins or 2000 strikeouts. These players were automatics, as were a few others who squeezed into the top ten lifetime in various pitching and batting categories, including stolen bases. One example of a player who benefitted from additional research was 19th century pitcher Willie Mains, who is now credited with 318 minor league victories. In the meantime, a modern hurler, ageless George Brunet, vaulted to the all-time leadership in strikeouts.

In addition to the "automatics," most of whom had long, but not necessarily exciting careers, the committee selected about 40 other players who had more recognizable names, sometimes in other sports. Included are football stars Joe Guyon, Fred Sington, and Ken Strong; basketball pro Bill Sharman; and hockey Hall of Famer Doug Harvey. Blacks with brief O.B. careers who merit inclusion are 19th century stars Frank Grant and George Stovey and 20th century great Ray Dandridge.

Other features of this second volume include the all-time top 15 players selected by the Society for American Baseball Research, and the records of some of the outstanding minor league managers.

The records compiled in this volume are the result of a substantial team effort by SABR members. Participants include advisory panel members Ed Brooks, Willie George, Bob Hoie, Tom Hufford, Bob Lindsay, Vern Luse, Bob McConnell, Ray Nemec, John Pardon, and Bill Weiss. Also, Craig Carter of The Sporting News. Others assisting in various ways include:

			Steve St. Martin
John Benesch	Jerry Jackson	Ralph LinWeber	Art Schott
Larry Bump	Cliff Johnson	Robert Lynch	Bill Schroeder
Jack Carlson	Richard Juline	Jim Maywar	John Schwartz
Merritt Clifton	Cliff Kachline	Stephen Milman	Jamie Selko
Dean Coughenour	David Kemp	Joe Overfield	Tom Strother
Peter Culter	Dan Krueckeberg	Frank Phelps	Sharon Trigilio
Jack Dougherty	Wally Kuczwara	Bill Plott	Gary Waddingham
Karl Green	Jim Laughlin	Allen Quimby	Karl Wingler
Robert Gill	Joe Lawler	Eves Raja	Gene Wood

Smead Jolley, one of the all-time greatest minor league batters.

The Top Minor League Players

The Society has worked since its inception to gain some special recognition for long service minor league stars. This was not a new concept. In the early years of the Hall of Fame in Cooperstown, this subject was raised by publisher J.G. Taylor Spink of The Sporting News. In an editorial in the April 27, 1939, edition, he said in part:

> So far, the names nominated to the Hall of Fame have a decidedly major league tinge. None whose career has been almost completely bound up with the minors has been proposed. Yet the minors have played as important a part in the propagation of the game as have the majors and should have their niche in Cooperstown.

When the so-called centennial of baseball was celebrated at Cooperstown in the summer of 1939, the National Association of Professional Baseball Leagues did have one day of activities on July 9. A bronze tablet dedicated to the seven founders of the National Association in 1902 was unveiled. Two of them, John Farrell and Thomas Hickey, were present. At the National Association All-Star game in the afternoon, 38 players from many different leagues participated, but the top players were not there because contending teams did not have the money or inclination to send their stars halfway across the country. Although there were some recognizable names in the lineup, the only real all-star was Joe Hauser and he was not playing in O.B. in 1939.

There was a better representation of managers with Mike Kelley heading one team and Spencer Abbott (assisted by Larry Gilbert) the other. Ed Brooks summarizes the situation in his 1981 Research Journal article:

> The first and last National Association all-star game, the birth and death of a novel idea which might have become an annual event, marks the only significant involvement of the minor leagues in Hall of Fame activities and the beginning of major league dominance.

SABR efforts to recognize minor league greats through the proposed use of an existing or a new facility were discussed at the National Convention in Columbus, Ohio, in 1977, but eventually came to nought because of the recognizable financial problems involved in such an undertaking.

The publication of *Minor League Baseball Stars* in 1978 reawakened interest in this subject and the suggestion was made to the Hall of Fame in Cooperstown to consider including a minor league section in its museum. No action was taken.

In 1983 the Society conducted a survey of its membership to determine the top minor league players. Originally the plan was to select the top ten, but the concept was broadened by a review committee in 1984. The original selections were largely limited to heavy hitting first basemen and outfielders of the 1920s and 1930s, with emphasis on the Pacific Coast League. The committee expanded the total to 15 players by focusing on players of the full period from 1877 to 1984, on catchers and infielders other than first basemen, and on additional pitchers. The result was a collection of stars that represented nearly the full history of the minor leagues, a fairly good geographic representation by league play, and an effort was made to broaden the selections by position.

Hector Espino of the Mexican League was the only modern player selected. Perry Werden won the nod from the 19th century over Count Campau and pitcher Willie Mains. Shortstop Buster Chatham, while not considered as good a middle infielder as Ray French, was the consensus choice over French (who batted only .267), Eddie Mulligan, and Harry Strohm. The three pitchers selected were Tony Freitas, a southpaw, and righthanders Joe Martina and Frank Shellenback. Sam Gibson and Bill Thomas also received serious consideration.

Since the full playing records of the 15 all-time all-stars are carried in the first volume of *Minor League Baseball Stars,* we will carry here only a brief profile of each player, along with an outstanding season and the career summary.

RUSSELL LOUIS (BUZZ) ARLETT — Born January 3, 1899 at Oakland, CA. Died May 16, 1964 at Minneapolis, MN. Batted left and right; threw right. Ht. 6.03; Wt. 225. Started out as a pitcher and won 29 games for Oakland in 1920. Became a full-time outfielder in 1923 and quickly developed into a power hitter from both sides of the plate. Twice hit four home runs in a game for Baltimore in 1932. He set a minor league career record in home runs with 432, since broken. A colorful and popular player, he was a lackadaisical fielder. Here is his best year and his career record.

Pos. OF-P	G	AB	R	H	2B	3B	HR	RBI	SB	BA
1929 Oakland, PC	200	722	146	210	70*	8	39	189	22	.374
1918-37 PC-Mixed	2390	8001	1610	2726	598	107	432	1786	200	.341

ISAAC MORGAN (IKE) BOONE — Born February 17, 1897 at Samantha, AL. Died August 1, 1958 at Northport, AL. Batted left; threw right. Ht. 6.00; Wt. 200. This University of Alabama alumnus and brother of Danny Boone was probably the best of the pure hitters with a .370 minor league career average. He hit well wherever he played and his single season records in the Southern Association, Texas League, and Pacific Coast rank among the all-time best in those circuits. A player-manager with Toronto in 1934-36, he was a slow runner but had a good assist record in the outfield.

Pos. Outfielder	G	AB	R	H	2B	3B	HR	RBI	SB	BA
1929 Missions, PC	198	794	195*	323*	49	8	55*	218*	9	.407
1920-37 PC-Mixed	1857	6807	1362	2521	477	128	215	1334+	120	.370

HEINRICH NICHOLAS (NICK) CULLOP — Born Oct. 16, 1900 at Weldon Spring, MO. Died December 8, 1978 at Westerville, Ohio. Batted right; threw right. Ht. 6.00; Wt. 200. Started out as pitcher, winning 19 games for Madison and Minneapolis in 1920. As full-time outfielder with Omaha in 1924, hit 40 home runs. Was an aggressive and popular player and a good outfielder. Collected 1090 long hits and is career leader in RBIs. Minor League manager of year with Columbus in 1943 and Milwaukee in 1947.

Pos. OF-P	G	AB	R	H	2B	3B	HR	RBI	SB	BA
1930 Minn. AA	139	515	150*	185	28	9	54*	152*	8	.359
1920-44 AA-Mixed	2484	8571	1607	2670	523	147	420	1857+	154	.312

SMEAD POWELL JOLLEY — Born January 14, 1902 at Wesson, AK. Batted left; threw right. Ht. 6.03½; Wt. 202. Began as hurler, working in 97 games with 41-34 won-lost record in six years. A tremendous batter who also hit for power (334 home runs). Was six-time batting champion with marks of .397 and .404 with San Francisco in 1927-28. He was a slow runner and a defensive liability in outfield. He currently resides in Alameda, California.

Pos. Outfielder	G	AB	R	H	2B	3B	HR	RBI	SB	BA
1928 San Fran. PC	191	765	143	309*	52	10	45*	188*	9	.404
1922-41, PC-Mixed	2231	8298	1455	3037	612	75	334	1593+	61	.366

ANTHONY VINCENT (BUNNY) BRIEF (Real name: Antonio Bordetski) — Born July 3, 1892 at Remus, MI. Died February 10, 1963 at Milwaukee, WI. Batted right; threw right. Ht. 6.00; Wt. 185. He was the top run producer in the high minors and also led in home runs eight seasons. He was the American Association career leader in hits, runs, doubles, homers and RBI. A good base stealer and good defensive player at first base and in the outfield.

Pos. OF-1B	G	AB	R	H	2B	3B	HR	RBI	SB	BA
1921 Kansas City AA	164	615	166	222	51*	11	42*	191*	8	.359
1910-28, AA-Mixed	2426	8945	1776	2963	594	152	340	1776+	247	.331

ANTHONY SPENCER HARRIS — Born August 12, 1900 at Duluth, MN. Died July 3, 1982 at Minneapolis, MN. Batted left; threw left. Ht. 5.09; Wt. 160. A steady and durable player who set minor league career records in runs, hits, doubles, and total bases. Incomplete records also indicate he led in bases on balls, giving him a good on-base average. Most of his 258 home runs were hit for Minneapolis, where he starred for ten years. Playing the majority of his games in center field, he was good to average defensively.

Pos. OF-1B	G	AB	R	H	2B	3B	HR	RBI	SB	BA
1928 Minn. AA	169	669*	133*	219	41*	4	32*	127	25	.327
1921-48 AA-Mixed	3258	11377	2287*	3617*	743*	150	258	1769	241	.318

HECTOR ESPINO — Born June 6, 1939 at Chihuahua, Mexico. Bats right; throws right. Ht. 5.11; Wt. 185. Best of the Mexican League players with five batting titles to his credit. He declined opportunity to go up to the majors. Holds the minor league career record with 484 home runs. Once a good fielding first baseman (led in assists four straight years, 1967-70), but has slowed down in recent years. He is 45 and has played 25 years.

Pos. First Base	G	AB	R	H	2B	3B	HR	RBI	SB	BA
1964 Monterrey, Mex.	126	448	118*	166	22	3	46*	117	5	.371*
1960-84 Mexican	2500	8605	1597	2898	403	49	484*	1678	54	.337

ARNOLD JOHN (JIGGER) STATZ — Born October 20, 1897 at Waukegan, IL. Batted right; threw right. Ht. 5.07½; Wt. 150. Excellent outfielder who played all 18 years in the minors at highest classification, with Los Angeles in PCL. Consequently set league records for career games, hits, runs, doubles, and triples. Good hitter but no power. Good base stealer, swiping six bases in one game on September 16, 1934, and leading the league three times. Lives in Los Angeles area.

Pos. Outfielder	G	AB	R	H	2B	3B	HR	RBI	SB	BA
1931 Los Angeles PC	184	748	141*	248	42	13	6	107	45*	.332
1920-42 Pac. Coast	2790	10657	1996	3356	595	137	66	1044	466	.315

JOSEPH JOHN (UNSER CHOE) HAUSER — Born January 12, 1899 at Milwaukee, WI. Batted left; threw left. Ht. 5.10½; Wt. 175. Powerful hitter whose home run totals mounted dramatically in favorable parks. Only player to hit more than 60 homers in a season twice, 63 with Baltimore in 1930 and 69 with Minneapolis in 1933 (50 of which were hit in Nicollet Park). Also hit 49 in 1932 and 33 in 287 at bats in 1934. Adequate fielder at first base. Manager of four pennant-winners at Sheboygan in Wisconsin State League. Lives in Sheboygan.

Pos. 1B-OF	G	AB	R	H	2B	3B	HR	RBI	SB	BA
1933 Minn. AA	153	570	153*	189	35	4	69*	182*	1	.332
1918-42 AA-Mixed	1854	6426	1430	1923	340	116	399	1353	109	.299

PERCIVAL WHERITT (PERRY) WERDEN — Born July 21, 1865 at St. Louis, MO. Died January 9, 1934 at Minneapolis, MN. Batted right; threw right. Ht. 6.02; Wt. 210. Broke in as hurler with St. Louis in Union Association in 1884 with 12-1 mark. Became primarily a first baseman the next year and developed into the top slugger of the 19th century with several big batting years in the Western League. He also ran the bases well for his size. He was a very colorful performer who drew fans to the park.

Pos. 1B-OF-P	G	AB	R	H	2B	3B	HR	RBI	SB	BA
1895 Minn. Western	123	563	179	241*	39	7	45*	-	32	.428
1884-08 West-Mixed	1539	6221	1214	2119	390	87	168	-	349	.341

OSCAR GEORGE (OX) ECKHARDT — Born December 23, 1901 at Yorktown, Texas. Died April 22, 1951 at Yorktown, Texas. Batted left; threw right. Ht. 6.01; Wt. 190. Was outstanding hitter with limited power over fairly short career of 13 full seasons. Batted incredible .382 over five seasons in PCL, including top mark of .414 in 1933. Hit 27 triples in Western League in 1928 and 55 doubles in Texas League in 1930. Was poor to average as defensive outfielder and was average base runner.

Pos. Outfielder	G	AB	R	H	2B	3B	HR	RBI	SB	BA
1933 Missions PC	189*	760	145	315*	56	16	12	143	15	.414
1925-40 PC-Mixed	1926	7563	1275	2773	455	146	66	1037	140	.367

CHARLES L. (BUSTER) CHATHAM — Born December 25, 1901, at West, Texas. Died December 15, 1975, at Waco, Texas. Batted right; threw right. Ht. 5.05; Wt. 150. Started out as center fielder in 1923 but was converted to shortstop. He was very fast in the field and on the bases and had surprising power at the plate. Scrappy, heads-up player who sparked Atlanta to three pennants in the 1930s and was hero of Dixie sweep of Beaumont in 1938. Reached base 15 consecutive times on 11 hits and 4 walks for Pueblo June 9-10, 1929.

Pos. SS-OF-3B	G	AB	R	H	2B	3B	HR	RBI	SB	BA
1929 Pueblo Western	116	446	112	172	32	10	13	81	23	.386*
1923-45 Southern-Mix.	2966	10578	1739	3067	504	182	132	1082+	312	.290

Frank Shellenback

Arnold (Jigger) Statz

Perry Werden in 1920

Buster Chatham in 1929

ANTONIO (TONY) FREITAS — Born May 5, 1908 at Mill Valley, CA. Threw left; batted right. Ht. 5.08; Wt. 161. Was top southpaw winner in minors with 342 victories, in spite of losing three years to military in WWII. Was great control pitcher and had most 20-win seasons in minors with nine. Led in complete games four straight years, 1937-40, and had fine ERA of 3.11 in robust hitting era. Presently resides at Orangevalle, California.

Pos. Pitcher	G	IP	W	L	H	R	ER	BB	SO	ERA
1938 Sacramento PC	38	290	24	11	298	103	86	46	159	2.79
1928-53, PC-Mixed	736	4905	342	238	5090	2073	1694	932	2324	3.11

JOHN JOSEPH (OYSTER JOE) MARTINA — Born July 8, 1889, at New Orleans, LA. Died March 22, 1962, at New Orleans, LA. Threw right; batted right. Ht. 6.00; Wt. 183. Hardworking and consistent hurler in Texas League and Southern Association who set career mark with 2770 strikeouts, since broken. Also Texas League career leader in strikeouts. Won 349 games, second highest in minors and won 20 or more games seven years.

Pos. Pitcher	G	IP	W	L	H	R	ER	BB	SO	ERA
1919 Beaumont, Texas	46	378*	28*	13	323	124	90	109	150	2.14
1910-31, Texas-South.	833	5417	349	277	4950	2307	1355	1868	2770	3.22

FRANK VICTOR (SHELLY) SHELLENBACK — Born December 16, 1898 at Joplin, MO. Died August 17, 1969, at Newton, MA. Threw right; batted right. Ht. 6.02; Wt. 200. As spitball hurler, was not eligible to return to majors after 1920, although he had some very good seasons. Won 295 games in PCL, including 26 in 1929 and 1932 and 27 in 1931. Won 15 straight games in 1931 and 33 of 34 over the 1930-31 seasons. Was good hitter as pitcher-pinch hitter with 63 home runs and .271 batting average.

Pos. Pitcher-PH	G	IP	W	L	H	R	ER	BB	SO	ERA
1931 Hollywood PC	36	306	27	7	305	118	97	61	127	2.85
1917-38, Pac. Coast	38	4514	315	192	4922	2110	1775	1021	1742	3.55

Minor League Managers

Almost all the top minor league players advanced to the major leagues, at least for one trial. This is not true of the most successful long-service managers. Only four of the 20 whose records we carry managed in the Big Time — John McCloskey, Billy Murray, Bob Coleman and Bill Meyer — and only Murray did reasonably well at that level. But success in the major leagues is not a criterion for selection of the top minor league pilots.

In this selection, primary emphasis is placed on longevity, particularly in the higher minors, on winning percentage, and on special contributions. Efforts also are made to have a reasonably balanced selection from the primary leagues and from the full period of minor league history. We were quite successful on the latter point as each year from 1888 to 1984 is covered by one or more managers — from John McCloskey to Stan Wasiak.

First let us deal with longevity, which is closely tied to success in managing. There was no minor league equivalent to Connie Mack and the Philadelphia Athletics. However, there were several minor league pilots who had long association with one club, some even to the extent of executive or ownership affiliation. For example, Jack Dunn managed 21 years at Baltimore; Bob Coleman had 20 years at Evansville; Mike Kelley 18 at St. Paul, Lefty O'Doul 17 at San Francisco; Jake Atz 16 at Forth Worth; and Larry Gilbert 15 at New Orleans.

Coleman managed a total of 35 years, most of it in the Three Eye League, between 1919 and 1957. This broke the old record of 34 years set by Spencer Abbott, who managed 24 different clubs between 1903 and 1947. Abbott, who was from the John McGraw school of belligerent and aggressively shrewd managers, never spent more than three years with one club, but always seemed to be in demand. Another long-service pilot who was seldom out of a job was William "Derby Bill" Clymer, whose tenure ran from 1898 to 1932. He had three straight pennant-winners at Columbus in 1905-06-07 and later in his career managed six clubs (Louisville, Seattle, Columbus, Toledo, Tulsa and Newark) in a five-year period (1918-22).

Coleman also shifted around in his early years but always seemed to return to Evansville, where, in 1951 he also became president and part-owner. During his total of 35 years, Coleman won 2496 games, still the record in the minor leagues. The previous leader in games won was Mike Kelley (2390), long associated with baseball in the twin cities of Minneapolis and St. Paul. He was the American Association manager who won the most games in one season (115 with St. Paul in 1920) and over his career (2293). In fact, that is the most games won by a manager in any one league. Larry Gilbert won the most in the Southern Association (2128); Jack Dunn won 2107 in the International League; Lefty O'Doul 2094 in the PCL; Coleman 1701 in the Three Eye; and Jake Atz 1565 in the Texas League.

Coleman ended his long managing career with 2103 losses, which exceeded Kelley's total by one. This stood as the record until 1984 when Stan Wasiak set a new mark of 2171. Wasiak is one of several modern managers to have long careers in the minors, a phenomenon which does not carry over to current players. Several of the others include Andy Gilbert with 29 years (1950-82); John (Red) Davis and Walt Dixon, both with 27 years (1949-76); Merrill (Pinky) May with 26 (1947-72) and Cal Ermer with 25 (1950-84). Another active manager, Dick Berardino, just completed his 16th consecutive season with Elmira in the New York-Penn League.

Wasiak, a faithful manager in the Brooklyn-Los Angeles Dodgers' organization for many years, started at Valdosta in the Georgia-Florida League in 1950 and gradually worked his way up to Albuquerque in 1973. He was 79-67 with Vero Beach in 1984, giving him a career total of 2395 wins and 2171 losses. This moved him into second place behind Coleman in wins and into first place in losses. His 35 consecutive years of managing was made possible by his appearance, after a lengthy illness, in one game in 1982. He will set a new record for years managed in 1985.

Billy Murray, who did most of his minor league managing in the late 19th century, tops the list of long-service managers when it comes to winning percentage. In 18 seasons he racked up a total of 1234 wins and 876 losses for a lofty .585 mark. Unfortunately, his total of wins is not that impressive because most leagues played a fairly short schedule in his era of 1889-1906.

Jack Dunn clearly stands out as the percentage leader since 1900. Thanks largely to his seven consecutive pennants with Baltimore, 1919 to 1925, he compiled a .579 winning percentage over 24 years. Dunn, who introduced Babe Ruth to Organized Baseball in 1914, was owner-manager of the Orioles and built the club into an International League powerhouse. The Orioles won 27 consecutive games in 1921. He is generally regarded as the top minor league pilot.

The chief challenger to Dunn probably was Larry Gilbert, who managed only two clubs, New Orleans and Nashville in the Southern Association. He established no dynasty with either club, but won nine pennants and had a .567 winning percentage over 25 years. He retired from the field in 1932 and became president of the New Orleans club. In that capacity he hired Texas League great Jake Atz to manage the Pelicans. The club finished in sixth place that season and Gilbert resumed the managerial reigns in 1933. He won the pennant and the playoffs. In 1939 he moved to Nashville and won four more pennants, the last one in 1948, his final year.

Other managers who had high career percentages in the minors include Jack Lelivelt .564, Johnny Dobbs and Ben Geraghty, both at .563. Jake Atz, Bill Meyer, and Bill Clymer were a few notches lower at .549, .548 and .546. The stress of managing at such a fast pace apparently was too much for three high-percentage performers who died in harness of heart attacks. Dunn died while riding horseback a month after the close of the 1928 season. Lelivelt, who had skippered Seattle to the Pacific Coast League title in 1940, succumbed January 20, 1941, at 55. Ben Geraghty was only 48 when he died June 18, 1963, in Jacksonville, Florida, where he was pilot of the International League club. His death came 17 years after he was severely injured June 24, 1946, in a roadtrip bus accident which took the lives of nine of his teammates on the Spokane club. This accident contributed to his transition from player to manager of Spokane in 1947.

Murray, Lelivelt, Dunn and Atz enhanced their career records with outstanding individual season marks. Murray, who led Joliet to a 32-4 first-half record in 1892, set the highest International (Eastern) League standard with Jersey City in 1903 when his club had a 92-32 (.742) record. In 1934, Lelivelt's Los Angeles Angels accumulated a 137-50 won-lost (.733) mark, easily the best in PCL history. Dunn, who won 100 or

John J. McCloskey, between managing assignments at age 64 in 1926.

more games for eight years in a row, 1919-26, compiled three percentage years over .700.

Ironically, in essentially the same years Dunn was dominating the International League, Jake Atz and his Fort Worth Panthers were riding roughshod over their Texas League opponents. Atz won the 1919 second-half championship and 1920 through 1925. In three of those seasons, the club's percentage was over .700. Finishing first was a special treat for him. He said his original name was Zimmerman but he changed it to Atz in 1900 after being in a baseball team payline where the money ran out before they got to him.

Some managers whose career won-lost records were not among the leaders were nevertheless much sought after for their recognized ability to get the best out of their players and to prepare them for the majors. In that category falls the aforementioned Abbott, along with John McCloskey, Bruno Betzel and Lefty O'Doul. O'Doul, who won only three pennants in 23 years, was a very popular manager on the West Coast. In the League's last 200-game schedule, in 1950, he split it down the middle with 100 wins and 100 losses. The next year the Seals finished eighth and he was through at San Francisco, but not in the PCL. San Diego, Oakland, Vancouver and Seattle all made use of his talents and popularity.

Betzel, whose full name was Christian Frederick Albert John Henry David Betzel, ended his 26-year career in 1956 by winning the pennant for Toronto. It was his seventh championship, each with a different club, but was not quite enough to put his career percentage over .500. He won 1887 games and lost 1892 for .499, but he was one of the better managers.

John McCloskey's won-lost record was not much over .500, but he merits inclusion because of his longevity and special contributions. His managerial career started in 1888 in the Texas League, which he organized. By the time he called it a career with the Akron club in 1932, he had organized five other leagues and managed 30 different clubs in O.B. When he would organize a new league, he usually would take over the weakest club in order to keep the league viable. He managed teams in such formerly remote areas as Great Falls, Montana; Boise, Idaho; Ogden, Utah; Vancouver, British Columbia; Salina, Kansas; and El Paso, Texas. He ran the gamut of high and low league classifications. He did get two trials in the majors, with Louisville in 1895-96 and the St. Louis Cardinals in 1906-08, and both clubs did poorly. A medicore player himself, he was good at spotting new talent. "Honest John" McCloskey was a popular and well respected leader who stimulated interest in baseball in many areas of the country over a period of 44 years.

Frank Shaughnessy was a pennant winner six times, his first title coming in his initial season as player-manager at Roanoke in the Virginia League in 1909. He won four consecutive pennants in 1912-15, the last three with Ottawa in the Canadian League. His managerial career was relatively short, however, as his remarkable executive ability drew him into the front office. While he was general manager of the Montreal club in 1933 he sold the proposal to the International League that the top four clubs engage in post-season playoffs. The "Shaughnessy Playoffs," which were adopted by many other leagues, were believed to have saved numerous clubs from financial failure, particularly during the Great Depression years. Shaughnessy returned as field manager at Montreal in 1935 and won his last pennant; ironically he lost the playoffs. The next year he began a 25-year stretch as president of the International League.

One manager who benefitted disproportionately from the playoff system was Clay Hopper. He won seven playoff championships and four of them came in years when his club didn't win the pennant. Hopper's main contribution in a 25-year managerial career probably resulted from his effective integration of black players into the Brooklyn Dodger organization when he was manager of Montreal in 1946-49. Such players as Jackie Robinson, Roy Campanella, and Don Newcombe gave the former Mississippi plantation owner good marks for the way he handled the sensitive racial situation.

Were there good players among the top 20 minor league managers? More than one-half appeared at least briefly in the majors. Lefty O'Doul was undoubtedly the best hitter. Frank Shaughnessy was a good base stealer in the lower classifications. Larry Gilbert and Jack Lelivelt were two others who had good playing records. Gilbert's record appeared in the first issue of Minor League Baseball Stars; Lelivelt's playing record is in this book.

Carried below is a summary of the top 20 minor league managers listed alphabetically. The full individual records follow.

Years	Manager	Won	Lost	Pct.	Pennants
34	Spencer Abbott	2180	2037	.517	4
27	Jake Atz	1972	1619	.549	7
35	Bob Coleman	2496*	2103	.543	4½
26	Bruno Betzel	1887	1892	.499	7
27	John (Red) Davis	1993	1927	.508	5
29	Bill Clymer	2122	1762	.546	7
25	Johnny Dobbs	1918	1487	.563	6
24	Jack Dunn	2107	1530	.579	9*
29	Andy Gilbert	2009	1899	.514	2½ + 3 Div.
25	Larry Gilbert	2128	1627	.567	9*
17	Ben Geraghty	1317	1021	.563	5 + 1 Div.
25	Clay Hopper	1916	1675	.534	5½
30	Mike Kelley	2390	2102	.532	5
20	Jack Lelivelt	1861	1439	.564	5
31	John McCloskey	1713	1632	.512	5½
19	Bill Meyer	1605	1325	.548	8
18	Billy Murray	1234	876	.585*	5
23	Lefty O'Doul	2094	1970	.515	3
19	Frank Shaughnessy	1148	1012	.531	6
35	Stan Wasiak	2395	2171*	.525	3 + 6½ Div.

SPENCER ABBOTT
Born August 27, 1877 at Chicago, IL.
Died December 18, 1951 at Washington, DC

Year	Club	League	Pos.	W	L	Pct.	
1903	Fargo	Northern		5	8	.375	(in 8/19)
1904	Topeka	Mo. Valley		23	23	.500	(in 7/28)
1905	Topeka	West. Assn.	7	54	80	.403	
1906	Hutchinson	West. Assn.		21	25	.457	(6/15 to 8/1)
1910	Wellington	Kansas St.		19	16	.543	(6/5 to 7/11)
1911	Lyons	Kansas St.	3	37	27	.578	
1913	San Diego	So. Calif.		31	13	.705	(out 6/4)
	Pasadena-S.B.	So. Calif.		7	17	.292	(in 6/5)
	Santa Barbara	So. Calif.	1	9	5	.643	(Second half)
1914	Keokuk	Cent. Assn.		37	44	.457	(out 7/23)

Spencer Abbott (continued)

Year	Club	League	Pos.	W	L	Pct.	
1919	Tulsa	Western	2	77	63	.550	
1920	Tulsa	Western	1	92	61	.601	
1921	Memphis	Southern A.	1	104	49	.680	
1922	Memphis	Southern A.	2	94	58	.618	
1923	Reading	Int.	3	85	79	.518	
1924	Reading	Int.	7	63	98	.391	
1925	Reading	Int.		20	22	.476	(out 5/30)
1926	Kansas City	A.A.	5	87	78	.527	
1927	Jersey City	Int.	7	66	100	.398	
1928	Pueblo	Western	2	45	36	.556	
			5	41	45	.477	
1929	Pueblo	Western		56	73	.434	(in 5/21)
1930	Omaha	Western	2	76	66	.535	
1931	Portland	PC	2	50	38	.568	
			4	49	49	.500	
1932	Portland	PC	1	111	78	.587	
1933	Portland	PC	2	105	77	.577	
1934	Atlanta	Southern A.	3	37	33	.529	
				31	40	.437	(out 9/8)
1936	Des Moines	Western	4	33	33	.500	
			3	31	31	.500	
1937	Seattle	PC		20	27	.426	(out 5/23)
	Trenton	NY-Penn		34	48	.415	(in 6/24)
1938	Trenton	Eastern	7	62	77	.446	
1939	Springfield	Eastern	3	74	66	.529	
1940	Springfield	Eastern	5	68	69	.496	
1941	Williamsport	Eastern	2	82	55	.599	
1942	Williamsport	Eastern	5	76	63	.547	
1943	Springfield	Eastern	7	46	88	.343	
1946	Charlotte	Tri-State	1	93	46	.669	(Won playoff)
1947	Charlotte	Tri-State		29	33	.468	(out 6/21)
				2180	**2037**	**.517**	

Coach with Washington Senators, 1935

JACOB HENRY ATZ
Born July 1, 1879 at Washington, DC
Died May 22, 1945 at New Orleans, LA

Year	Club	League	Pos.	W	L	Pct.	
1911	Providence	Eastern		39	69	.361	(in 6/10)
1914	Ft. Worth	Texas		29	34	.460	(in 7/7)
1915	Ft. Worth	Texas		50	41	.549	(in 6/15)
1916	Ft. Worth	Texas		46	34	.575	(out 7/4)
1917	Ft. Worth	Texas	2	91	70	.565	
1918	Ft. Worth	Texas	2	47	39	.547	
1919	Ft. Worth	Texas	2	38	30	.559	(Lost playoff)
			1	56	30	.651	
1920	Ft. Worth	Texas	1	45	19	.703	
			1	63	21	.750	
1921	Ft. Worth	Texas	1	56	25	.691	
			1	51	26	.662	
1922	Ft. Worth	Texas	1	50	22	.694	
			1	59	24	.711	
1923	Ft. Worth	Texas	1	96	56	.632	
1924	Ft. Worth	Texas	1	51	23	.689	
			1	58	18	.763	
1925	Ft. Worth	Texas	1	54	22	.711	
			1t	49	26	.653	
1926	Ft. Worth	Texas	3	83	73	.532	
1927	Ft. Worth	Texas	4	77	79	.494	

Jacob Henry Atz (continued)

Year	Club	League	Pos.	W	L	Pct.	
1928	Ft. Worth	Texas	2	46	32	.590	
			4	37	41	.474	
1929	Ft. Worth	Texas	4	41	39	.513	(out 7/1)
1930	Dallas	Texas	8	23	51	.311	
			6	35	42	.455	
1931	Shreveport	Texas	7	33	46	.418	
			7	33	48	.407	
1932	New Orleans	Southern A	6	66	84	.440	
1933	Ft. Worth	Texas		49	66	.426	(in 5/18)
1934	Tulsa	Texas	5	77	75	.507	
1936	Galveston	Texas		42	69	.378	(in 5/29)
1938	Harlingen	Tex. Valley	2	84	53	.613	(Won playoff)
1939	Henderson	E. Texas	1	85	55	.607	
1940	Henderson	E. Texas	5	23	24	.489	
			1	56	31	.644	(Lost playoff)
1941	Winston-Salem	Piedmont	8	54	82	.397	
				1972	**1619**	**.549**	

Infielder in majors four years between 1902 and 1909.

BRUNO BETZEL
(Full name: Christian Frederick Albert John Henry David Betzel)
Born December 6, 1894 in Chattanooga, OH
Died February 7, 1965, in West Hollywood, FL

Year	Club	League	Pos.	W	L	Pct.	
1927	Indianapolis	A.A.	6	70	98	.417	
1928	Indianapolis	A.A.	1	99	68	.593	
1929	Indianapolis	A.A.	4	78	89	.468	
1930	Topeka	Western	7	66	84	.440	
1932	Louisville	A.A.	8	67	101	.399	
1933	Louisville	A.A.	6	70	83	.458	
1934	Louisville	A.A.		29	34	.460	(out 6/22)
1935	Ft. Wayne	III	5	21	33	.389	
			4	31	38	.449	
1936	Allentown	NY-Penn	6	34	35	.493	
			4	37	33	.529	
1937	Elmira	NY-Penn	1	84	51	.622	(Won playoff)
1938	Binghamton	Eastern	1	84	51	.622	(Lost playoff)
1939	Binghamton	Eastern	6	71	69	.507	
1940	Binghamton	Eastern	2	77	62	.554	(Won playoff)
1941	Durham	Piedmont	1	84	53	.613	(Won playoff)
1942	Durham	Piedmont	5	65	70	.481	
1943	Durham	Piedmont	6	44	86	.338	
1944	Montreal	Int.	6	73	80	.477	
1945	Montreal	Int.	1	95	58	.621	(Lost playoff)
1946	Jersey City	Int.	8	57	96	.373	
1947	Jersey City	Int.	1	94	60	.610	(Lost playoff)
1948	Jersey City	Int.	7	69	83	.454	
1950	Syracuse	Int.	6	74	79	.484	
1951	Syracuse	Int.	3	82	71	.536	
1952	Syracuse	Int.	2	88	66	.571	
1953	Syracuse	Int.	7	58	95	.379	
1956	Toronto	Int.	1	86	66	.566	(Lost playoff)
				1887	**1892**	**.499**	

Infielder with St. Louis Cardinals, 1914-18

WILLIAM JOHNSTON (DERBY BILL) CLYMER
Born December 18, 1873 at Philadephia, PA
Died December 26, 1936 at Philadelphia, PA

Year	Club	League	Pos.	W	L	Pct.	
1898	Rochester	Eastern		9	4	.692	(5/25 to 6/6)
1900	Wilkes-Barre	Atlantic	2	24	13	.649	
1902	Louisville	A.A.	2	92	45	.672	
1903	Louisville	A.A.	2	87	54	.617	
1904	Columbus	A.A.	2	88	61	.591	
1905	Columbus	A.A.	1	100	52	.658	
1906	Columbus	A.A.	1	91	57	.615	
1907	Columbus	A.A.	1	90	64	.584	
1908	Columbus	A.A.	3	86	68	.558	
1909	Columbus	A.A.		71	76	.483	(out 9/12)
1910	Wilkes-Barre	NY State	1	85	53	.616	
1911	Wilkes-Barre	NY State	1	82	61	.573	
1912	Wilkes-Barre	NY State	2	81	57	.587	
1913	Buffalo	Int.	4	78	75	.510	
1914	Buffalo	Int.	2	89	61	.593	
1915	Toronto	Int.	3	72	67	.518	
1916	Louisville	A.A.	1	101	66	.605	
1917	Louisville	A.A.	3	88	66	.571	
1918	Louisville	A.A.	4	41	36	.532	
1919	Seattle	PC		38	70	.352	(out 8/5)
1920	Columbus	A.A.	7	66	99	.400	
1921	Toledo	A.A.		31	39	.443	(out 7/1)
	Tulsa	Western		36	47	.434	(in 7/12)
1922	Newark	Int.	8	54	112	.325	
1926	Buffalo	Int.	4	92	72	.561	
1927	Buffalo	Int.	1	112	56	.667	
1928	Buffalo	Int.	2	92	76	.548	
1929	Buffalo	Int.	5	83	84	.497	
1930	Buffalo	Int.		31	30	.508	(out 6/20)
1932	Scranton	NY-Penn		30	41	.423	(out 7/10)
				2122	**1762**	**.546**	

Shortstop in three games for Philadelphia (AA) in 1891. Coach, Cincinnati Reds, 1925

ROBERT HUNTER COLEMAN
Born September 26, 1890 at Huntingburg, IN
Died July 16, 1959 at Boston, MA

Year	Club	League	Pos.	W	L	Pct.	
1919	Mobile	Southern A	4	67	69	.493	
1920	Mobile	Southern A	6	68	86	.442	
1921	Terre Haute	III	3	70	65	.519	
1922	Terre Haute	III	1	85	51	.625	
1923	San Antonio	Texas	2	81	68	.544	
1924	San Antonio	Texas	5	38	36	.514	
			3	37	39	.487	
1925	San Antonio	Texas	3	42	33	.560	
			4	39	31	.557	
1927	Knoxville	Sally	3	79	68	.537	
1928	Evansville	III	6	30	31	.492	
			4t	32	37	.464	
1929	Evansville	III	3	79	57	.581	
1930	Evansville	III	4t	33	33	.500	
			1	46	22	.676	(Lost playoff)
1931	Evansville	III	6	25	30	.455	
			2	42	28	.600	
1932	Decatur	III	6	20	37	.351	
			4	4	6	.400	
1933	Beaumont	Texas	5	73	79	.480	

Robert Hunter Coleman (continued)

Year	Club	League	Pos.	W	L	Pct.	
1934	St. Paul	A.A.	7	67	84	.444	
1935	Springfield	III	1	36	17	.679	
			2	38	28	.576	(Lost playoff)
1936	San Antonio	Texas	6	73	77	.487	
1937	Scranton	NY-Penn	6	63	75	.457	
1938	Evansville	III	1	77	47	.621	
1939	Evansville	III	2	73	48	.603	
1940	Evansville	III	4	68	55	.553	
1941	Evansville	III	1	80	45	.640	
1942	Evansville	III	3	65	54	.546	
1944	Boston	National	6	65	89	.422	
1945	Boston	National	7	42	49	.462	(out 7/30)
1946	Evansville	III	3	68	51	.571	(Won playoff)
1947	Evansville	III	5	70	55	.560	
1948	Evansville	III	3	67	54	.554	(Won playoff)
1949	Evansville	III	1	74	51	.592	(Lost playoff)
1950	Milwaukee	A.A.	6	68	85	.444	
1951	Evansville	III	2	69	60	.535	
1952	Evansville	III	1	74	47	.612	
1953	Evansville	III	3	70	59	.543	
1954	Evansville	III	1	81	54	.600	
1955	Evansville	III	5	60	66	.476	
1956	Evansville	III	1	47	19	.712	
			1	37	17	.685	
1957	Evansville	III	1	81	49	.623	
		Majors		**107**	**138**	**.437**	
		Minors		**2496**	**2103**	**.543**	

Catcher in majors 1913-16; Coach, Boston Red Sox 1926; Detroit 1932; Boston Braves 1943

JOHN HUMPHREY (RED) DAVIS
Born July 15, 1915 at Laurel Run, PA

Year	Club	League	Pos.	W	L	Pct.	
1949	Greenville	Big State	6	66	82	.446	
1950	Corpus Christi	R.G. Valley	3	79	64	.552	(Won playoffs)
1951	Corpus Christi	Gulf Coast	1	98	56	.636	(Lost playoffs)
1952	Paris	Big State	5	79	68	.537	
1953	Paris	Big State	8	48	96	.333	
1954	Mayfield	Kitty	2	37	22	.627	
			6	27	30	.474	
1955	Dallas	Texas	1	93	67	.581	(Lost playoffs)
1956	Dallas	Texas	2	94	60	.610	
1957	Minneapolis	A.A.	3	85	69	.552	
1958	Phoenix	PC	1	89	65	.578	
1959	Phoenix	PC	8	64	90	.416	
1960	Tacoma	PC	2	81	73	.526	
1961	Tacoma	PC	1	97	57	.630	
1962	Tacoma	PC	3	81	73	.526	
1963	Rocky Mount	Carolina	3E	72	72	.500	
1964	Macon	Southern	3	75	65	.536	
1965	Knoxville	Southern	4	73	66	.525	
1966	Buffalo	Int.	5	72	74	.493	
1967	Pawtucket	Eastern	4E	67	71	.486	
1968	Portland	PC	3W	72	72	.500	
1969	Portland	PC	4N	57	89	.390	
1970	Waterbury	Eastern	1	79	62	.560	
1971	Waterbury	Eastern	3	68	70	.493	
1972	Charleston	Int.	2	80	64	.556	
1974	Oklahoma City	A.A.	3W	62	73	.459	
1975	Oklahoma City	A.A.	4W	50	86	.368	
1976	Williamsport	Eastern	4S	48	91	.345	
				1993	**1927**	**.508**	

Played third base for New York Giants, 1941.

JOHN GORDON DOBBS
Born June 3, 1876 at Chattanooga, TN
Died September 9, 1934 at Charlotte, NC

Year	Club	League	Pos.	W	L	Pct.	
1907	Nashville	Southern A	8	59	78	.431	
1909	Chattanooga	Sally	1	45	16	.738	
			2	37	20	.649	(Won playoff)
1910	Chattanooga	Southern A	4	66	71	.482	
1911	Montgomery	Southern A	2	77	58	.570	
1912	Montgomery	Southern A	6	64	75	.460	
1913	Montgomery	Southern A	5	68	69	.496	
1914	New Orleans	Southern A	3	80	65	.552	
1915	New Orleans	Southern A	1	91	63	.591	
1916	New Orleans	Southern A	2	73	61	.545	
1917	New Orleans	Southern A	2	89	61	.593	
1918	New Orleans	Southern A	1	49	21	.700	
1919	New Orleans	Southern A	3	74	61	.548	
1920	New Orleans	Southern A	2	86	62	.581	
1921	New Orleans	Southern A	2	97	57	.630	
1922	New Orleans	Southern A	3	89	64	.582	
1923	Memphis	Southern A	3	76	70	.521	
1924	Memphis	Southern A	1	104	49	.680	
1925	Birmingham	Southern A	7	67	85	.441	
1926	Birmingham	Southern A	3	87	61	.588	
1927	Birmingham	Southern A	2	91	63	.591	
1928	Birmingham	Southern A	1	50	26	.658	
			2	49	28	.636	(Won playoff)
1929	Birmingham	Southern A	1	93	60	.608	
1930	Atlanta	Southern A	4	84	69	.549	
1931	Atlanta	Southern A	6	63	65	.492	(Spd. 5/26 to 6/20)
1933	Charlotte	Piedmont		10	9	.526	(out 5/16)
				1918	**1487**	**.563**	

Outfielder in major leagues 1901-05
Co-owner of Charlotte club when he died in 1934

Johnny Dobbs

Jack Dunn

JOHN JOSEPH (JACK) DUNN
Born October 6, 1872 at Meadville, PA
Died October 22, 1928 at Baltimore, MD

Year	Club	League	Pos.	W	L	Pct.
1905	Providence	Eastern	1	83	47	.638
1906	Providence	Eastern	6	65	75	.464
1907	Baltimore	Eastern	6	68	69	.496
1908	Baltimore	Eastern	1	83	57	.593
1909	Baltimore	Eastern	7	67	86	.438
1910	Baltimore	Eastern	3	83	70	.542
1911	Baltimore	Eastern	2	95	58	.621
1912	Baltimore	Eastern	4	74	75	.497
1913	Baltimore	Int.	3	77	73	.513
1914	Baltimore	Int.	6	72	77	.483
1915	Richmond	Int.	7	59	81	.421
1916	Baltimore	Int.	4	74	66	.529
1917	Baltimore	Int.	3	88	61	.591
1918	Baltimore	Int.	3	74	53	.583
1919	Baltimore	Int.	1	100	49	.671
1920	Baltimore	Int.	1	110	43	.719
1921	Baltimore	Int.	1	119	47	.717
1922	Baltimore	Int.	1	115	52	.689
1923	Baltimore	Int.	1	111	53	.677
1924	Baltimore	Int.	1	117	48	.709
1925	Baltimore	Int.	1	105	61	.633
1926	Baltimore	Int.	2	101	65	.608
1927	Baltimore	Int.	5	85	82	.509
1928	Baltimore	Int.	6	82	82	.500
				2107	**1530**	**.579**

Pitcher and utility player in majors 1897-1904
Transferred club to Richmond in 1915 to avoid competition with Baltimore Federal League club.
Eastern League and International League were same organization in this period; only the name was changed.

BENJAMIN RAYMOND GERAGHTY
Born July 19, 1914 at Jersey City, NJ
Died June 18, 1963 at Jacksonville, FL

Year	Club	League	Pos.	W	L	Pct.	
1947	Spokane	West Int.	2	87	67	.565	
1948	Meridian	Southeastern		15	31	.326	(out 5/30)
	Palatka	Fla. St.	8	17	44	.279	(in 6/30)
1949	Bristol	Appalach.	3	76	41	.650	
1950	Bristol	Appalach.	5	34	30	.531	
			2	40	16	.714	(Won playoffs)
1951	Jacksonville	Sally	2	79	58	.577	
1952	Jacksonville	Sally	7	69	85	.448	
1953	Jacksonville	Sally	1	93	44	.679	(Lost playoffs)
1954	Jacksonville	Sally	1	83	57	.593	(Lost playoffs)
1955	Jacksonville	Sally	2	79	61	.564	
1956	Jacksonville	Sally	1	87	53	.621	(Won playoffs)
1957	Wichita	A.A.	1	93	61	.604	(Lost playoffs)
1958	Wichita	A.A.	2	83	71	.539	
1959	Louisville	A.A.	1E	97	65	.599	(Lost playoffs)
1960	Louisville	A.A.	2	85	68	.556	(Won playoffs)
1961	Louisville	A.A.	2	80	70	.533	(Won playoffs)
1962	Jacksonville	Int.	1	94	60	.610	(Lost playoffs)
1963	Jacksonville	Int.	4S	26	39	.400	(Died 6/18)
				1317	**1021**	**.563**	

Infielder in majors parts of three seasons, 1936-44.

ANDREW GILBERT
Born July 18, 1916 at Bradenville, PA

Year	Club	League	Pos.	W	L	Pct.	
1950	Springfield	Ohio-Ind.	4	72	64	.529	
1951	Springfield	Ohio-Ind.	3	30	27	.526	
			2	24	31	.436	
1952	Muskogee	West. Assn.	1	40	24	.625	
			4	33	42	.440	(Lost playoffs)
1953	Danville	Carolina	2	79	59	.572	(Won playoffs)
1954	Danville	Carolina	5	70	69	.504	
1955	Danville	Carolina	2	73	64	.533	(Won playoffs)
1956	Johnstown	Eastern	8	16	33	.327	(out 6/18)
1957	Muskogee	Sooner St.	3	71	55	.563	
1958	Springfield	Eastern	2	36	35	.507	
			2	32	30	.516	
1959	Springfield	Eastern	1	85	55	.607	(Won playoffs)
1960	Springfield	Eastern	3	69	70	.496	
1961	Springfield	Eastern	1	85	54	.612	
1962	Springfield	Eastern	4	68	71	.489	
1963	Tacoma	PC	3N	79	79	.500	
1964	Springfield	Eastern	3	77	63	.550	
1965	Springfield	Eastern	3	63	77	.450	
1966	Waterbury	Eastern	5	64	76	.457	
1967	Waterbury	Eastern	3E	71	69	.507	
1968	Amarillo	Texas	3W	67	71	.486	
1969	Amarillo	Texas	1W	80	55	.593	(Lost playoffs)
1970	Amarillo	Texas	4W	57	78	.422	
1971	Amarillo	Texas	1W	88	54	.620	(Lost playoffs)
1976	Fresno	California	2	41	29	.586	
			3	36	34	.514	
1977	Waterbury	Eastern	2NE	77	63	.550	
1978	Waterbury	Eastern	6	28	42	.400	
			3	37	32	.536	
1979	Shreveport	Texas	3E	30	33	.476	
			1E	43	29	597	(Lost playoffs)
1980	Shreveport	Texas	4E	25	40	.385	
			4E	24	47	.338	
1981	Savannah	Southern	5E	34	37	.479	
			1E	36	33	.522	(Lost playoffs)
1982	Savannah	Southern	3E	37	34	.521	
			4E	32	41	.438	
				2009	**1899**	**.514**	

Played outfield in 8 games with Boston Red Sox, 1942-46
Coach, San Francisco Giants, 1972-75

LAWRENCE WILLIAM (LARRY) GILBERT
Born December 2, 1891 at New Orleans, LA
Died February 17, 1965 at New Orleans, LA

Year	Club	League	Pos.	W	L	Pct.	
1923	New Orleans	Southern A	1	89	57	.610	
1924	New Orleans	Southern A	3	93	60	.608	
1925	New Orleans	Southern A	2	85	68	.556	
1926	New Orleans	Southern A	1	101	53	.656	
1927	New Orleans	Southern A	1	96	57	.627	
1928	New Orleans	Southern A	3	40	33	.548	
			6	33	41	.446	
1929	New Orleans	Southern A	3	89	64	.582	
1930	New Orleans	Southern A	2	91	61	.599	
1931	New Orleans	Southern A	5	78	75	.510	
1933	New Orleans	Southern A	2	41	34	.547	
			1	47	31	.603	(Won playoffs)

Lawrence William (Larry) Gilbert (continued)

Year	Club	League	Pos.	W	L	Pct.	
1934	New Orleans	Southern A	2	40	32	.556	
			1	54	28	.659	(Won playoffs)
1935	New Orleans	Southern A	2	86	67	.562	
1936	New Orleans	Southern A	4	81	71	.533	
1937	New Orleans	Southern A	4	84	65	.564	
1938	New Orleans	Southern A	3	79	70	.530	
1939	Nashville	Southern A	3	85	68	.556	(Won playoffs)
1940	Nashville	Southern A	1	101	47	.682	(Won playoffs)
1941	Nashville	Southern A	2	83	70	.542	(Won playoffs)
1942	Nashville	Southern A	2	85	66	.563	(Won playoffs)
1943	Nashville	Southern A	1	49	26	.653	
			3	34	29	.540	(Won playoffs)
1944	Nashville	Southern A	5	32	36	.471	
			1	47	25	.653	(Won playoffs)
1945	Nashville	Southern A	7	55	84	.396	
1946	Nashville	Southern A	5	75	78	.490	
1947	Nashville	Southern A	3	80	73	.523	
1948	Nashville	Southern A	1	95	58	.621	(Lost playoffs)
				2128	**1627**	**.567**	

President, New Orleans Pelicans, in 1932
(Playing record carried in Minor League Baseball Stars, Volume I)

ROBERT CLAY HOPPER
Born October 3, 1902 at Portersville, MS
Died April 17, 1976 at Greenwood, MS

Year	Club	League	Pos.	W	L	Pct.	
1929	Laurel	Cot. St.	3	32	27	.542	
			7	27	36	.429	
1931	Scottdale	Mid. Atl.	5	37	29	.561	
			4	41	26	.612	
1932	Mobile	Southeastern	1	19	13	.594	(League fld.)
	Elmira	NY-Penn		30	39	.435	(in 7/11)
1933	Springfield	Miss. Val.	6	18	38	.321	
			5	25	32	.439	
1934	Greensburg	Penn St. A	4	24	25	.490	
			1	33	20	.623	(Won playoff)
1935	Greenwood	E. Dixie	8	20	46	.303	
			7	32	38	.457	
1936	Greensburg	Penn St. A	2	31	24	.564	
			1	33	20	.623	(Lost playoff)
1937	Springfield	West. Assn.	4	76	67	.531	(Won playoff)
1938	Springfield	West. Assn.	2	79	56	.585	
1939	Columbus	Sally	1	83	55	.601	(Lost playoff)
1940	Columbus	Sally	2	88	63	.583	(Won playoff)
1941	Columbus	Sally	3	68	69	.496	
1942	Houston	Texas	5	81	70	.536	
1945	Mobile	Southern A	3	74	65	.532	(Won playoff)
1946	Montreal	Int.	1	100	54	.649	(Won playoff)
1947	Montreal	Int.	2	93	60	.608	
1948	Montreal	Int.	1	94	59	.614	(Won playoff)
1949	Montreal	Int.	3	84	70	.545	(Won playoff)
1950	St. Paul	A.A.	4	83	69	.546	
1951	St. Paul	A.A.	2	85	66	.563	
1952	Portland	PC	4	92	88	.511	
1953	Portland	PC	4	92	88	.511	
1954	Portland	PC	8	71	94	.430	
1955	Portland	PC	5	86	86	.500	
1956	Hollywood	PC	4	85	83	.506	
				1916	**1675**	**.534**	

Hopper, who did not play in majors, hit four home runs in one game for Danville, Ill,
July 17, 1927

MICHAEL JOSEPH KELLEY
Born December 2, 1875 at Otter River, MA
Died June 6, 1955 at Minneapolis, MN

Year	Club	League	Pos.	W	L	Pct.	
1901	Des Moines	Western	7	49	74	.398	
1902	St. Paul	A.A.	3	72	66	.522	
1903	St. Paul	A.A.	1	88	46	.657	
1904	St. Paul	A.A.	1	95	52	.646	
1905	St. Paul	A.A.	5	73	77	.487	
1906	Minneapolis	A.A.	3	79	66	.545	
1907	Des Moines	Western		13	7	.650	(out 5/13)
1908	Toronto	Int.		35	39	.473	(out 7/21)
	St. Paul	A.A.		18	23	.439	(in 8/9)
1909	St. Paul	A.A.	5	80	83	.491	
1910	St. Paul	A.A.	4	88	80	.524	
1911	St. Paul	A.A.	4	79	85	.482	
1912	St. Paul	A.A.	6	77	90	.461	
1913	Indianapolis	A.A.	8	68	99	.407	
1915	St. Paul	A.A.	2	90	63	.588	
1916	St. Paul	A.A.	4	86	79	.521	
1917	St. Paul	A.A.	2	88	66	.571	
1918	St. Paul	A.A.	6	39	38	.506	
1919	St. Paul	A.A.	1	94	60	.610	
1920	St. Paul	A.A.	1	115	49	.701	
1921	St. Paul	A.A.	6	80	87	.479	
1922	St. Paul	A.A.	1	107	60	.641	
1923	St. Paul	A.A.	1	111	57	.661	
1924	Minneapolis	A.A.	6	77	89	.464	
1925	Minneapolis	A.A.	4	86	80	.518	
1926	Minneapolis	A.A.	7	72	94	.434	
1927	Minneapolis	A.A.	5	88	80	.524	
1928	Minneapolis	A.A.	2	97	71	.577	
1929	Minneapolis	A.A.	3	89	78	.533	
1930	Minneapolis	A.A.	4	77	76	.503	
1931	Minneapolis	A.A.	6	80	88	.476	
				2390	**2102**	**.532**	

President and primary owner of the Minneapolis Millers, 1923-46
Played first base with Louisville, NL, in 1899

JOHN FRANK (JACK) LELIVELT
Born November 14, 1885 at Chicago, IL
Died January 20, 1941 at Seattle, WA

Year	Club	League	Pos.	W	L	Pct.	
1920	Omaha	Western	4	76	77	.497	
1921	Omaha	Western		7	9	.438	(out 5/3)
1922	Tulsa	Western	1	103	64	.617	
1923	Tulsa	Western	2	101	67	.601	
1924	Tulsa	Western	3	89	69	563	
1925	St. Joseph	Western	5	77	87	.470	
1926	Milwaukee	A.A.	3	93	71	.567	
1927	Milwaukee	A.A.	2t	99	69	.589	
1928	Milwaukee	A.A.	3	90	78	.536	
1929	Milwaukee	A.A.		21	37	.362	(out 6/21)
	Los Angeles	PC (2nd H.)	3t	48	44	.522	(in 7/12)
1930	Los Angeles	PC	1	57	42	.576	
			2	56	42	.571	(Lost playoff)
1931	Los Angeles	PC	5	43	47	.478	
			2	55	42	.567	
1932	Los Angeles	PC	5	96	93	.508	
1933	Los Angeles	PC	1	114	73	.610	

John Frank (Jack) Lelivelt (continued)

Year	Club	League	Pos.	W	L	Pct.	
1934	Los Angeles	PC	1	66	18	.786	
			1	71	32	.689	
1935	Los Angeles	PC	1	46	25	.648	
			4	52	51	.505	(Lost playoff)
1936	Los Angeles	PC	5	88	88	.500	
1938	Seattle	PC	2	100	75	.571	
1939	Seattle	PC	1	101	73	.580	(Lost playoff)
1940	Seattle	PC	1	112	66	.629	(Won playoff)
				1861	**1439**	**.564**	

Jack Leliveit, one of the better players as well as managers, dressed like a successful businessman in Washington in 1910.

JOHN J. McCLOSKEY

Born April 4, 1862 at Louisville, KY
Died November 17, 1940 at Louisville, KY

Year	Club	League	Pos.	W	L	Pct.	
1888	Austin-San Ant.	Texas	2	31	24	.564	
	San Antonio	Tex-Southern	3	12	9	.571	
1889	Houston	Texas	1	54	44	.551	
1890	Houston	Texas	4	23	23	.500	
1891	Sacramento	California	3	75	73	.507	
1892	Houston	Texas	1	40	14	.741	
			1	19	12	.613	
1893	Montgomery	Southern	8	26	38	.406	
			9	12	19	.387	
1894	Savannah	Southern (1st H)	4	30	26	.536	
1895	Louisville	National	12	35	96	.267	
1896	Louisville	National		2	17	.105	(out 5/10)
1897	Dallas	Tex-Southern	7	28	40	.412	
			4	23	33	.411	
1898	Dallas	Texas Assn.		13	7	.650	(Team out 5/1)
1898	Dallas	Southwestern		3	2	.600	(May 3/9)
1900	Great Falls	Montana St.	3	15	21	.417	
			1	24	11	.686	(Won playoff)
1901	Tacoma	Pacific NW	2	57	51	.528	
1902	Butte	Pacific NW	1	73	47	.608	
1903	San Francisco	Pacific Nat.	5	56	52	.519	
1904	Boise	Pacific Nat.	1	82	49	.626	
1905	Vancouver	Northwestern	1t	34	24	.586	
			4	11	28	.282	
1906	St. Louis	National	7	52	98	.347	
1907	St. Louis	National	8	52	101	.340	
1908	St. Louis	National	8	49	105	.318	
1909	Milwaukee	A.A.	2	90	77	.539	
1910	Milwaukee	A.A.	6	76	91	.455	
1911	Butte	Union Assn.	3	77	60	.562	
1912	Ogden	Union Assn.	4	71	68	.511	
1913	Salt Lake	Union Assn.	2	75	47	.615	
1915	El Paso	Rio G. Assn.	3	12	7	.632	
			1	24	15	.615	
1919	Beaumont	Texas	3	36	32	.529	
				19	24	.442	(out 8/14)
1920	Memphis	Southern A	5	72	77	.483	
1921	Bartlesville	Southwestern	6	30	38	.441	
			6	34	42	.447	
1922	Salina	Southwestern	8	17	51	.250	
			6	27	39	.409	
1923	Wilmington	Atlantic		12	5	.706	(Club fld. 5/23)
	Milford	E. Shore		17	13	.567	(5/27 to 7/5)
1924	Newton	Southwestern	1	42	20	.677	
	New/Black/Ottawa	Southwestern	3	34	29	.540	(Lost playoff)
1928	Akron	Central	4	33	29	.532	
			4	34	36	.486	
1929	Akron	Central	6	58	76	.433	
1930	Richmond	Central	4	31	36	.463	
			5	32	39	.451	
1932	Akron	Central	5	19	34	.358	(Club fld. 6/20)
		Majors		**190**	**417**	**.313**	
		Minors		**1713**	**1632**	**.512**	

WILLIAM ADAM (BILL) MEYER
Born January 14, 1893 at Knoxville, TN
Died March 31, 1957 at Knoxville, TN

Year	Club	League	Pos.	W	L	Pct.	
1926	Louisville	A.A.	1	105	62	.629	
1927	Louisville	A.A.	7	65	103	.387	
1928	Louisville	A.A.	8	62	106	.369	
1932	Springfield	Eastern	1	53	26	.671	(Lg. fld. 7/17)
	Binghamton	NY-Penn	5	34	28	.548	(in 7/19)
1933	Binghamton	NY-Penn	1	79	55	.590	
1934	Binghamton	NY-Penn	1	41	28	.594	
			3	35	34	.507	(Lost playoff)
1935	Binghamton	NY-Penn	5	35	31	.530	
			1	40	29	.580	(Won playoff)
1936	Oakland	P C	2t	95	81	.540	
1937	Oakland	P C	7	79	98	.446	
1938	Kansas City	A.A.	2	84	67	.556	
1939	Kansas City	A.A.	1	107	47	.695	
1940	Kansas City	A.A.	1	95	57	.625	
1941	Kansas City	A.A.	3	85	69	.552	
1942	Newark	Int.	1	92	61	.601	
1943	Newark	Int.	2	85	68	.556	
1944	Newark	Int.	2	85	69	.552	
1945	Newark	Int.	2	89	64	.582	
1946	Kansas City	A.A.	7	67	82	.450	
1947	Kansas City	A.A.	1	93	60	.608	
1948	Pittsburgh	National	4	83	71	.539	
1949	Pittsburgh	National	6	71	83	.461	
1950	Pittsburgh	National	8	57	96	.373	
1951	Pittsburgh	National	7	64	90	.416	
1952	Pittsburgh	National	8	42	112	.273	
		Majors		**317**	**452**	**.412**	
		Minors		**1605**	**1325**	**.548**	

Catcher in the American League, 1913-17

WILLIAM J. (BILLY) MURRAY
Born April 13, 1864 at Peabody, MA
Died March 25, 1937 at Youngstown, OH

Year	Club	League	Pos.	W	L	Pct.
1889	Quincy	Cen. InterSt	3	59	52	.532
1890	Quincy	West InterSt	4	42	44	.488
1891	Quincy	Illinois-Iowa	1	65	35	.650
1892	Joliet	Illinois-Iowa	1	55	27	.671
1893	Atlanta	Southern	3	55	39	.585
1894	Providence	Eastern	1	78	34	.696
1895	Providence	Eastern	2	74	44	.627
1896	Providence	Eastern	1	71	47	.602
1897	Providence	Eastern	5	69	60	.535
1898	Providence	Eastern	5	58	60	.492
1899	Providence	Eastern	7	54	62	.466
1900	Providence	Eastern	1	84	52	.618
1901	Providence	Eastern	2	74	57	.565
1902	Providence	Eastern	5	67	68	.496
1903	Jersey City	Eastern	1	92	32	.742
1904	Jersey City	Eastern	3	76	57	.571
1905	Jersey City	Eastern	3	81	49	.623
1906	Jersey City	Eastern	2	80	57	.584
1907	Philadelphia	National	3	83	64	.565
1908	Philadelphia	National	4	83	71	.539
1909	Philadelphia	National	5	74	79	.484
		Majors		**240**	**214**	**.529**
		Minors		**1234**	**876**	**.585** *

FRANCIS JOSEPH (LEFTY) O'DOUL
Born March 4, 1897 at San Francisco, CA
Died December 7, 1969 at San Francisco, CA

Year	Club	League	Pos.	W	L	Pct.	
1935	San Francisco	PC	2t	41	30	.577	
1936	San Francisco	PC	7	83	93	.472	
1937	San Francisco	PC	2	98	80	.551	
1938	San Francisco	PC	4	93	85	.522	
1939	San Francisco	PC	2	97	78	.554	
1940	San Francisco	PC	7	81	97	.455	
1941	San Francisco	PC	5t	81	95	.460	
1942	San Francisco	PC	5	88	90	.494	
1943	San Francisco	PC	2	89	66	.574	(Won playoffs)
1944	San Francisco	PC	3t	86	83	.509	(Won playoffs)
1945	San Francisco	PC	4	96	87	.525	(Won playoffs)
1946	San Francisco	PC	1	115	68	.628	(Won playoffs)
1947	San Francisco	PC	2	105	82	.561	
1948	San Francisco	PC	2	112	76	.596	
1949	San Francisco	PC	7	84	103	.449	
1950	San Francisco	PC	5	100	100	.500	
1951	San Francisco	PC	8	74	93	.443	
1952	San Diego	PC	5	88	92	.489	
1953	San Diego	PC	7	88	92	.489	
1954	San Diego	PC	1	102	67	.604	(Lost playoffs)
1955	Oakland	PC	7	77	95	.448	
1956	Vancouver	PC	8	67	98	.406	
1957	Seattle	PC	5	87	80	.521	
				2094	**1970**	**.515**	

Pitcher and outfielder in major leagues, 1919-34

FRANK J. (SHAG) SHAUGHNESSY
Born April 8, 1883 at Amboy, IL
Died May 15, 1969 at Montreal, Canada

Year	Club	League	Pos.	W	L	Pct.	
1909	Roanoke	Virginia	1	73	49	.598	
1910	Roanoke	Virginia	2	68	52	.567	
1911	Roanoke	Virginia	3	63	56	.529	
1912	Ft. Wayne	Central	1	77	52	.597	
1913	Ottawa	Canadian	1	66	39	.629	
1914	Ottawa	Canadian	1	76	45	.628	
1915	Ottawa	Canadian	1	72	39	.649	
1916	Wells/Brad/Warren	InterSt.	4	41	37	.526	
1919	Hamilton	Mich-Ont.	2	75	36	.676	
1920	Hamilton	Mich-Ont.	2	71	46	.607	
1921	Syracuse	Int.		29	38	.433	(in 7/30)
1922	Syracuse	Int.	7	64	102	.386	
1923	Syracuse	Int.	6	73	92	.442	
1924	Syracuse	Int.	6	79	83	.488	
1925	Syracuse	Int.		9	29	.237	(out 5/28)
	Providence	Int.		49	69	.415	(in 6/4)
1926	Reading	Int.		1	8	.111	(out 4/23)
1934	Montreal	Int.		15	18	.455	
1935	Montreal	Int.	1	92	62	.597	(Lost playoff)
1936	Montreal	Int.		55	60	.478	(out 8/5)
				1148	**1012**	**.531**	

Outfielder, American League, 1905-08. Coach, Detroit, 1928. General Manager, Montreal, 1932-34. President, International League, 1936-60

STANLEY WASIAK
Born April 8, 1920 at Chicago, IL

Year	Club	League	Pos.	W	L	Pct.
1950	Valdosta	Georgia-Fla.	2	81	56	.591
1951	Valdosta	Georgia-Fla.	1	81	45	.643
1952	Greenwood	Cotton States	3	70	56	.556
1953	Newport News	Piedmont	3	80	56	.588
1954	Mobile	Southern A		25	35	.417 (out 6/9)
1954	Valdosta	Georgia-Fla.	5	39	28	.582 (in 7/1)
1955	Valdosta	Georgia-Fla.	4	68	70	.493
1956	Idaho Falls	Pioneer	7	30	37	.448 (out 7/7)
	Hazle-Baxley	Georgia St.	5	21	21	.500 (in 7/12)
1957	Valdosta	Georgia-Fla.	1	42	28	.600
			3	35	34	.507
1958	Great Falls	Pioneer	1	39	28	.582
			7	24	42	.364
1959	Green Bay	III	1	39	24	.619
			3	35	27	.565 (Won playoffs)
1960	Green Bay	III	6	65	73	.471
1961	Salem	Northwest	2	40	29	.580
			4	34	37	.479
1962	Salem	Northwest	2	38	33	.535
			2t	36	34	.514
1963	Salem	Northwest	3	38	28	.576
			2	43	31	.581
1964	Salem	Northwest	3	34	30	.531
			2	44	32	.579
1965	Salem	Northwest	6	26	44	.371
			6	21	46	.313
1966	Fox Cities	Midwest	1	42	19	.689
			3	35	28	.556 (Won playoffs)
1967	Lynchburg	Carolina	4W	68	68	.500
1968	Evansville	Southern	6	55	84	.396
1969	Lynchburg	Carolina	4W	60	84	.417
1970	Daytona Beach	Florida St.	3E	76	55	.580
1971	Daytona Beach	Florida St.	1W	82	58	.586
1972	Daytona Beach	Flordia St.	1N	40	28	.588
	El Paso	Texas	1W	47	32	.595 (Won playoffs)
1973	Albuquerque	PC	4E	62	82	.431
1974	Albuquerque	PC	1E	76	66	.535
1975	Albuquerque	PC	3E	71	73	.493
1976	Albuquerque	PC	3E	66	78	.458
1977	Lodi	California	3	33	37	.471
			1	48	22	.686 (Won playoffs)
1978	Lodi	California	1N	42	28	.600
			1N	43	27	.614
1979	Lodi	California	1N	42	28	.600
			5N	25	44	.362
1980	Vero Beach	Florida St.	2N	82	59	.582
1981	Vero Beach	Florida St.		23	35	.397 (ill; left club)
1982	Vero Beach	Florida St.		1	0	1.000 (August 24)
1983	Vero Beach	Florida St.	4S	28	41	.406
			1S	41	24	.631 (Won playoffs)
1984	Vero Beach	Florida St.	3S	40	38	.513
			1St	39	29	.574
				2395	**2171***	**.525**

Left club twice because of illness in 1981; Managed only one game in 1982.

Jake Atz

Larry Gilbert

Frank Shaughnessy

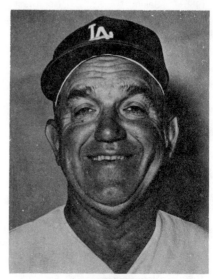

Stan Wasiak

Minor League Cavalcade

Highest Level of Performance in Minors and Majors

Many players have had truly great seasons in the minor leagues but failed to measure up in the majors; some others were just average in the minors but really blossomed in the Big Time. There were a few who had really outstanding seasons in both classifications. One of these was Joe DiMaggio who, in 1933, knocked in 169 runs for San Francisco in the Pacific Coast League, and in 1937 drove across 167 for the New York Yankees. That was the highest level of performance in that particular category. DiMaggio did even better when it came to consecutive game hitting streaks, hitting in 61 straight games in 1933 and 56 with the Yankees in 1941, but that is a special category.

In compiling a list of players with the top season figures in both minors and majors, two factors must be noted. The Pacific Coast League had a longer schedule of games, giving their players dominance in some season totals. The other factor is that hurlers worked more innings in the 19th century, giving them an edge in some totals. Consequently, Nolan Ryan, who has pitched in an era of high strikeouts, and who did fan 307 batters in the minors in 1966, lost out to oldtimer John Clarkson. In wins, Kid Nichols got the nod over Joe McGinnity, who was the only pitcher since 1900 to win at least 30 games in a season in both the minors and majors, but that wasn't enough. With those two caveats, we have compiled the season highs in all the appropriate categories. There are some familiar names and some surprises.

Batting

Runs	Lefty O'Doul	1925	Salt Lake, Pacific Coast	185
		1929	Philadelphia, National	152
Hits	Lefty O'Doul	1925	Salt Lake, Pacific Coast	309
		1929	Philadelphia, National	254
Doubles	Paul Waner	1925	San Fran., Pacific Coast	75
		1932	Pittsburgh, National	62
Triples	Adam Comorosky	1926	Williamsport, NY-Penn	26
		1930	Pittsburgh, National	23
Homers	Gorman Thomas	1974	Sacramento, Pacific Coast	51
		1979	Milwaukee, American	45
RBI	Joe DiMaggio	1933	San Fran., Pacific Coast	169
		1937	New York, American	167
SB	Rickey Henderson	1979	Modesto, California	95
		1982	Oakland, American	130

Bat. Ave.	Billy Hamilton	1894	Philadelphia, National	.404
		1904	Haverhill, New England	.414
Sl. Ave.	Lou Gehrig	1924	Hartford, Eastern	.720
		1927	New York, American	.765

Pitching

Games	Dan McGinn	1968	Asheville, Southern	74
		1969	Montreal, National	74
IP	Joe McGinnity	1903	New York, National	434
		1913	Tacoma, Northwestern	436
Wins	Kid Nichols	1889	Omaha, Western	36
		1892	Boston, National	35
SO	John Clarkson	1884	Saginaw, Northwest	388
		1886	Chicago, National	340
Shutouts	Grover Alexander	1910	Syracuse, NY State	14
		1916	Philadelphia, National	16
W. Pct.	Chief Bender	1914	Philadelphia, American	.850(17-3)
		1919	Richmond, Virginia	.932(29-2)

Highest Level of Career Performance

When it comes to compiling the players with the highest level of career performance in both the minors and majors, the totals are not especially significant except for those of Joe McGinnity. He worked more than 3400 innings in each classification, winning 239 games in the minors and 247 in the majors. In spite of his large number of innings pitched, he neither led in strikeouts nor bases on balls. Babe Herman dominated the batting departments, although Lefty O'Doul compiled the highest batting and slugging marks. George Brunet is credited with the most years of play with 26 in the minors and 15 in the majors. These figures are not additive as he split many of those seasons.

		Minors	Majors
Years	George Brunet	26	15
Games	Babe Herman	1431	1552
Runs	Dolph Camilli	886	936
Hits	Babe Herman	1545	1818
Doubles	Babe Herman	361	399
Triples	Buck Freeman	98	130
Homers	Dick Stuart	222	228

		Batting			
		Minors		Majors	
RBI	Babe Herman	850+		997	
SB	Billy Hamilton	369		936	
Bat. Ave.	Lefty O'Doul	.352	(3253/1146)	.349	(3264/1140)
Sl. Ave.	Lefty O'Doul	.521	(3253/1696)	.532	(3264/1736)

		Pitching			
		Minors		Majors	
Games	Joe McGinnity	593		467	
IP	Joe McGinnity	3863		3455	
Wins	Joe McGinnity	239		247	
Losses	Joe McGinnity	212		145	
BB	Vern Kennedy	1035		1049	
SO	Diego Segui	1490		1298	
W. Pct.	Lefty Grove	.742	(112-38)	.682	(300-141)

Babe Herman, who split his long career between majors and minors.

Annual Minor League Home Run Leader

While Babe Ruth led the two major leagues in home runs ten different seasons, no player came anywhere near that domination in the minors. The reason, of course, is that there are many more individual leagues in the minors. Looking back 100 years, we find that the annual minor league home run leader played for teams from all parts of the U.S. as well as Mexico, and the Canadian provinces of British Columbia, Alberta, Ontario, and Quebec. Minneapolis (Nicollet Park) had the most team leaders with seven. By state, Texas had 11 home run leaders from 10 different jurisdictions.

In regard to individual players, Joe Bauman, who set the O.B. record with 72 home runs for Roswell (Longhorn League) in 1954, led the minors four different seasons.

Bunny Brief led three years and nine other players led twice. Did any minor league leader ever repeat as the major league champ? Only three — Buck Freeman, Cliff Cravath, and Frank Howard.

Ironically, three of the top all-time season leaders in the minors did not get the individual honor of leading all the minor leagues. Bob Lennon, who hit 64 homers for Nashville (Southern) in 1954, lost out to the aforementioned Joe Bauman, who hit 72 that season. Similarly, while Ken Guettler was blasting 62 for Shreveport (Texas League) in 1956, and Frosty Kennedy was socking 60 for Plainview (Southwest), it was Dick Stuart of Lincoln (Western) who was out front with 66.

Here are the annual minor league leaders from 1884 to 1984. In several seasons, totals result from play in two different leagues.

1884	Thomas P. Burns	Wilmington	Eastern	11
1885	Richard Johnston	Richmond	Eastern	16
1886	Theodore Sheffler	Portland	New England	11
	Guerdon Whitley	Newburyport/Lynn	New England	11
	George Wilson	Newburyport/Lynn	New England	11
1887	Walter Andrews	Memphis	Southern	28
1888	John Carroll	St. Paul	Western Assoc.	16
1889	Charles Reilly	St. Paul	Western Assoc.	23
1890	John Carroll	St. Paul	Western Assoc.	21
1891	Dell Darling	Minneapolis	Western Assoc.	18
1892	Ed Breckenridge	Columbus	Western	17
1893	Abel Lezotte	Lewiston	New England	25
1894	Perry Werden	Minneapolis	Western	42
1895	Perry Werden	Minneapolis	Western	45
1896	Ed Breckenridge	Brockton	New England	25
1897	James Williams	St. Joseph	Western Assoc.	31
1898	Buck Freeman	Toronto	Eastern	23
1899	Charles Campau	Rochester	Eastern	8
1900	Kitty Bransfield	Worcester	Eastern	17
1901	Frank C. Roth	Ced. Rap/Evansv.	III	36
1902	Clarence Foster	Prov/Montreal	Eastern	14
1903	William Marshall	San Francisco	Pacific National	25
1904	Charles Eagan	Tacoma	Pacific Coast	25
1905	Charles Eagan	Tacoma	Pacific Coast	21
1906	Robert Unglaub	Williamsport	Interstate	14
1907	Buck Freeman	Minneapolis	American Assoc.	18
1908	Patrick Newnam	San Antonio	Texas	18
1909	Cy Perkins	Hartford	Connecticut	23
1910	Frank (Ping) Bodie	San Francisco	Pacific Coast	30
1911	Cliff Cravath	Minneapolis	American Assoc.	29
1912	Albert Durham	Bay City Oshkosh	South Michigan (25) Wis.-Illinois (5)	30
1913	Charles Swain	Victoria	Northwestern	34
1914	Wilborn Bankston	Cordele	George State	31
1915	Otto Besse	McAlester	Western Assoc.	34
1916	Bunny Brief	Salt Lake City	Pacific Coast	33

1917	Ernest Calbert	Muskogee	Western Assoc.	43
1918	Arthur Griggs	San Francisco	Pacific Coast	12
	Earl Sheely	Salt Lake City	Pacific Coast	12
1919	Earl Sheely	Salt Lake City	Pacific Coast	28
1920	Clarence Yaryan	Wichita	Western	41
1921	Bunny Brief	Kansas City	American Assoc.	42
1922	Bunny Brief	Kansas City	American Assoc.	40
1923	Moses Solomon	Hutchinson	Southwestern	49
1924	Clarence Kraft	Fort Worth	Texas	55
1925	Tony Lazzeri	Salt Lake City	Pacific Coast	60
1926	Moose Clabaugh	Tyler	East Texas	62
1927	Elmer J. Smith	Portland	Pacific Coast	40
1928	Smead Jolley	San Francisco	Pacific Coast	45
1929	Ike Boone	S.F. Missions	Pacific Coast	55
1930	Joe Hauser	Baltimore	International	63
1931	David Barbee	Hollywood	Pacific Coast	47
1932	Buzz Arlett	Baltimore	International	54
1933	Joe Hauser	Minneapolis	American Assoc.	69
1934	Buzz Arlett	Birmingham	Southern Assoc. (7)	48
		Minneapolis	American Assoc. (41)	
1935	Gene Lillard	Los Angeles	Pacific Coast	56
1936	Tom Winsett	Columbus	American Assoc.	50
1937	Maurice Van Robays	Ogdensburg	Canadian-Amer.	43
1938	Ollie Carnegie	Buffalo	International	45
1939	Tony Robello	Pocatello	Pioneer	58
1940	Lou Novikoff	Los Angeles	Pacific Coast	41
1941	Leslie Burge	Atlanta	Southern Assoc.	38
	Howard Murdeski	Johnstown	Penn. State As.	38
1942	Donald Manno	Welch	Mountain State	34
1943	Ted Norbert	Milwaukee	American Assoc.	25
1944	John Cappa	Allentown	Inter-State	30
1945	Frank Skaff	Baltimore	International	38
1946	Joe Bauman	Amarillo	West Tex-N. Mex.	48
1947	Buck Frierson	Sherman-Denison	Big State	58
1948	Bobby Crues	Amarillo	West Tex-N. Mex	69
1949	D.C. Miller	Gladewater	East Texas (3)	55
		Lamesa	West Tex-N. Mex (52)	
1950	Jesse McClain	Harlingen	Rio Gr. Valley	53
1951	Jack Harshman	Nashville	Southern Assoc.	47
1952	Joe Bauman	Artesia	Longhorn	50
1953	Joe Bauman	Artesia	Longhorn	53
1954	Joe Bauman	Roswell	Longhorn	72
1955	Keith Little	Corpus Christi	Big State	47
1956	Dick Stuart	Lincoln	Western	66
1957	Steve Bilko	Los Angeles	Pacific Coast	56
1958	Rocky Nelson	Toronto	International	43
1959	Frank Howard	Victoria	Texas (27)	43
		Spokane	Pacific Coast (16)	

1960	Raymond Reed	Boise	Pioneer	37
	R.C. Stevens	Salt Lake City	Pacific Coast	37
1961	Robert Sanders	Magic Valley	Pioneer	40
1962	Ramiro Caballero	Guanajuato	Mexican Center	59
1963	Arlo Engel	El Paso	Texas	41
1964	Hector Espino	Monterrey Jacksonville	Mexican (46) International (3)	49
1965	Bobby Prescott	Poza Rica	Mexican	39
1966	Heriberto Vargas	Guanajuato	Mexican Center	55
1967	Elrod Hendricks	Jalisco	Mexican	41
1968	Tolia Solaita	High Pt.-Thomas	Carolina	49
1969	Frank Herrera	Carmen Miami	Mexican S.E. (39) Florida State (4)	43
1970	Harold Breeden	Richmond	International	37
1971	Adrian Garrett	Tacoma	Pacific Coast	43
1972	Hector Espino	Tampico	Mexican	37
1973	James Fuller	Rochester	International	39
1974	William McNulty	Sacramento	Pacific Coast	55
1975	Andres Mora	Saltillo	Mexican	35
1976	Roger Freed	Denver	American Assoc.	42
1977	Danny Walton	Albuquerque	Pacific Coast	42
1978	William Foley	Burlington	Midwest	34
	Champ Summers	Indianapolis	American Assoc.	34
1979	Dick Lancellotti	Buffalo	Eastern	41
1980	Randy Bass	Denver	American Assoc.	37
1981	Tim Laudner	Orlando	Southern	42
1982	Ron Kittle	Edmonton	Pacific Coast	50
1983	Stanley Holmes	Visalia	California	37
1984	Derek Bryant	Tampico	Mexican	40

20-Game Winners Fading Out

No pitcher has won 20 games in a minor league season in the last three years. In 1983, Dwight Gooden won 19 for Lynchburg in the Carolina League, and in 1984 Mike Bielecki racked up 19 victories for Hawaii in the Pacific Coast League.

Why has the 20-game winner become such a rarity in the minors? One reason is that most of the league seasons have been shortened. Another is that starting pitchers give way to relief hurlers more readily and if the starter does an outstanding job he is likely to be called up in mid-season to help the parent club.

The lack of 20-game winners in recent years contrasts sharply with the old days. There was one case in 1887, for example, of a pitcher who won 20 games in two different leagues. This was Tom Lovett, who started the season with Bridgeport in the Eastern League and chalked up a smashing 21-3 mark. He then shifted to Oshkosh in the Northwest League and racked up a 20-2 record. He not only led both circuits in percentage but accumulated a 41-5 mark for the season. In the three minor league seasons of 1886-87-88, he won 103 games.

One other hurler won 41 games in one season but the victories were not so evenly distributed. In 1906 Stoney McGlynn had a great season with York (TriState), but in mid-August jumped to Steubenville in the Penn-Ohio-Mich. League. He won five of six games there but, when he didn't get the money he was promised, went back to York where he pitched a doubleheader win over Harrisburg. He closed the season with a 36-10 mark at York and 5-1 at Steubenville. If that wasn't enough, the St. Louis Cardinals called him up and he was 2-2 in six games, one of which was a 7-inning no-hitter which ended in a tie. He pitched 511 innings in all that season.

The Pacific Coast League was playing more than 200 games at that time and the seasons would run to late November. Consequently most of the big winners were in that circuit. In 1906, for example, Rube Vickers won 39 and lost 20 for Seattle. But later, in spite of its long schedule, the Coast League did not produce any more big winners than certain other loops. In the 1920s, for example, Jakie May was the only 30-game winner in the PCL (35-9 in 1922). The International League has three 30-game winners in that decade — John Ogden in 1921, Rube Parnham in 1923, and Tommy Thomas in 1925. George Boehler set the high mark with 38 victories for Tulsa in the Western League in 1922. In the Texas League, Joe Pate twice won 30 games for Ft. Worth — in 1921 and 1924 — the only minor leaguer to achieve that lofty status twice in the last 70 years. Rube Vickers did it in 1906 and 1911.

Bill Thomas provided further proof that a 30-game winner did not need a long schedule when he won 35 games for Houma in the Evangeline League in 1946. The club played 132 games. Wenceslao Gonzalez was the last minor league hurler to win 30 games, going 32-11 for Juarez in the Southwest International League in a 140-game schedule in 1951.

Baseball's Boyer Brothers

When the subject of brothers in baseball comes up, the force of numbers causes one to focus on the five Delahanty's and the four O'Neills, all of whom made it to the major leagues. However, if the subject is broadened to cover the minor leagues as well, the numbers of these two Irish families do not increase very much. There were no additional O'Neill players. There was a sixth Delahanty, William, who played 1906-10 with Mansfield, Wilkes-Barre, Binghamton, and Waterbury. Consideration then has to shift to the Bannons of Massachusetts, the Sowders of Indiana, and the Boyers of Missouri.

At the turn of the century, there were ten Bannon brothers playing hither and yon. They might play an off-season game together in northeastern Massachusetts, where most of them lived, but during the summer a Bannon could pop up in a box score most anywhere in the east. A check of old records in the 1890s indicates that only five actually played under the umbrella of Organized Baseball. They were Tom and Jim, who made the majors, and William, George, and Daniel. The others would have to be classified as semi-pro.

Even less is known of the Seven Sowders brothers, most of whom were born in Louisville, but lived their lives in Indianapolis. Len, Bill and John made it to the majors in the late 1880s, but Len died at age 27 in 1888 and Bill's pitching career was ended by illness and surgery in 1890 when he was only 26. A fourth brother, David, had an extensive career in the minors, and it is believed the three others also played some minor league ball. Unfortunately, the fragmentary reporting of those days does not provide their first names. One, characterized as the youngest of the seven Sowders brothers, played in the Indiana State League in 1896.

Documentation is easier on the Boyers of Missouri because of their recent vintage. Seven of the 14 offspring of Mr. and Mrs. Vernon Boyer played in O.B. There might have been more but the other seven children were girls. Five of the boys signed with the Cardinals, one with Kansas City, and one with the Yankees. Cloyd, Ken and Clete became well known as players and/or coaches. The other four tried hard but made little impression. Here is a brief run-down on the seven Boyer brothers.

Cloyd, born in 1927, broke in as a pitcher with Lynchburg in the Piedmont League in 1945. He had winning seasons with Duluth, Houston, and Rochester before going up to the Cardinals in late 1949. He spent four seasons with the Cards and one with Kansas City before going back to the minors for seven more years. He closed out in 1961 with 117 minor league victories.

Wayne, born in 1929, started as a pitcher with Lenoir in the Blue Ridge and Carthage in the KOM in 1947. The next year he was 8-10 for Tallassee (Georgia-Alabama) and played 20 games in the outfield while batting .268. He quit to become a dentist.

Ken, born in 1931, also broke in as a hurler for Lebanon (North Atlantic) in 1949. He switched to third base and played for Hamilton (Pony) and Omaha (Western). After military service during the Korean War, he had a good season at Houston before launching a long career with the Cardinals.

Lynn, born in 1935, played first base for Hannibal in the Miss.-Ohio Valley League in 1954 and hit .252. The next year he hit .219 for Ardmore in the Sooner State and .152 for Albany (Georgia-Florida). That was the end of his pro baseball career.

Clete, born in 1937, pulled a switch by starting in the majors as a bonus baby infielder with Kansas City. In 1957 he was sold to the Yankees and they farmed him to Binghamton and Richmond. He went up to the parent club in 1959 and participated in five World Series before being traded to Atlanta. After playing for Hawaii in 1971, he concluded his active career in Japan.

Ron, born in 1944, started in the Yankee chain at Harlan in the Appalachian League in 1962. He spent two years at Shelby in the Western Carolinas, one at Greensboro, and the 1966 season at Columbus, Ga., in the Southern League, where he batted only .200. Then it was on to Syracuse in 1967, Binghamton in 1968 and Manchester in the Eastern League in 1969, each year batting under .200. He was a good fielder but couldn't hit.

Len, The youngest son, was born in 1946, one year after Cloyd had broken in. He made progress in the Cardinal chain from Rock Hill (Western Carolinas) in 1965 to St. Petersburg (Florida State) to Modesto (California), to Arkansas (Texas League). He also was a third baseman with a weak stick. He was batting .230 for Arkansas in 1970 when the manager made the decision to ship him back to Modesto for more seasoning. The manager was his older brother Ken.

That was essentially the end of baseball's biggest brother act, but a second generation is giving it a try. Ken's son Dave also followed the third base route in the Cardinals' organization. He spent two years (1976-77) at St. Petersburg, but he also was a poor hitter. Clete's son Mickey played third for Idaho Falls in the Pioneer League in 1984 and hit .273. That is an Oakland farm club.

The Mysterious Malmquist

Who had the highest season batting average in minor league history? Minor league record books (including **Minor League Baseball Stars**) have reported for years that it was Walter Malmquist with York in the Nebraska State League in 1913. According to the official averages published in the annual Reach Guide, he played 110 games and collected 154 hits in 323 at bats for an astounding .477 batting percentage.

There were two strange features about this high average. First, Malmquist had only 323 at bats in 110 games, slightly less than three per game, and for a very heavy hitting club. Almost all the other players in approximately 110 games had well over 400 at bats. Secondly, Malmquist had hit only .241 with York the preceding year, and .248 with Waco the following year. Why the unusual spurt in 1913? SABR researcher David Kemp, who recently moved to Nebraska, decided that this fabulous record should be documented.

He found that the year-end stats published in the York and Grand Island newspapers were the same as those carried in the Reach Guide. He then conducted a box score search in the league newspapers. He found 97 box scores of York games, plus brief narrative accounts of three additional games. From this material he was able to establish that Malmquist had 129 hits in 377 at bats for a .342 percentage. Dave says the schedule of dates he logged for York games indicates little opportunity to squeeze in the ten additional games credited to Malmquist in the guides, but it would have been possible with some doubleheaders. Curiously, if he had played the additional games he would have wound up with approximately 423 at bats rather than the published figure of 323. The main point, however, is that he could not have raised his average from .342 to anywhere near .477. Even though all the loose ends have not been secured on this project, it is apparent there was a statistical disaster in the Nebraska State League in 1913, and the mystical mantle of leadership must be removed from Mr. Malmquist. The question is, who should take his place as the all-time season batting king?

The apparent heir is Bill Krieg, first baseman with Rockford in the Western Association in 1895. He conducted a blitzkrieg of opposing pitchers and achieved a .452 mark based on 237 hits in 524 at bats. With the pitchers box moved back about 10 feet, the mid-1890s were heavy hitting days, not only in the majors (Hugh Duffy .438, Willie Keeler .432), but in the minors as well (Perry Werden hit .428 with 45 homers for Minneapolis in 1895).

If Krieg is the new king, mention at least must be made of Gary Redus, who hit .462 for Billings in the short-schedule Pioneer League in 1978. In fact, because of the widely varying schedule of games in the minors, past and present, it might be appropriate to list the all-time leaders in the various category levels of at bats.

In the 400-499 category, it should be noted that Bill Diester hit .444 with Salina in the Southwestern League in 1926. However, in 44 at bats with Tulsa in the Western League he hit "only" .341, which lowered his season average to .434.

AB Range	Player, Team and League	Year	AB	H	BA
200-299	Gary Redus, Billings, Pioneer	1978	253	117	.462
300-399	Ike Boone, Missions, Pacific Coast	1930	310	139	.448
400-499	Robert Schmidt, Duluth, Northern	1939	440	194	.441
500-599	Bill Krieg, Rockford, Western Assn.	1896	524	237	.452
600-699	Jack Lelivelt, Omaha, Western	1921	659	274	.416
700-Up	Oscar Eckhardt, Missions, Pac. Cst.	1933	760	315	.414

From Joe Relford To Hub Kittle

There is a logical limit to how young a person may be to play in the minors — although that limit has been stretched on a couple of occasions — but historically there hasn't been any restriction on how old a player may be. At least it doesn't seem that way.

The youngest player to take part in a minor league game was Joe Relford, a 12-year-old Negro batboy for the Fitzgerald club in the Georgia State League on July 19, 1952. The game was being lost 13-0 to Statesboro when the crowd yelled "Put in the batboy." Relford went in as a pinch hitter and grounded sharply to the third baseman. He then went to center field where he fielded a grounder cleanly and made a sensational catch of a line drive. That was the extent of play for Relford, who, incidentally, broke the color line in the Georgia State League.

On the last day of the 1932 Texas League season (one source says it was 1931 but the apparent date was September 11, 1932), Houston manager Joe Schultz inserted his son Joe Jr., who had just turned 14, as a pinch hitter in a game against Galveston. Young Joe, later to become a major league player like his father, shared the Houston batboy duties with a young black named Fritz, who also pinch hit in that game. His age was not given.

In 1974, Jorge Lebron, a talented Latin youngster, played two games at short for Auburn in the New York-Penn. League. He was 14. Rafael Montalvo also was 14 when he won four games and lost two for Lethbridge in the Pioneer League in 1980.

Omar Moreno played 25 games with the Bradenton Pirates in the Gulf Coast League in 1969 when he was 15. Back in the war year of 1943, catcher Bill Sarni got into 33 games with the Los Angeles Angels at age 15. He was frequently paired with veteran hurler Charlie Root, then 44.

A longer bridge between the fuzzy cheeks and the graybeards was erected May 11, 1925, when Joe McGinnity, the 55-year-old iron-man hurler of Dubuque, beat 18-year-old John Welch of Ottumwa 7-3 in a Mississippi Valley League game.

McGinnity was one of the oldest minor leaguers to perform on a regular basis. He was 6-6 in wins and losses in 1925, his last O.B. effort. Two years before, he was 15-12 and pitched a couple of shutouts at age 53. Satchel Paige also pitched steadily for Miami in 1958 when he was 52. Irked at being passed over for the International League All-Star game by Toronto manager Dixie Walker, Paige shut out the Maple Leafs 3-0 on July 27, 1958. Lefty George turned 57 in the war year of 1943 when he pitched for York in the Inter-State League. His seven victories included one complete-game shutout.

The non-pitcher who played regularly the longest was James O'Rourke, owner-manager of the Bridgeport club of the Connecticut League at the turn of the century. He played in 93 games for his club in 1906 and observed his 54th birthday in August. In spite of his many years as a catcher, he stole five bases. The next year he got into 24 games, but after that it was token appearances for "Orator Jim." His final appearance was on September 14, 1912, when he caught a full game for New Haven. He was president of the Connecticut League by that time and was 60 years old.

In the period 1903-04, it was common to see in the Bridgeport line-up O'Rourke, Sr., and O'Rourke, Jr. The latter was Jim's son, also a Yale man. The senior O'Rourke was the oldest minor league player in 11 different seasons. He took the honor away from such contemporaries as Dan Brouthers and Roger Connor, both of whom continued in the minors for some years after leaving the major leagues. George Jackson was the oldest player from 1926 to 1932, edging out such grizzled veterans as Gabby Street and Elmer Knetzer. The oldest minor leaguer for six of the most recent years has been George Brunet, who was 49 in 1984.

There have been 25 oldtimers who played in the minors after age 50 and five who participated in official games at age 60 or over. All of the latter made token appearances. The oldest was Hub Kittle, 63, who pitched one hitless inning for Springfield in the American Association on August 27, 1980. The former hurler was a minor league instructor for the St. Louis Cardinals at the time. The next oldest was Kid Elberfeld, who still went by that nickname at age 61 when he pinch hit for his Fulton, Kitty League club on September 12, 1936. He grounded out to third.

The accompanying list shows the oldest player in the minors each season from 1900 through 1984. In 29 of those years the oldest player made a token appearance of one or two games. Almost all player positions are represented, with pitcher being most dominant. The only player to make an appearance as a pinch runner was Pepper Martin, a coach for Tulsa in the Texas League in 1958. The Wild Horse of the Osage was 54.

Oldest Minor League Player Each Year
(Age, position, team and league)

1900   Jim O'Rourke, 48, C, Bridgeport, Connecticut
1901   Jim O'Rourke, 49, C, Bridgeport, Connecticut
1902   Jim O'Rourke, 50, C, Bridgeport, Connecticut
1903   Jim O'Rourke, 51, C, Bridgeport, Connecticut
1904   Jim O'Rourke, 52, C, Bridgeport, Connecticut
1905   Jim O'Rourke, 53, C, Bridgeport, Connecticut
1906   Jim O'Rourke, 54, 1B, Bridgeport, Connecticut
1907   Jim O'Rourke, 55, 1B, Bridgeport, Connecticut
1908   Jim O'Rourke, 56, C-OF, Bridgeport, Connecticut
1909   *Jim O'Rourke, 57, C, Bridgeport, Connecticut
1910   William Hart, 45, P, Chattanooga, Southern
1911   *John McCloskey, 49, SS, Butte, Union Assoc.
1912   *Jim O'Rourke, 60, C, New Haven, Connecticut
         *John McCloskey, 50, PH, Ogden, Union Assoc.
1913   Jesse Burkett, 43, OF, Worcester, Eastern
1914   Deacon Van Buren, 43, OF, Sacramento, Pacific Coast
1915   *John McCloskey, 53, PH, El Paso, Rio Grande Valley
1916   Jesse Burkett, 46, OF, Three teams, Eastern
1917   Joe McGinnity, 46, P, Butte-Great Falls, Northwest
1918   Joe McGinnity, 47, P, Vancouver, Pacific Coast Int.
1919   *Jack Dunn, 45, P, Baltimore, International
1920   Dave Altizer, 43, OF, Madison, South Dakota
1921   Bobby Wallace, 47, SS, Muskogee, Southwestern

*Indicates token appearances
Runnersup over 50 also listed. See 1912, for example

1922	Joe McGinnity, 51, P, Dubuque, Mississippi Valley
1923	Joe McGinnity, 52, P, Dubuque, Mississippi Valley
1924	Walter Kay, 46, OF, Wilkes-Barre, NY-Penn.
1925	Joe McGinnity, 54, P, Dubuque, Mississippi Valley
1926	George Jackson, 44, OF-1B, Greenville, East Texas
1927	George Jackson, 45, 1B, Tyler, Lone Star
1928	George Jackson, 46, 1B-OF, Tyler, Lone Star
1929	George Jackson, 47, 1B, Laurel-El Dor. Cotton States
1930	George Jackson, 48, 1B, El Dorado, Cotton States
1931	George Jackson, 49, 1B, El Dorado, Cotton States
1932	George Jackson, 50, 1B, El Dorado, Cotton States
1933	*Howard Holmes, 50, PH, Dayton, Middle Atlantic
1934	*Gabby Street, 51, C, Mission, Pacific Coast
1935	*Jack Quinn, 51, P, Johnstown, Middle Atlantic
1936	*Kid Elberfeld, 61, PH, Fulton, Kitty
	*Howard Holmes, 53, PH, Dayton, Middle Atlantic
1937	*Bill McCorry, 50, P, Albany, Eastern
1938	*Bill McCorry, 51, P, Albany, Eastern
	Grover Hartley, 50, C, Findlay, Ohio State
1939	*Bill McCorry, 52, P, Ogden, Pioneer
	Wally Schang, 50, C, Ottawa, Canadian-American
	*Grover Hartley, 51, C, Findlay, Ohio State
1940	Lefty George, 53, P, York, Interstate
	Ray Caldwell, 52, P, Fremont, Ohio State
	*Truck Hannah, 51, C, Memphis, Southern
	Wally Schang, 51, C, Three Rivers, Provincial
1941	*Bill McCorry, 54, P, Ogden, Pioneer
	Ben Tincup, 50, P, Paducah, Kitty
1942	*Bill McCorry, 55, P, Ogden, Pioneer
	Wally Schang, 53, C, Augusta, South Atlantic
	Bruno Haas, 51, P-OF, Grand Forks, Northern
	*Ben Tincup, 51, P, Fargo-Moorhead, Northern
	*Steve O'Neill, 51, C, Beaumont, Texas
1943	Lefty George, 57, P, York, Interstate
	Wally Schang, 54, C, Utica, Eastern
1944	*Lefty George, 57, P, York, Interstate
1945	Wally Schang, 56, C, Marion, Ohio State
	Jim Poole, 50, 1B, Statesville, No. Caro. State
1946	Wally Schang, 57, C, Marion, Ohio State
	*Bruno Haas, 55, P, Fargo-Moorhead, Northern
	Jim Poole, 51, 1B, Moultrie, Georgia-Florida
1947	Sam Gibson, 48, P, Radford, Blue Ridge
1948	Charlie Root, 49, P, Billings, Pioneer
1949	Sam Gibson, 50, P, Griffin, Georgia-Alabama
1950	*Charles Milner, 59, P, Valley, Georgia-Alabama
1951	*Charles Milner, 60, P, Valley, Georgia-Alabama
1952	Albert Reitz, 48, P, Blackwell, K.O.M.

1953	*Charles Shaney, 53, P, Asheville, Tri-State
1954	*Charles Shaney, 54, P, Asheville, Tri-State
	*Herb Brett, 54, P, Winston-Salem, Carolina
	*Pepper Martin, 50, PH, Portsmouth, Piedmont
1955	*Charles Shaney, 55, P, Asheville, Tri-State
	*Mike Ryba, 52, P, Houston, Texas
1956	*Lefty O'Doul, 59, PH, Vancouver, Pacific Coast
	Satchel Paige, 50, P, Miami, International
1957	Satchel Paige, 51, P, Miami, International
1958	*Pepper Martin, 54, PR, Tulsa, Texas
	Satchel Paige, 52, P, Miami, International
1959	*Frank Scalzi, 46, PH, Charleston, South Atlantic
1960	Luke Easter, 45, 1B, Rochester, International
1961	Satchel Paige, 55, P, Portland, Pacific Coast
1962	Luke Easter, 47, 1B, Rochester, International
1963	Luke Easter, 48, 1B, Rochester, International
1964	Luke Easter, 49, 1B, Rochester, International
1965	*Ray Hathaway, 48, P, Raleigh, Carolina
1966	*Satchel Paige, 60, P, Peninsula, Carolina
1967	*Warren Spahn, 46, P, Tulsa, Texas
1968	Art Fowler, 46, P, Denver, Pacific Coast
1969	*Hub Kittle, 52, P, Savannah, Southern
1970	Art Fowler, 48, P, Denver, Pacific Coast
1971	Minnie Minoso, 48, 1B, Gomez Palacio, Mexican
1972	Minnie Minoso, 49, 1B, Gomez Palacio, Mexican
1973	Minnie Minoso, 50, 1B, Gomez Palacio, Mexican
1974	Jose Guerrero, 48, OF, Gomez Palacio, Mexican
1975	Moises Camacho, 42, 1B, Poza Rica, Mexican
1976	*Vern Rapp, 48, C, Denver, American Association
1977	Pilo Gaspar, 47, C, Chihuahua, Mexican
1978	George Brunet, 43, P, Poza Rica, Mexican
1979	George Brunet, 44, P, Coatza.-MC Tigers, Mexican
1980	*Hub Kittle, 63, P, Springfield, American Assoc.
1981	George Brunet, 46, P, Augila, Mexican
1982	George Brunet, 47, P, Veracruz, Mexican
1983	George Brunet, 48, P, Veracruz, Mexican
1984	George Brunet, 49, P, Saltillo-Monterrey, Mexican

Vangilder in the Vanguard as Streak-Stopper

Two of the greatest minor league batting records were the 69-game hitting streak of Joe Wilhoit of Wichita in 1919 and the 15 consecutive hits by George Quellich of Reading in 1929. Although these two spectacular streaks occurred ten years apart and in different areas of the country, they were both stopped by the same hurler. His name was Elam Vangilder, a better-than-average hurler with the St. Louis Browns in the ten-year interval.

First, let us review the 1919 streak. Wilhoit, who had played the outfield for the Braves, Pirates, and Giants from 1916 to 1918, started the 1919 season with Seattle in the Pacific League. He batted poorly and was soon shipped to Wichita in the Class A Western League. There he also started slowly, but after a few weeks he caught fire and his record for sustained batting performance has never been equalled in the history of baseball.

Wilhoit started his streak on June 14 when Wichita was in last place. On August 1 he ran his string to 50 games to surpass the existing Organized Baseball record of Jack Ness of Oakland in 1915. Wilhoit remembered that occasion because he had homered in the 2-1 victory for Vernon when Ness' record was snapped on July 22, 1915. Wilhoit tacked 19 more games on his streak, moving up to 69 games by August 19. The next day Vangilder took the mound for Tulsa and got the Wichita wonder to fly out, to ground out to the shortstop, and then set him down on strikes. Wilhoit came up for the last time in the seventh inning and was walked by recruit hurler Jack Williams, who was wild in his debut and ultimately was charged with the loss. One report had Tulsa manager Spencer Abbott ordering the base on balls.

As a result of the blanking, Wilhoit's batting average "dropped" to .445. During the 69-game streak he had batted a phenomenal .505, and his 151 hits included 23 doubles, 8 triples, and 5 home runs. He had helped raise the club from the cellar to third place and closed out the season with a batting mark of .422, easily tops in the league.

In regard to Vangilder, he went up to the St. Louis Browns where he had some productive seasons. He was 19-13 in 1922, and led the majors in relief wins with 11 in 1925. He also was a good hitter, batting .244 lifetime. Van was traded to the Tigers in 1928 and after a brief appearance with Detroit the next season was released. He caught on with Montreal in the International League, and this brings us up to date with the second great batting streak he squelched.

The Reading Keys had a strong hitting club in 1929. Outfielder Danny Taylor led the league in batting with a .371 average. Another hard-hitting gardener was left fielder George Quellich, who enhanced his record considerably in the period of August 9 to 12. He started his consecutive hit streak by connecting for a homer, double, and single in the last three at bats against Toronto on August 9. The next day he splurged with a homer and five singles in six trips against Montreal. On August 11 he had two homers and two singles, as well as an intentional walk in four trips. That gave him 13 consecutive hits, one above the O.B. mark of 12 held by Jim Cooney of Milwaukee in 1923.

On August 12, Montreal sent Vangilder to the hill to face Reading. He gave up a single to Quellich in the first, walked him in the third, gave up a grand slam homer in the 4th and permitted him a sacrifice fly in the sixth. In the eighth he got Quellich to loft a fly to center fielder Hinky Haines to close out the remarkable string. Although hit hard, Vangilder went the distance in the 11-7 loss. However, he had stopped the redhot Reading record-setter and he collected three hits himself.

Quellich quit with 15 hits in 15 trips, including five homers and one double. He also scored nine runs and knocked in 14. Actually, he didn't cool off for several days. Through games of August 9 to 16, he had 29 hits in 36 trips, an .806 pace. He finished the 1929 season with 31 home runs and a .349 batting average. After two more years in the International League, the Tigers had him up for a trial in 1931, when he batted .222 in 13 games.

As for Vangilder, he went on pitching for many years. And he didn't neglect his hitting, either. Hurling his first game for Jackson in the Kitty League in 1936, he collected two homers and three singles in five trips. He was 40 years old.

Batting Average During Hitting Streaks

A review of the minor leagues' longest consecutive game hitting streaks reveals a great disparity in production during those streaks. Ironically, the player with the longest string, Joe Wilhoit, who hit in 69 consecutive games, had by far the highest average — .505. This was 65 percentage points higher than Jack Ness hit in his 49-game streak in 1915.

The lowest average for players with hit streaks of 42 or more games was the .327 mark achieved by Eddie Marshall of Milwaukee in 1935. It is surprising that he could sustain a string of 43 games at that level. One reason is that he batted leadoff which gave him the maximum at bats. His American Association record lasted until 1961 when it was tied by Howie Bedell of Louisville. Bedell batted only .340 in his 43-game string.

Here is the list of players with the longest hitting streaks and their batting averages during those streaks. Full information was not available on one player.

Games	Player, Club, and League	Streak Ended		Batted
69	Joe Wilhoit, Wichita, Western	Aug. 21, 1919	151-299	.505
61	Joe DiMaggio, San Fran., Pacific Coast	July 26, 1933	104-257	.405
55	Roman Mejias, Waco, Big State	Aug. 2, 1954	97-223	.435
50	Otto Pahlman, Danville, III	Sep. 9, 1922	78-196	.398
49	Jack Ness, Oakland, Pacific Coast	July 22, 1915	81-184	.440
49	Harry Chozen, Mobile, Southern	July 25, 1945	70-177	.395
46	John Bates, Nashville, Southern	Sep. 16, 1925	72-194	.371
43	Eddie Marshall, Milwaukee, AA	June 14, 1935	66-202	.327
43	Orlando Moreno, Big Spring, Longhorn	Aug. 5, 1947	(not available)	
43	Howie Bedell, Louisville, AA	June 23, 1961	66-197	.340
42	Herb Chapman, Gadsden, Southeastern	June 4, 1950	63-172	.366

Akin To Get Even

Unassisted triple plays are very unusual happenings, but there was one minor leaguer who participated in two — one on offense and one on defense.

In the only unassisted triple play performed by an outfielder, on July 19, 1911, Roy Akin was the Los Angeles batter who lofted the ball into shallow center field with runners on first and second. Vernon's center fielder, Walter Carlisle, dashed in, made a spectacular catch, touched second, and ran to first for the third out. (See Minor League Stars, Volume 1, pp. 3-4 for details.)

The next year, Akin was playing third base for Waco in the Texas League. In a game against Houston on May 9, 1912, the opposition tried to "double squeeze" both runners home from second and third by bunting down the third base line. However, the bunt was tapped harder than planned and into the air. Akin grabbed it for one out, stepped on third for another, and tagged the player coming in from second. In a few seconds the embarrassment of the previous year was wiped away.

The Men In Blue

The Society has never made a specific study of minor league umpires. Such a project would take considerable research because umpires, unlike players and managers, do not have a published record of game and season statistics to review. Survival and acceptance might be better guides, and the comments would have to come from fellow arbiters and, sometimes grudgingly, from players and managers. There were several "men in blue" who had long service in the high minors. Here are a few of the better known examples.

Bill Carpenter, the chief supervisor of umpires for the National Association from 1945 to his death in 1952, was an umpire in the National League first in 1897 when he was only 23 years old. He moved around considerably in the next 15 years — Inter-State in 1900, New York State 1901-02; Southern Association 1903, 1905, 1908-11; American 1904; National 1906-07 — before landing in the International League in 1912. He was an active ump there until 1933 when he was made chief of staff of the league office. His duties included supervision of umpires and schedule-making. He became so adept at the latter that many leagues used his services. At the 1939 baseball centennial in Cooperstown, NY, he was one of the umpires in the Minor League All-Star game. Two others were Harry (Steamboat) Johnson and Ollie Anderson (see below).

Ollie Anderson started umpiring in the Northern League in 1903 and in his first six years in the lower classifications he was the only umpire to last the season in his particular league. Looking back in 1941, he said "those were not the good old days." He tried to do something about it, designing new ballparks in such southeast towns as High Point, Spartanburg, Augusta, and Macon which permitted umpires to reach their dressing room without passing through the crowd. Anderson, less than six feet tall and weighing only 140 pounds, survived. He officiated in 14 different circuits, including the Texas, Pacific Coast, and the American Association. He also spent 1914 in the Federal League. From 1934 to 1941 he was umpire in chief of the Western Association. He had umpired in approximately 5000 consecutive games prior to an auto accident which hospitalized him in 1936. Minor league officials, players, and fans showed enthusiastic appreciation at his retirement at the Topeka park on August 22, 1941. Wartime shortage of personnel caused his return to service in the California League in 1942. He was 68 and it was his 40th year as an ump. His frequent response when players objected to his calls was "I wish I were Santa Claus so I could give you everything you want."

William (Big Bill) Guthrie was a sharply contrasting figure to Anderson, not only in appearance but in manner of speaking. He was a bull-necked, barrel-chested native of Chicago who talked like a Capone henchman. He was officiating in the American Association in 1925 when Hack Wilson was playing with Toledo. Guthrie called a third strike on the squat one, who angrily threw his bat high in the air. Big Bill barked, "Listen kid, if dat bat comes down to oith, youse is otta de game." This was a story subsequently adopted by other umpires but without the peculiar accent. Actually, under that domineering facade Guthrie was a capable umpire. He started in the Missouri Valley League in 1904 when he was 19 and moved around considerably in the next 30 years. He wasn't in as many leagues as Anderson but he had second and third tours in some circuits — the III, AA, PCL, and SA. He also worked in the National in

1913-15 and the AL 1922 and 1928-32. His final tour was back in the AA, 1935-43, where he became fast friends with **George (Tiny) Johnson,** dean of AA umpires. Johnson confirmed that Guthrie, so fully in charge on the field, was docile and caring in the home environment. Big Bill died in Chicago in 1950 at age 64.

"Tiny" was not a reverse nickname for Johnson. He really was small — but smart and resourceful. He lacked the playing ability of his brother Ernie, a major league shortstop between 1912 and 1925, so launched his career as an umpire in the Central League in 1909. He was in the New York State League in 1913 and the next year began a lenghty career in the AA. The National League offered him a job, but AA President Tom Hickey refused to give up his prize arbiter. Johnson retired after the 1943 season. He later became a regional supervisor of umpires for the National Association, serving until 1955. He died in Hinsdale, Illinois, on Christmas Day, 1971.

Harry (Steamboat) Johnson started in the Western League in 1912, went to the III in 1913, and then the NL in 1914. Then it was the New York State League, 1915-18, and the Southern Association, 1919-20. After one year in the South Atlantic, he returned to the Southern, where he continued to call balls and strikes through 1946. He was supervisor of SA umps 1947-51. Johnson, who was behind the plate in the longest SA game, a 23-inning tie between Atlanta and Chattanooga in 1919, became a Dixie institution long before his death at age 66 in 1951. He got his nickname because his booming voice "resembled the blast of a Mississippi River sidewheeler." In 1935 he published a book about his chosen profession entitled "Standing the Gaff."

Cornelius (Jack) Powell started his umpiring career a little later than some because he was a minor league player for 12 years. He started calling balls and strikes in the Michigan-Ontario League in 1922 and "upward mobility" landed him in the National League in 1924. He was there only one year and blamed his short tenure on several run-ins with New York Giants manager John McGraw. He then moved to the Western League in 1925, the AA in 1926-28, and the PCL for his first tour in 1929-32. Powell was back in the NL in 1933 (John McGraw having retired), but for less than a year. He worked the IL in 1933-34 and then spent 18 straight years in the PCL. He retired in 1952 and served as supervisor of umpires for the National Association in 1953-54.

Powell had two unusual traits. He thrived on boos. "The more the better," he said. "If the fans didn't boo, I might as well pack my bags and quit. I just wouldn't be doing a good or honest job." He also refused to use a balls-and-strikes indicator most of the time when he worked behind the plate, insisting that he could keep the count in his head. In 1951, near the end of his active career, he was given a "night" at Gilmore Field in Hollywood. Powell died in Lynwood, California, in 1971 at age 85.

Of the six umpires cited above, only Anderson and Guthrie failed to settle in for a lengthy tour in one circuit. Powell had 22 years in the PCL; Carpenter 21 in the IL; Steamboat Johnson 28 in the SA; and Tiny Johnson more than 20 in the AA.

Have Toe-Plate, Will Travel

In the National Association office there are contract records of almost every one who played or managed in Organized Baseball since the Association was established in 1902. The person with the largest number of individual entries is some one (no, not George Brunet) most readers have never heard of. His name is Bill Sisler, a diminutive southpaw pitcher and occasional outfielder and no relation to the George Sisler baseball family.

In an odyssey that began in 1923 with Elmira of the New York-Penn League and ended in 1950 with Auburn of the Border League, Bill signed contracts with 50 clubs. Because most of his stops were very brief, he may, in fact, have signed additional contracts which were never filed with the National Association. In only one year, 1939, was he without a professional affiliation. Amazingly, Clarksburg, West Virginia, was the only city in which he made two stops.

Some Minor League Committee members have become fascinated with the record or "non-record" of this man, probably the most nomadic of all minor leaguers. They have tried to track his performance, but the old guides usually did not carry records of players in fewer than 10 games. This necessitated going to the newspaper box scores. Committee member Ed Brooks of Delmar, NY, went beyond the paper search and tried to locate the elusive Sisler in upstate New York. The pitcher was a native of Rochester and played and umpired semi-pro baseball in that area when he was unable to make an OB connection. Sisler could not be found, but it is perhaps no coincidence that his last known address was on a street near Silver Stadium, the home of the Rochester Red Wings.

Not making direct contact with Sisler, we must focus on his incomplete record, shown on the accompanying page. He had a pitching log of 36-57 in 175 games, most of them incomplete. In 1942 he remained with Staunton of the Virginia League long enough to appear in 23 games with an 8-10 showing. That was a war year and the shortage of personnel undoubtedly made Sisler more employable. He reached his highest league classification in 1944 and 1945, going 1-0 with Syracuse and 0-2 with Minneapolis. Almost all of his career work was in the lower classifications. In 1948 at the age of 45, Bill appeared in four games with Harlan, breaking even at 1-1. He managed at Granby in 1946, Rehoboth Beach in 1949, and Auburn in 1950, but was let go in mid-season by all three clubs.

We can only speculate that in his over-riding desire to play baseball or be associated with the game in some capacity he must have oversold himself to management time after time. When he couldn't perform up to expectations — again time after time — he was released and moved on to the next opportunity. It was probably somewhat like Harold Hill in "The Music Man" but with no malice intended. One imagines that Sisler still might be out there somewhere, battered suitcase and round trip bus ticket in hand, heading for another opportunity to get involved in a game which he must have loved very much.

WILLIAM J. SISLER
Born November 17, 1903 at Rochester, NY.
Batted and threw left. Height 5.06. Weight 150.

Year	Club	League	G	W	L
1923	Elmira	NY-Penn	3	0	0
1924	Montreal/Rutland	Que.-Ont.-Vt.	2	0	0
1925	Moline	Miss. Valley			
1926	Lawrence	New England			

Year	Team	League			
1927	Shamokin	NY-Penn			
	Muskogee	Western Assn.	4	0	1
1928	Martinsburg	Blue Ridge	2	1	0
	Clarks/Charleroi	Mid. Atl.		3	1
1929	Lewiston/Auburn	New England	2	1	0
1930	Scranton	NY-Penn	5	0	0
	St. Thomas	Ontario	11	5	2
1931	Clarksburg	Mid. Atl.	1	1	0
1932	Dayton	Central	(Did not play)		
1933	Johnstown	Mid. Atl.	16	5	8
	York	NY-Penn	5	1	3
1934	Muskegon	Central	(Did not play)		
1935	Terre Haute	III	(Did not play)		
1936	Ogdensburg	Can.-Am.	8	2	2
1937	South Boston	Bi-State	3	1	1
	Thomasville	N.Caro. St.	15	5	4
1938	Portsmouth	Piedmont	(Did not play)		
	Bluefield	Mt. State	(Less than 10 games)		
	Danville	Bi-State	1	0	1
1939	(Not in Organized Baseball)				
1940	Sunbury	Interstate	2	0	1
	Oneonta	Can.-Am.	1	0	0
	St. Joseph	Mich. St.			
	London	Pony	6	0	2
1941	Newport News	Virginia	4	3	0
	Gadsden	Southeastern	2	0	0
1942	Ft. Pierce	Flordia E.C.			
	Staunton	Virginia	23	8	10
	Quebec City	Can.-Am.	2	1	1
1943	Trenton	Interstate	9	1	6
	Springfield	Eastern	16	1	8
1944	Syracuse	International	8	1	0
1945	Binghamton	Eastern	2	0	0
	Memphis	Southern Assn.	6	0	2
	Minneapolis	American Assn.	2	0	2
1946	Granby	Border	(Manager)		
	Anderson	Tri-State	8	0	0
1947	Gainesville	Big State	6	1	1
	Daytona Beach	Florida St.			
	Bridgeport	Colonial	1	0	1
	Nyack	No. Atlantic	6	2	2
	Smithfield-Selma	Tobacco State	1	0	0
1948	Harlan	Mt. State	4	1	1
1949	Rehoboth Beach	East. Shore	(Manager)		
1950	Auburn	Border	(Manager)		

Luke Easter, a big drawing card at Buffalo.

Player records of certain minor leagues which, for some technical or other reason did not come under the supervision of the National Association in specific years, are included in the minor league totals in this book. Some examples are the American League in 1900, the American Association and California League in 1902, the Pacific Coast League in 1903, TriState League (Penn-NJ-Del) in 1904-07, Provincial League in 1937-39 and 1947-49, and the pre-1955 Mexican League. On the other hand, the Vermont League of 1904-06, which employed such name hurlers as Rube Vickers, Andy Coakley, Ed Reulbach, and Jack Coombs, is not included because of direct violations.

Player Records (Non-Pitchers)

THOMAS WOODLEY (WOODY) ABERNATHY
Born October 16, 1908 at Athens, AL. Died March 1, 1961 at Houston, TX
Batted left. Threw right. Height 6.01½. Weight 195.

Year	Club	League	Pos	G	AB	R	H	2B	3B	HR	RBI	SB	BA
1928	Vicksburg	Cot St	1B-OF	123	472	60	169	33	16	2	-	6	.358
1929	Montgomery	SEastern	OF	138	507	85	172	30	13	3	80	12	.339
1930	Montgomery	SEastern	OF	136	508	79	172	22	11	4	77	15	.339
1931	Birmingham	South A	1B-OF	118	427	67	133	17	12	10	74	6	.311
1932	Birmingham	South A	OF-1B	78	284	47	91	12	6	8	55	4	.320
1933	Birmingham	South A	1B-OF	150	577	77	186	35	12	10	101	4	.322
1934	Baltimore	Int	OF-1B	151	563	102	174	24	9	32*	120	5	.309
1935	Baltimore	Int	OF-1B	149	544	97	150	25	9	31	110	12	.276
1936	Baltimore	Int	OF-1B	149	554	132*	171	24	3	42*	127	11	.309
1937	Baltimore	Int	OF	148	546	94	155	29	2	21	71	3	.284
1938	Buffalo	Int	OF	103	375	76	121	27	5	21	74	3	.323
1939	Knoxville	South A	OF	135	485	84	161	32	4	16	103	5	.332
1940	St. Paul/Mil	A A	OF	135	506	60	142	35	4	10	87	5	.281
	Minors			1713	6348	1060	1997	345	106	210	1079	91	.315

TEOLINDO ANTONIO ACOSTA
Born July 23, 1937 at Maracaibo, Venezuela
Batted left. Threw left. Height 5.06. Weight 158.

Year	Club	League	Pos	G	AB	R	H	2B	3B	HR	RBI	SB	BA
1958	Dothan	Ala-Fla	OF	124*	520*	95	163*	19	3	6	76	36*	.313
1959	Dothan	Ala-Fla	OF	119	457	92	154	29	7	7	46	46*	.337
1960	Billings/Miss	Pioneer	OF	121	491	114	181	17	6	6	69	45*	.369*
1961	Columbia	Sally	OF	125	487	104	167*	11	9	1	27	40*	.343*
1962	San Diego	P C	OF	13	29	6	8	1	2	0	3	0	.276
	Macon	Sally	OF	89	313	53	92	10	4	0	28	16	.294
1963	Macon	Sally	OF	141*	544	79	152	18	5	1	36	21	.279
1964	Macon	South A	OF	121	405	66	109	20	0	1	33	15	.269
1965	Peninsula	Carolina	OF	141	497	100	167*	21	8	2	53	23	.336
1966	Knoxville	South A	OF	15	51	12	14	5	0	0	4	3	.275
	Buffalo	Int	OF	113	377	59	108	17	3	5	37	9	.286
1967	Buffalo	Int	OF	49	160	14	38	5	1	0	6	3	.238
1968	Puebla	Mexican	OF	99	354	53	115	16	6	4	39	15	.325
1969	Puebla	Mexican	OF	142	534	87	189*	29	9	6	82	18	.354*
1970	Yucatan	Mexican	OF	140	469	76	158	26	14*	3	55	14	.337
1971	Yucatan	Mexican	OF	133	441	75	173	22	11	7	71	17	.392*
1972	Yucatan	Mexican	OF	134	492	77	170	25	11	4	51	11	.346
1973	Yucatan/Pueb	Mexican	OF	121	419	64	157	17	8	9	66	11	.375
1974	Puebla	Mexican	OF	122	464	93*	170*	17	6	2	43	20	.366*
1975	Villahermosa	Mexican	OF	109	416	43	133	9	8	0	30	19	.320
1976	Nuevo Laredo	Mexican	OF	101	384	48	106	5	0	0	19	7	.276
	Minors			2272	8304	1410	2724	339	121	64	874	389	.328

DAVID TILDEN ALTIZER
Born November 6, 1876 at Pearl, IL. Died May 14, 1964 at Pleasant Hill, IL
Batted left. Threw right. Height 5.10½. Weight 160.
Set American Association season record with 61 sacrifice hits in 1910.

Year	Club	League	Pos	G	AB	R	H	2B	3B	HR	SB	BA
1902	Buffalo	Eastern	SS	1	2	0	0	0	0	0	1	.000
	Meriden	Conn	3B	91	351	77	107	12	2	0	39	.305
1903	Meriden	Conn	3B	66	253	39	65	5	0	0	26	.257
	Toledo	A A	SS-3B	22	79	5	12	1	0	0	1	.152
1904	Meri/Spring	Conn	IF	107	383	61	108	10	2	0	51	.282
1905	Springfield	Conn	SS	91	356	79	125	26	0	1	39	.351
1906	Lancaster	Tri-St	SS	27	105	25	38	6	3	1	12	.362
	Washington	American	SS-OF	115	433	56	111	9	5	1	37	.256
1907	Washington	American	SS-1B	147	540	60	145	15	5	2	38	.269
1908	Wash/Clev	American	UT	96	294	30	65	2	3	0	15	.221
1909	Chicago	American	OF-1B	116	382	47	89	6	7	1	27	.233
1910	Cincinnati	National	SS	3	10	3	6	0	0	0	0	.600
	Minneapolis	A A	SS	163	580	111*	174	18	10	2	65*	.300
1911	Cincinnati	National	SS	37	75	8	17	4	1	0	2	.227
	Minneapolis	A A	SS	73	284	64	95	13	3	1	30	.335
1912	Minneapolis	A A	SS	162	625	125	184	21	4	6	68*	.294
1913	Minneapolis	A A	SS	166	640	141*	187	37	6	4	24	.292
1914	Minneapolis	A A	SS	170	635	132	210	37	9	14	32	.331
1915	Minneapolis	A A	SS	149	582	118*	176	26	11	8	19	.302
1916	Minneapolis	A A	IF-OF	164	597	108*	178	22	9	8	17	.298
1917	Minneapolis	A A	OF-IF	149	525	85	169	20	4	7	18	.322
1918	Minneapolis	A A	OF-IF	52	174	16	42	2	1	1	5	.241
1919	(Not in OB)											
1920	Aber/Mad	S Dak	UT	93	336	-	101	-	-	-	-	.301
1921	Madison	Dakota	UT	52	174	42	56	6	4	2	7	.322
	Majors			**514**	**1734**	**204**	**433**	**36**	**21**	**4**	**119**	**.250**
	Minors			**1798**	**6681**	**1228**	**2027**	**262**	**68**	**55**	**454**	**.303**

ROGELIO ALVAREZ (HERNANDEZ)
Born April 18, 1938 at Santa Lucia, Pinar del Rio, Cuba.
Batted right. Threw right. Height 5.11. Weight 185.

Year	Club	League	Pos	G	AB	R	H	2B	3B	HR	RBI	SB	BA
1956	Yuma	Ariz-Mex	1B-OF	12	40	2	13	2	1	1	11	1	.325
	Port Arthur	Big St	1B-OF	82	308	34	93	8	4	4	38	4	.302
1957	Clovis	SWestern	1B	48	210	59	77	10	1	24	86	2	.367
	Wenatchee	NWest	1B	80	291	50	86	14	6	15	74	4	.296
1958	Havana	Int	1B-OF	146	485	67	130	23	5	25	88	2	.268
1959	Havana	Int	1B-P	145	506	51	99	19	1	22	65	3	.196
1960	Jersey City	Int	1B-P	151	527	61	134	20	1	17	72	2	.254
	Cincinnati	National	1B	3	9	1	1	0	0	0	0	0	.111
1961	Jersey City	Int	1B	140	443	56	101	13	6	12	58	3	.228
1962	San Diego	P C	1B-3B	132	481	88	153	27	5	18	73	3	.318
	Cincinnati	National	1B	14	28	1	6	0	0	0	2	0	.214
1963	San Diego	P C	1B-OF	103	367	51	95	19	2	15	63	1	.259
1964	Macon	Southern	1B-OF	56	144	16	39	7	0	10	42	0	.271
1965	San Diego	P C	1B-OF	31	67	2	14	1	0	2	8	0	.209
	Knoxville	Southern	1B-OF	80	234	25	56	9	0	14	42	0	.239
1966	Knoxville	Southern	1B	114	369	56	115	20	1	27	78	2	.312
	Buffalo	Int	1B	10	39	3	6	3	0	1	4	0	.154
1967	Knoxville/Evans	South A	1B	133	459	46	110	21	1	19*	84	0	.240
1968	Aguila	Mexican	1B-OF	95	310	57	90	11	0	24	72	1	.290
1969	Aguila	Mexican	1B	148	462	86	123	10	1	28	84	0	.266
1970	Aguila	Mexican	1B	146	465	66	134	16	0	33*	93	0	.288
1971	Aguila	Mexican	1B	129	387	29	98	5	0	12	44	0	.253
1972	Poza Rica	Mexican	1B	23	61	8	15	1	0	2	7	0	.246
1973	Yucatan	Mexican	1B-P	104	316	36	74	9	1	12	44	3	.234
	Majors			**17**	**37**	**2**	**7**	**0**	**0**	**0**	**2**	**0**	**.189**
	Minors			**2108**	**6971**	**949**	**1855**	**268**	**36**	**337**	**1230**	**31**	**.266**

JAMES FRED (RED) BENNETT

Born March 15, 1902 at Atkins, AK. Died May 12, 1957 at Atkins, AK
Batted right. Threw right. Height 5.09. Weight 185.

Year	Club	League	Pos	G	AB	R	H	2B	3B	HR	RBI	SB	BA
1924	Ardmore/Musk	West A	1B-OF	48	197	53	68	14	5	7	29	10	.345
1925	Muskogee	West A	OF-2B	149	548	120	189	45	7	32	137	12	.345
1926	Muskogee	West A	OF	87	333	89	126	28	8	25	-	8	.378
	Tulsa	Western	OF	69	254	53	89	20	5	13	-	3	.350
1927	Tulsa	Western	OF	153	608	151	234	55*	14	21	-	11	.385
1928	Tulsa	Western	OF	136	507	136	188	28	5	35	-	5	.371
	St. Louis	American	OF	7	8	0	2	1	0	0	0	0	.250
1929	Wichita Falls	Texas	OF	154	552	127	203	39	11	27	145*	13	.368
1930	Milwaukee	A A	OF	92	301	47	91	23	7	4	52	4	.302
1931	Pittsburgh	National	OF	32	89	6	25	5	0	1	7	0	.281
	Ft. Worth	Texas	OF	18	57	6	16	4	0	1	6	1	.281
	Newark	Int	OF	17	42	5	15	3	0	2	6	0	.357
1932	Albany/Buff	Int	OF	94	299	52	97	26	0	11	66	6	.324
1933	Buffalo/JC	Int	OF	15	42	10	13	3	1	0	7	1	.310
	Dallas	Texas	OF	97	327	56	107	22	2	7	63	13	.327
1934	Dallas	Texas	OF	102	339	50	89	21	4	6	62	8	.263
1935	Little Rock	South A	OF	14	56	5	10	0	1	0	4	1	.179
1936-37	(Not in O.B.)												
1938	Marshall	E Texas	OF	(Less than 10 games)									
	Monroe/Green	Cot St	OF	95	338	70	115	21	4	6	71	9	.340
	Nashville	South A	PH	4	2	1	0	0	0	0	2	0	.000
1939	Richmond	Piedmont	PH	2	1	0	0	0	0	0	0	0	.000
	Kannapolis	N Car St	OF	17	60	3	19	5	0	0	17	0	.317
	Majors			**39**	**97**	**6**	**27**	**6**	**0**	**1**	**7**	**0**	**.278**
	Minors			**1363**	**4863**	**1034**	**1669**	**357**	**74**	**197**	**667**	**109**	**.343**

JOSEPH AUGUST BERGER

Born December 20, 1886 at St. Louis, MO. Died March 6, 1956 at Rock Island, IL
Batted right. Threw right. Height 5.10½. Weight 170.

Year	Club	League	Pos	G	AB	R	H	2B	3B	HR	SB	BA
1907	Rock Island	III	SS	116	421	36	84	-	-	-	14	.200
1908	Rock Island	III	SS	133	450	34	96	15	9	0	10	.213
1909	Rock Island	III	SS	137	474	67	119	17	6	3	31	.251
1910	Mobile	South A	SS	146	453	57	91	15	5	2	13	.201
1911	Pueblo	Western	SS	172	652	128*	198	41	17*	6	20	.304
1912	Los Angeles	P C	SS	197	722	120	201	36	7	8	29	.278
1913	Chicago	American	2-S-3	77	223	27	48	6	2	2	5	.215
1914	Chicago	American	S-2-3	47	148	11	23	3	1	0	2	.155
1915	Vernon	P C	SS	202	737	92	185	29	5	5	23	.251
1916	Oakland	P C	SS	169	565	40	136	16	1	0	10	.241
1917	Rock Island	III	SS	62	222	33	53	11	0	2	13	.239
	Wichita	Western	SS	67	245	37	69	11	4	0	3	.282
1918	Wichita	Western	SS	63	230	34	70	19	2	3	6	.304
	Louisville	A A	SS	10	32	5	6	1	1	0	2	.188
1919	Wichita	Western	SS	103	371	71	116	23	11	1	6	.313
1920	Wichita	Western	SS	154	582	119	178	42	3	5	19	.306
1921	Wichita	Western	SS	165	651	155	213	61	6	8	14	.327
1922	Wichita	Western	SS	159	634	150	229	55	8	6	21	.361
1923	Wichita Falls	Texas	SS	145	519	83	158	36	4	6	12	.304
1924	Denver	Western	SS	166	663	133	210	35	7	12	28	.317
1925	Denver	Western	SS	150	552	116	184	33	10	6	17	.333
1926	Denver	Western	SS	21	48	6	12	6	1	0	2	.250
1927	Denver	Western	1B	53	135	19	39	7	2	1	1	.289
1928	Augusta	Sally	2B	18	57	6	12	1	0	1	0	.211
	Majors			**124**	**371**	**38**	**71**	**9**	**3**	**2**	**7**	**.191**
	Minors			**2608**	**9415**	**1541**	**2659**	**510**	**109**	**75**	**294**	**.282**

JAMES TILTON (SUNNY JIM) BLAKESLEY

Born October 16, 1896 at Mulhall, OK. Died July 8, 1965 at Inglewood, CA
Batted left. Threw right. Height 5.10. Weight 190.

Year Club	League	Pos	G	AB	R	H	2B	3B	HR	RBI	SB	BA
1920 Henryetta	West A	OF	116	466	73	138	29	6	6	41	9	.296
Wichita	Western	OF	16	62	19	25	7	4	0	-	0	.403
1921 Wichita	Western	OF	150	548	105	192	46	8	25	-	18	.350
1922 Wichita	Western	OF	159	649	141	222	60	5	14	-	21	.342
1923 Wichita	Western	OF	169	685	151*	246	53	16*	36	-	25	.359
1924 Vernon	P C	OF	181	692	138	218	51	14	11	101	9	.315
1925 Vernon	P C	OF	121	420	59	120	26	13	13	62	8	.286
1926 Omaha	Western	OF	140	541	129	208	49	10	39	-	15	.384*
1926 New Orleans	South A	OF	11	31	6	9	0	1	0	3	0	.290
1927 New Orleans	South A	OF	117	426	67	130	24	12	3	70	7	.305
1928 New Haven	Eastern	OF	152	568	119	217*	50*	13	19	108	10	.382*
1929 New Orleans	South A	OF	135	482	94	162	22	14	8	106	11	.336
1930 New Orleans	South A	OF	140	521	94	173	24	16	6	99	10	.332
1931 Dallas	Texas	OF	25	86	10	20	6	1	0	7	4	.233
New Haven/Rich	Eastern	OF	114	428	64	125	18	12	9	66	7	.292
1932 Richmond	Eastern	OF	58	230	35	73	11	2	4	34	3	.317
1933 Durham	Piedmont	OF	46	182	38	60	11	1	8	45	11	.330
Minors			**1850**	**7017**	**1342**	**2338**	**487**	**148**	**201**	**742**	**168**	**.333**

JOE JOHN BONOWITZ

Born August 12, 1899 at Columbus, OH. Died September 4, 1969 at Hollywood, FL
Batted right. Threw right. Height 5.10½. Weight 165.

Year Club	League	Pos	G	AB	R	H	2B	3B	HR	RBI	SB	BA
1918 St. Jospeh	Western	C-3-1	35	98	7	15	1	0	2	-	0	.153
1919 St. Joseph	Western	OF	115	419	49	112	26	3	2	-	2	.267
1920 St. Joseph	Western	OF	146	586	70	158	16	9	3	-	8	.270
1921 St. Joseph	Western	OF	49	211	39	65	15	6	3	-	3	.308
1922 St. Joseph	Western	OF	159	648	96	205	44	12	11	-	5	.316
1923 Omaha	Western	OF	166	655	99	185	47	7	5	-	15	.282
1924 Omaha	Western	OF	166	665	111	213	37	11	18	-	25	.320
1925 Shreveport	Texas	OF	148	571	83	141	26	6	21	93	12	.247
1926 Shreveport	Texas	OF	136	487	58	154	36	2	7	79	7	.316
1927 Ft. Worth	Texas	OF	152	563	61	165	43	5	8	92	15	.293
1928 Ft. Worth	Texas	OF	155	578	87	193	54*	3	3	117	6	.334
1929 Ft. Worth	Texas	OF	140	571	108	205	43	7	16	104	12	.359
Hollywood	P C	OF	22	79	10	22	6	1	1	24	0	.278
1930 Ft. Worth	Texas	OF	152	631	89	205	47	7	17	105	5	.325
1931 Mobile/Knox	South A	OF	152	605	77	181	22	11	6	82	12	.299
1932 Chattanooga	South A	OF	141	577	73	202	34	8	3	85	4	.350
1933 Atlanta	South A	OF	142	556	79	173	35	14	10	104	4	.311
1934 Williamsport	NY-Penn	OF	132	535	85	173	24	13	6	76	2	.323
1935 Norfolk	Piedmont	OF	9	42		15	2	1	1	12	0	.357
1936 Americus	Ga-Fla	OF	48	200	46	72	15	4	8	40	3	.360
Chattanooga	South A	OF	67	258	29	71	6	6	0	29	2	.275
Minors			**2432**	**9535**	**1356**	**2925**	**579**	**136**	**151**	**1042**	**142**	**.307**

Who was the best minor league player who never played a game in the majors? Probably Mexican League great Hector Espino, who declined the opportunity. There were some other long-service candidates, however, including Larry Barton, Joe Bauman, Ollie Carnegie, Stanley Keyes, Ted Norbert, Al Pinkston, Bill Raimondi, Harry Strohm, Spider Baum, Ed Greer, Bill Thomas, and Hal Turpin.

HENRY JOHN (ZEKE) BONURA

Born September 20, 1908 at New Orleans, LA
Batted right. Threw right. Height 6.00. Weight 210.

Year	Club	League	Pos	G	AB	R	H	2B	3B	HR	RBI	SB	BA
1929	New Orleans	South A	2B-1B	131	460	81	148	24	14	9	86	6	.322
1930	New Orleans	South A	1B	55	182	35	64	12	2	8	38	3	.352
1931	New Orleans	South A	1B-2B	85	234	34	84	16	4	1	57	0	.359
	Indianapolis	A A	1B	23	52	9	14	2	0	0	8	0	.269
1932	Dallas	Texas	1B	144	509	101	164	39	3	21	110	9	.322
1933	Dallas	Texas	1B	152	516	141*	184	43	3	24*	111*	19	.357
1934	Chicago	American	1B	127	510	86	154	35	4	27	110	0	.302
1935	Chicago	American	1B	138	550	107	162	34	4	21	92	4	.295
1936	Chicago	American	1B	148	587	120	194	39	7	12	138	4	.330
1937	Chicago	American	1B	116	447	79	154	41	2	19	100	5	.345
1938	Washington	American	1B	137	540	72	156	27	3	22	114	2	.289
1939	New York	National	1B	123	455	75	146	26	6	11	85	1	.321
1940	Washington	American	1B	79	311	41	85	16	3	3	45	2	.273
	Chicago	National	1B	49	182	20	48	14	0	4	20	1	.264
1941	Minneapolis	A A	1B	46	172	47	63	9	1	7	38	2	.366
1942-45	(Military Service)												
1946	Minneapolis	A A	1B	9	25	1	5	1	0	0	6	0	.200
	Thibodaux	Evang	1B	77	247	47	87	13	1	11	54	2	.352
1947	Stamford	Colonial	1B	99	327	78	126	17	1	17	100	6	.385
1948	Stamford	Colonial	1B	105	281	87	108	19	0	23*	68	2	.384
1949	Kingston	Border	1B	70	206	45	68	12	1	6	38	2	.330
1950	(Not in O.B.)												
1951	Midland	Longhorn	1B	48	109	30	44	10	0	5	23	0	.404
1952	Midland	Longhorn	1B	2	8	1	4	0	0	0	3	0	.500
	Majors			**917**	**3582**	**600**	**1099**	**232**	**29**	**119**	**704**	**19**	**.307**
	Minors			**1046**	**3328**	**737**	**1163**	**217**	**30**	**132**	**740**	**51**	**.349**

EDGAR DUDLEY (DUD) BRANOM

Born November 30, 1897 at Sulphur Springs, TX. Died February 4, 1980 at Sun City, AZ
Batted left. Threw left. Height 6.01. Weight 190.

Year	Club	League	Pos	G	AB	R	H	2B	3B	HR	RBI	SB	BA
1920	Enid	West A	1B	129	499	56	160	33	7	4	74	4	.321
	Kansas City	A A	1B	15	60	4	18	4	2	0	4	2	.300
1921	Kansas City	A A	1B	31	58	9	16	2	3	1	7	0	.276
	Tulsa	Western	1B	80	317	44	85	21	3	1	–	4	.268
1922	Enid	West A	1B	119	511	99	200	36	6	14	–	8	.391
	Kansas City	A A	1B	8	20	4	8	1	0	0	3	1	.400
1923	Kansas City	A A	1B	120	379	71	132	18	14	9	76	2	.348
1924	Kansas City	A A	1B	164	629	98	200	37	22*	11	105	9	.318
1925	Kansas City	A A	1B	138	514	66	151	20	9	7	99	3	.294
1926	Kansas City	A A	1B	163	632	98	222	34	7	10	116	10	.351
1927	Philadelphia	American	1B	30	94	8	22	1	0	0	13	2	.234
	Portland	P C	1B	102	377	59	141	22	3	13	81	5	.374
1928	Louisville	A A	1B	170	659	69	204	33	11	17	128	11	.310
1929	Louisville	A A	1B	151	597	92	198	35	8	17	129	8	.332
1930	Louisville	A A	1B	154	617	90	194	20	4	14	123	9	.314
1931	Louisville	A A	1B	168	670	98	201	30	6	15	134	3	.300
1932	Louisville	A A	1B	168	652	71	177	27	6	17	110	3	.271
1933	Baltimore	Int	1B	29	109	11	23	3	0	1	14	0	.211
	Minneapolis	A A	1B	4	4	0	2	1	0	0	2	0	.500
	Wilkes Barre	NY-Penn	1B	69	245	19	78	15	3	0	39	3	.318
1934	Milwaukee	A A	1B	18	75	7	20	2	0	1	8	2	.267
	Little Rock	South A	1B	23	99	10	22	2	2	0	12	1	.222
	Bartlesville	West A	1B	45	171	19	51	7	0	0	35	0	.298
	Majors			**30**	**94**	**8**	**22**	**1**	**0**	**0**	**13**	**2**	**.234**
	Minors			**2068**	**7894**	**1094**	**2503**	**403**	**116**	**152**	**1299**	**88**	**.317**

EARL JAMES BROWNE
Born March 5, 1911 at Louisville, KY
Batted left. Threw left. Height 6.00. Weight 175.

Year Club	League	Pos	G	AB	R	H	2B	3B	HR	RBI	SB	BA
1928 Louisville	A A	OF-P	3	11	0	1	1	0	0	2	0	.091
1929 Dayton	Central	P	57	136	21	41	9	1	5	25	0	.301
Louisville	A A	P	7	13	0	2	0	0	0	0	0	.154
1930 Dayton	Central	OF-P	62	143	19	44	6	0	4	23	2	.308
Louisville	A A	P	4	4	0	2	0	1	0	1	0	.500
1931 Huntington	Mid Atl	OF-P	63	164	25	48	13	1	9	30	1	.293
Mobile-Knox	South A	OF-P	7	12	0	4	0	0	0	2	0	.333
1932 Asheville	Piedmont	P	20	51	7	13	2	0	2	9	0	.255
Little Rock	South A	P	20	36	8	9	1	1	0	4	0	.250
1933 Little Rock	South A	1B-OF	139	483	77	156	26	14	5	74	10	.323
1934 Little Rock	South A	1B-OF	155	592	77	152	34	10	5	72	15	.257
1935 Little Rock	South A	1B	140	510	94	176	26	19	13	96	25	.345
Pittsburgh	National	1B	9	32	6	8	2	0	0	6	0	.250
1936 Pittsburgh	National	1B-OF	8	23	7	7	1	2	0	3	0	.304
Minneapolis	A A	1B-OF	155	629	135	206	39	11	35	126	4	.328
1937 Philadelphia	National	1B-OF	105	332	42	97	19	3	6	52	4	.292
1938 Philadelphia	National	1B-OF	21	74	4	19	4	0	0	8	0	.257
Columbus	A A	OF-1B	125	469	79	143	23	6	17	98	7	.305
1939 Columbus	A A	OF	116	369	49	99	13	3	12	62	3	.268
1940 New Orleans	South A	1B	153	559	83	153	16	15	14	87	4	.274
1941 Chattanooga	South A	OF	152	539	75	148	24	7	12	89	4	.275
1942 Atlanta	South A	1B	130	446	63	131	22	3	6	64	9	.294
Louisville	A A	1B	11	28	1	6	0	0	0	3	0	.214
1943 Louisville	A A	1B	144	543	62	147	26	9	4	46	3	.271
1944 Louisville	A A	1B	143	564	90	176	30	6	7	99	9	.312
1945 Louisville	A A	1B	146	539	72	147	16	7	5	83	7	.273
1946 Owensboro	Kitty	1B	92	350	84	150	18	3	21	104	2	.429*
1947 Owensboro	Kitty	1B	107	344	100	146	37	3	7	93	4	.424*
1948 Hartford	Eastern	1B	15	29	2	5	0	0	0	4	0	.172
1949 Hartford	Eastern	1B	1	2	0	0	0	0	0	0	0	.000
Majors			**143**	**461**	**59**	**131**	**26**	**5**	**6**	**69**	**4**	**.284**
Minors			**2167**	**7580**	**1222**	**2309**	**383**	**119**	**185**	**1301**	**105**	**.304**

RAMIRO S. CABALLERO
Born in 1930 at Monterrey, Nuevo Leon, Mexico.
Batted right. Threw right. Height 6.00. Weight 205.

Year Club	League	Pos	G	AB	R	H	2B	3B	HR	RBI	SB	BA
1955 Nogales	Ariz-Mex	1B	18	64	9	17	4	0	2	7	0	.266
Monterrey	Mexican	1B	21	64	9	14	3	0	2	12	0	.219
1956 Chihuahua	Cent Mex	1B	102	423*	60	127	21	0	13	77	7	.300
1957 Chihuahua	Cent Mex	1B	99	415	87	152	20	8	24	109	18	.366
1958 Chihuahua	Ariz-Mex	1B	78	330	65	118	16	4	21	86	8	.358
Poza Rica	Mexican	1B	38	141	17	43	5	2	7	28	1	.305
1959 Poza Rica	Mexican	1B	15	28	2	5	2	0	1	6	0	.179
1960 (Not in O.B.)												
1961 Vera Cruz	Mexican	1B	87	214	34	60	9	0	8	25	0	.280
1962 Guanajuato	Mex Cent	1B-3B	113	423	123	175*	25	0	59*	170	3	.414*
1963 MC Reds	Mexican	1B	23	45	4	9	2	1	0	3	0	.200
Guanajuato	Mex Cent	1B	22	71	20	25	7	0	6	25	0	.352
1964 Leon	Mex Cent	1B	121	460	135*	175*	29	1	35*	145*	3	.380*
1965 Leon	Mex Cent	1B	128	425	133	151	18	3	34	113	5	.355
Minors			**865**	**3103**	**698**	**1071**	**161**	**19**	**212**	**806**	**45**	**.345**

ERNEST ELGIN (CRAZY SNAKE) CALBERT

Born January 13, 1887 at Eagle, NE. Died July 16, 1966 at Decatur, IL
Batted right. Threw right. Height 5.10. Weight 190.
Pitched a no-hitter for Jackson against Hopkinsville, August 28, 1911, and lost 1-to-0.

Year	Club	League	Pos	G	AB	R	H	2B	3B	HR	RBI	SB	BA
1910	Harrisburg	S III	OF-P				(Record not available)						
	Harrisburg	Kitty	OF-P	44	126	14	33	8	1	3	-	15	.262
1911	Harris/Jackson	Kitty	OF-P	114	415	60	112	22	12	10*	-	27	.270
1912	Wheeling/TH	Central	OF-P	92	287	32	77	8	5	4	-	10	.268
1913	Terre Haute	Central	OF-P	26	56	7	17	4	1	0	-	4	.304 *
	Steubenville	Inter-St	OF-P	40	152	25	46	7	4	5	-	11	.303
	Huntington	Ohio St	OF	66	240	37	75	12	2	3	-	30	.313
1914	Hunt/Charles	Ohio St	OF	139	516	85	138	30	9	17*	-	25	.267
1915	Savannah	Sally	OF	5	19	1	2	0	0	0	1	1	.105
	Ironton	Ohio St	OF	106	387	46	101	14	6	13*	-	36*	.261
1916	Charleston	Ohio St	OF	54	208	43	71	16*	13*	4	-	19	.341
	Rocky Mount	Virginia	OF	50	174	14	47	11	2	3	-	12	.270
1917	Muskogee	West A	OF	158*	596	101*	177*	27	5	43*	109*	32	.297
1918-19	(In U.S. Army)												
1920	London	Mich-Ont	OF	98	379	64	118	20	8	8	54	13	.311
1921	London/Kitch	Mich-Ont	OF	96	346	43	87	16	9	7	38	15	.251
1922	Hamilton	Mich-Ont	OF	129	488	83	174*	36	7	28*	110*	17	.357
1923	Decatur	III	OF	127	486	94	152	23	7	18*	-	1	.313
1924	Decatur	III	OF	138	532	68	160	28	12	13	72	5	.301
1925	Bloomington	III	OF	17	60	7	9	1	1	0	-	1	.150
	Saginaw	Mich-Ont	OF	97	365	55	110	24	4	13	70	8	.301
1926	Saginaw	Michigan	OF	88	334	58	109	23	12*	9	64	12	.326
1927	Quincy/Evans	III	OF	49	181	25	59	8	7	2	32	2	.326
1928	Erie	Central	OF	11	39	3	7	2	1	0	-	0	.179
	Minors			1744	6386	965	1881	340	128	203	549	296	.295

MOISES CAMACHO (MUNIZ)

Born March 31, 1933 at Teahualilo, Durango, Mexico.
Batted right. Threw right. Height 5.10. Weight 170.

Year	Club	League	Pos	G	AB	R	H	2B	3B	HR	RBI	SB	BA
1951	Torreon	Mexican	2B	53	154	10	31	6	1	0	7	3	.201
1952	Torreon	Mexican	2B	92	348	48	73	11	4	3	22	6	.210
1953	Mexicali	Ariz-Tex	2B	139	589	128	201	35	9	13	105	10	.341
1954	Mexicali	Ariz-Tex	2B	76	311	85	108	27	7	15	65	2	.347
1955	Mexicali	Ariz-Mex	2B	114	460	124	167	38	12	16	113	7	.363*
	Peoria	III	2B	12	40	11	13	2	0	3	4	0	.325
1956	Allentown	Eastern	2B	132	465	72	125	21	3	12	70	1	.269
1957	Nuevo Laredo	Mexican	2B	121	449	62	131	20	2	19	74	5	.292
1958	Nuevo Laredo	Mexican	2B	120	475	87	132	25	2	21	97	4	.278
1959	Nuevo Laredo	Mexican	2B	143	548	85	152	28	4	24	93	4	.277
1960	Puebla	Mexican	2B	141	502	81	151	31	4	17	94	4	.301
1961	Puebla	Mexican	2B	125	433	77	145	29	6	15	71	2	.335
1962	Puebla	Mexican	2B	121	463	72	139	21	0	10	75	2	.300
1963	Puebla	Mexican	2B	134*	485	83	145	24	1	29	105	2	.299
1964	Puebla	Mexican	2B	138	516	78	168	24	7	9	106	1	.326
1965	Puebla	Mexican	2B	130	493	91	166	28	2	17	95	1	.337
1966	MC Reds	Mexican	2B-3B	134	469	71	160	22	11	4	81	4	.341
1967	MC Reds	Mexican	2B-3B	132	475	62	139	20	8	3	66	2	.293
1968	MC Reds	Mexican	2B	115	399	41	111	15	4	3	54	1	.278
1969	MC Reds-Poza	Mexican	2B	145	485	55	140	23	2	6	62	0	.289
1970	Poza Rica	Mexican	2B-3B	129	391	35	85	17	0	4	46	0	.217
1971	Poza Rica	Mexican	2B-3B	60	140	8	32	5	0	1	10	0	.229
1972	Poza Rica	Mexican	PH	5	4	0	3	0	0	0	2	0	.750
1973	Poza Rica	Mexican	1B	8	10	0	2	0	0	0	1	0	.200
1974	Poza Rica	Mexican	PH	20	17	0	6	3	0	0	10	0	.353
1975	Poza Rica	Mexican	1B	4	6	0	0	0	0	0	1	0	.000
	Minors			2543	9127	1466	2725	475	89	244	1529	60	.299

CHARLES COLUMBUS (COUNT) CAMPAU
Born October 17, 1863 at Detroit, MI. Died April 3, 1938 at New Orleans, LA.
Batted left. Threw right. Height 5.11. Weight 160.

Year	Club	League	Pos	G	AB	R	H	2B	3B	HR	SB	BA
1887	Savan/NO	Southern	OF	109	504	133	198	24	18*	17	100	.393*
1888	Kansas City	West A	OF	42	185	36	40	3	7	2	17	.216
	Detroit	National	OF	70	251	28	51	5	3	1	27	.203
1889	Detroit	Int A	OF	112	442	111	126	14	11	6	62	.285
1890	Detroit	Int A	OF-3B	39	158	29	49	5	4	3*	19	.310
	St. Louis	A A	OF	75	314	68	101	9	12	9*	36	.322
1891	Troy	East A	OF	122	471	86	111	18	10	3	45	.236
1892	Columbus	Western	OF	65*	233	46	61	7	7*	3	23	.262
	New Orleans	Southern	OF	40	151	43	50	11	3	3	39	.331
1893	New Orleans	Southern	OF-1B	94	359	98	121	27	6	9	44	.337
	Wilkes-Barre	Eastern	OF	20	86	15	28	6	6	1	3	.326
1894	New Orleans	Southern	OF	65	244	66	73	17	1	11	45	.299
	Washington	National	OF	2	7	1	1	0	0	0	0	.143
	Milw/Detroit	Western	OF	59	264	66	97	26	13	9	11	.367
1895	Detroit	Western	OF	118	476	115	171	41	9	13	29	.359
1896	Seattle	Pac NW	OF	32	124	55*	50	9	6	13*	19	.403
	Kansas City	Western	OF	88	326	83	106	8	10	10	8	.325
1897	Grand Rapids	Western	OF	132	548	109	166	25	11	12	25	.303
1898	Minn/St P/KC	Western	OF	130	539	101	143	22	10	6	50	.265
1899	Rochester	Eastern	OF	113	462	92	129	17	12	8	36	.279
1900	Rochester	Eastern	OF	130	507	70	127	20	11	2	25	.250
1901	Binghamton	NY St	1B	112	420	67	128	21	3	1	19	.305
1902	Binghamton	NY St	1B	102	418	46	100	14	4	0	25	.239
1903	New Orleans	South A	1B	9	27	4	7	0	0	0	2	.259
	Binghamton	NY St	1B	64	232	39	73	11	3	2	9	.315
1904	Binghamton	NY St	1B	118	429	43	97	13	6	2	18	.226
1905	Binghamton	NY St	OF	57	199	24	35	9	1	0	9	.176
	Majors			**147**	**572**	**97**	**153**	**14**	**15**	**10**	**63**	**.267**
	Minors			**1972**	**7804**	**1577**	**2286**	**368**	**172**	**136**	**682**	**.293**

HIRAM CLEO CARLYLE
Born September 7, 1902 at Fairburn, GA. Died November 12, 1967 at Los Angeles, CA
Batted left. Threw right. Height 6.00. Weight 170.
Brother of Roy Carlyle

Year	Club	League	Pos	G	AB	R	H	2B	3B	HR	RBI	SB	BA
1924	Charlotte	Sally	OF	127	488	98	173	28	25*	14	103	10	.355
1925	Toronto	Int	OF	130	422	86	139	15	5	17	78	4	.329
1926	Toronto	Int	OF	122	386	85	117	28	8	14	74	5	.303
1927	Boston	American	OF	95	278	31	65	12	8	1	28	4	.234
1928	Hollywood	P C	OF	126	440	77	127	16	4	14	72	8	.289
1929	Hollywood	P C	OF	195	666	146	231	42	12	20	136	21	.347
1930	Hollywood	P C	OF	172	616	142	201	41	4	12	97	14	.326
1931	Hollywood	P C	OF	135	490	89	157	25	4	10	89	3	.320
1932	Hollywood	P C	OF	181	673	123	233	54	9	16	106	16	.346
1933	Hollywood	P C	OF	158	584	105	187	40	7	9	94	14	.320
1934	Hollywood	P C	OF	122	459	71	125	22	0	4	58	9	.272
	Newark	Int	OF	35	126	19	32	5	3	0	4	3	.254
1935	Los Angeles	P C	OF	173	653	104	194	25	2	11	100	13	.297
1936	Los Angeles	P C	OF	167	654	118	222	29	7	3	82	15	.339
1937	Los Angeles	P C	OF	139	488	74	145	24	4	7	63	15	.297
1938	New Orleans	South A	OF	131	474	64	138	24	6	2	61	7	.291
1939	Tulsa	Texas	OF	52	195	28	46	15	4	0	22	2	.236
	San Diego	P C	OF	77	258	30	70	12	3	2	31	1	.271
	Majors			**95**	**278**	**31**	**65**	**12**	**8**	**1**	**28**	**4**	**.234**
	Minors			**2242**	**8072**	**1459**	**2537**	**445**	**107**	**155**	**1270**	**160**	**.314**

ROY EDWARD CARLYLE
Born December 10, 1900 at Buford, GA. Died November 22, 1956 at Norcross, GA
Batted left. Threw right. Height 6.02½. Weight 195.
Brother of Cleo Carlyle.

Year	Club	League	Pos	G	AB	R	H	2B	3B	HR	RBI	SB	BA
1921	Griffin	Ga St	OF	16	67	14	30	2	1	6	-	3	.448
1922	(Not in O.B.)												
1923	Charlotte	Sally	OF	110	424	68	143	25	10	15	81	2	.337
1924	Memphis	South A	OF	157	633	117	233*	47*	20*	12	122*	8	.368
1925	Wash/Boston	American	OF	94	277	36	90	20	3	7	49	1	.325
1926	Boston/NY	American	OF	80	217	25	67	11	3	2	27	0	.309
1927	Newark	Int	OF	163	629	100	216	34	16	18	122	9	.343
1928	Newark	Int	OF	23	71	9	18	6	0	1	12	0	.254
	Birmingham	South A	OF	69	205	23	72	10	9	3	52	2	.351
1929	Oakland	P C	OF	166	604	90	210	36	11	22	108	2	.348
1930	Kansas City	A A	OF	10	27	7	11	2	0	0	-	0	.407
	Atlanta	South A	OF	90	313	51	104	20	10	5	69	1	.332
1931	Atlanta	South A	OF	123	446	91	159	34	11	19	104	5	.357
1932	Atlanta	South A	OF	28	90	16	29	10	0	6	19	0	.322
	Scranton	NY-Penn	OF	16	67	14	23	1	0	3	12	0	.343
	Indianapolis	A A	OF	2	8	0	2	0	0	0	0	0	.250
1933	(Not in O.B.)												
1934	Charlotte	Piedmont	OF	5	17	-	5	1	0	0	0	0	.294
	Majors			**174**	**494**	**61**	**157**	**31**	**6**	**9**	**76**	**1**	**.318**
	Minors			**978**	**3601**	**600**	**1255**	**228**	**88**	**110**	**701**	**32**	**.349**

DORSEY LEE (DIXIE) CARROLL
Born May 19, 1891 at Paducah, KY. Died October 13, 1984 at Jacksonville, FL.
Batted left. Threw right. Height 5.11. Weight 165.

Year	Club	League	Pos	G	AB	R	H	2B	3B	HR	SB	BA
1910	Paducah	Kitty	OF	20	69	5	12	3	1	0	0	.174
1911	Paducah	Kitty	OF	111	403	44	102	15	6	4	22	.253
1912	Jacksonville	Sally	OF	119	464	59	117	18	2	2	15	.252
1913	Jacksonville	Sally	OF	61	208	25	44	7	1	3	6	.212
1914	Jacksonville	Sally	OF	122	449	60	126	-	-	-	25	.281
1915	Jacksonville	Sally	OF	90	333	42	95	-	-	-	33	.285
	Shreveport	Texas	OF	34	118	16	37	3	1	0	6	.314
1916	Shreveport	Texas	OF	144	540	78	165	24	7	3	40	.306
1917	Shreveport	Texas	OF	165	592	81	179	28	5	3	36	.302
1918	Memphis	South A	OF	73	256	40	75	12	3	0	16	.293
1919	Memphis	South A	OF	134	471	71	138	23	3	5	20	.293
	Boston	National	OF	15	49	10	13	3	1	0	5	.265
1920	Memphis	South A	OF	148	551	106	186	28	7	8	54*	.338
1921	Los Angeles	P C	OF	180	686	109	200	28	22	3	45	.292
1922	Los Angeles	P C	OF	186	710	99	211	28	13	3	35	.297
1923	Los Angeles	P C	OF	79	190	26	60	11	2	1	4	.316
1924	Louisville	A A	OF	4	4	0	0	0	0	0	0	.000
	Chattanooga	South A	OF	126	467	79	150	21	14	3	19	.321
1925	Chattanooga	South A	OF	149	588	102	195	40	11	4	20	.332
1926	Chattanooga	South A	OF	137	521	96	193	26	13	2	18	.370
1927	Chattanooga	South A	OF	147	537	101	184	26	10	0	18	.343
1928	Newark	Int	OF	95	270	33	79	13	3	1	5	.293
1929	Mobile	South A	OF	105	414	54	127	21	3	3	5	.307
	Majors			**15**	**49**	**10**	**13**	**3**	**1**	**0**	**5**	**.265**
	Minors			**2429**	**8841**	**1326**	**2675**	**375**	**127**	**47**	**442**	**.303**

FRANK WILLIS CARSWELL
Born November 6, 1919 at Palestine, TX.
Batted right. Threw right. Height 6.00. Weight 195.

Year	Club	League	Pos	G	AB	R	H	2B	3B	HR	RBI	SB	BA
1941	Jamestown	Pony	3B	70	275	44	93	17	9	3	44	4	.338
1942-45	(Military Service)												
1946	Dallas	Texas	3B	77	254	23	69	15	2	2	31	5	.272
1947	Paris	Big St	3B	135	552	116	201	36	7	36	145	12	.364
1948	Paris	Big St	3B	86	351	85	124	23	5	8	65	12	.353
	Dallas	Texas	3B	47	156	22	50	12	1	2	21	0	.321
1949	Texarkana	Big St	OF-1B	146	594	115	229*	42	7	21	145*	11	.386
1950	Texarkana	Big St	3-0-1	126	478	106	191	51*	2	18	131	2	.400*
1951	Buffalo	Int	OF-1B	124	444	59	134	37	3	9	79	4	.302
1952	Buffalo	Int	OF	141	511	88	176	34	0	30*	101	4	.344*
1953	Detroit	American	OF	16	15	2	4	0	0	0	2	0	.267
	Buffalo	Int	OF	105	362	60	117	28	1	23	75	3	.323
1954	Buffalo	Int	OF	130	421	60	134	26	1	16	87	3	.318
1955	Houston	Texas	OF	29	79	8	19	4	0	0	11	0	.241
	Omaha	A A	OF	107	356	52	125	29	1	11	74	1	.351
1956	Tulsa	Texas	OF	62	207	23	59	10	1	8	38	1	.285
	Portland	P C	OF	79	229	33	71	12	1	13	54	0	.310
1957	Portland	P C	OF-1B	115	217	20	57	11	0	9	49	1	.263
1958	Decatur	Midwest	PH	1	1	0	1	0	0	0	0	0	1.000
	Majors			**16**	**15**	**2**	**4**	**0**	**0**	**0**	**2**	**0**	**.267**
	Minors			**1580**	**5487**	**914**	**1850**	**387**	**41**	**209**	**1150**	**63**	**.337**

ROBERT LEE CHURCHILL
Born August 12, 1918 at Sapa, MS
Batted left. Threw right. Height 5.11. Weight 175.

Year	Club	League	Pos	G	AB	R	H	2B	3B	HR	RBI	SB	BA
1940	Hopkins/Owens	Kitty	OF	28	73	13	20	3	2	2	7	0	.274
1941	Hopkins/B G	Kitty	OF	110	477	80	143	35	5	9	45	9	.300
1942	Bowling Green	Kitty	OF	46	190	34	66	13	2	9	38	9	.347
	Charleston	Sally	OF	50	183	30	54	10	4	1	18	2	.295
1943	Portsmouth	Piedmont	OF	82	319	48	92	14	13	1	34	5	.288
	Nashville	South A	OF	18	36	9	14	4	0	0	4	0	.389
1944-45	(Military Service)												
1946	Macon/Green	Sally	OF	123	469	64	151	27	9	1	69	1	.322
1947	Greenville	Sally	OF	136	503	62	159	25	16	6	96	3	.316
1948	Knoxville	Tri-St	OF	140	566	101	230*	33	28*	6	102	7	.406*
1949	Rock Hill	Tri-St	OF	97	378	68	136	19	11	6	66	2	.360*
	New Castle	Mid Atl	OF	12	50	8	17	0	0	1	13	0	.340
1950	Durham	Carolina	OF	20	69	13	23	4	3	0	10	0	.333
	Anderson	Tri-St	OF	113	463	72	165	34	13	6	69	2	.356*
1951	Anderson	Tri-St	OF	58	201	38	65	17	6	6	44	1	.323
1952	Greenville	Cot St	OF	74	312	39	96	16	7	7	67	1	.308
	Baton Rouge	Evang	OF	55	233	40	77	19	0	6	59	2	.330
	Minors			**1162**	**4522**	**719**	**1508**	**273**	**119**	**67**	**741**	**44**	**.333**

The *Story of Minor League Baseball,* published in 1952, gave Buster Chatham credit for six consecutive assists at shortstop for Pueblo in a game against Wichita (Western League) August 24, 1929. Actually, it was his younger brother Chester who performed the unusual feat and at third base. Buster, the league batting champ, had just been transferred to Portland in the PCL and Chester had come in from the Nebraska State League. With the bases loaded in the fourth and nobody out, Chester, on successive plays, threw three runners out at the plate. The next inning he threw three runners out at first base, giving him six straight assists. Chester now lives near Dallas. Buster died in Waco in 1975.

JOHN WILLIAM (BUD) CLANCY

Born September 15, 1900 at Odell, IL. Died September 27, 1968 at Ottumwa, IA
Batted left. Threw left. Height 6.00. Weight 170.

Year	Club	League	Pos	G	AB	R	H	2B	3B	HR	RBI	SB	BA
1923	Grand Rapids	Mich-Ont	1B	86	344	37	96	13	5	5	43	4	.279
1924	Muskegon	Mich-Ont	1B	124	483	48	159	25	13	2	52	15	.329
	Chicago	American	1B	13	35	5	9	1	0	0	6	3	.257
1925	Little Rock	South A	1B	113	431	69	128	22	7	1	49	6	.297
	Chicago	American	1B	4	3	0	0	0	0	0	0	0	.000
1926	Little Rock	South A	1B	141	544	64	185	28	10	4	84	15	.340
	Chicago	American	1B	12	38	3	13	2	2	0	7	0	.342
1927	Chicago	American	1B	130	464	46	139	21	2	3	53	4	.300
1928	Chicago	American	1B	130	487	64	132	19	11	2	37	6	.271
1929	Chicago	American	1B	92	290	36	82	14	6	3	45	3	.283
1930	Chicago	American	1B	68	234	28	57	8	3	3	27	3	.244
1931	Jersey City	Int	1B	167*	625	80	195	33	4	13	93	6	.312
1932	Jersey City	Int	1B	111	436	77	134	27	3	13	88	9	.307
	Brooklyn	National	1B	53	196	14	60	4	2	0	16	0	.306
1933	Jersey City	Int	1B	161	605	68	174	34	4	6	90	2	.288
1934	Buffalo	Int	1B	108	390	54	105	22	6	6	63	4	.269
	Philadelphia	National	1B	20	49	8	12	0	0	1	7	0	.245
1935	Birmingham	South A	1B	159*	638*	85	191	31	11	6	71	8	.299
1936	Birmingham	South A	1B	143	564	103	181	37	8	13	77	3	.321
1937	Birmingham	South A	1B	154*	597	83	186	25	5	7	55	5	.312
1938	Birmingham	South A	1B	156*	626*	82	189	25	4	3	58	4	.302
1939	Birmingham	South A	1B	149	565	71	174	24	10	6	77	4	.308
1940	Helena	Cot St	1B	134	522	94	178	35	12	4	111	8	.341
1941	Santa Barbara	Calif	1B	108	398	67	137	25	4	4	82	6	.344*
1942	Santa Barbara	Calif	1B	59	219	28	72	15	0	1	41	2	.329
	Valdosta	Ga-Fla	1B	48	167	36	48	10	3	0	31	5	.287
	Majors			**522**	**1796**	**204**	**504**	**69**	**26**	**12**	**198**	**19**	**.281**
	Minors			**2121**	**8154**	**1146**	**2532**	**431**	**109**	**94**	**1165**	**106**	**.311**

PARKE EDWARD (ED) COLEMAN

Born December 1, 1901 at Canby, OR. Died August 5, 1964 at Oregon City, OR
Batted left. Threw right. Height 6.02. Weight 200.

Year	Club	League	Pos	G	AB	R	H	2B	3B	HR	RBI	SB	BA
1926	Logan	Utah-Ida	OF	44	129	22	49	10	5	2		1	.380
1927	Idaho Falls	Utah-Ida	OF	50	202	45	74	15	9	7		1	.366
1928	Boise/TF	Utah-Ida	OF	110	433	89	167*	28	12	26*		6	.386
1929	San Francisco	P C	OF	121	405	73	139	24	2	16	72	2	.343
1930	San Francisco	P C	OF	125	396	55	119	18	2	12	68	3	.301
1931	Portland	P C	OF	187*	768*	134*	275*	53*	14	37	183*	4	.358
1932	Philadelphia	American	OF	26	73	13	25	7	1	1	13	1	.342
1933	Philadelphia	American	OF	102	388	48	109	26	3	6	68	0	.281
1934	Philadelphia	American	OF	101	329	53	92	14	6	14	60	0	.280
1935	Phil/St. L	American	OF	118	410	66	115	15	9	17	71	0	.280
1936	St. Louis	American	OF	92	137	13	40	5	4	2	34	0	.292
1937	Toledo	A A	OF	138	517	95	159	29	5	25	123	1	.308
1938	Toledo	A A	OF	119	437	77	145	27	8	15	89	3	.332
1939	Portland	P C	OF	105	320	56	110	17	1	16	77	0	.344
1940	Portland	P C	OF	73	268	38	85	10	0	9	47	0	.317
	Oklahoma City	Texas	OF	22	72	6	15	4	0	0	9	0	.208
1941	Salem	West Int	OF	6	12	1	2	1	0	0	1	0	.167
	Majors			**439**	**1337**	**193**	**381**	**67**	**23**	**40**	**246**	**1**	**.285**
	Minors			**1100**	**3959**	**691**	**1339**	**236**	**58**	**165**	**669**	**21**	**.338**

ANNA SEBASTIAN (PETE) COMPTON

Born September 28, 1889 at San Marcos, TX. Died February 3, 1978 at Kansas City, MO
Batted left. Threw left. Height 5.11. Weight 170.

Year	Club	League	Pos	G	AB	R	H	2B	3B	HR	RBI	SB	BA
1910	Beeville	SW Tex	OF	115	419	51	106	14	5	1	-	41	.253
1911	Battle Creek	S Mich	OF	125	511	86	180	28	25*	4	-	49	.352
	St. Louis	American	OF	28	107	9	29	4	0	0	5	2	.271
1912	St. Louis	American	OF	101	268	26	75	6	4	2	30	11	.280
1913	St. Louis	American	OF	61	100	14	18	5	2	2	17	2	.180
	Kansas City	A A	OF	36	130	15	34	4	4	4	-	7	.262
1914	Kansas City	A A	OF	166	607	89	197	33	13	11	-	58*	.325
1915	St. Louis	Federal	OF	2	8	0	2	0	0	0	3	0	.250
	Kansas City	A A	OF	104	414	83	142	19	9	9	-	19	.343
	Boston	National	OF	35	116	10	28	7	1	1	12	4	.241
1916	Boston/Pitt	National	OF	39	114	14	21	2	0	0	8	5	.184
	Louisville	A A	OF	73	278	42	81	12	5	3	-	9	.291
1917	Louisville	A A	OF	61	215	30	48	6	3	1	-	5	.223
	New Orleans	South A	OF	66	238	36	62	9	5	1	-	13	.261
1918	New Orleans	South A	OF	70	224	36	72	11	5	3	-	13	.321
	Louisville	A A	OF	15	59	14	23	1	2	1	-	5	.390
	New York	National	OF	21	60	5	13	0	1	0	5	2	.217
1919	Seattle	P C	OF	167	629	100	185	24	8	10	-	31	.294
1920	Sacramento	P C	OF	200	742	90	228	33	4	14	-	31	.307
1921	Sacramento	P C	OF	168	616	108	171	29	7	18	95	24	.278
1922	Sac/San Fran	P C	OF	126	432	55	132	12	8	8	43	12	.306
1923	San Francisco	P C	OF	134	527	81	171	37	5	7	68	7	.324
1924	Houston	Texas	OF	151	635	125	201	36	14	11	89	11	.317
1925	Houston	Texas	OF	143	534	96	168	33	3	10	92	16	.315
1926	Ft. Worth	Texas	OF	80	286	38	87	13	3	1	38	3	.304
	Wichita	Western	OF	59	230	47	82	24	5	3	-	2	.357
1927	Denver	Western	OF	70	281	57	96	14	5	6	-	1	.342
1928	Miami	Ariz St	OF	67	261	47	81	9	9*	3	-	25	.310
	Majors			**287**	**773**	**78**	**186**	**24**	**8**	**5**	**80**	**26**	**.241**
	Minors			**2196**	**8268**	**1326**	**2547**	**401**	**147**	**129**	**425**	**382**	**.308**

WILLIAM MILLAR (BUNK) CONGALTON

Born January 24, 1875 at Guelph, Ontario. Died August 19, 1937 at Cleveland, OH
Batted left. Threw left. Height 5.10. Weight 165.

Year	Club	League	Pos	G	AB	R	H	2B	3B	HR	SB	BA
1895	Toronto	Eastern	OF	13	43	9	8	2	1	0	3	.186
	Port Huron	Mich St	OF	3	13	2	4	1	0	0	1	.308
1896	Guelph	Canadian	OF-P	31	130	23	28	4	3	2	-	.215
1897	Guelph	Canadian	OF	46	182	35	58	9	7	3	19	.319
1898	Hamilton	Int	OF	58	232	41	77	13	6*	5	19	.332
	Hamilton	Canadian	OF	57	224	55	74	11	9*	5	11	.330
1899	Hamilton	Canadian	OF	63	255	57	88	12	6	4	19	.345
	Milwaukee	Western	OF	40	168	24	50	6	4	0	9	.298
1900	Wheeling	Int St	OF	131	539		158	23	7	6	23	.293
1901	Minneapolis	Western	OF	102	425	75	132	27	11	5	17	.311
1902	Chicago	National	OF	45	179	14	40	3	0	1	3	.223
	Colo. Springs	Western	OF	78	313	57	106	10	11	8	10	.339
1903	Colo. Springs	Western	OF	123	507	84	184*	23	18	7	30	.363*
1904	Colo. Springs	Western	OF	129	538	113	176	25	9	5	22	.327*
1905	Columbus	A A	OF	153	592	88	186	36	8	2	27	.314
	Cleveland	American	OF	12	47	4	17	0	0	0	3	.362
1906	Cleveland	American	OF	117	419	51	134	13	5	2	12	.320
1907	Cleve/Boston	American	OF	136	518	46	146	11	7	2	13	.282
1908	Columbus	A A	OF	152	594	76	179	41	4	3	18	.301

Year	Club	League	Pos	G	AB	R	H	2B	3B	HR	SB	BA
1909	Columbus	A A	OF	168	669	63	183	26	7	2	11	.274
1910	Columbus	A A	OF	144	543	58	158	29	2	1	16	.291
1911	Columbus	A A	OF	165	669	99	211	49	5	3	9	.315
1912	Colum/Toledo	A A	OF	143	550	75	154	27	4	2	9	.280
1913	Omaha	Western	OF	164	649	117	227*	50*	4	19	15	.350
1914	Omaha	Western	OF	136	516	97	173	31	4	11	18	.335
	Majors			**310**	**1163**	**115**	**337**	**27**	**12**	**5**	**31**	**.290**
	Minors			**2099**	**8351**	**1248**	**2614**	**455**	**130**	**93**	**306**	**.313**

MERVIN THOMAS (BUD) CONNALLY

Born April 25, 1901 at San Francisco, CA. Died June 12, 1964 at Berkeley, CA
Batted right. Threw right. Height 5.08. Weight 154.

Year	Club	League	Pos	G	AB	R	H	2B	3B	HR	RBI	SB	BA
1922	Portland	P C	2B-OF	7	14	1	3	0	0	0	0	1	.214
	Tacoma	West Int	SS	37	144	9	36	7	4	2	-	4	.250
	Des Moines	Western	2-3-S	50	167	17	40	6	1	1	-	4	.240
1923	Portland	P C	SS	10	33	5	8	2	0	0	2	0	.242
	Bay City	Mich-Ont	3B	133	481	80	144	34	15	8	78	18	.299
1924	Bay City	Mich-Ont	3B	136	518	92	171	43	13	6	85	31	.330
1925	Boston	American	SS-3B	43	107	12	28	7	1	0	21	0	.262
	Mobile	South A	3B	43	167	34	52	11	1	1	13	2	.311
1926	Toledo/Colum	A A	2-3-S	129	461	79	141	23	4	2	62	15	.306
1927	Toledo/Ind	A A	S-2-3	132	474	67	130	28	7	2	48	18	.274
1928	Indianapolis	A A	2B	147	525	65	153	29	8	1	62	7	.291
1929	Indianapolis	A A	2B	163	575	64	157	32	1	5	83	11	.273
1930	Indianapolis	A A	2-S-1	133	479	85	162	33	7	7	75	8	.338
1931	Milwaukee	A A	2B-3B	161	670	118	211	35	5	15	85	22	.315
1932	Milwaukee	A A	2B	165	657	111	190	26	4	14	84	18	.289
1933	Milwaukee	A A	2B-SS	148	550	100	166	33	3	18	79	11	.302
1934	San Antonio	Texas	2B	148	574	101	171	36	1	5	77	6	.298
1935	New Orleans	South A	3B-2B	125	439	55	124	27	6	6	67	3	.282
1936	New Orleans	South A	3B-2B	157	534	66	142	29	10	4	95	5	.266
1937	New Orleans	South A	3B	89	265	30	69	12	2	0	31	5	.260
	Montgomery	SEastern	3B	36	126	20	40	7	0	0	28	2	.317
1938	Montgomery	SEastern	3B	137	431	68	124	18	3	0	52	9	.288
1939	Bloomington	III	3B	117	393	72	117	23	1	8	72	9	.298
1940	Madison	III	3B	36	84	18	21	3	0	0	16	2	.250
	Majors			**43**	**107**	**12**	**28**	**7**	**1**	**0**	**21**	**0**	**.262**
	Minors			**2439**	**8761**	**1357**	**2572**	**497**	**96**	**105**	**1194**	**211**	**.294**

COSMO COMO (TONY) COTELLE

Born November 5, 1904 at St. James, LA. Died December 25, 1975 at Chicago, IL
Batted left. Threw left. Height 5.05. Weight 155.

Year	Club	League	Pos	G	AB	R	H	2B	3B	HR	RBI	SB	BA
1926	Rock Island	Miss Val	OF-P	117	417	59	140	21	6	10	-	7	.336
1927	Marshalltown	Miss Val	OF-P	107	402	64	128	22	12	5	-	15	.318
1928	Danville	III	OF	118	438	50	142	14	8	3	65	15	.324
1929	Houston	Texas	OF	48	153	26	45	7	6	0	23	5	.294
	Laurel	Cot St	OF-P	12	42	4	14	2	2	0	-	0	.333
	Danville	III	OF-P	46	163	14	51	5	5	0	23	0	.313
1930	Danville	III	OF	59	238	51	92	16	5	2	53	11	.387
	St. Joseph	Western	OF	77	308	52	99	18	4	8	52	5	.321
1931	Rochester/JC	Int	OF	91	306	43	94	21	1	5	44	4	.307
	Albany	Eastern	OF	46	175	29	51	6	4	3	20	5	.291
1932	Jersey City	Int	OF	22	76	7	19	5	2	0	10	4	.250
	Hartford	Eastern	OF	54	210	32	59	14	5	2	28	7	.281
1933	Davenport	Miss Val	OF	91	378	106	154	28	7	11	86	31	.407*
1934	Indianapolis	A A	OF	114	420	66	126	22	5	3	53	8	.300
1935	Indianapolis	A A	OF-P	109	381	55	122	15	3	1	45	11	.320

Year	Club	League	Pos	G	AB	R	H	2B	3B	HR	RBI	SB	BA
1936	Indianapolis	A A	OF	25	101	15	27	1	0	0	12	2	.267
	Memphis	South A	OF	98	375	48	116	14	8	2	53	5	.309
1937	Albany	NY-Penn	OF	122	479	68	162	27	7	1	60	22	.338*
1938	Albany	Eastern	OF	121	436	63	120	23	8	2	63	16	.275
1939	Williamsport	Eastern	OF-P	114	405	50	120	21	5	0	50	4	.296
1940	Portsmouth	Piedmont	OF	9	33	2	10	3	0	0	3	0	.303
	Greenville	Sally	OF	29	134	21	50	3	3	0	12	6	.373
	Dayton	Mid Atl	OF	77	273	38	92	14	5	1	36	8	.337
1941	Dayton/Erie	Mid Atl	OF	112	409	73	150	21	11	1	56	17	.367*
1942	Erie	Mid Atl	OF-P	123	422	66	138	22	2	1	46	21	.327*
1943	Syracuse	Int	OF	4	4	1	0	0	0	0	0	0	.000
	Hartford	Eastern	OF	114	407	78	124	15	8	0	44	17	.305
1944	Ind/Louisville	A A	OF	115	385	53	132	18	9	1	68	5	.343
1945	Louisville	A A	OF	58	188	29	51	9	2	1	23	6	.271
	Scranton	Eastern	OF	47	159	24	50	12	2	0	26	3	.314
1946	El Paso	Mex Nat	OF	32	139	32	52	-	-	-	-	-	.374
Minors				**2311**	**8456**	**1319**	**2730**	**419**	**145**	**63**	**1054**	**260**	**.323**

RAYMOND DANDRIDGE

Born August 31, 1913 at Richmond, VA.
Batted right. Threw right. Height 5.06. Weight 185.
Played in the Negro National League 1933-38, 1942 and 1944, and the Negro American League in 1949.

Year	Club	League	Pos	G	AB	R	H	2B	3B	HR	RBI	SB	BA
1940	Vera Cruz	Mexican	3B	27	127	27	44	8	3	1	27	6	.346
1941	Vera Cruz	Mexican	3B-SS	101	430	94	158	32	5	8	86	12	.367
1942	Vera Cruz	Mexican	3B	35	142	27	44	7	1	4	37	8	.310
	Newark	Neg Nat				(Record not available)							
1943	Vera Cruz	Mexican	3B	90	370	67	131*	24	4	8	70*	17	.354
1944	Newark	Neg Nat	3-2-S	47	189	38	70	12	5	2	21	8	.370
1945	Mexico City	Mexican	3B-SS	83	344	67	126	29	4	1	58	20	.366
1946	Mexico City	Mexican	3B	98	418	79	135	24	0	7	51	24	.323
1947	Mexico City	Mexican	3B-SS	122	514	90	169*	24	6	2	65	23	.329
1948	Mexico City	Mexican	3B	88	370	65	138*	22	6	3	52	10	.373*
1949	New York	Neg Amer				(Record not available)							
	Minneapolis	A A	3B-2B	99	398	60	144	22	5	6	64	4	.362
1950	Minneapolis	A A	3B-2B	150	627*	106	195*	24	1	11	80	1	.311
1951	Minneapolis	A A	3B	107	423	59	137	24	1	8	61	1	.324
1952	Minneapolis	A A	3B	145	618	86	180	27	1	10	68	3	.291
1953	Sac/Oakland	P C	2B-3B	87	254	32	68	10	1	0	13	1	.268
Minors				**1232**	**5035**	**859**	**1669**	**277**	**38**	**69**	**732**	**130**	**.331**

HARRY ALBERT DAVIS

Born May 7, 1908 at Shreveport, LA
Batted left. Threw left. Height 5.10½. Weight 175.

Year	Club	League	Pos	G	AB	R	H	2B	3B	HR	RBI	SB	BA
1928	Syracuse	NY-Penn	1B	124	478	68	133	20	5	2	43	10	.278
1929	Syra/Hazleton	NY-Penn	1B	137	527	90	176	40	10	6	76	14	.334
	Toronto	Int	1B	10	34	6	9	2	0	0	6	2	.265
1930	Toronto	Int	1B	128	397	43	111	20	5	3	35	15	.280
1931	Toronto	Int	1B	133	459	73	144	22	11	6	46	7	.314
1932	Detroit	American	1B	140	590	92	159	32	13	4	74	12	.269
1933	Detroit	American	1B	66	173	24	37	8	2	0	14	2	.214
1934	Toledo	A A	1B	136	508	93	161	25	9	15	90	12	.317
1935	Portland	P C	1B	153	566	81	178	33	4	2	64	7	.314
1936	Toledo	A A	1B	147	563	93	168	29	6	12	90	22	.298

Year	Club	League	Pos	G	AB	R	H	2B	3B	HR	RBI	SB	BA
1937	St. Louis	American	1B	120	450	89	124	25	3	3	35	7	.276
1938	Kansas City	A A	1B	147	602	107	180	31	7	10	64	25	.299
1939	Rochester	Int	1B	145	585	103	174	38	7	21	92	10	.297
1940	Rochester	Int	1B	160	588	96	179	38	1	17	101	10	.304
1941	Rochester	Int	1B	152	514	84	152	29	3	14	88	8	.296
1942	Rochester	Int	1B	127	423	58	104	23	2	7	57	4	.246
	Columbus	A A	1B	29	102	9	23	5	0	1	8	0	.225
1943	Toronto	Int	1B	148	477	62	139	27	1	6	64	18	.291
1944	Toronto	Int	1B	140	458	68	129	32	3	6	57	10	.282
1945	Toronto	Int	1B	152	478	94	125	26	1	7	62	8	.262
1946	Toronto	Int	1B	11	9	0	4	0	0	0	0	0	.444
	Williamsport	Eastern	1B	110	375	50	101	22	6	1	64	5	.269
1947	Greenville	Big St	1B	142	541	110	160	44	2	10	78	11	.296
1948	Marshall	LoneStar	1B	62	228	40	66	14	1	2	35	3	.289
	Gadsden	SEastern	1B	55	193	45	58	12	1	0	25	8	.301
1949	Gadsden	SEastern	1B	15	52	8	9	3	0	0	7	1	.173
1950	Amarillo	WTNM	1B	27	99	17	28	9	2	1	21	0	.283
Majors				326	1213	205	320	65	18	7	123	21	.264
Minors				2590	9256	1498	2711	544	87	149	1273	210	.293

JOHN WILBUR (BUD) (COUNTRY) DAVIS

Born December 7, 1896 at Merry Point, VA. Died May 26, 1967 at Williamsburg, VA
Batted left. Threw right. Height 6.00. Weight 207.
Started as a pitcher, compiling 47-49 won-lost record, including 20-13 in 1921.

Year	Club	League	Pos	G	AB	R	H	2B	3B	HR	RBI	SB	BA
1915	Philadelhia	American	P	21	26	4	8	2	1	0	3	0	.308
1916	Atlanta	South A	P	26	62	4	18	2	1	2	-	1	.290
	Newnan	Ga-Ala	OF-P	52	173	33	52	7	0	16	-	7	.301
1917	Winston-Salem	N Caro	OF-P	18	68	11	20	0	0	4	10	1	.294
	Memphis	South A	OF-P	24	76	11	24	1	1	1	-	2	.316
	Ft. Worth/Waco	Texas	P	33	69	8	14	3	1	1	-	1	.203
1918	Waco	Texas	P	28	71	4	21	2	0	1	-	2	.296
1919	(Military Service)												
1920	Augusta	Sally	1-0-P	105	336	38	88	11	17	5	40	5	.262
1921	Augusta	Sally	0-1-P	98	288	38	98	18	6	5	-	9	.340
1922	Augusta/Charl	Sally	1-3-P	119	427	64	135	17	8	5	48	5	.316
1923	Okmulgee	West A	1B	117	450	82	158	38	9	15	-	14	.351
1924	Okmulgee	West A	1B	160	650	151	260*	50*	11	51*	190*	6	.400*
1925	Sacramento	P C	1B	179	690	89	228	42	13	13	119	10	.330
1926	Sacramento	P C	1B	164	585	84	180	37	5	12	93	6	.308
1927	New Orleans	South A	1B	152	591	107	222	46	11	11	121	5	.376*
1928	New Orleans	South A	1B	142	534	74	168	28	9	11	96	0	.315
1929	Dallas	Texas	1B	132	468	74	149	31	2	13	97	2	.318
1930	Reading	Int	1B	162	606	95	207	32	15	26	150	8	.342
1931	Nashville	South A	1B	68	259	33	79	12	1	9	37	3	.305
	Raleigh	Piedmont	1B	21	83	10	30	4	3	3	20	1	.361
	Baton Rouge	Cot St	1B	38	153	14	52	7	0	3	24	3	.340
1932	Norfolk	Eastern	1B	76	288	51	96	12	1	18*	59	2	.333
1933	(Not in O.B.)												
1934	Joplin	West A	1B	130	517	87	182	33	10	12	113	10	.352
1935	Bentonville	Ark St	1B	105	412	63	146	20	5	12	93*	14	.354
1936	(Not in O.B.)												
1937	Bassett/Reids.	Bi-State	1B	68	262	32	63	17	1	4	-	5	.240
Majors				21	26	4	8	2	1	0	3	0	.308
Minors				2217	8118	1257	2690	470	130	253	1310	122	.331

YANCY (YANK) DAVIS
Born in 1889.
Batted left. Threw left. Height 5.10. Weight 170.

Year	Club	League	Pos	G	AB	R	H	2B	3B	HR	SB	BA
1909	Sapulpa	West A	OF-P	62	187	21	62	10	1	0	4	.332
1910	Sapulpa	West A	OF	116	454	66	137	14	8	2	22	.302
	Wichita	Western	OF	34	109	13	27	3	2	0	6	.248
1911	Pueblo	Western	OF	116	427	82	138	19	13	7	13	.323
1912	Wichita	Western	OF	145	560	72	174	19	14	4	19	.311
1913	Wichita	Western	OF	60	187	18	50	8	0	1	4	.267
1914	St. Joseph	Western	OF	50	177	29	49	9	1	2	8	.277
	Terre Haute	Central	OF	79	285	39	78	10	5	0	3	.274
1915	Moline	III	OF	121	433	54	122	22	8	3	5	.282
1916	Moline	III	OF	136	492	78	170	27	14	7	22	.346
1917	Moline	III	OF	65	264	29	79	10	2	2	7	.299
	Joplin	Western	OF	59	205	22	47	4	0	0	3	.229
1918	Hutchinson	Western	OF	11	38	1	9	3	0	0	1	.237
1919	Tulsa	Western	OF	140	497	72	150	21	3	9	13	.302
1920	Tulsa	Western	OF	151	532	88	149	28	10	20	10	.280
1921	Tulsa	Western	OF	144	549	93	200	42	2	21	4	.364
1922	Tulsa	Western	OF	166	676	162	230	54	7	35*	3	.340
1923	Tulsa	Western	OF	166	681	141	240	54	6	32	7	.352
1924	Tulsa	Western	OF	158	684	148	231	39	6	42	7	.338
1925	Nashville	South A	OF	150	596	98	191	35	8	11	2	.320
1926	Beaumont	Texas	OF	93	371	61	111	16	6	9	3	.299
	Corsicana	Tex A	OF	20	72	7	20	3	0	1	2	.278
1927	Muskogee	West A	OF	40	151	20	37	8	0	0	3	.245
	Minors			2282	8627	1414	2701	458	116	208	171	.313

STEPHEN DEMETER
Born January 27, 1935 at Homer City, PA
Batted right. Threw right. Height 5.10. Weight 185.

Year	Club	League	Pos	G	AB	R	H	2B	3B	HR	RBI	SB	BA
1953	Wausau	Wis St	3B	124	475	98	166	29	6	15	123	16	.349
1954	Durham	Carolina	3B	138	550	86	169	48	7	23	111	4	.307
1955	Buffalo	Int	3B	142	516	68	147	28	9	17	79	4	.285
1956	Charlston	A A	3B	47	174	23	42	12	1	4	21	0	.241
	Augusta	Sally	3B	73	280	36	76	14	4	8	40	0	.271
1957	Birmingham	South A	3B	126	478	63	128	30	6	13	79	1	.268
1958	Birmingham	South A	3B	151	550	88	170	36	6	18	88	8	.309
1959	Detroit	American	3B	11	18	1	2	1	0	0	1	0	.111
	Charlston	A A	3B	137	512	79	151	25	2	13	77	0	.295
1960	Cleveland	American	3B	4	5	0	0	0	0	0	0	0	.000
	Toronto	Int	3B	121	375	45	98	14	2	11	63	1	.261
1961	Toronto	Int	3B	132	438	62	115	19	3	25	77	2	.263
1962	Toronto	Int	3B	131	494	60	131	25	3	26	86	1	.265
1963	Toronto	Int	3B	56	204	23	51	11	1	6	30	1	.250
	Denver	P C	3B	92	351	61	120	23	4	17	75	3	.342
1964	Rochester	Int	3B	152	542	68	144	28	5	16	65	3	.266
1965	Rochester	Int	3B	147	552	64	165	28	2	15	90	3	.299
1966	Rochester	Int	3B	142	530	91	166	32	3	18	82	0	.313
1967	Rochester	Int	3B	127	457	56	145	32	2	5	67	3	.317
1968	Rochester	Int	3B	111	369	46	111	27	1	10	63	2	.301
1969	Syracuse	Int	3B	134	486	64	136	23	3	10	76	4	.280
1970	Tulsa	A A	3B-1B	26	50	2	11	1	0	1	6	0	.220
1972	Sherbrooke	Eastern	3B	47	69	2	13	0	0	1	6	0	.188
	Majors			15	23	1	2	1	0	0	1	0	.087
	Minors			2356	8452	1185	2455	485	70	272	1404	56	.290

WILLIAM M. DIESTER
Batted right. Threw right.
Achieved one of highest season batting averages (.444) with Salina in 1926.

Year	Club	League	Pos	G	AB	R	H	2B	3B	HR	RBI	SB	BA
1923	Bartlesville	SWestern	OF-P	64	229	39	72	7	6	7	-	2	.314
1924	Inde/Eureka	SWestern	OF-P	112	431	70	139	25	5	12	-	3	.323
1925	Independence	West A	OF	9	22	1	5	2	0	0	3	0	.227
	Salina	SWestern	OF	121	488	85	163	-	-	-	-	-	.334
1926	Salina	SWestern	OF	106	428	110*	190*	33*	4	27	-	10	.444*
	Tulsa	Western	OF	11	44	5	15	4	0	0	-	0	.341
1927	Dallas	Texas	OF	31	121	11	32	8	0	1	12	4	.264
	C.C./Edinburg	Tex Val	OF	116	446	63	144	33	2	10	-	8	.323
1928	Joplin/Inde	West A	OF	134	536	98	188*	44*	10	13	107	10	.351
1929	Joplin	West A	OF	130	496	79	178	40	11	12	120	12	.359
1930	Joplin	West A	OF	127	520	89	176	39	9	5	84	10	.338
1931	Hend/Ral/W-S.	Piedmont	OF	134	542	72	158	31	3	10	99	5	.292
1932	Bridgeport	Eastern	OF	5	21	4	5	0	0	0	1	0	.238
	Dubuque	Miss Val	OF	66	271	32	78	14	3	1	51	4	.288
	Minors			**1166**	**4595**	**758**	**1543**	**280**	**53**	**98**	**477**	**68**	**.336**

FRANK EDWARD (POP) DILLON
Born October 17, 1873 at Normal, IL. Died September 12, 1931 at Los Angeles, CA.
Batted left. Threw right.
Cousin of Clark Griffith. Player-manager for Los Angeles, 1905-15.

Year	Club	League	Pos	G	AB	R	H	2B	3B	HR	SB	BA
1894	Peoria	West A	P	24	106	26	31	5	2	1	1	.292
1895	Bloomington	W Int St	P-1-2	9	33	7	9	0	1	1	1	.273
	Ottumwa	Iowa St	O-P-S	5	12	1	3	0	0	0	0	.250
	Dubuque	West A	P-OF	19	67	12	21	-	-	-	-	.313
1896	Rockford	West A	OF	81	344	60	106	16	11	4	11	.308
1897	Rockford	West A	OF	106	457	102	150	21	12	7	27	.328
1898	Rock Island	West A	OF	39	146	31	42	7	6	0	10	.288
1899	Scranton	Atlantic	OF-1B	62	233	-	72	-	-	-	-	.309
	Buffalo	Western	1B	60	244	38	76	-	-	-	14	.311
	Pittsburgh	National	1B	30	121	21	31	5	0	0	5	.256
1900	Pittsburgh	National	1B	5	18	3	2	1	0	0	0	.111
	Detroit	American	1B	123	470	57	137	21	7	2	25	.291
1901	Detroit	American	1B	74	281	40	81	14	6	1	14	.288
1902	Det/Balt	American	1B	68	250	22	52	6	4	0	2	.208
	Los Angeles	Calif	1B	83	318	53	108	-	-	-	12	.340
1903	Los Angeles	P C	1B	190	752	115	271	45	12	4	43	.360
1904	Brooklyn	National	1B	135	511	60	132	18	6	0	13	.258
1905	Los Angeles	P C	1B	216	779	101	212	35	6	2	33	.272
1906	Los Angeles	P C	1B	165	549	61	181	21	10	1	18	.330
1907	Los Angeles	P C	1B	181	631	88	192	33	5	5	34	.304
1908	Los Angeles	P C	1B	168	620	77	168	24	7	0	33	.271
1909	Los Angeles	P C	1B	119	416	44	101	14	5	1	12	.243
1910	Los Angeles	P C	1B	189	629	63	150	20	4	2	27	.238
1911	Los Angeles	P C	1B	172	580	63	147	13	8	3	18	.253
1912	Los Angeles	P C	1B	121	368	52	108	18	0	1	13	.293
1913	Los Angeles	P C	1B	22	55	4	20	1	0	0	1	.364
1914	Los Angeles	P C	PH	3	2	0	1	0	1	0	0	.500
1915	Los Angeles	P C	1B	18	37	4	7	0	1	0	1	.189
	Majors			**312**	**1181**	**146**	**298**	**44**	**16**	**1**	**34**	**.252**
	Minors			**2175**	**7848**	**1059**	**2313**	**294**	**98**	**34**	**334**	**.295**

JOHN JAMES DUFFY
Born May 24, 1877 at Albany, NY. Died April 24, 1970 at Albany, NY.

Year	Club	League	Pos	G	AB	R	H	2B	3B	HR	SB	BA
1898	New Haven	Conn	OF	95	391	84	121	9	1	2	9	.309
1899	New Haven	Conn	OF	43	171	36	38	-	-	-	23	.222
	Albany	NY St	OF	53	210	37	67	4	3	0	21	.319
1900	Albany	NY St	OF	95	387	81	125	11	2	0	52	.323
1901	Albany	NY St	OF	88	340	61	97	11	1	0	37	.285
1902	Albany	NY St	OF	88	363	63	110	-	-	-	39	.303
	St. Joseph	Western	OF	32	115	29	31	-	-	-	6	.270
1903	Birmingham	South A	OF	124	497	82	131	17	8	1	37	.264
1904	Birmingham	South A	OF	128	487	100	140	19	4	2	56	.287
1905	Memphis	South A	OF	117	436	79	124	11	2	0	44*	.284
1906	Rochester	Eastern	OF	107	426	53	97	4	5	3	22	.228
1907	Scranton	NY St	OF	116	450	65	123	11	3	0	35	.273
1908	Troy	NY St	OF	141	542	77	135	16	3	0	53	.249
1909	Troy	NY St	OF	137	554	83	149	11	0	0	41	.269
1910	Troy	NY St	OF	134	505	75	124	13	2	0	43	.246
1911	Troy	NY St	OF	143	576	71	153	12	0	0	33	.266
1912	Troy	NY St	OF	130	510	86	145	10	3	1	34	.284
1913	Albany	NY St	OF	132	526	68	141	10	8	1	20	.268
1914	Albany	NY St	OF	132	496	44	108	8	0	0	21	.218
	Minors			**2035**	**7982**	**1274**	**2159**	**177**	**45**	**10**	**626**	**.270**

ALBERT L. (BULL) DURHAM
Born in 1885 in Richmond, IN. Died September 17, 1949 at Oshkosh, WI.
Batted right. Threw right.

Year	Club	League	Pos	G	AB	R	H	2B	3B	HR	SB	BA
1909	Fairmont	Pa-WV	OF	54	221	26	59				11	.267
	McKeesport	Ohio-Pa	OF	54	188	38	59				10	.314
1910	McKeesport	Ohio-PA	OF	124	422	67	125	27	4	15	15	.296
1911	Wheeling	Central	OF	92	326	52	103	22	5	11*	9	.316
1912	Bay City	S Mich	OF-1B	102	354	68	108	18	6	25*	18	.305
	Oshkosh	Wis-III	OF	27	97	21	32	10	1	5	7	.330
1913	Oshkosh	Wis-III	OF	111	394	71	121	26	0	26*	12	.307
1914	Oshkosh	Wis-III	OF	118	410	87*	112	25	0	25*	14	.273
1915	Racine	Bi-State	OF-1B	48	174	28	62	17*	1	4	10	.356*
	Muscatine	Cent A	OF	61	209	39	77	18	2	8	6	.368*
1916	Mus/Marshaltn	Cent A	OF	117	422	64	116	15	6	18*	11	.275
	Minors			**908**	**3217**	**561**	**974**	**178**	**25**	**137**	**123**	**.303**

When Tony Lazzeri set a new O.B. record with 60 home runs for Salt Lake City (P C) in 1925, his final roundtripper came in the seventh inning of the last game of the season on October 18 and was an inside-the-park drive to left-center which the outfielders played casually. The game was at Sacramento and the ball was hit off Frank Shellenback, who went all the way for a 12-10 victory. The Salt Lake City newspapers, which spelled the name LaZerre, headlined the event but provided few details of the free-hitting contest. The *Tribune* did call it a world record which would last for many years (it was a 17-homer increase in the PCL). The next season Moose Clabaugh hit 62 homers in 121 games for Tyler in the East Texas League. The important feature for Lazzeri, who played 197 games in 1925, was that he was a power-hitting shortstop. His Sacramento counterpart at that position was Ray French, who hit no four-baggers in 167 games.

JOSEPH MICHAEL (DOUBLE) DWYER

Born March 27, 1907 at Orange, NJ.
Batted left. Threw left. Height 5.09. Weight 155.

Year	Club	League	Pos	G	AB	R	H	2B	3B	HR	RBI	SB	BA
1924	Rochester	Int	OF	4	6	1	1	0	0	1	1	0	.167
1925	(Not in O.B.)												
1926	Salem	New Eng	OF	88	350	79	129	17	5	8	50	11	.369
	Scranton	NY-Penn	OF	16	56	8	14	4	0	0	8	0	.250
1927	Salem/Lynn	New Eng	OF	92	367	55	106	13	6	4	42	6	.289
1928	Lynn	New Eng	OF	106	414*	74	114	20	10	6	54	6	.275
1929	Lynn	New Eng	OF	127	536*	98	192*	21	8	4	54	8	.358
1930	Wilkes-Barre	NY-Penn	OF	129	515	116	187	28	13	3	78	20	.363
1931	Shreveport	Texas	OF	11	33	7	7	0	0	0	1	1	.212
	Wilkes-Barre	NY-Penn	OF	140*	562*	100	181*	40	8	0	61	10	.322
1932	Wilkes-Barre	NY-Penn	OF	120	491	75	156	27	14	3	54	5	.318
1933	Wilkes-Barre	NY-Penn	OF	139	533	77	187	38	15	1	95	5	.351
1934	Wilkes-Barre	NY-Penn	OF	133	510	81	175	36	11	2	76	7	.343
1935	Wilkes-Barre	NY-Penn	OF	105	432	68	157	25	9	2	77	5	.363
1936	Nashville	South A	OF	154	600	127*	230*	65*	7	4	117	7	.383
1937	Cincinnati	National	OF	12	11	2	3	0	0	0	1	0	.273
	Jersey City	Int	OF	88	304	26	80	17	2	1	28	1	.263
1938	JC/Baltimore	Int	OF	56	194	19	43	8	1	0	19	0	.222
1939	Toledo	A A	OF	79	260	27	82	13	3	2	24	0	.315
1940	Toledo	A A	OF	74	239	31	74	8	4	1	28	3	.310
	Little Rock	South A	OF	46	192	30	67	13	7	0	26	5	.349
1941	Little Rock	South A	OF	151	589	98	191	33	5	2	70	3	.324
1942	Binghamton	Eastern	OF	59	208	28	58	9	2	0	19	0	.279
1943	Newark	Int	OF	94	252	25	69	8	0	3	14	1	.274
1944	Newark	Int	OF	76	160	24	45	7	0	2	15	0	.281
1945	Newark	Int	OF	11	15	0	4	1	0	0	1	0	.267
	Majors			12	11	2	3	0	0	0	1	0	.273
	Minors			2098	7818	1274	2549	451	130	49	1012	104	.326

LUSCIOUS LUKE EASTER

Born April 4, 1915 at St. Louis, MO. Died March 29, 1979 at Euclid, OH.
Batted left. Threw right. Height 6.04½. Weight 240.

Year	Club	League	Pos	G	AB	R	H	2B	3B	HR	RBI	SB	BA
1949	San Diego	P C	1B	80	273	56	99	23	0	25	92	1	.363
	Cleveland	Amer	OF	21	45	6	10	3	0	0	2	0	.222
1950	Cleveland	Amer	1B-OF	141	540	96	151	20	4	28	107	0	.280
1951	Cleveland	Amer	1B	128	486	65	131	12	5	27	103	0	.270
1952	Indianapolis	A A	1B	14	50	13	17	2	0	6	12	1	.340
	Cleveland	Amer	1B	127	437	63	115	10	3	31	97	1	.263
1953	Cleveland	Amer	1B	68	211	26	64	9	0	7	31	0	.303
1954	Cleveland	Amer	PH	6	6	0	1	0	0	0	0	0	.167
	Ottawa	Int	1B	66	230	49	80	10	0	15	48	1	.348
	San Diego	P C	1B	56	198	43	55	8	1	13	42	0	.278
1955	Charleston	A A	1B	144	477	78	135	25	5	30	102	0	.283
1956	Buffalo	Int	1B	145	483	75	148	20	3	35*	106*	0	.306
1957	Buffalo	Int	1B	154	534	87	149	27	2	40*	128*	0	.279
1958	Buffalo	Int	1B	148	502	89	154	33	0	38	109	1	.307
1959	Buf/Rochester	Int	1B	143	478	68	125	32	2	22	76	0	.262
1960	Rochester	Int	1B	115	275	36	83	12	1	14	57	0	.302
1961	Rochester	Int	1B	82	203	24	59	13	1	10	51	0	.291
1962	Rochester	Int	1B	93	249	39	70	11	1	15	60	0	.281
1963	Rochester	Int	1B	77	188	20	51	8	1	6	35	0	.271
1964	Rochester	Int	PH	10	10	0	2	0	0	0	1	0	.200
	Majors			491	1725	256	472	54	12	93	340	1	.274
	Minors			1327	4150	677	1227	224	17	269	919	6	.296

ROSS C. (BRICK) ELDRED

Born July 26, 1893 at Sacramento, CA.
Batted right. Threw right. Height 5.06½. Weight 162.
Averaged 64 doubles a season for six years, 1920-25.

Year	Club	League	Pos	G	AB	R	H	2B	3B	HR	RBI	SB	BA
1916	Salt Lake City	P C	OF	19	32	3	7	2	0	0	-	-	.219
	Seattle	NWest	OF	92	340	59	113	19	9	8	-	17	.332
1917	Newark	Int	OF	143	487	67	131	26	5	6	-	27	.269
1918	San Francisco	P C	OF	97	398	54	105	26*	5	4	-	22	.264
1919	Sacramento	P C	OF	166	617	111	192	34	13	4	-	41	.311
1920	Seattle	P C	OF	188	682	111	231	59*	17	3	-	35	.339
1921	Seattle	P C	OF	154	590	109	188	60	3	6	84	17	.319
1922	Seattle	P C	OF	187	734	102	260	55	10	9	131	23	.354
1923	Seattle	P C	OF	193	742	129	262	71	11	7	116	23	.353
1924	Seattle	P C	OF	177	684	129	240	71	5	7	131	21	.351
1925	Seattle	P C	OF	191	739	120	242	66	6	7	142	21	.327
1926	Seattle	P C	OF	125	312	49	106	30	2	2	59	3	.340
1927	Seattle	P C	OF	122	369	53	120	31	1	2	48	10	.325
1928	Seattle	P C	OF	11	19	2	6	1	0	0	2	0	.316
	Wichita Falls	Texas	OF	91	317	67	113	26	2	9	56	4	.356
1929	Wichita Falls	Texas	OF	25	48	3	16	2	0	0	6	0	.333
	Milwaukee	A A	OF	38	108	14	23	3	2	0	-	1	.213
1930	Sacramento	P C	OF	79	203	31	75	10	1	6	42	3	.369
Minors				**2098**	**7421**	**1213**	**2430**	**592**	**92**	**80**	**817**	**268**	**.327**

CHARLES DEWIE ENGLISH

Born April 8, 1910 at Darlington, SC.
Batted right. Threw right. Height 5.09½. Weight 160.

Year	Club	League	Pos	G	AB	R	H	2B	3B	HR	RBI	SB	BA
1931	Florence	Palmetto	OF	76	282	61	81	15	4	11	58	6	.287
1932	Muskog/Hutch.	West A	3B	83	335	81	114	21	9	11	57	7	.340
	Chicago	American	3B-SS	24	63	7	20	3	1	1	8	0	.317
1933	Chicago	American	2B	3	9	2	4	2	0	0	1	0	.444
	Galveston	Texas	2B	153	604	87	169	29	9	5	85	31	.280
1934	Galveston	Texas	2B	147	564	81	184	37	8	10	116	15	.326
1935	Galveston	Texas	2B	161	612	99	186	42	10	13	104	29	.304
1936	Ft. Worth	Texas	2B	122	485	78	146	38	3	12	72	13	.301
	New York	National	2B	6	1	0	0	0	0	0	0	0	.000
1937	Kansas City	A A	3B-2B	154	624	80	204	44	15	1	98	2	.327
	Cincinnati	National	3B-2B	17	63	1	15	3	1	0	4	0	.238
1938	Los Angeles	PCL	2B	176	709	102	215	43	7	19	143	3	.303
1939	Los Angeles	PCL	3B-OF	171	660	114	184	39	4	13	89	2	.279
1940	Milwaukee	A A	3B	148	568	80	171	29	4	17	93	7	.301
1941	Milwaukee	A A	3B	14	36	4	11	0	0	0	1	0	.306
	Ft. Worth	Texas	3-2-0	33	112	17	27	7	0	4	16	1	.241
	Nashville	South A	3B-2B	59	205	31	59	15	0	4	33	1	.288
1942	Nashville	South A	3B	150	590	99	201*	50*	4	10	139*	1	.341*
1943	Los Angeles	P C	3B	157	591	101	191	31	5	16	98	2	.323
1944	L.A./Oakland	P C	3B-2B	124	447	56	131	23	5	2	59	7	.293
1945	Portland	P C	2B-3B	129	449	62	127	26	5	4	52	2	.283
1946	Baton Rouge	Evang	3B	51	178	26	56	9	1	1	28	1	.315
1947	Lancaster	Int St	3B	23	81	10	22	3	2	2	16	0	.272
1948	(Not in O.B.)												
1949	Balinger	Longhorn	3B	25	72	9	20	1	0	0	12	0	.278
Majors				**50**	**136**	**10**	**39**	**8**	**2**	**1**	**13**	**0**	**.287**
Minors				**2156**	**8204**	**1278**	**2499**	**502**	**95**	**155**	**1369**	**130**	**.305**

74

ROBERT SHAW (BUCK) FAUSETT

Born April 8, 1908 at Sheridan, AK.
Batted left. Threw right. Height 5.10. Weight 170.
Stole five bases in one game for Indianapolis, May 14, 1936.

Year Club	League	Pos	G	AB	R	H	2B	3B	HR	RBI	SB	BA
1931 Longview	E Texas	3B	7	28	4	7	1	0	0		1	.250
1932 Galveston	Texas	3B	126	446	53	117	14	7	0	45	20	.262
1933 Galveston	Texas	3B	153	609*	90	197*	35	7	0	51	16	.323
1934 Galveston	Texas	3B	154	634*	106	179	20	15	4	52	14	.282
1935 Galveston	Texas	3B	153	616	88	159	20	12	4	56	31	.258
1936 Indianapolis	A A	3B	157	688*	101	194	25	15	3	78	20	.282
1937 Indianapolis	A A	SS-3B	133	508	66	141	14	7	3	53	18	.278
1938 Indianapolis	A A	3B	139	502	89	170	27	11	3	40	28	.339
1939 Minneapolis	A A	3B-OF	131	463	66	141	18	6	3	53	23	.305
1940 Minneapolis	A A	3B	129	456	59	129	10	4	2	52	27	.283
1941 Minneapolis	A A	3B	93	294	37	67	12	1	1	22	15	.228
1942 Little Rock	South A	3B	138	563	96	188	27	8	2	46	19	.334
1943 Little Rock	South A	3B-P	140	567	92	205*	26	13	2	92	23	.362
1944 Cincinnati	National	3B-P	13	31	2	3	0	1	0	1	0	.097
Hollywood	P C	3B	94	381	44	120	18	6	0	35	11	.315
1945 Hollywood	P C	3B-P	167	644	100	203	28	6	2	60	21	.315
1946 Hollywood	P C	3B	84	252	29	65	7	2	0	22	12	.258
Albuquerque	WTNM	3B	19	57	11	25	3	6	0	12	3	.439
1947 Albuquerque	WTNM	3B	136	545	134	223	30	21*	20	142	12	.409
1948 Amarillo	WTNM	3B	109	369	71	147	35	1	12	101	7	.398
1949 Amarillo	WTNM	3B	5	5	0	2	0	0	0	0	0	.400
Majors			13	31	2	3	0	1	0	1	0	.097
Minors			2267	8627	1336	2679	370	148	61	1012	321	.311

ROBERTO FERNANDEZ (TAPANES)

Born October 22, 1927 at Campo, FL
Batted right. Threw right. Height 6.00. Weight 170.

Year Club	League	Pos	G	AB	R	H	2B	3B	HR	RBI	SB	BA
1948 Big Spring	Longhorn	OF	136	586	112	203	41	10	7	113	24	.346
1949 Abilene	WTNM	OF	137	591	118	241*	56*	5	14	111	24	.408
1950 Havana	Fla Int	OF	144	562	73	168	26	11	5	83	8	.299
1951 Havana	Fla Int	OF	93	370	45	115	27	1	3	53	3	.311
1952 St. P/Lake/Hav	Fla Int	OF	100	390	33	92	14	0	1	33	6	.236
Lubbock	WTNM	OF	51	201	32	83	23	4	2	51	4	.413
1953 Lubbock	WTNM	OF	142	589	146	233	53	15	29	134	45*	.396
1954 Lubbock	WTNM	OF	113	454	102	170	34	11	25	116	23	.374
1955 Lubbock	WTNM	OF	135	573	110	215	49	4	23	130	7	.375
1956 Roswell	SWestern	OF-3B	143	629*	132*	231*	64*	4	13	116	7	.367
1957 Nuevo Laredo	Mexican	OF-1B	40	169	27	58	9	4	3	25	3	.343
Havana	Int	1B	23	70	2	14	3	0	0	4	0	.200
1958 Yucatan	Mexican	1B	118	435	46	123	19	3	9	71	5	.283
1959 Veracruz	Mexican	1B	34	114	8	30	1	0	2	19	0	.263
Minors			1409	5733	986	1976	419	72	136	1059	159	.345

Fred Merkle had problems at both ends of his career. Not only did he fail to touch second base as the apparent winning run crossed the plate for the New York Giants in a crucial game with the Cubs late in the 1908 season, but he was the playing-manager for Reading in the International League in 1927 when that club lost 31 consecutive games. However, he did have some good years in between, both in the majors and minors. He drove in 166 runs for Rochester (IL) in 1923.

GEORGE ALOYS (SHOWBOAT) FISHER
Born January 16, 1899 at Jennings, IA.
Batted left. Threw right. Height 5.10. Weight 170.

Year	Club	League	Pos	G	AB	R	H	2B	3B	HR	RBI	SB	BA
1919	Minneapolis	A A	P	1	2	0	0	0	0	0	0	0	.000
1920	Minneapolis	A A	P	4	7	1	1	1	0	0	1	0	.143
	Miller	S Dak St	OF-P	51	201	10	76	4	1	3	6	1	.378*
1921	St. Joseph	Western	OF	163	634	131	223	38	15	14	-	8	.352
1922	St. Joseph	Western	OF	169*	675	160	242	55	17	16	-	9	.359
1923	New Haven	Eastern	OF	115	458	93	167	31	15	4	-	9	.365
	Washington	American	OF	13	23	4	6	2	0	0	2	0	.261
1924	Washington	American	OF	15	41	7	9	1	0	0	6	2	.220
	Minneapolis	A A	OF	112	398	58	123	27	7	10	72	12	.309
1925	Minneapolis	A A	OF	123	431	83	151	23	6	19	96	15	.350
1926	Minn/Indian	A A	OF	139	484	101	159	29	8	14	89	19	.329
1927	Buffalo	Int	OF	111	400	62	128	21	5	10	62	5	.320
1928	Buffalo	Int	OF	146	499	90	167	30	6	17	89	6	.335
1929	Buffalo	Int	OF	150	572	119	192	28	12	36	124	3	.336
1930	St. Louis	National	OF	92	254	49	95	18	6	8	61	4	.374
1931	Rochester	Int	OF	120	400	77	130	24	5	17	78	4	.325
1932	Rochester	Int	OF	49	189	34	54	15	1	6	29	2	.286
	St. Louis	American	OF	18	22	2	4	0	0	0	2	0	.182
	Milwaukee	A A	OF	36	122	28	44	8	3	2	21	4	.361
1933	Milwaukee	A A	OF	38	116	15	25	6	0	2	-	3	.216
	LR/Nashville	South A	OF	48	167	27	49	11	1	2	17	5	.293
	Majors			**138**	**340**	**62**	**114**	**21**	**6**	**8**	**71**	**6**	**.335**
	Minors			**1575**	**5755**	**1089**	**1931**	**351**	**102**	**172**	**684**	**105**	**.336**

JOSEPH LEO FORTIN
Born June 20, 1923 at Highland Park, MI
Batted right. Threw right. Height 6.03. Weight 215.

Year	Club	League	Pos	G	AB	R	H	2B	3B	HR	RBI	SB	BA
1942	Lockport	Pony	OF	34	134	17	32	10	2	0	9	0	.239
1943-45	(Not in O.B.)												
1946	Lamesa/Pampa	WTNM	OF	131	531	82	169	26	6	7	131	8	.318
1947	Pampa	WTNM	OF	41	168	38	63	17	4	3	56	1	.375
1948	Pampa	WTNM	OF	138	570	123	216	52	4	34	183	3	.379
1949	Richmond	Piedmont	OF	140	558	84	155	34	6	15	96	5	.278
1950	Pampa	WTNM	OF	145	588	151	236*	50	3	28	171*	7	.401
1951	Augusta	Sally	OF	15	53	6	12	3	1	0	4	0	.226
	Pampa/Albuq	WTNM	OF	107	387	100	120	31	6	19	85	5	.310
1952	Lamesa	WTNM	OF-1B	139	530	113	185	33	7	32	142*	7	.349
1953	Artesia	Longhorn	OF	86	310	59	102	26	2	19	78	9	.329
	Grand Forks	Northern	OF	34	120	23	36	3	3	3	24	0	.300
1954	Amar/Pampa/Pl	WTNM	OF	21	83	26	30	8	0	4	22	0	.361
1955	Pampa	WTNM	1B	137	540	138*	198	31	3	41	154	6	.367
1956	Pampa	SWestern	1B	46	172	37	58	10	0	14	44	2	.337
	Minors			**1214**	**4744**	**997**	**1612**	**334**	**47**	**219**	**1199**	**53**	**.340**

Eddie Rose collected 2517 hits in the minors and the most unusual probably was achieved when he was playing for the New Orleans Pelicans in a game at Birmingham on August 11, 1935. In the second inning he hit a high pop-up in the second baseman's territory. However, some pigeons were flying over and the ball hit one. The bird and ball fell in front of shortstop Moore and were both pronounced dead. Rose was given a single and romped home on a double by Bud Connally.

CLARENCE FRANCIS (POP) FOSTER
Born April 8, 1878 at New Haven, CT. Died April 16, 1944 at Princeton, NJ.
Threw right.

Year	Club	League	Pos	G	AB	R	H	2B	3B	HR	SB	BA
1897	Bridgeport	Conn			(No record available)							.261
1898	New Brittain	Conn	OF-SS	66	253	45	66	-	-	-	-	.261
	New York	National	O-3-S	32	112	10	30	6	1	0	0	.268
1899	Bridgeport	Conn	OF	27	114	18	47	9	4	2	9	.412
	New York	National	OF	84	301	48	89	9	7	3	7	.296
1900	New York	National	O-S-2	31	84	19	22	3	1	0	0	.262
	Worcester	Eastern	OF-SS	17	51	6	12	-	-	-	-	.235
1901	Chicago/Wash	American	OF-SS	115	427	69	119	18	11	7	10	.279
1902	Prov/Montreal	Eastern	OF	129	465	72	117	-	-	14*		.252
1903	Bridgeport	Conn	OF	104	455	75	138	22	12	0	30	.303
1904	Bridgeport	Conn	OF	109	420	79	158*	-	-	-	-	.376*
1905	Bridgeport	Conn	OF	114	437	91	143	32	16*	7*	55	.327
	Newark	Eastern	OF	15	48	13	22	8	0	3	6	.458
1906	Lancaster	Tri-St	OF	39	138	22	37	6	4	2	9	.268
1907	Lancaster	Tri-St	OF	124	443	77	130	21	15	4	40	.293
1908	Lancaster	Tri-St	OF	119	440	74	139	26	17*	5	27	.316
1909	Reading	Tri-St	OF	113	405	70	127	14	14	5	25	.314
1910	Holyoke	Conn	OF	124	453	68	155	36	5	15*	24	.342*
1911	New Haven	Conn	OF	115	394	58	128	27	5	7*	24	.325*
1912	New Haven	Conn	OF	120	418	59	125	24	7	9*	29	.299
1913	New Haven	East A	OF	118	419	55	120	26	5	4	22	.286
1914	Trenton	Tri-St	OF	87	294	58	114	22	4	5	13	.388*
1915	Portsmouth	Virginia	OF	65	210	26	58	11	2	3	4	.276
	Majors			**262**	**924**	**146**	**260**	**36**	**20**	**10**	**17**	**.281**
	Minors			**1605**	**5857**	**966**	**1836**	**284**	**110**	**85**	**317**	**.313**

JOHN HENRY FREDERICK
Born January 26, 1901 at Denver, CO. Died June 18, 1977 at Tigard, OR.
Batted left. Threw left. Height 5.11. Weight 165.
Set major league record by hitting six pinch home runs for Brooklyn in 1932.

Year	Club	League	Pos	G	AB	R	H	2B	3B	HR	RBI	SB	BA
1921	Regina	W. Can.	OF	59	271	42	66	5	8	1		15	.244
1922	(Not in O.B.)												
1923	Salt Lake City	P C	OF	160	585	111	192	37	10	16	82	4	.328
1924	Salt Lake City	P C	OF	186	790	171	279	67	7	28	132	8	.353
1925	Salt Lake City	P C	OF	162	640	120	198	40	7	10	79	3	.309
1926	Hollywood	P C	OF	186	667	87	185	33	4	8	63	3	.277
1927	Hollywood	P C	OF	180	623	95	190	40	3	9	93	9	.305
1928	Memphis	South A	OF	150	616	133	221*	44*	11	9	85	14	.359
1929	Brooklyn	National	OF	148	628	127	206	52*	6	24	75	6	.328
1930	Brooklyn	National	OF	142	616	120	206	44	11	17	76	1	.334
1931	Brooklyn	National	OF	146	611	81	165	34	8	17	71	2	.270
1932	Brooklyn	National	OF	118	384	54	115	28	2	16	56	1	.299
1933	Brooklyn	National	OF	147	556	65	171	22	7	7	64	9	.308
1934	Brooklyn	National	OF-1B	104	307	51	91	20	1	4	35	4	.296
1935	Sacramento	P C	1B-OF	170	628	116	228	34	11	3	93	6	.363
1936	Portland	P C	OF-1B	170	644	132	227	44	9	9	103	4	.352
1937	Portland	P C	OF-1B	177	667	110	201	46	8	12	107	0	.301
1938	Portland	P C	OF-1B	176	617	92	197	37	5	5	102	3	.319
1939	Portland	P C	OF-1B	150	479	86	156	27	4	4	85	1	.326
1940	Portland	P C	1B-OF	135	415	55	127	17	0	2	43	5	.306
	Majors			**805**	**3102**	**498**	**954**	**200**	**35**	**85**	**377**	**23**	**.308**
	Minors			**2061**	**7642**	**1350**	**2467**	**471**	**87**	**116**	**1067**	**75**	**.323**

ROBERT LAWRENCE (BUCK) FRIERSON
Born July 29, 1917 at Chicota, TX
Batted right. Threw right. Height 6.03. Weight 195.
Had 100 long hits and 197 RBI in 1947.

Year	Club	League	Pos	G	AB	R	H	2B	3B	HR	RBI	SB	BA
1937	Texarkana	E Texas	1B	18	64	8	15	1	2	1	9	0	.234
1938	Texarkana	E Texas	1-3	135	479	92	164	28	5	15	101	5	.342
1939	Texarkana	E Texas	3B	140	557	84	161	44	5	11	80	12	.289
1940	Cedar Rapids	III	OF	124	472	96	158	35	9	14	87	7	.335
1941	Wilkes-Barre	Eastern	OF	139	542	92	168	25	16*	5	78	20*	.310
	Cleveland	American	OF	5	11	2	3	1	0	0	2	0	.273
1942	Wilkes-Barre	Eastern	O-1	138	512	79	148	16	9	5	67	8	.289
1943-45	(Military Service)												
1946	Sherman	E Texas	O-3	84	348	84	136	23	2	25	102	6	.391
1947	Sherman-Den	Big St	OF	156*	660	188*	248*	36	6	58*	197*	2	.376
1948	Sherman-Den	Big St	OF	100	414	102	152	31	5	24	118	13	.367
	Dallas	Texas	OF	50	203	34	66	10	2	4	40	1	.325
1949	Dallas	Texas	OF	154	622	104	200	48	7	19	116	4	.322
1950	Dallas/OC	Texas	OF	128	371	46	100	27	1	9	55	0	.270
1951	Oklahoma City	Texas	OF	42	119	13	26	7	0	1	13	0	.218
	Denver	Western	OF	71	221	38	67	14	1	5	48	1	.303
1952	Paris	Big St	OF	147	591	115	222*	52*	2	24	140	4	.376
1953	Paris	Big St	OF	89	331	42	93	19	0	4	37	5	.281
	Harlingen	Gulf Cst	OF	46	172	24	52	8	3	3	35	1	.302
Majors				**5**	**11**	**2**	**3**	**1**	**0**	**0**	**2**	**0**	**.273**
Minors				**1761**	**6678**	**1241**	**2176**	**424**	**75**	**227**	**1323**	**89**	**.326**

JOHN EMIL FRISK
Born October 15, 1875 at Kalkaska, MI. Died January 27, 1922 at Seattle, WA.
Batted left. Threw right. Height 6.01. Weight 190.

Year	Club	League	Pos	G	AB	R	H	2B	3B	HR	SB	BA
1898	Port Huron	Int	P	46	183	32	60	7	3	1	12	.328
	Hamilton	Canadian	P	23	74	12	23	5	3	0	5	.311
1899	Cincinnati	National	P	9	25	5	7	1	0	0	0	.280
	Detroit	Western	P-OF	50	156	31	44	6	5	3	3	.282
1900	Detroit	American	P-OF	31	75	12	21	5	1	0	2	.280
1901	Detroit	American	P-OF	20	48	10	15	3	0	1	0	.313
	Denver	Western	P-OF	23	74	7	21	1	1	0	0	.284
1902	Denver	Western	OF	123	450	89	168	-	-	-	20	.373
1903	Denver	Western	OF	65	249	41	68	-	-	-	11	.273
1904	Seattle	P C	OF		808	179*	272*	46	14*	11	26	.337*
1905	St. Louis	American	OF	127	429	58	112	11	6	3	7	.261
1906	St. Paul	A A	OF	127	485	85	155	36	11	6	13	.320
1907	St. Paul	A A	OF	147	568	89	162	33	8	8	18	.285
	St. Louis	American	PH	4	4	0	1	0	0	0	0	.250
	Seattle	NWestern	OF	19	68	14	25	9	0	4	5	.368
1908	Seattle	NWestern	OF	132	470	72	124	19	4	11	17	.264
1909	Seattle	NWestern	OF	169	631	107	194	49*	6	10	20	.307
1910	Seattle/Spok	NWestern	OF	152	560	82	148	26	13*	7	22	.264
1911	Spokane/Van	NWestern	OF	159	588	104	171	23	16*	9	20	.291
1912	Vancouver	NWestern	OF	162	583	105	174	29	4	8	19	.298
1913	Vancouver	NWestern	OF	168	609	86	173	29	5	7	7	.284
1914	Van/Seattle	NWestern	OF	150	557	69	178	32	8	4	16	.320
1915	Spok/Sea/Van	NWestern	OF	107	384	59	103	10	5	7	10	.268
Majors				**160**	**506**	**73**	**135**	**15**	**6**	**4**	**7**	**.267**
Minors				**1853**	**7572**	**1275**	**2284**	**365**	**107**	**96**	**246**	**.302**

VINICIO UZCANGA (CHICO) GARCIA
Born December 24, 1924 at Vera Cruz, Mexico.
Batted right. Threw right. Height 5.08. Weight 170.

Year	Club	League	Pos	G	AB	R	H	2B	3B	HR	RBI	SB	BA
1944	Mexico City	Mexican	2B	8	18	0	4	0	0	0	2	1	.222
1946	San Luis Potosi	Mexican	2B-3B	92	383	55	122	8	6	0	28	11	.319
1947	San Luis Potosi	Mexican	2B	96	371	59	106	10	10	0	39	10	.286
1948	Puebla	Mexican	2B	82	331	67	105	16	5	3	41	14	.317
1949	Juarez	Ariz-Tex	2B	148	602	170*	227*	42	20*	4	88	41	.377*
1950	Shreveport	Texas	2B	142	485	53	104	17	1	1	35	9	.214
1951	Corpus Christi	Gulf Cst	2B	34	145	35	52	6	4	1	21	6	.359
	Shreveport	Texas	2-3-S	77	235	28	57	10	1	0	20	4	.243
1952	Shreveport	Texas	2B	158	585	88	162	20	7	2	62	6	.277
1953	Shreveport	Texas	2B	155	601	82	183*	34	4	2	51	8	.304
1954	Baltimore	American	2B	39	62	6	7	0	2	0	5	0	.113
1955	Toledo	A A	2B	154	577	93	173	34	4	10	68	8	.300
1956	Wichita	A A	2B-3B	144	516	60	144	25	1	3	65	5	.279
1957	Indianapolis	A A	2B	153	593	92	177	30	6	4	68	1	.298
1958	Indianapolis	A A	2B-3B	101	316	44	84	11	1	2	23	6	.266
1959	Dallas	A A	2B	158	573	55	152	27	1	2	53	6	.265
1960	Monterrey	Mexican	2B	127	493	102	173	41	4	16	75	3	.351
1961	Monterrey	Mexican	2B	121	488	85	169	49	3	5	63	6	.346
1962	Monterrey	Mexican	2B	126	504	91	172*	28	5	9	76	9	.341
1963	Monterrey	Mexican	2B	122	475	107*	175	36*	5	21	88	3	.368*
1964	Monterrey	Mexican	2B-1B	130	498	91	167	28	2	11	79	2	.335
1965	Monterrey	Mexican	2B-1B	131	464	79	146	27	3	9	70	0	.315
1966	Vera Cruz	Mexican	2B-1B	119	414	52	125	18	4	3	45	2	.302
1967	Aguila	Mexican	1B-2B	81	257	26	65	12	0	3	25	0	.253
1968	Aguila	Mexican	1B-2B	75	170	21	54	9	0	1	25	2	.318
1969	Aguila	Mexican	1B	57	77	4	14	2	0	0	10	0	.182
1970	Mont/MC Tigers	Mexican	1B	12	11	2	4	0	0	1	3	0	.364
Majors				**39**	**62**	**6**	**7**	**0**	**2**	**0**	**5**	**0**	**.113**
Minors				**2803**	**10182**	**1641**	**3116**	**540**	**97**	**113**	**1223**	**163**	**.306**

WILLIAM M. GEORGE
Born January 27, 1865 at Bellair, OH. Died August 23, 1916 at Wheeling, WV.
Batted right. Threw left. Height 5.07. Weight 158.

Year	Club	League	Pos	G	AB	R	H	2B	3B	HR	SB	BA
1887	New York	National	P-OF	13	53	6	9	0	0	0	2	.170
1888	New York	National	OF-P	9	39	7	9	1	0	1	1	.231
1889	New York	National	OF	3	15	1	4	0	0	0	1	.267
	Springfield	C Int St	OF	26	112	24	37	12	2	0	2	.330
	Columbus	A A	OF-P	5	17	1	4	0	0	0	1	.235
1890	Wheeling	Tri-St	OF	49	215	39	76	15	4	2	11	.353
1891	Portland	Pac NW	OF	94	422	102	143	40*	11	5	29	.339
1892	Portland	Pac NW	OF	74	312	67	92	12	5	2	37	.295
1893	Mont/Mob/Sav	Southern	OF	78	322	69	100	17	6	7	8	.311
1894	Grand Rapids	Western	OF	115	515	137	218	42	17	11	32	.423
1895	GR/St. Paul	Western	OF	124	595	169	240	63*	13	13	38	.403
1896	St. Paul	Western	OF	138	637	159	244	58	17	14	39	.383
1897	St. Paul	Western	OF	139	615	141	208	35	11	10	49	.338
1898	Norf/Newark	Atlantic	OF	74	279	50	83	15	4	0	25	.297
Majors				**30**	**124**	**15**	**26**	**1**	**0**	**1**	**5**	**.210**
Minors				**911**	**4024**	**957**	**1441**	**309**	**90**	**64**	**270**	**.358**

JACOB JOHN GETTMAN
Born October 25, 1875 at Frank, Russia. Died October 4, 1956 at Denver, CO.
Batted both. Threw right. Height 5.11. Weight 185.

Year Club	League	Pos	G	AB	R	H	2B	3B	HR	SB	BA
1897 Ft. Worth	Texas	OF	110	490	122	159	-	-	-	55	.324
Washington	National	OF	36	143	28	45	7	3	3	8	.315
1898 Washington	National	OF-1B	142	567	75	157	16	5	5	32	.277
1899 Washington	National	OF-1B	19	62	5	13	1	0	0	4	.210
Kansas City	Western	OF	59	238	48	64	-	-	-	22	.269
1900 Buffalo	American	1B-OF	121	516	82	154	26	12	2	35	.298
1901 Buffalo	Eastern	OF	99	403	76	119	-	-	3	39	.295
1902 Buffalo	Eastern	OF	116	489	121	166	-	-	9	-	.339
1903 Buffalo	Eastern	OF	91	359	96	120	-	-	4	26	.334
1904 Buffalo	Eastern	OF	60	233	47	60	11	2	0	13	.258
1905 Buffalo	Eastern	OF	137	558	84	152	27	10	2	16	.272
1906 Buffalo	Eastern	OF	136	516	90	150	22	7	1	22	.291
1907 Buffalo	Eastern	OF	95	348	49	96	16	8	1	15	.276
1908 Toronto	Eastern	OF	115	462	50	117	9	4	4	16	.253
1909 Newark	Eastern	OF	149	561	78	162	30	8	6	16	.289
1910 Newark	Eastern	OF	132	485	54	130	19	7	2	24	.268
1911 JC/Baltimore	Eastern	OF	123	487	54	124	14	9	1	14	.255
1912 Baltimore	Int	OF	94	349	57	120	26	19	3	10	.344
1913 Indianapolis	A A	OF	61	237	33	54	7	4	1	8	.228
1914 Hastings	Neb St	OF	109	381	54	128	-	-	-	-	.336*
Majors			**197**	**772**	**108**	**215**	**24**	**8**	**8**	**44**	**.278**
Minors			**1807**	**7112**	**1195**	**2075**	**207**	**90**	**39**	**331**	**.292**

FRANK PATRICK GILHOOLEY
Born June 10, 1892 at Toledo, OH. Died July 11, 1959 at Toledo, OH.
Batted left. Threw right. Height 5.08. Weight 155.

Year Club	League	Pos	G	AB	R	H	2B	3B	HR	RBI	SB	BA
1910 Saginaw	S Mich	2B-3B	32	123	9	19	2	0	0	-	6	.154
1911 Adrian	S Mich	OF	128	522	103	190	33	11	1	-	47	.364
St. Louis	National	OF	1	0	0	0	0	0	0	0	0	.000
1912 Erie	Central	OF	126	484	104	148	16	3	1	-	47	.306
St. Louis	National	OF	13	49	5	11	0	0	0	2	0	.224
1913 Montreal	Int	OF	117	458	74	150	13	3	0	-	36	.328
New York	American	OF	24	85	10	29	2	1	0	14	6	.341
1914 New York	American	OF	1	3	0	2	0	0	0	0	0	.667
Buffalo	Int	OF	142	562	116	174	13	15	0	-	62*	.310
1915 Buffalo	Int	OF	122	450	92	145	19	11	3	-	53*	.322
New York	American	OF	1	4	0	0	0	0	0	0	0	.000
1916 New York	American	OF	58	223	40	62	5	3	1	10	16	.278
1917 New York	American	OF	54	165	14	40	6	1	0	8	6	.242
1918 New York	American	OF	112	427	58	118	13	5	1	23	7	.276
1919 Boston	American	OF	48	112	14	27	4	0	0	1	2	.241
1920 Buffalo	Int	OF	148	583	139	200	30	10	2	-	45	.343
1921 Buffalo	Int	OF	164	641	131	201	28	17	1	-	55	.314
1922 Reading	Int	OF	164	636	124	230*	35	13	0	64	22	.362
1923 Reading	Int	OF	56	223	45	66	10	3	0	19	7	.296
1924 Toronto	Int	OF	148	576	119	187	25	4	3	47	13	.325
1925 Toronto	Int	OF	162	654	128	206	29	3	5	64	10	.315
1926 Toronto	Int	OF	156	631	118	193	29	8	0	67	17	.306
1927 Rochester	Int	OF	102	399	71	138	17	7	0	37	19	.346
1928 Jersey City	Int	OF	130	426	64	134	17	7	1	33	12	.315
1929 Jersey City	Int	OF	24	55	4	14	1	0	0	2	3	.255
Majors			**312**	**1068**	**141**	**289**	**30**	**10**	**2**	**58**	**37**	**.271**
Minors			**1921**	**7423**	**1441**	**2395**	**317**	**115**	**17**	**333**	**454**	**.323**

ROBERT JAMES GILKS

Born July 2, 1867 at Cincinnati, OH. Died August 20, 1944 at Brunswick, GA.
Batted right. Threw right.

Year	Club	League	Pos	G	AB	R	H	2B	3B	HR	SB	BA
1885	Chattanooga	Southern	OF-P	72	264	21	45	2	0	0	-	.170
1886	Binghamton	Int	O-3-P	85	386	51	103	15	4	0	23	.267
1887	Binghamton	Int	OF-P	75	372	68	121	19	0	1	29	.325
	Cleveland	A A	P-1B-OF	22	83	12	26	2	0	0	5	.313
1888	Cleveland	A A	OF-IF-P	119	484	59	111	14	4	1	16	.229
1889	Cleveland	National	OF-IF	53	210	17	50	5	2	0	6	.238
1890	Cleveland	National	OF-IF-P	130	544	65	116	10	3	0	17	.213
1891	Rochester	East	OF	71	318	38	67	10	1	0	7	.211
	Oconto	Wis		(No record available)								
1892	Omaha	Western	OF-2B	58	249	41	69	8	3	1	10	.277
	Mobile	Southern	2B	39	170	29	42	1	0	0	3	.247
1893	Mobile	Southern	OF-2B	88	357	74	122	19	3	2	21	.342
	Baltimore	National	OF	15	64	10	17	2	0	0	3	.266
1894	Toledo	Western	OF-SS	120	577	139	223	32	14	6	19	.386
1895	Toledo	Western	OF-1-P	120	560	113	169	23	2	2	21	.302
1896	Grand Rapids	Western	OF	121	529	71	146	15	1	0	11	.276
1897	Toledo	Inter St	OF-1-P	126	626	109	208	37	4	2	20	.332
1898	Toledo	Inter St	OF-P	150	669	100	195	28	4	1	45	.291
1899	Toledo	Inter St	OF-P	137	592	66	166	18	2	1	13	.280
1900	Toledo	Inter St	OF-P	115	468	31	111	14	0	0	19	.237
1901	Toledo	Western	OF-P	135	539	60	152	30	2	1	8	.282
1902	Toledo	A A	OF	141	561	60	141	15	1	0	18	.251
1903	Shreveport	South A	OF	61	215	19	58	-	-	-	5	.270
1904	Shreveport	South A	OF-1B	86	326	38	84	12	1	0	10	.258
1905	Shreveport	South A	OF	14	52	3	8	1	0	0	0	.154
1906	Shreveport	South A	OF	17	55	1	8	0	0	0	0	.145
1907	Gulfport	Cot St	1B	134	510	31	98	-	-	-	7	.192
1908	Gulf/Biloxi	Cot St	1B	98	366	23	84	-	-	-	10	.230
1909	Savan/Charl	Sally	1B	35	118	2	25	-	-	-	2	.212
	Galveston	Texas	OF	28	86	5	24	5	0	0	2	.279
	Majors			**339**	**1385**	**163**	**320**	**33**	**9**	**1**	**47**	**.231**
	Minors			**2126**	**8965**	**1193**	**2469**	**304**	**42**	**17**	**303**	**.275**

ROLAND EDOUARD GLADU

Born May 10, 1913 at Montreal, Quebec, Canada.
Batted left. Threw right. Height 5.08½. Weight 185.

Year	Club	League	Pos	G	AB	R	H	2B	3B	HR	RBI	SB	BA
1932	Montreal	Int	OF	15	17	5	4	0	0	1	4	0	.235
1933	Montreal	Int	OF	20	21	1	4	0	0	1	2	0	.190
	York	NY-Penn	OF	10	30	2	6	1	0	0	3	0	.200
1934	Richmond	Piedmont	1B-OF	72	194	36	50	13	3	4	25	2	.258
1935-37				(Not in O.B.)									
1938	Quebec	Provincl	1B-OF	42	144	27	49	-	-	-	17	-	.340
1939	Quebec	Provincl	1B	74	283	51	92	23	8	5	54	-	.325
1940	Quebec	Que Prov	1B	70	273	53	89	20	0	8	55	5	.326
1941	Quebec	Can-Amer	1B-3B	125	469	95	164	46*	7	13	91	14	.350
1942	Quebec	Can-Amer	3B-OF	115	404	85	140	37*	7	12	97	14	.347
1943				(Not in O.B.)									
1944	Hartford	Eastern	3B-OF	119	417	92	155	28	14	7	102	8	.372
	Boston	National	3B-OF	21	66	5	16	2	1	1	7	0	.242
1945	Montreal	Int	3B-OF	153*	603	126	204*	45*	14*	12	105	14	.338
1946	Nuevo Laredo	Mexican	3B-OF	91	342	61	110	17	11	4	62	-	.322
1947	San Luis	Mexican		115	429	77	138	27	12	6	75	-	.322
	St. Hyacinthe	Provincl	1B	2	5	0	0	0	0	0	0	0	.000
1948	Sherbrooke	Provincl	1B	89	303	82	116	27	1	10	69	-	.383
1949	Sherbrooke	Provincl	1B	94	321	72	98	22	3	19	81	-	.305
1950	Sherbrooke	Provincl	1B	92	309	59	105	15	1	5	52	2	.340
1951	Sherbrooke	Provincl	1B	96	321	66	106	25	0	7	71	2	.330
	Majors			**21**	**66**	**5**	**16**	**2**	**1**	**1**	**7**	**0**	**.242**
	Minors			**1394**	**4885**	**990**	**1630**	**346**	**81**	**114**	**965**	**61**	**.334**

WILBUR DAVID GOOD

Born September 28, 1885 at Punxsutawney, PA. Died December 30, 1963 at Brooksville, FL.
Batted left. Threw left. Height 5.06. Weight 165.

Year	Club	League	Pos	G	AB	R	H	2B	3B	HR	RBI	SB	BA
1905	Johnstown	Tri-St	P	28	80	11	23	3	3	0	10	0	.287
	New York	American	P	5	8	2	3	0	0	0	0	0	.375
1906	Johnstown	Tri-St		10	26	2	7	0	0	0	0	8	.269
1907	Akron	Ohio-Pa	P	38	136	17	35	3	3	0	-	9	.257
1908	Akron	Ohio-Pa	OF	96	387	58	143	19	14	2	28	37	.370*
	Cleveland	American	OF	46	154	23	43	1	3	1	14	7	.279
1909	Cleveland	American	OF	94	318	33	68	6	5	0	17	13	.214
1910	Baltimore	Eastern	OF	130	504	76	151	9	12	7	-	22	.300
	Boston	National	OF	23	86	15	29	5	4	0	11	5	.337
1911	Boston-Chicago	National	OF	101	310	48	83	14	7	2	36	13	.268
1912	Chicago	National	OF	39	35	7	5	0	0	0	1	3	.143
1913	Chicago	National	OF	49	91	11	23	3	2	1	12	5	.253
1914	Chicago	National	OF	154	580	70	158	24	7	2	43	31	.272
1915	Chicago	National	OF	128	498	66	126	18	9	2	27	19	.253
1916	Philadelphia	National	OF	75	136	25	34	4	3	1	15	7	.250
1917	Kansas City	A A	OF	75	300	51	89	20	4	0	-	16	.297
1918	Kansas City	A A	OF	73	271	44	87	10	4	1	32	13	.321
	Chicago	American	OF	35	148	24	37	9	4	0	11	1	.250
1919	Kansas City	A A	OF	140	586	91	204*	31	12	7	-	23	.348
1920	Kansas City	A A	OF	166	686	110	229*	37	15	11	119	26	.334
1921	Kansas City	A A	OF	164	711	165	248	38	9	23	157	25	.349
1922	Kansas City	A A	OF	165	707*	149*	249*	31	13	6	97	13	.352
1923	Kansas City	A A	OF	155	662	136	232	40	15	11	91	17	.350
1924	Kansas City	A A	OF	71	292	50	77	19	8	2	18	8	.264
	Atlanta	South A	OF	68	266	61	95	16	9	1	27	4	.357
1925	Atlanta	South A	OF	152	622*	130	236*	33	22	10	126	30	.379*
1926	Atlanta	South A	OF	126	475	64	143	20	5	1	60	21	.301
	San Antonio	Texas	OF	20	79	12	28	4	4	0	12	1	.354
1927	Macon	Sally	OF	140	523	99	180	22	7	16	99	24	.344
1928	Macon	Sally	OF	136	494	81	158	19	4	6	93	11	.320
1929	Atlanta	South A	OF	29	110	13	27	3	1	0	6	0	.245
1930	Johnstown	Mid Atl	OF	79	282	54	102	17	3	4	58	7	.362
1931	Johnstown	Mid Atl	OF	27	28	3	7	1	0	0	3	0	.250
	Majors			**749**	**2364**	**324**	**609**	**84**	**44**	**9**	**187**	**104**	**.258**
	Minors			**2088**	**8227**	**1477**	**2750**	**395**	**167**	**108**	**1036**	**315**	**.334**

FRANK GRANT

Born about 1865 at Pittsfield, MA. Died May 26, 1937 in New York City.
Batted right. Threw right. Height 5.07½. Weight 155.
One of top black players of 19th century, he played with Cuban Giants at Trenton in 1889 and at
Ansonia in 1891. The Giants were an all-black team in O.B. those two years.

Year	Club	League	Pos	G	AB	R	H	2B	3B	HR	SB	BA
1886	Meriden	Eastern	2B	44	177	23	56	17	1	1	3	.316
	Buffalo	Int	2B	49	192	38	66	13	7	2	12	.344
1887	Buffalo	Int	2B	105	459	81	162	26	10	11*	40	.353
1888	Buffalo	Int A	2B-OF	84	347	95	120	18	5	11	28	.346
1889	Trenton	Mid St	2-3-C	67	252	72	79	19	3	1	34	.313
1890	Harrisburg	E In-St	3-0-2	59	252	66	84	12	6	5	22	.333
	Harrisburg	Atl A	SS	47	187	33	62	17	2	0	10	.332
1891	Ansonia	Conn St	2B	3	13	2	5	1	0	0	0	.385
	Minors			**458**	**1879**	**410**	**634**	**123**	**34**	**31**	**149**	**.337**

82

WILLIAM HAYDEN (STUBBY) GREER
Born in 1920 at Carbon, TX.
Batted right. Threw right. Height 5.08. Weight 160.

Year	Club	League	Pos	G	AB	R	H	2B	3B	HR	RBI	SB	BA
1940	Midland	WTNM	SS	94	390	80	119	26	3	10	51	11	.305
1941	Big Spring	WTNM	SS	135	531	99	178	30	11	16	115	18	.335
1942	Santa Barbara	Calif	2B	68	276	60	88	26	6	3	39	11	.319
	Dayton	Mid Atl	2B	71	270	48	70	19	4	3	38	11	.259
1943-45	(Military Service)												
1946	Abilene	WTNM	SS-2B	135	565	146	202	39	8	23	131	38*	.358
1947	Abilene	WTNM	S-2-3	112	432	110	149	27	4	16	89	25	.345
	Mobile	South A	SS	24	82	12	30	7	2	0	12	0	.366
1948	Mobile	South A	3B	110	351	38	97	14	5	4	46	4	.276
1949	Abilene	WTNM	SS	118	475	122	155	29	3	19	106	28	.326
1950	Abilene	WTNM	SS-2B	96	300	67	99	23	1	14	68	9	.330
1951	Artesia	Longhorn	SS-2B	111	408	83	135	24	5	18	89	18	.331
1952	Roswell	Longhorn	S-3-2	130	534	89	192	44	8	15	117	2	.360
1953	Brownsville	Gulf Cst	SS	57	216	33	67	15	1	5	41	6	.310
	Amarillo	WTNM	2B	32	126	34	46	11	3	6	30	4	.365
1954	Roswell	Longhorn	3B-OF	103	400	122	159	35	4	13	101	12	.398
1955	Roswell	Longhorn	SS-3B	123	489	111	165	39	8	22	113	7	.337
1956	Victoria	Big St	3B	37	119	13	25	3	0	1	12	2	.210
1957	Ballinger	SWestern	SS	113	443	81	139	30	4	16	76	6	.314
	Minors			**1669**	**6407**	**1348**	**2115**	**441**	**80**	**204**	**1274**	**212**	**.330**

IVY MOORE GRIFFIN
Born January 16, 1896 at Thomasville, AL. Died August 25, 1957 at Gainesville, FL.
Batted left. Threw right. Height 5.11. Weight 180.

Year	Club	League	Pos	G	AB	R	H	2B	3B	HR	RBI	SB	BA
1919	Atlanta	South A	1B	118	429	41	130	18	6	0	-	12	.303
	Philadelphia	American	1B	17	68	5	20	2	2	0	6	0	.294
1920	Philadelphia	American	1B-2B	129	467	46	111	15	1	0	20	3	.238
1921	Philadelphia	American	1B	39	103	14	33	4	2	0	13	1	.320
1922	Milwaukee	A A	1B	168	673	107	204	31	13	11	92	8	.303
1923	Milwaukee	A A	1B	166	660	98	239	33	15	9	112	18	.362
1924	Milwaukee	A A	1B	138	550	72	168	25	7	2	64	7	.305
1925	Milwaukee	A A	1B	161	632	112	212	35	10	6	92	20	.335
1926	Milwaukee	A A	1B	149	612	103	205	28	9	9	105	19	.335
1927	Milwaukee	A A	1B	138	566	90	183	28	8	4	88	11	.323
1928	Milwaukee	A A	1B	115	428	72	139	22	7	6	55	13	.325
1929	Mil/Louisville	A A	1B	97	351	63	115	22	4	5	49	9	.328
1930	Little Rock	South A	1B	129	502	87	181	33	4	8	103	10	.361
1931	Little Rock	South A	1B	148	580	104	182	33	7	7	95	11	.314
1932	Little Rock	South A	1B	151	584	88	175	34	6	2	95	4	.300
1933	Williamsport	NY-Penn	1B	135	514	83	166	22	4	1	57	9	.323
1934	Asheville	Piedmont	1B	95	378	71	123	16	4	2	34	7	.325
1935	Jeanerette	Evang	1B	129	467	92	136	19	2	3	49	12	.291
1936	Cordele	Ga-Fla	1B	113	432	67	125	17	3	4	63	12	.289
1937	Cordele	Ga-Fla	1B	118	424	83	130	-	-	2	62	6	.307
1938	Selma	SEastern	1B	13	13	1	2	0	0	0	1	0	.154
1939	Eau Claire	Northern	1B	19	23	1	6	0	1	0	2	1	.261
1940	Eau Claire	Northern	1B	(Less than 10 games)									
	Majors			**185**	**638**	**65**	**164**	**21**	**5**	**0**	**39**	**4**	**.257**
	Minors			**2300**	**8818**	**1435**	**2821**	**416**	**110**	**81**	**1218**	**189**	**.320**

83

JOHN (BUNNY) GRIFFITHS
Born December 2, 1904 at Wilkes-Barre, PA
Batted right. Threw right. Height 5.06. Weight 155.

Year	Club	League	Pos	G	AB	R	H	2B	3B	HR	RBI	SB	BA
1925	Martinsburg	Blue Rdg	SS	98	372	48	84	12	0	1	-	11	.226
1926	Martinsburg	Blue Rdg	SS	74	295	61	95	18	0	3	-	11	.322
1927	Chambersburg	Blue Rdg	SS	100*	369	49	79	7	1	0	-	11	.214
1928	Chambersburg	Blue Rdg	SS	100	361	62	104	23	6	4	-	13	.288
1929	Chambersburg	Blue Rdg	SS	117	428	92	131	27	2	2	-	19	.306
1930	Hazleton	NY-Penn	SS	139*	523	80	142	15	1	4	43	8	.272
1931	Albany	Eastern	SS	33	125	16	28	3	1	0	14	2	.224
	Binghamton	NY-Penn	SS	77	286	35	69	11	1	0	21	11	.241
1932	Binghamton	NY-Penn	SS	78	296	52	90	16	4	0	33	7	.304
	Cumberland	Mid Atl	SS	50	168	20	42	7	1	0	12	8	.250
1933	Wilkes-Barre	NY-Penn	SS	139	550	84	155	27	0	0	38	19	.282
1934	Wilkes-Barre	NY-Penn	SS	133	496	54	157	21	4	0	66	8	.317
1935	Wilkes-Barre	NY-Penn	SS	110	437	50	137	15	4	0	51	14	.314
1936	Wilkes-Barre	NY-Penn	SS	21	86	9	27	4	0	0	18	2	.314
	Syracuse	Int	SS	18	55	11	16	3	2	0	7	1	.291
	Little Rock	South A	SS	92	360	36	107	19	6	0	41	6	.297
1937	Little Rock	South A	SS	153	543	63	143	22	5	0	54	6	.263
1938	San Diego	P C	SS	169	613	78	173	27	0	0	69	6	.282
1939	San Diego	P C	SS	119	384	34	87	12	1	0	25	4	.227
1940	Salem	West Int	SS	97	348	40	83	14	1	2	41	8	.239
1941	Salem	West Int	SS	131	464	53	129	20	2	1	63	4	.278
1942	Rome	Can-Amer	SS	12	44	7	11	3	2	0	8	1	.250
1943	York	Inter-St	SS	139	488	71	167	29	3	0	66	27	.342
1944	York	Inter-St	SS	104	384	70	136	28	8	0	65	18	.354
1945	York	Inter-St	SS	120	381	62	104	13	3	2	50	6	.273
1946	Hagerstown	Inter-St	SS	52	160	18	45	10	0	0	16	5	.281
1947	Hagerstown	Inter-St	SS	15	23	1	5	0	0	0	2	1	.217
Minors				**2490**	**9039**	**1256**	**2546**	**406**	**58**	**19**	**803**	**237**	**.282**

MARVIN JOHN GUDAT
Born August 27, 1904 at Weser, TX. Died March 1, 1954 at Los Angeles, CA.
Batted left. Threw left. Height 5.11. Weight 162.
Compiled 56-35 record as pitcher in 143 games.

Year	Club	League	Pos	G	AB	R	H	2B	3B	HR	RBI	SB	BA
1926	Monroe/Vicks	Cot St	P-OF	44	127	18	35	6	2	3		4	.276
1927	Topeka	West A	P-OF	38	87	5	22	2	2	0	8	1	.253
	Houston	Texas	P	1	0	0	0	0	0	0	0	0	.000
1928	Dayton	Central	P-OF	38	106	23	36	8	2	0	12	2	.340
1929	Cincinnati	National	P	9	10	0	2	0	0	0	0	0	.200
1930	Peoria	III	P-OF	39	116	11	27	4	3	3	22	0	.233
1931	Columbus	A A	P-O-1	102	213	37	73	10	1	4	34	6	.343
1932	Chicago	National	O-1-P	60	94	15	24	4	1	1	15	0	.255
1933	Los Angeles	P C	OF-P	183	741	154	247	41	8	10	113	25	.333
1934	Los Angeles	P C	OF	188*	758	150	242	36	13	4	125	43	.319
1935	Los Angeles	P C	OF	176*	735*	125	227	28	4	2	65	52	.309
1936	Los Angeles	P C	OF	102	346	52	112	15	3	1	46	13	.324
1937	Los Angeles	P C	OF-1B	164	621	100	206	45	6	6	73	7	.332
1938	L.A./Oakland	P C	OF-P	73	216	37	64	13	1	2	32	6	.296
1939	Oakland	P C	OF-1B	153	516	80	167	30	12	1	71	10	.324
1940	Oakland	P C	OF	173	626	81	196	26	7	1	67	13	.313
1941	Oakland	P C	OF-1B	174	640	74	186	41	2	2	65	9	.291
1942	Oakland	P C	OF-1B	112	369	32	100	18	3	0	41	4	.271
1943	Holly/SD	P C	OF-1B	128	407	47	104	14	1	0	26	8	.256
1944	San Diego	P C	OF-1B	113	369	38	104	14	2	0	31	8	.282
1945	San Diego	P C	1B-OF	102	238	21	63	11	2	0	25	3	.265
Majors				**69**	**104**	**15**	**26**	**4**	**1**	**1**	**15**	**0**	**.250**
Minors				**2103**	**7231**	**1085**	**2211**	**362**	**74**	**39**	**856**	**214**	**.306**

JOSEPH NAPOLEON GUYON

Born November 26, 1892 at White Earth, MN. Died November 27, 1971 at Louisville, KY.
Batted left. Threw right. Height 5.11½. Weight 172.
A Chippewa Indian, Guyon played NFL football 1920-27, and was named to the Professional Football Hall of Fame in 1966. An All American at Georgia Tech in 1918, he was named to National Football Foundation Hall of Fame in 1971.

Year Club	League	Pos	G	AB	R	H	2B	3B	HR	RBI	SB	BA
1920 Augusta	Sally	OF	5	16	1	4	0	0	0	0	0	.250
Atlanta/LR	South A	OF	44	134	23	31	6	0	1		6	.231
1921 Atlanta	South A	OF	135	505	78	158	20	13	1	32	45	.313
1922 Atlanta	South A	OF	152	556	89	166	30	6	11		19	.299
1923 Atlanta	South A	OF	140	544	104	172	12	9	10	50	32	.316
1924 Little Rock	South A	OF	151	593	106	205	35	11	7	51	28	.346
1925 Louisville	A A	OF	157	628	152	228	38	17	9	106	18	.363
1926 Louisville	A A	OF	154	609	132	209	36	13	2	86	21	.343
1927 Louisville	A A	OF	129	506	93	181	20	9	3	62	12	.358
1928 Louisville	A A	OF	25	79	9	19	3	3	0	9	1	.241
1929-30 (Not in O.B. because of serious injury sustained in 1928)												
1931 Anders/Spart	Palmetto	OF		146	36	46	6	2	4	23	8	.315
1932 Asheville	Piedmont	OF	66	242	46	88	14	6	0	25	13	.364
1933-35 (Not in O.B.)												
1936 Fieldale	Bi-State	OF	33	132	31	35	7	2	1	12	0	.265
Minors			**1191**	**4690**	**900**	**1542**	**227**	**91**	**49**	**456**	**203**	**.329**

BRUNO PHILIP HAAS

Born May 5, 1891 at Worcester, MA. Died June 5, 1952 at Sarasota, FL.
Batted both. Threw left. Height 5.10. Weight 180.
Played NFL football in 1921. Collected six hits in six trips in game for St. Paul, June 7, 1925.

Year Club	League	Pos	G	AB	R	H	2B	3B	HR	RBI	SB	BA
1915 Philadelphia	American	P-OF	12	18	1	1	0	0	0	0	0	.056
1916 Wilkes-Barre	NY St	OF-3B	125	472	64	141					25	.299
1917 Newark	Int	OF	132	497	52	127	20	8	5		18	.256
1918			(Did not play)									
1919 Milwaukee	A A	OF	129	459	76	135	20	8	7		13	.294
1920 St. Paul	A A	OF-2-P	130	446	73	137	24	5	11	64	12	.307
1921 St. Paul	A A	OF-2B	144	527	100	171	27	7	6	72	14	.324
1922 St. Paul	A A	OF-1B	146	547	105	181	35	14	8	90	24	.331
1923 St. Paul	A A	OF	156	554	112	186	37	15	14	111	22	.336
1924 St. Paul	A A	OF	155	536	85	157	22	13	11	100	24	.293
1925 St. Paul	A A	OF-P	117	419	70	133	24	6	10	78	18	.317
1926 St. Paul	A A	OF	158	590	75	194	51	8	8	76	20	.329
1927 St. Paul	A A	OF	115	440	64	147	32	5	6	63	24	.334
1928 St. Paul	A A	OF-1B	151	564	76	185	34	5	10	76	18	.328
1929 St. Paul	A A	OF	135	510	56	151	31	4	3	60	6	.296
1930 St. Paul	A A	OF	82	262	40	98	11	5	3	40	6	.374
1931 Toledo/Milw	A A	OF	138	488	65	139	26	2	6	73	3	.285
1932 New Orleans	South A	OF	84	320	49	98	13	5	6	58	2	.306
Des Moines	Western	OF	26	82	8	18	7	1	0	17	0	.220
1933 Winnipeg	Northern	OF-P	49	141		34	6	1	4		3	.241
1934-36 Winnipeg	Northern		(Manager — did not play)									
1937 Winnipeg	Northern	P-OF	29	51	9	10	3	1	2	9	0	.196
1938 Winnipeg	Northern	P-OF	24	48	4	14	3	0	1	6	0	.292
1939-41			(Did not play)									
1942 Grand Forks	Northern	P-OF	20	25	1	4	1	0	0	3	0	.160
1943-45			(Did not play)									
1946 Fargo-Moorhd	Northern	P	1	2	0	1	1	0	0	0	0	.500
Majors			**12**	**18**	**1**	**1**	**0**	**0**	**0**	**0**	**0**	**.056**
Minors			**2246**	**7980**	**1184**	**2461**	**428**	**113**	**121**	**996**	**252**	**.308**

WILLIAM ROBERT (BILLY) HAMILTON

Born February 16, 1866 at Newark, NJ. Died December 15, 1940 at Worcester, MA.
Batted left. Threw left. Height 5.06. Weight 165.
Named to Baseball Hall of Fame in 1961. Holds major league record for scoring most runs in a season with 192 in 1894.

Year	Club	League	Pos	G	AB	R	H	2B	3B	HR	RBI	SB	BA
1887	Waterbury	Eastern	OF	71	313	75	116	19	5	0	-	18	.371
1888	Worcester	New Eng	OF	61	248	76	87	10	4	0	-	72	.351
	Kansas City	A A	OF	35	129	21	34	4	4	0	11	19	.264
1889	Kansas City	A A	OF	137	534	144	161	17	12	3	77	111*	.301
1890	Philadelphia	National	OF	123	496	133	161	13	9	2	49	102*	.325
1891	Philadelphia	National	OF	133	527	141*	179*	23	7	2	60	111*	.340*
1892	Philadelphia	National	OF	139	554	132	183	21	7	3	53	57	.330
1893	Philadelphia	National	OF	82	355	110	135	22	7	5	44	43	.380*
1894	Philadelphia	National	OF	129	544	192*	220	25	15	4	87	98*	.404
1895	Philadelphia	National	OF	123	517	166*	201	22	6	7	74	97*	.389
1896	Boston	National	OF	131	523	152	191	24	9	3	52	83	.365
1897	Boston	National	OF	127	507	152*	174	17	5	3	61	66	.343
1898	Boston	National	OF	110	417	110	154	16	5	3	50	54	.369
1899	Boston	National	OF	84	297	63	92	7	1	1	33	19	.310
1900	Boston	National	OF	136	520	103	173	20	5	1	47	32	.333
1901	Boston	National	OF	102	348	71	100	11	2	3	38	20	.287
1902	Haverhill	New Eng	OF	66	243	67	82	23	2	2	-	26	.337
1903	Haverhill	New Eng	OF	37	132	37	60	15	2	4	-	27	.455
1904	Haverhill	New Eng	OF	113	408	113*	168*	32	8	0	-	74*	.412*
1905	Harrisburg	Tri-St	OF	110	386	82	132	15	8	2	-	45	.342
1906	Haverhill	New Eng	OF	14	51	1	10	1	0	0	-	5	.196
	Harrisburg	Tri-St	OF	43	155	33	43	5	1	0	-	16	.277
1907	Haverhill	New Eng	OF	91	324	50	108	16	4	0	-	29	.333*
1908	Haverhill	New Eng	OF	85	300	63	87	19	0	1	-	39	.290
1909	Lynn	New Eng	OF	109	376	61	125	17	2	0	-	23	.332*
1910	Lynn	New Eng	OF	41	112	14	28	1	2	0	-	5	.250
	Majors			1591	6268	1690	2158	242	94	40	736	912	.344
	Minors			841	3048	672	1046	173	38	9		379	.343

WILLIAM G. (SKEETER) HARTMAN

Born in 1874 at Fort Wayne, IN. Died June 27, 1945 at Toledo, OH.

Year	Club	League	Pos	G	AB	R	H	2B	3B	HR	SB	BA
1895	P. Huron/Kala	Mich St	3B-SS	72	344	79	114	17	14*	6	29	.331
1896	Tacoma	Pac NW	OF	31	137	35	54	13	2	0	13	.394
	Toledo	InterSt	OF-2B	54	204	40	64	15	3	3	24	.314
1897	Toledo	InterSt	OF	126	571	152	192	35	9	6	58	.336
1898	Toledo	InterSt	OF	152	629	167	214	50	12	9	42	.340
1899	Toledo	InterSt	OF-2B	135	528	117	142	29	6	10	45	.269
1900	Toledo	InterSt	OF	135	541	119	142	33	6	7	44	.262
1901	Kansas City	Western	OF	124	482	101	141	23	16	2	21	.293
1902	St. Joseph	Western	OF	139	546	68	150	-	-	-	33	.275
1903	St. Jospeh	Western	OF	116	447	71	126	-	-	-	27	.282
1904	St. Jospeh	Western	OF	141	565	85	165	-	-	-	57	.292
1905	Little Rock	South A	OF	30	109	20	25	1	0	0	12	.229
1906	Harr/Alt/Lan	Tri-St	OF	117	419	52	102	22	2	0	29	.243
1907	Johns/Alt	Tri-St	OF	113	407	47	96	13	1	2	34	.236
1908	Dayton	Central	OF	134	452	62	120	11	-	0	23	.265
1909	Dayton	Central	OF	126	458	53	109	13	6	0	24	.238
1910	Quincy	Cent A	OF	140	567	77	132	21	4	0	30	.233
1911	Quincy	Cent A	OF	129	481	62	123	-	-	-	12	.256
1912	Quincy/Bloom	Cent A		(Less than 10 games)								
	Minors			2014	7887	1407	2211	296	81	45	557	.280

DOUGLAS NORMAN HARVEY

Born December 19, 1924 at Montreal, Quebec, Canada.
Batted left. Threw right. Height 5.11. Weight 190.
Star defenseman in the National Hockey League, 1947-68. Named to Hockey Hall of Fame in 1973.

Year	Club	League	Pos	G	AB	R	H	2B	3B	HR	RBI	SB	BA
1947	Ottawa	Border	OF	10	15	4	6	1	0	0	0	0	.400
1948	Ottawa	Border	OF	109	423	107	144	22	10	4	73	24	.340
1949	Ottawa	Border	OF	109	422	121*	148	27	10	14	109*	30	.351*
1950	Ottawa	Border	OF	10	35	11	10	1	2	0	5	4	.286
	Minors			238	895	243	308	51	22	18	187	58	.344

MINOR WILSON (MICKEY) HEATH

Born October 30, 1903 at Toledo, OH.
Batted left. Threw left. Height 6.00. Weight 175.
Collected 12 consecutive hits September 2-3-4, 1930.

Year	Club	League	Pos	G	AB	R	H	2B	3B	HR	RBI	SB	BA
1923	Ottumwa	Miss Val	1B	121	435	67	129	27	7	3	-	15	.297
1924	Ottumwa	Miss Val	1B	119	445	117	157	42	12	8	-	23	.353
1925	Toronto	Int	1B	123	365	55	82	18	4	3	46	5	.225
1926	Toronto	Int	1B	164	537	83	180	27	15	10	115	19	.335
1927	Toronto	Int	1B	17	40	8	10	3	0	2	4	0	.250
	Hollywood	P C	1B	106	330	56	93	24	3	9	51	7	.282
1928	Hollywood	P C	1B	191	662	118	203	38	12	19	109	10	.307
1929	Hollywood	P C	1B	201	680	149	237	44	5	38	156	20	.349
1930	Hollywood	P C	1B	174	546	149	177	16	3	37	136	19	.324
1931	Cincinnati	National	1B	7	26	2	7	0	0	0	3	0	.269
1932	Cincinnati	National	1B	39	134	14	27	1	3	0	15	0	.201
	Rochester	Int	1B	36	116	17	31	7	1	7	18	1	.267
1933	Rochester	Int	1B	62	226	37	64	11	1	9	42	4	.283
	Columbus	A A	1B	92	333	46	77	14	5	8	61	5	.231
1934	Columbus	A A	1B	150	508	115	142	14	5	29	123	10	.280
1935	Indianapolis	A A	1B	153	551	115	166	32	7	20	98	20	.301
1936	Indianapolis	A A	1B	77	277	50	81	16	6	7	46	8	.292
	Montreal	Int	1B	64	213	36	56	16	2	3	34	0	.263
1937	Milwaukee	A A	1B	156	537	107	159	31	11	25	113	11	.296
1938	Milwaukee	A A	1B	141	514	117	151	21	4	32	81	13	.294
1939	Milwaukee	A A	1B	117	336	65	87	15	7	16	53	6	.259
1940	Milwaukee	A A	1B	4	3	0	1	0	0	0	0	0	.333
	Majors			46	160	16	34	1	3	0	18	0	.213
	Minors			2268	7654	1507	2283	416	110	285	1286	196	.298

JOHN EDWARD HENDEE

Born March 7, 1903 at Flagler, IA.
Batted left. Threw left. Height 5.10½. Weight 175.

Year	Club	League	Pos	G	AB	R	H	2B	3B	HR	SB	BA
1924	Marshalltown	Miss Val	1B	16	60	4	17	3	2	0	3	.283
1925	Marshalltown	Miss Val	1B	113	443	68	150	30	7	7	11	.339
1926	Salisbury	Piedmont	1B	24	102	17	29	7	2	0	3	.284
1927	(Not in O.B.)											
1928	Rock Island	Miss Val	1B	114	470	58	173	28	13	5	5	.368
1929	Davenport	Miss Val	1B	124	505	97	183*	30	14	11	16	.362
	Kansas City	A A	1B	3	6	0	1	0	0	0	0	.167
1930	Davenport	Miss Val	1B	118	478	90	161	34	15*	5	21	.337
1931	Davenport/Dub	Miss Val	1B	109	462	71	156	35	6	6	10	.338
1932	Richmond	Eastern	1B	80	327	44	107	19	7	1	6	.327
	Waterloo	Miss Val	1B	6	24		10	1	0	0	1	.417
1933	Richmond	Piedmont	1B	118	475	74	157	26	6	3	26	.331
1934	Richmond	Piedmont	1B	106	414	69	124	20	4	2	14	.300
	Rock Is/SC	Western	1B	22	79	6	20	2	0	1	2	.253
1935	Wilkes-Barre	NY-Penn	1B	4	20		4	0	0	0	0	.200
	Minors			957	3865	598	1292	235	76	41	118	.334

RICHARD BROOKS HOLDER
Born November 2, 1915 at Rising Star, TX.
Batted left. Threw right. Height 5.10. Weight 180.

Year	Club	League	Pos	G	AB	R	H	2B	3B	HR	RBI	SB	BA
1935	Des Moines	Western	2B-SS	88	345	69	105	14	13	1	46	15	.304
	San Francisco	P C	2B	18	48	9	12	0	0	0	4	4	.250
1936	San Francisco	P C	2B	152	581	110	168	27	11	1	50	17	.289
1937	San Francisco	P C	OF	135	486	87	155	27	8	2	65	10	.319
1938	San Francisco	P C	OF	172	585	122	193	26	8	2	95	11	.330
1939	San Francisco	P C	OF	173	636	115	200	34	24*	5	87	14	.314
1940	San Francisco	P C	OF	152	521	63	143	19	7	1	60	6	.274
1941	San Francisco	P C	OF	170	624	119	175	30	10	2	53	11	.280
1942	San Francisco	P C	OF	179	652	113	194	36	9	6	51	4	.298
1943	Hollywood	P C	OF	149	543	83	148	27	5	6	62	12	.273
1944	Hollywood	P C	OF	161	583	119	163	28	8	6	54	21	.280
1945	Hollywood	P C	OF	109	312	54	80	16	2	5	41	13	.256
1946	Oakland	P C	OF	155	477	88	135	15	3	13	59	14	.283
1947	Oakland	P C	OF	172	599	137	186	40	4	16	78	9	.311
1948	Oakland	P C	OF	148	482	99	143	15	3	10	57	11	.297
1949	San Francisco	P C	OF	76	237	45	74	17	0	5	36	0	.312
1950	San Francisco	P C	OF	158	511	113	151	26	1	11	77	2	.295
1951	Portland	P C	OF	125	377	65	115	20	1	6	54	0	.305
	Minors			**2492**	**8599**	**1610**	**2540**	**417**	**117**	**98**	**1029**	**174**	**.295**

LEROY LUCIEN (COWBOY) JONES
Born October 2, 1900 at McCall Creek, MS.
Batted left. Threw right. Height 5.11. Weight 168.

Year	Club	League	Pos	G	AB	R	H	2B	3B	HR	RBI	SB	BA
1924	Durham	Piedmont	OF	116	425	52	124	21	16*	10	72	7	.292
1925	Mobile	South A	OF	149	550	85	172	41	16	12	106	12	.313
1926	Birmingham	South A	OF	22	72	11	18	1	1	0	3	3	.250
	Hartford	Eastern	OF	28	105	17	31	5	0	2	-	0	.295
	Peoria	III	OF	9	26	10	8	0	0	3	9	1	.308
1927	Little Rock	South A	OF	25	87	13	21	7	2	2	15	0	.241
	Columbia	Sally	OF	48	168	25	41	5	8	4	29	5	.244
	Salis-Spencer	Piedmont	OF	73	235	74	93	20	11	10	63	11	.396
1928	Columbia	Sally	OF	25	85	17	25	8	4	1	14	0	.294
	Salis-Spencer	Piedmont	OF	119	415	105	160	47*	4	23	100	5	.386
1929	Salis-Spencer	Piedmont	OF	132	440	101	157	37	9	12	60	1	.357
1930	Toledo	A A	OF	8	24	6	9	3	1	1	7	0	.375
	Ft. Wayne	Central	OF	139	525	162*	213	35	7	36	152	10	.406
1931	St. Paul	A A	OF	13	9	4	5	2	0	0	-	0	.556
	Dallas	Texas	OF	114	374	66	115	33	3	6	90	4	.307
1932	Dallas/Beau	Texas	OF	51	171	26	50	10	3	2	25	5	.292
	Decatur	III	OF	18	62	11	18	5	2	0	-	0	.290
1933	Jackson	Dixie	OF	123	450	90	148	43*	8	4	99	4	.329
1934	Jackson	E Dixie	OF	90	331	65	83	16	5	2	50	5	.251
1935	Pine Bluff	E Dixie	OF	119	447	69	128	31	4	2	72	5	.286
1936	Pine Bluff	Cot St	OF	139	486	101	138	36	10	7	74	7	.284
1937	Pine Bluff	Cot St	OF	132	475	92	135	39	5	7	84	6	.284
1938	Pine Bluff	Cot St	OF	83	273	41	78	20	2	1	43	2	.286
	Taft	Tex Val	OF	39	129	31	48	15	3	6	28	2	.372
1939	Clarksdale	Cot St	OF	133	469	104	156	31	6	5	99	4	.333
1940	Clarksdale	Cot St	OF	118	392	70	130	27	8	6	89	3	.332
1941	Clarks/Marsh	Cot St	OF	52	154	35	43	13	0	0	17	1	.279
	Minors			**2117**	**7379**	**1483**	**2347**	**551**	**138**	**164**	**1400**	**103**	**.318**

IRWIN V. (FUZZY) HUFFT
Born August 2, 1903 at Lebanon, MO.
Batted left. Threw right. Height 5.10. Weight 175.

Year	Club	League	Pos	G	AB	R	H	2B	3B	HR	RBI	SB	BA
1921	Parsons	SWestern	OF	32	123	7	22	5	1	0	-	7	.179
	Drumwright	West A	OF	13	44	2	11	2	0	0	-	0	.250
1923	Springfield	West A	OF	(Less than 10 games)									
1924	Springfield	West A	OF	23	84	19	24	6	2	4	10	0	.286
	Arkansas City	SWestern	OF	101	384	86	141	24	6	28*	-	9	.367*
1925	Arkansas City	SWestern	OF	95	373	85	134	29	7	25	107	20	.359
	Wichita	Western	OF	14	56	16	17	3	0	5	-	0	.304
1926	Seattle	P C	OF	165	550	86	171	23	8	16	94	8	.311
1927	Seattle	P C	OF	147	496	85	176	37	5	19	138	10	.355
1928	Seattle/Miss	P C	OF	160	561	108	208	46	8	30	143	7	.371
1929	Missions	P C	OF	194	754	140	286	57	7	39	187	7	.379
1930	Missions	P C	OF	187	721	140	257	51	6	37	178	8	.356
1931	Missions/Oak	P C	OF	176	645	119	221	49	9	14	92	10	.343
1932	Oakland	P C	OF	125	449	57	127	31	3	11	70	5	.283
	Indianapols	A A	OF	38	133	15	31	10	2	2	21	0	.233
1933	Indianapolis	A A	OF	10	25	1	7	0	0	0	-	0	.280
	OC/Galveston	Texas	OF	123	445	61	132	33	8	5	81	10	.297
	Minors			**1603**	**5843**	**1027**	**1965**	**406**	**72**	**235**	**1121**	**101**	**.336**

LYLE LEROY JUDY
Born November 15, 1913 at Lawrenceville, IL.
Batted right. Threw right. Height 5.10. Weight 150.
Stole 107 bases in 1935, creating a sensation in that heavy hitting era.

Year	Club	League	Pos	G	AB	R	H	2B	3B	HR	RBI	SB	BA
1934	Springfield	West A	C-SS	100	343	66	108	19	5	2	62	6	.315
1935	Springfield	West A	2B	135	496	127	167	33	20	0	65	107*	.337
	St. Louis	National	2B	8	11	2	0	0	0	0	0	2	.000
1936	Sacramento	P C	2B	36	100	10	22	3	1	0	5	4	.220
	Columbus	A A	2B	31	102	10	26	1	2	1	14	2	.255
	Huntington	Mid Atl	OF	3	10	0	2	0	0	0	0	0	.200
	Hopkinsville	Kitty	2B	18	70	21	20	1	4	0	6	10	.286
1937	Baltimore	Int	2B	2	7	0	1	0	0	0	0	0	.143
	Albany/Trent	NY-Penn	2B	85	281	35	60	9	0	1	23	11	.214
1938	St. Augustine	Fla St	2B	126	461	82	132	12	2	2	44	35	.286
1939	St. Augustine	Fla St	2B	139	529	103	161	23	7	0	53	51*	.304
1940	Reading	Int St	2B	128	478	107*	140	21	3	5	51	46*	.293
1941	Reading/Trent	Int St	2B	75	224	48	64	10	0	0	21	10	.286
	Dayton	Mid Atl	2B	23	82	12	22	4	0	0	11	5	.268
1942-45 (Not in O.B.)													
1946	St. Augustine	Fla St	2B	95	361	67	102	8	0	1	42	31	.283
1947	St. Augustine	Fla St	2B	120	431	98	131	24	1	2	45	32	.304
1948	St. Augustine	Fla St	2B	138	506	99	146	24	2	3	87	24	.289
1949	St. Augustine	Fla St	2B	130	509	85	131	20	2	1	57	24	.257
1950	St. Augustine	Fla St	2B	134	447	97	119	12	0	1	32	21	.266
1951	Palataka	Fla St	2B	131	503	100	139	23	2	2	46	23	.276
	Majors			**8**	**11**	**2**	**0**	**0**	**0**	**0**	**0**	**2**	**.000**
	Minors			**1649**	**5940**	**1167**	**1693**	**247**	**51**	**21**	**664**	**442**	**.285**

Kyle Rote was one of many college football stars who gave minor league baseball a fling. An All-American at Southern Methodist in 1951, he joined the Corpus Christi baseball club in the Gulf Coast League in April 1952 and played in 22 games. Although he had missed spring training, he hit three home runs in a game against Galveston and had a batting average of .348 and slugging percentage of .712 when he left to report for football training with the New York Giants.

JOSEPH KATZ

Year	Club	League	Pos	G	AB	R	H	2B	3B	HR	SB	BA
1889	Greenville	Mich St	OF	95	423	100	154*	-	-	-	4	.364*
1890	Burlington	W Int St	OF	82	353	67	103	17	8	5	13	.292
	Seattle	Pac NW	OF	17	70	7	16	3	1	0	3	.229
1891	Grand Rapids	NWestern	OF	70	288	60	93*	20*	6	5	12	.323
	Kansas City	West A	OF	25	102	17	23	4	2	2	2	.225
1892	Minneapolis	Western	OF	45	192	27	55	11	4	6	7	.286
1893	Chattanooga	Southern	OF	67	236	49	86	19	2	11	1	.364
1894	Rock Is/Mol	West A	OF	115	450	149	182	45	10	20	23	.404*
1895	Jacksonville	West A	OF	82	452	121	153	-	-	-	-	.338
1896	Portsmouth	Virginia	OF	59	244	37	73	18	5	3	19	.299
	Birmingham	Southern	OF	66	276	46	99	22	10	0	11	.359
1897	Mansfield	Inter St	OF	98	504	127	177	36	13	15	24	.351
1898	Mans/Youngs	Inter St	1B	96	442	72	140	31	8	8	13	.317
	Minors			**917**	**4032**	**879**	**1354**	**226**	**69**	**75**	**132**	**.336**

WALTER BROCTON (BILL) KAY

Born February 14, 1878 at New Castle, VA. Died December 3, 1945 at Roanoke, VA.
Batted left. Threw right. Height 6.02. Weight 180.

Year	Club	League	Pos	G	AB	R	H	2B	3B	HR	SB	BA
1907	Washington	American	OF	25	60	8	20	1	1	0	0	.333
1908	Minneapolis	A A	OF	16	46	0	12	1	1	0	1	.261
1909	Albany	NY St	OF	140	527	71	185*	34	11	2	21	.351*
1910	Albany	NY St	OF	127	443	72	161	22	12	3	26	.363*
1911	Montgomery	South A	OF	33	116	19	30	4	3	0	5	.259
	Albany	NY St	OF	99	356	51	120	16	6	2	35	.337
1912	Newark	Int	OF	7	4	0	1	0	0	0	0	.250
	Albany/Scran	NY St	OF	67	243	39	83	12	7	0	10	.342
1913	Albany	NY St	OF	134	472	67	149	23	12	5	27	.316
1914	Binghamton	NY St	OF	126	422	83	136	22	14	4	32	.322
1915	Binghamton	NY St	OF	125	447	98*	169*	22	25*	7	35	.378*
1916	Binghamton	NY St	OF	124	461	85*	166*	25	11	2	18	.360*
1917	Binghamton	NY St	OF	89	325	43	102	9	3	3	14	.314
1918	Binghamton	Int	OF	90	339	61	110	16	12	1	9	.324
1919	Binghamton	Int	OF	5	13	0	4	1	0	0	0	.308
	Springfield	Eastern	OF	33	115	10	27	8	1	0	4	.235
1920	Greenville	Sally	OF	54	186	29	57	10	2	4	4	.306
1921-23	(Not in O.B.)											
1924	Bing/W-B	NY-Penn	OF	94	264	36	83	8	6	5	2	.314
1925	Columbia	Sally	OF	23	79	11	17	3	1	3	1	.215
	Majors			**25**	**60**	**8**	**20**	**1**	**1**	**0**	**0**	**.333**
	Minors			**1386**	**4858**	**775**	**1612**	**236**	**127**	**41**	**244**	**.332**

JAMES WARD KEESEY

Born October 27, 1902 at Perryville, MO. Died September 5, 1951 at Boise, ID.
Batted right. Threw right. Height 6.00½. Weight 170.

Year	Club	League	Pos	G	AB	R	H	2B	3B	HR	RBI	SB	BA
1923	Frederick	Blue Rdg	1B	94	342	71	125	17	4	20	-	6	.365
1924	Portsmouth	Virginia	1B	137	522	93	170	31	9	17	97	10	.326
1925	Portsmouth	Virginia	1B	122	451	91	154	27	4	16	81	7	.341
	Philadelphia	American	1B	5	5	1	2	0	0	0	1	0	.400
1926	Reading	Int	1B	151	513	61	142	22	6	4	61	2	.277
1927	Hartford	Eastern	1B	156	594	114	204*	36	16	15	115*	14	.343
1928	Portland	P C	1B	186	678	107	228	52	7	9	104	18	.336
1929	Portland	P C	1B	185	705	107	246	54	8	12	124	17	.349

Year	Club	League	Pos	G	AB	R	H	2B	3B	HR	RBI	SB	BA
1930	Philadelphia	American	1B	11	12	2	3	1	0	0	2	0	.250
	Jersey City	Int	1B	89	327	51	85	14	6	1	40	4	.260
1931	San Francisco	P C	1B	163	665	103	238	40	10	10	113	14	.358
1932	SF/Portland	P C	1B	175	674	105	208	35	8	5	122	6	.309
1933	Portland	P C	1B	83	334	33	100	19	2	4	56	1	.299
	Kansas City	A A	1B	65	257	31	87	10	5	1	39	0	.339
1934	Dallas	Texas	1B	72	283	40	83	18	8	1	36	6	.293
1935	Oklahoma City	Texas	1B	161	581	83	155	29	7	4	72	8	.267
1936	Oklahoma City	Texas	1B	150	537	87	152	38	7	4	93	14	.283
1937	Oklahoma City	Texas	1B	157	586	86	186	37	2	9	97	12	.317
1938	Oklahoma City	Texas	1B	134	482	60	147	26	1	1	56	13	.305
1939	Portsmouth	Piedmont	1B	32	70	4	23	1	0	1	7	1	.329
1940	Oklahoma City	Texas	1B	42	116	17	38	8	2	2	14	2	.328
1941	Boise	Pioneer	1B	93	285	52	92	18	3	2	52	6	.323
1942	Boise	Pioneer	1B	94	317	49	91	21	3	0	67	9	.287
1943	(Not in O.B.)												
1944	Seattle	P C	1B	18	50	2	12	2	0	0	5	1	.240
	Majors			**16**	**17**	**3**	**5**	**1**	**0**	**0**	**3**	**0**	**.294**
	Minors			**2559**	**9369**	**1447**	**2966**	**555**	**118**	**138**	**1451**	**171**	**.317**

JUDSON FABIAN (JAY) KIRKE

Born June 16, 1888 at Fleischmans, NY. Died August 31, 1968 at New Orleans, LA.
Batted left. Threw right. Height 6.00. Weight 195.

Year	Club	League	Pos	G	AB	R	H	2B	3B	HR	RBI	SB	BA
1906	Kingston	Hudson R	SS	22	69	4	22	2	1	0	-	0	.319
1907	Poughkeepsie	Hudson R	SS	16	61	11	25	6	0	0	-	4	.410
1907	Wilmington	Tri-St	SS	23	82	7	18	4	0	0	-	2	.220
1908	Binghamton	NY St	2B-SS	133	488	43	130	9	9	1	-	11	.266
1909	Bing/Wilkes-Ba	NY St	2B-3B	144*	547	62	158	26	3	1	-	22	.289
1910	Scranton	NY St	2B	139*	541*	78	182*	25	9	1	-	31	.336
	Detroit	American	2B-OF	8	25	3	5	1	0	0	3	1	.200
1911	New Orleans	South A	2B	137	519	68	160	25	5	5	-	24	.308
	Boston	National	O-3-2	20	89	9	32	5	5	0	12	3	.360
1912	Boston	National	O-3-1	103	359	53	115	11	4	4	62	7	.320
1913	Boston	National	OF	18	38	3	9	2	0	0	3	0	.237
	Toledo	A A	O-1-3	136	525	56	168	26	9	8	-	15	.320
1914	Cleveland	A A	1B-OF	74	307	44	107	17	6	3	-	6	.349
	Cleveland	American	1B-OF	67	242	18	66	10	2	1	25	5	.273
1915	Cleveland	American	1B	87	339	35	105	19	2	2	40	5	.310
	Cleveland	A A	1B-OF	68	266	28	76	19	3	1	-	9	.286
1916	Mil/Louisville	A A	1B	168	633	78	192	40*	5	5	-	14	.303
1917	Louisville	A A	1B-OF	148	550	70	175	37*	8	2	84	16	.318
1918	Louisville	A A	1B-OF	75	278	29	76	10	4	1	18	6	.273
	New York	National	1B	17	56	1	14	1	0	0	3	0	.250
1919	Louisville	A A	1B	145	524	67	158	24	15	4	85	19	.302
1920	Louisville	A A	1B	161	634	84	209	32	6	8	114	19	.330
1921	Louisville	A A	1B	168*	730*	125	282*	43	17	21	157	13	.386*
1922	Louisville	A A	1B	168	664	112	236*	38	16	9	123	8	.355
1923	Indianapolis	A A	1B	128	468	50	117	19	5	4	74	4	.250
1924	Minneapolis	A A	1B-OF	151	521	70	170	45	2	14	97	8	.326
1925	Ft.W/Beau/Shrev	Texas	1B	131	531	77	171	41	4	15	82	5	.322
1926	Shreveport	Texas	1B	110	430	61	143	32	0	3	63	4	.333
1927	Decatur	Ill	1B	112	434	47	133	30	4	1	58	5	.306
1928-34	(Not in O.B.)												
1935	Opelousas	Evang	1B	60	203	26	57	7	0	4	42	1	.281
	Majors			**320**	**1148**	**122**	**346**	**49**	**13**	**7**	**148**	**21**	**.301**
	Minors			**2617**	**10005**	**1297**	**3165**	**557**	**131**	**111**	**997**	**246**	**.316**

JOSEPH WILLIAM (QUIET JOE) KNIGHT
(Sometimes called Jonas Knight)
Born September 28, 1859 at Port Stanley, Ontario, Canada. Died October 18, 1938 at St. Thomas, Ontario.
Batted left. Threw left. Height 5.11. Weight 185.

Year	Club	League	Pos	G	AB	R	H	2B	3B	HR	SB	BA
1883	Bay City/Quin	NWestern	P	31	125	9	25	-	-	-	-	.200
1884	Philadelphia	National	P	6	24	2	6	3	0	0	-	.250
	Muskegon	NWestern	P	7	26	1	8	0	0	0	-	.308
1885	London	Canadian	P-OF	36	165	35	41	3	5	2	-	.248
1886	Hamilton	Int	OF-P	78	329	47	91	21	6	1	6	.277
1887	Hamilton	Int	OF	100	442	86	148	24	8	5	41	.335
1888	Hamilton	Int A	OF	111	496	99	148	32*	6	1	64	.298
1889	London	Int A	OF	103	472	81	165	28	15	3	41	.350
1890	Cincinnati	National	OF	127	481	67	150	26	8	4	17	.312
1891	Rochester	East A	OF	95	394	75	118	27	11	0	25	.299
1892	Syr/Utica/Bing	Eastern	OF	107	416	93	158	40*	7	3	22	.380
1893	Binghamton	Eastern	OF	94	437	110	170*	28	17*	2	26	.389
1894	W-B/Provi	Eastern	OF	113	494	107	180	37	10	1	25	.364
1895	Providence	Eastern	OF	116	504	98	183	32	10	3	20	.363
1896	Providence	Eastern	OF	119	523	112	197	35	6	3	21	.377
1897	Providence	Eastern	OF	128	528	127	177	36	8	0	12	.335
1898	W-B/Ottawa	Eastern	OF	90	358	62	121	17	3	0	8	.338
	St. Thomas	Canadian	OF	9	39	4	10	4	1	1	2	.256
1899	St. Thomas	Canadian	OF	17	65	7	21	-	-	-	4	.323
	Buffalo	Eastern	OF	6	25	3	9	0	0	0	1	.360
	Majors			**133**	**505**	**69**	**156**	**29**	**8**	**4**	**17**	**.309**
	Minors			**1360**	**5838**	**1156**	**1970**	**364**	**113**	**25**	**318**	**.337**

EDWARD A. KNOBLAUCH
Born January 31, 1918 at Bay City, MI.
Batted left. Threw left. Height 5.10. Weight 160.

Year	Club	League	Pos	G	AB	R	H	2B	3B	HR	RBI	SB	BA
1938	Monett	Ark-Mo	OF	63	253	57	90	17	3	2	43	13	.356
	Asheville	Piedmont	OF	55	195	31	58	7	1	0	11	4	.297
1939	Kilgore	E Texas	OF	139	564	125*	189	37	4	2	48	28	.335
1940	Columbus	Sally	OF	150	595	135*	205	33	9	0	72	25	.345
1941	Columbus	Sally	OF	139	568	114*	191	18	11	2	71	12	.336
1942	Houston	Texas	OF	151	558	77	172	22	9	0	52	20	.308
1943-45	(Military Service)												
1946	Houston	Texas	OF	110	356	54	109	8	5	2	42	9	.306
1947	Houston	Texas	OF	156	570	93	157	17	9	0	68	6	.275
1948	Houston	Texas	OF	153	553	102	163	20	8	1	44	5	.295
1949	Hou/Shr/Tulsa	Texas	OF	139	504	95	158	26	10	2	72	7	.313
1950	Tulsa	Texas	OF	146	534	86	159	22	15	2	67	22	.298
1951	Tulsa/Dallas	Texas	OF	158	555	89	171	35	8	1	44	15	.308
1952	Dallas	Texas	OF	147	558	84	171	31	12	2	51	11	.306
1953	Dallas	Texas	OF	154	592	98	180	23	7	0	44	6	.304
1954	Dallas/Beau	Texas	OF	146	583	82	178	27	4	0	43	3	.305
1955	Beau/Dallas	Texas	OF	157	588	98	192	48	2	4	60	4	.327*
	Minors			**2163**	**8126**	**1420**	**2543**	**391**	**117**	**20**	**832**	**190**	**.313**

What player played for a major league team and a minor league team in the same city in the same year? Jay Kirke (see his record on page 91) did it in both 1914 and 1915 when the Cleveland Indians operated an American Association farm team in the same city to keep the Federal League out. Ironically, Kirke hit better for the Cleveland major league club than he did for the minor league team in 1915.

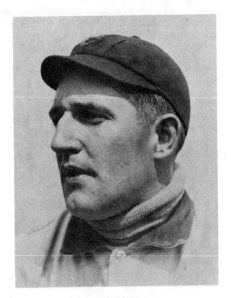

Joe Munson (self portrait)   **Jay Kirke**

Brooklyn outfielders in 1932 — Johnny Frederick, Lefty O'Doul, and Hack Wilson. All contributed to minor league records and lore.

HORACE L. (PIP) KOEHLER
Born January 16, 1902 at Gilbert, PA.
Batted right. Threw right. Height 5.10. Weight 165.

Year	Club	League	Pos	G	AB	R	H	2B	3B	HR	RBI	SB	BA
1925	New York	National	OF	12	2	1	0	0	0	0	0	0	.000
	Reading	Int	OF	71	222	38	61	15	3	2	25	5	.275
1926	Toledo	A A	OF	153	553	70	157	18	4	2	44	20	.284
1927	Toledo	A A	OF-3B	137	465	49	134	27	7	3	85	7	.288
1928	Toledo	A A	O-S-3	154	588	83	167	23	10	1	57	10	.284
1929	Toledo	A A	OF-3B	156	640	98	198	30	12	3	70	17	.309
1930	Toledo	A A	3B-OF	149	616	101	199	36	11	4	94	12	.323
1931	Tol/Milwaukee	A A	3B-OF	158	619	83	168	28	7	3	80	12	.271
1932	Milwaukee	A A	3B	152	571	79	167	27	4	8	91	5	.292
1933	Milwaukee	A A	3B-OF	155	644	96	205	30	6	6	85	8	.318
1934	Atlanta	South A	2-0-3	116	410	56	119	18	1	1	51	7	.290
1935	Portsmouth	Piedmont	SS-3B	136	527	97	171	32	5	7	70	13	.324
1936	Portsmouth	Piedmont	OF-SS	140	545	85	154	25	4	10	86	12	.283
1937	Portsmouth	Piedmont	OF	140	585	92	152	26	3	6	80	11	.260
1938	Akron	Mid Atl	0-3-2	122	466	76	162	37	2	3	56	9	.348
1939	Akron	Mid Atl	0-3-2	114	417	45	122	20	1	2	51	7	.293
1940	Akron	Mid Atl	3B	14	42	6	10	3	0	0	4	0	.238
1941	Tacoma	West Int	0-2-3	91	289	28	81	9	0	0	35	3	.280
1942	Tacoma	West Int	0-2-1	100	330	38	86	15	0	0	45	11	.261
	Majors			12	2	1	0	0	0	0	0	0	.000
	Minors			2258	8529	1220	2513	419	80	61	1109	169	.295

ARTHUR CLIFFORD HIRAM (HI) LADD
Born February 9, 1870 at Willamantic, CT. Died May 7, 1948 at Cranston, RI.
Batted left. Threw right. Height 6.04. Weight 180.

Year	Club	League	Pos	G	AB	R	H	2B	3B	HR	SB	BA
1892	Woonsocket	New Eng	OF-P	98	454	90	140	31	6	2	25	.308
1893	Charleston	Southern	OF	18	72	13	19	4	1	0	1	.264
	Fall River	New Eng	OF-P	87	351	83	114	26	8	7	46	.327
1894	Fall River	New Eng	OF-P	99	434	85	142	32	4	5	21	.325
1895	Fall River	New Eng	OF-P	107	485	111	176	33	15	6	16	.363
1896	Fall River	New Eng	OF-P	106	487	103	160	28	6	14	12	.329
1897	Fall River	New Eng	OF	103	435	83	144	33	4	4	19	.331
1898	Fall River	New Eng	OF	54	219	50	70	19	3	3	12	.320
	Pitt/Boston	National	OF	2	5	1	1	0	0	0	0	.200
1899	Paterson	Atlantic	OF	71	288	44	99	8	3	3	9	.344
	Worcester	Eastern	OF	14	53	7	16	3	2	1	0	.302
1900	Newark	Atlantic	OF	19	77	12	32	8	3	1	1	.416
	Derby	Conn	OF	84	318	67	118	26	2	9	6	.371*
1901	Derby	Conn	OF	109	479	97	171	-	-	-	-	.357
1902	Bridgeport	Conn	OF	107	428	54	119	23	5	4	21	.278
1903	Bridgeport	Conn	OF	106	423	63	145	23	6	1	9	.343
1904	Bridgeport	Conn	OF	116	460	63	148	-	-	-	-	.322
1905	Bridgeport	Conn	OF	114	456	70	147	30	6	0	15	.322
1906	Bridgeport	Conn	OF	124	489	64	157	22	4	2	13	.321
1907	Bridgeport	Conn	OF	125	493	60	168*	-	-	-	-	.341*
1908	Bridgeport	Conn	OF	127	488	59	144	27	4	1	11	.295
1909	Bridgeport	Conn	OF	124	490	55	156	27	8	3	17	.318
1910	Bridgeport	Conn	OF	123	470	68	158	15	9	0	13	.336
1911	Bridgeport	Conn	OF	120	490	60	143	25	9	4	13	.292
	Majors			2	5	1	1	0	0	0	0	.200
	Minors			2155	8839	1461	2886	443	108	70	280	.327

DANIEL J. (BUD) LALLY
Born August 12, 1867 at Jersey City, NJ. Died April 14, 1936 at Milwaukee, WI.
Batted right. Threw right. Height 5.11½. Weight 210.
Scored 205 runs for Mineapolis in 1895.

Year	Club	League	Pos	G	AB	R	H	2B	3B	HR	SB	BA
1887	Haverhill	New Eng	OF-P	77	348	61	126	21	3	7	-	.362
1888	Toronto	Int A	P	2	8	0	6	1	0	0	0	.750
	Belleville	East Int	P	(No record available)								
1889	New Haven	Atl A	OF	85	345	62	111	18	11	7	17	.322
1890	New Haven	Atl A	OF	119	480	89	159	24*	11	12*	23	.331
1891	New Haven	East A	OF	84	353	56	98	20	8	5*	16	.278
	Pittsburgh	National	OF	41	143	24	32	6	2	1	0	.224
1892	Columbus	Western	OF	65	267	44	74	12	5	3	23	.277
	Memphis	Southern	OF	36	145	19	38	5	3	1	1	.262
1893	Atlanta	Southern	OF	24	97	15	22	3	1	1	2	.227
	Erie	Eastern	OF	82	339	79	113	25	6	7	14	.333
1894	Erie	Eastern	OF	108	458	78	152	22	7	8	8	.332
1895	Minneapolis	Western	OF	123	590	205*	236	49	13	36	44	.400
1896	Minneapolis	Western	OF	139	599	153	197	38	14	15	39	.329
1897	Minneapolis	Western	OF	25	112	37	45	5	2	2	3	.402
	St. Louis	National	OF-1B	87	355	56	99	15	5	2	12	.279
1898	Columbus	Western	OF	114	435	66	131	27	6	3	12	.301
1899	Columbus	Western	OF	122	496	84	156	13	13	4	14	.315
1900	Chicago/Minn	American	OF	138	576	71	151	24	6	1	21	.262
1901	Grand Rapids	West A	OF	129	552	-	164	36	9	2	39	.297
1902	Columbus/Minn	A A	OF	130	526	84	143	26	13	1	25	.272
1903	Minneapolis	A A	OF	134	543	80	156	31	4	3	10	.287
1904	Minneapolis	A A	1B	26	93	10	22	3	1	0	0	.237
	Crookston	Northern	1B	4	15	1	4	1	0	0	0	.267
	Butte	Pac Nat	OF	69	295	53	106	12	2	0	17	.359
1905	Nashville	South A	OF-1B	34	141	15	29	5	2	0	3	.206
	Charleston	Sally	1B-OF	42	146	12	27	5	0	0	4	.185
	Majors			**128**	**498**	**80**	**131**	**21**	**7**	**3**	**12**	**.263**
	Minors			**1907**	**7944**	**1373**	**2462**	**425**	**140**	**118**	**335**	**.308**

SAMUEL H. J. LaROQUE
Born February 26, 1864 at St. Mathias, Quebec, Canada. Reportedly died in 1917 in Texas.
Threw right. Height 5.11. Weight 190.

Year	Club	League	Pos	G	AB	R	H	2B	3B	HR	SB	BA
1884	Rockland	Conn		-	-	-	-	-	-	-	-	.320
1885	New Brit/Hart	S New Eng		-	-	-	-	-	-	-	-	.338
1886	Newbury/Lynn	New Eng	OF-2B	103	443	89	134	23	8	7	28	.302
1887	Des Moines	NWestern	0-3-S	98	463	108	162	21	9	6	59	.350
1888	Lynn	New Eng	2B	64	283	82	96	21*	5	11	39	.339
	London	Int	OF	38	145	33	42	4	4	2	17	.290
	Detroit	National	2B	2	9	1	4	0	0	0	0	.444
1889	Quincy	C Int St	2B-SS	35	157	45	57	9	11	5	7	.363
	London	Int A	3B-OF	68	243	40	51	9	4	0	27	.210
1890	Pittsburgh	National	1-0-2	111	434	59	105	20	4	1	27	.242
1891	Pittsburgh	National	2B	1	4	0	0	0	0	0	0	.000
	Louisville	A A	2-3-1	10	35	6	11	2	1	1	1	.314
	St. Paul/Dul	West A	2B	57	224	40	59	8	1	7	21	.263
	Green Bay	Wis St	1B	16	70	20	24	0	0	0	12	.343
1892	Seattle	Pac NW	2B	23	78	15	17	3	1	2	9	.218
	Terre Haute	Ill-Iowa	SS	20	70	9	16	4	0	2	5	.229
1893	Nashville	Southern	2B-SS	69	264	50	78	12	0	2	11	.295
	Easton	Penn St	1B	40	168	37	43	6	1	1	12	.256
1894	Savannah	Southern	2B	54	210	51	56	8	1	4	14	.267
	Lewiston	New Eng	2B	68	278	44	64	9	3	4	5	.230
1895	Quincy	West A	2B	82	323	84	117	24	8	10	-	.362
1896	Dubuque	West A	2B	80	306	79	101	24	4	7	28	.330
	Lancaster	Atlantic	2B	24	108	27	37	8	4	2	4	.343

Year Club	League	Pos	G	AB	R	H	2B	3B	HR	SB	BA
1897 Lancaster	Atlantic	1B	120	507	128	157	31	15	1	37	.310
1898 Paterson	Atlantic	1B	58	220	32	65	12	2	0	12	.295
London	Canadian	1B	60	234	49	79	18	7	1	12	.338
1899 Lancaster	Atlantic		65	250	51	75	-	-	-	-	.300
1900 St. Hyacinthe	Provincl	1B-2B	11	46	10	15	1	0	0	-	.326
1901 Birmingham	Southern	1B	114	435	56	134	21	5	0	12	.308
1902 Birm/Memphis	Southern	1B	108	420	73	121	29	7	3	-	.288
1903 Butte	Pac Nat	1-2-3	107	435	88	134	28	6	4	29	.308
1904 Savan/Charl	Sally	1B	113	406	47	99	24	7	2	23	.244
1905 Greenville	Cot St	1B	78	297	42	76	-	-	-	11	.256
1906 Beaumont	S Texas	2B	115	395	49	125*	-	-	-	20	.316*
1907 San Antonio	Texas	2B	41	151		31	-	-	-	1	.205
Majors			**124**	**482**	**66**	**120**	**22**	**5**	**2**	**28**	**.249**
Minors			**1929**	**7629**	**1478**	**2265**	**357**	**113**	**83**	**455**	**.297**

HARRY LAYNE

Born February 13, 1901 at New Haven, WV
Batted right. Threw right. Height 5.07. Weight 165.
Twin brother of Herman Layne (see player record below)

Year Club	League	Pos	G	AB	R	H	2B	3B	HR	RBI	SB	BA
1922 Bristol	Appal	OF	120	463	82	143	14	10	4	-	26	.309
1923 Greenville	Cot St	OF	30	106	19	30	2	1	3	-	4	.283
1924 Evansville	III	OF	137	509	94	160	20	9	13	92	18	.314
1925 Peoria	III	OF	106	413	81	136	15	10	7	-	24	.329
Columbus	A A	OF	17	67	10	10	2	1	1	7	0	.149
1926 Columbus	A A	OF	9	21	1	6	0	0	0	0	0	.286
Peoria	III	OF	107	381	95	137	21	6	17	95	57	.360*
Syracuse	Int	OF	15	57	16	22	1	2	4	12	6	.386
1927 Syracuse	Int	OF	163	619	138	200	29	10	21	114	50	.323
1928 Rochester	Int	OF	122	439	83	137	17	13	6	56	26	.312
1929 Roch/Balt	Int	OF	145	517	79	157	26	8	10	74	23	.304
1930 Newark	Int	OF	142	568	111	185	32	12	20	85	25	.326
1931 Newark/JC	Int	OF	105	369	49	97	10	6	2	38	21	.263
1932 Jersey City	Int	OF	13	31	2	6	0	0	2	3	1	.194
Bridgeport	Eastern	OF	67	286	51	97	11	6	3	28	17	.339
1933 Zanesville	Mid Atl	OF	30	127	29	48	5	3	4	25	6	.378
1934 Zanesville	Mid Atl	OF	29	113	19	36	4	1	2	23	7	.319
Minors			**1357**	**5086**	**959**	**1607**	**209**	**98**	**119**	**652**	**311**	**.316**

HERMAN LAYNE

Born February 13, 1901 at New Haven, WV. Died August 27, 1973 at Gallipolis, OH.
Batted right. Threw right. Height 5.06. Weight 165.
Twin brother of Harry Layne.

Year Club	League	Pos	G	AB	R	H	2B	3B	HR	RBI	SB	BA
1922 Bristol	Appal	OF	121	455	83	161	25	14	4	-	26	.354
1923 Augusta	Sally	OF	129	473	72	162	20	9	7	72	23	.342
1924 Toronto	Int	OF	134	496	96	169	23	11	12	111	17	.341
1925 Toronto	Int	OF	110	374	63	129	17	5	6	51	9	.345
1926 Toronto	Int	OF	148	560	107	196	32	16	7	114	32	.350
1927 Pittsburgh	Nat	OF	11	6	3	0	0	0	0	0	0	.000
Indianapolis	A A	OF	123	440	81	143	25	10	10	86	20	.325
1928 Indianapolis	A A	OF	115	412	68	143	25	7	7	65	16	.347
1929 Indianapolis	A A	OF	151	570	107	175	41	6	4	60	23	.307
1930 Louisville	A A	OF	151	628	124	209	33	19	10	88	40	.333
1931 Louisville	A A	OF	150	564	102	195	22	7	3	44	25	.346
1932 Louisville	A A	OF	150	557	91	168	23	9	2	56	41	.302
1933 Louis/Indian	A A	OF	135	559	83	153	21	10	5	40	21	.274
1934 Charleston	Mid Atl	OF	79	317	68	94	14	6	3	39	22	.297
Majors			**11**	**6**	**3**	**0**	**0**	**0**	**0**	**0**	**0**	**.000**
Minors			**1696**	**6405**	**1145**	**2097**	**321**	**129**	**80**	**826**	**315**	**.327**

ERNEST DUDLEY LEE (Played under name of Dud Dudley in 1920-21)
Born August 22, 1899 at Denver, CO. Died January 7, 1971 at Denver, CO.
Batted left. Threw right. Height 5.09. Weight 150.

Year	Club	League	Pos	G	AB	R	H	2B	3B	HR	RBI	SB	BA
1920	Chattanooga	South A	SS	138	478	57	111	13	5	1	-	22	.232
	St. Louis	American	SS	1	2	2	2	0	0	0	1	1	1.000
1921	St. Louis	American	S-2-3	72	180	18	30	4	2	0	11	1	.167
1922	Columbus	A A	SS	38	108	14	20	2	1	1	5	0	.185
	Chattanooga	South A	SS	80	300	39	79	6	5	0	-	10	.263
1923	Tulsa	Western	SS	161	617	142	210	44	7	12	-	22	.340
1924	Boston	American	SS	94	288	36	73	9	4	0	29	8	.253
1925	Boston	American	SS	84	255	22	57	7	3	0	19	2	.224
1926	Boston	American	SS	2	7	2	1	0	0	0	0	0	.143
	Hollywood	P C	SS	165	558	58	127	19	5	0	42	8	.228
1927	Hollywood	P C	SS	190	689	100	167	31	6	2	39	7	.242
1928	Hollywood	P C	SS	191	802	119	219	35	4	5	77	7	.273
1929	Hollywood	P C	SS	205*	848*	161	222	37	4	4	71	9	.262
1930	Hollywood	P C	SS	187	717	122	197	24	4	3	57	27	.275
1931	Hollywood	P C	SS	161	651	117	179	31	4	3	55	14	.275
1932	Hollywood	P C	SS	163	611	85	162	26	2	1	44	10	.265
1933	Indianapolis	A A	SS	130	514	81	143	14	4	2	37	11	.278
1934	Indianapolis	A A	SS	132	505	69	126	19	4	1	42	22	.250
1935	Dallas	Texas	SS	30	91	7	21	1	0	0	6	4	.231
	New Orleans	South A	SS	115	381	44	92	10	0	0	42	6	.241
1936	Portland	P C	SS	162	613	77	153	23	3	0	49	9	.250
1937	Portland	P C	SS	174	631	85	148	22	3	0	49	2	.235
1938	Portland	P C	SS	69	227	16	56	8	1	0	14	2	.247
1939	Dayton	Mid Atl	SS	70	214	30	56	9	1	0	33	2	.262
	Pine Bluff	Cot St	SS	39	131	20	34	6	2	2	13	0	.260
	Majors			**253**	**732**	**80**	**163**	**20**	**9**	**0**	**60**	**12**	**.223**
	Minors			**2600**	**9686**	**1443**	**2522**	**380**	**65**	**37**	**675**	**194**	**.260**

JOHN FRANK (JACK) LELIVELT
Born November 14, 1885 at Chicago, IL. Died January 20, 1941 at Seattle, WA.
Batted left. Threw left. Height 5.11. Weight 180.
Brother of Bill Lelivelt, pitcher for Detroit Tigers 1909-10.

Year	Club	League	Pos	G	AB	R	H	2B	3B	HR	SB	BA
1906	Lake Linden	N Copper	OF-P	93	351	43	105	21	8	2	13	.299
1907	Hartford	Conn	OF	89	302	42	80	23	6	1	13	.265
	Reading	Tri-St	OF	29	95	8	25	2	1	0	7	.263
1908	Reading	Tri-St	OF	124	462	59	141	12	11	4	32	.305
1909	Reading	Tri-St	OF	41	168	27	58	7	7	2	12	.345
	Washington	American	OF	91	318	25	93	8	6	0	8	.292
1910	Washington	American	OF	110	347	40	92	10	3	0	20	.265
1911	Washington	American	OF	72	225	29	72	12	4	0	7	.320
1912	Rochester	Int	OF	125	478	78	168	33	14	3	23	.351
	New York	American	OF	36	149	12	54	6	7	2	7	.362
1913	NY/Cleveland	American	OF	40	51	2	15	2	1	0	2	.294
1914	Cleveland	American	1B-OF	32	64	6	21	5	1	0	2	.328
	Cleveland	A A	1B	92	369	56	109	11	7	3	8	.295
1915	Kansas City	A A	1B	152	575	85	199*	41*	9	7	16	.346*
1916	Kansas City	A A	OF-1B	154	517	80	158	28	12	3	14	.306
1917	Kansas City	A A	OF	102	343	40	101	15	7	6	4	.294
1918	Louisville	A A	1B-OF	72	265	30	86	11	11	1	10	.325
1919	Minneapolis	A A	1B-OF	153	600	75	172	34	7	3	21	.287
1920	Omaha	Western	1B	149	550	77	170	36	10	2	24	.309
1921	Omaha	Western	1B	166	659	149	274*	70*	9	14	24	.416*
1922	Tulsa	Western	1B	154	594	114	219	48	2	16	18	.369
1923	Tulsa	Western	1B	157	582	114	200	48	2	12	18	.344
1924	Tulsa	Western	1B	155	594	124	228	56	8	11	16	.384
1925	St. Joseph	Western	1B	156	557	83	178	37	4	2	15	.320

Year Club	League	Pos	G	AB	R	H	2B	3B	HR	SB	BA
1926-30 (Did not play)											
1931 Los Angeles	P C	P	1	0	0	0	0	0	0	0	.000
Majors			381	1154	114	347	43	22	2	46	.301
Minors			2164	8061	1284	2671	533	135	92	288	.331

THOMAS F. LETCHER

Born in 1868 at Grand Rapids, MI. (No death data).

Year Club	League	Pos	G	AB	R	H	2B	3B	HR	SB	BA
1890 Joliet	Ill-Iowa	1B	-	-	-	-	-	-	-	-	.237
1891 Marinette	Wis St	OF-1B	84	353	71	87	-	-	-	21	.246
Milwaukee	A A	OF	6	21	3	4	1	0	0	1	.190
1892 Indianapolis	Western	OF	53	230	38	68	8	2	1	14	.296
Seattle	Pac NW	OF	13	60	6	15	4	0	0	1	.250
1893 Atlanta/Nash	Southern	OF	47	179	25	49	3	5	3	4	.274
1894 Jacksonville	West A	OF	117	548	157	182	41	14	10	34	.332
1895 Des Moines	West A	OF	86	512	115	184	27	13	1	-	.359
1896 Des Moines	West A	OF	71	313	88	98	25	11	3	30	.313
Grand Rapids	Western	OF	24	109	21	40	6	3	0	3	.367
1897 Des Moines	West A	OF	23	104	19	29	-	-	-	9	.279
Minneapolis	Western	OF	104	446	76	125	21	9	2	23	.280
1898 Minneapolis	Western	OF	141	584	86	168	25	12	3	15	.288
1899 Fort Wayne	Inter St	OF	137	573	112	184	40	9	4	18	.321
1900 Fort Wayne	Inter St	OF	104	452	66	123	27	4	4	10	.272
1901 Omaha	Western	OF	121	476	66	125	22	5	1	22	.263
1902 Tacoma	Pac NW	OF	114	480	76	127	28	4	1	21	.265
1903 Marion	Central	OF	119	460	77	142	-	-	-	-	.309
1904 Marion	Central	OF	39	165	13	43	4	2	0	-	.261
1905 South Bend	Central	OF	135	561	70	149	16	7	2	25	.266
1906 TH/Evansville	Central	OF	123	475	43	90	13	5	0	22	.189
1907 Fond du Lac	Wis-Ill	OF	100	359	27	103	-	-	-	-	.287
1908 Madison	Wis-Ill	OF	122	463	51	117	-	-	-	-	.253
1909 Appleton	Wis-Ill	OF	62	243		55	-	-	-	-	.226
1910 Regina	West Can	OF	86	309	32	89	5	3	0	9	.288
1911 Brandon/Sask	West Can	OF	32	119	23	27	6	1	0	9	.227
Majors			6	21	3	4	1	0	0	1	.190
Minors			2057	8573	1358	2419	321	109	35	290	.282

JOSEPH JOHN MACKO

Born February 19, 1928 at Port Clinton, OH.
Batted right. Threw right. Height 6.02. Weight 195.
Father of the late Steven Macko, infielder, Chicago NL, 1979-80.

Year Club	League	Pos	G	AB	R	H	2B	3B	HR	RBI	SB	BA
1948 Batavia	Pony	1B-OF	95	308	47	97	18	4	11	59	11	.315
1949 Burlington	Cent A	1B	128	504	110	157	21	10	19	97	12	.312
1950 Dayton	Central	1B	118	439	79	132	28	2	12	65	10	.301
1951 Dallas	Texas	1B	30	99	11	24	3	0	1	6	2	.242
Wichita	Western	1B	127	489	77	140	26	5	14	96	19	.286
1952 Dallas	Texas	1B	142	574	67	156	21	7	16	93	8	.272
1953 Indianapolis	A A	1B	153	543	64	127	22	2	20	74	10	.234
1954 Tulsa	Texas	1B	155	519	74	120	23	3	29	92	6	.231
1955 Tulsa	Texas	1B	154	566	89	160	38	1	28	102	4	.283
1956 San Diego	P C	1B	21	43	3	10	1	0	1	4	0	.233
Dallas	Texas	1B	129	469	100	133	24	5	36	97	3	.284
1957 Portland	P C	1B	22	67	6	14	4	0	2	8	0	.209
Louisville	A A	1B	61	198	36	45	9	1	13	35	0	.227
1958 Ft. Worth	Texas	1B	137	504	76	146	25	0	24	81	1	.290
1959 Ft. W./Minn	A A	1B-3B	147	494	71	138	23	1	25	85	2	.279
1960 Houston	A A	1B-3B	152	547	79	131	18	1	27	91	2	.239
1961 St. Cloud	Northern	1B-3B	102	325	69	86	11	3	17	76	8	.265
1962 Wenatchee	NWestern	1B-3B	41	69	19	22	6	0	4	15	0	.319
1963 Amarillo	Texas	1B-3B	67	143	27	41	8	1	7	22	1	.287
1964 Wenatchee	NWestern	1B	2	3	1	1	0	0	0	0	0	.333
1970 Dallas-Ft. W.	Texas	1B	4	10	0	0	0	0	0	0	0	.000
Minors			1987	6913	1105	1880	329	46	306	1198	99	.272

MANUEL MAGALLON
Born April 9, 1928 at Mazatlan, Sinaloa, Mexico.
Batted right. Threw right. Height 6.00. Weight 185.

Year Club	League	Pos	G	AB	R	H	2B	3B	HR	RBI	SB	BA
1948 Juarez	Ariz-Tex	1B	33	141	22	38	3	3	2	31	0	.270
1949 Juarez	Ariz-Tex	1B-OF	135	547	101	174	37	14	9	124	13	.318
1950 Juarez	Ariz-Tex	1B-OF	31	99	17	29	2	0	1	16	1	.293
1951 Juarez	SW Int	OF	109	444	85	157	29	13	3	97	5	.354
1952 Bisbee-Doug	Ariz-Tex	1B	45	194	46	80	15	3	13	61	1	.412
1953 Bisbee-Doug	Ariz-Tex	1B-OF	132	544	120	200	40	4	20	116	3	.368
1954 Bisbee-Doug	Ariz-Tex	1B	132	567	113	217	37	3	20	141	3	.383
1955 Bisbee-Doug	Ariz-Mex	OF-1B	139	579	106	197	40	6	15	136	5	.340
1956 Tijuana/Mexi	Ariz-Mex	1B-OF	111	441	72	129	23	4	18	79	2	.293
1957 Mexicali	Ariz-Mex	1B	117	462	88	161	37	1	18	92	1	.348
Minors			984	4018	770	1382	263	51	119	893	34	.344

JAMES WALTER MATTHEWS
Born October 20, 1921 at DeQueen, AK.
Batted right. Threw right. Height 5.10. Weight 190.

Year Club	League	Pos	G	AB	R	H	2B	3B	HR	RBI	SB	BA
1939 New Iberia	Evang	OF	3	4	0	0	0	0	0	0	0	.000
Hamilton	Pony	OF	35	133	27	39	8	2	3	14	3	.293
Union City	Kitty	OF	44	178	33	51	9	3	5	19	4	.287
1940 Kilgore	E Texas	OF	48	171	33	44	13	1	6	29	7	.257
Pine Bluff	Cot St	OF	18	55	8	14	2	0	2	6	1	.255
Cooleemee	N Caro St	OF	35	137	20	44	10	1	4	15	1	.321
1941 New Iberia	Evang	OF	95	344	53	82	15	5	5	64	9	.238
Beaumont	Texas	OF	30	108	9	21	4	1	1	10	1	.194
1942 Winston-Salem	Piedmont	OF	85	265	35	54	8	2	10	38	3	.204
Beaumont	Texas	OF	8	19	4	3	1	0	0	2	0	.158
1943 Knoxville	South A	OF	132	453	66	120	19	8	12	81	5	.265
1944-45 (Military Service)												
1946 Mobile	South A	OF	18	45	8	9	1	0	1	7	1	.200
Abilene	WTNM	C-OF	111	386	113	115	17	2	31	91	9	.298
1947 Wichita Falls	Big St	OF-C	152	561	152	192	30	9	40	135	25	.342
1948 SA/Tulsa/Dall	Texas	OF-C	33	86	18	19	5	0	1	9	1	.221
Little Rock	South A	OF	24	86	11	20	7	0	0	8	3	.233
Texarkana	Big St	OF-C	62	226	43	73	18	1	14	53	1	.323
1949 Texarkana	Big St	C-OF	139	486	103	137	19	0	18	91	5	.282
1950 Texarkana	Big St	C-OF	98	309	54	75	19	0	14	60	4	.243
1951 Texarkana	Big St	OF-C	145	492	100	137	29	1	31	95	4	.278
1952 Clovis	WTNM	OF-C	134	444	123	142	22	4	39	130	15	.320
1953 Amarillo	WTNM	OF-C	139	473	162	186	35	2	50*	152	13	.393
1954 Gal/Bryan	Big St	OF-C	41	128	18	25	5	0	2	18	7	.195
Abilene	WTNM	OF-C	78	288	67	78	10	2	18	69	5	.271
1955 Port Arthur	Big St	OF-C	4	18	0	4	0	0	0	0	0	.222
Minors			1711	5895	1260	1684	306	44	307	1196	127	.286

WILLIAM MAC McGHEE
Born September 5, 1908 at Shawmut, AL.
Batted left. Threw left. Height 5.10½. Weight 185.

Year Club	League	Pos	G	AB	R	H	2B	3B	HR	RBI	SB	BA
1929 Carrollton	Ga-Ala	OF	61	222	26	69	9	2	0	-	2	.311
1930 Anniston	Ga-Ala	1B	96	387	66	127	22	9	2	46	26	.328
1931 Augusta	Palmetto	OF-1B	76	328	81	133*	16	14*	3	73*	12	.405*
Galveston	Texas	1B	50	185	13	48	8	3	0	28	3	.259
1932 Galv/Tyler	Texas	1B	68	234	21	58	10	0	1	25	2	.248
1933-34			(Not in O.B.)									
1935 Galveston	Texas	1B	159	554	68	161	25	9	2	80	13	.291

Year	Club	League	Pos	G	AB	R	H	2B	3B	HR	RBI	SB	BA
1936	Galveston	Texas	1B	2	5	0	0	0	0	0	0	0	.000
	Nashville	South A	1B	23	104	13	32	5	2	0	17	3	.308
	Albany	Int	1B	8	24	0	6	0	1	0	4	0	.250
	Clarksdale	Cot St	1B	10	43	8	15	8	0	0	12	2	.349
1937	Jackson	SEastern	1B	44	178	25	41	8	1	1	29	1	.230
	Winston-Salem	Piedmont	1B	86	305	41	93	13	6	1	42	7	.305
1938	Winston-Salem	Piedmont	1B	65	250	37	67	13	2	3	39	6	.268
	Elmira	Eastern	1B	71	266	35	74	16	5	1	27	4	.278
1939	Winston-Salem	Piedmont	1B	44	168	21	45	10	3	0	18	0	.268
	Meridian	SEastern	1B	87	328	43	126	26	2	4	55	7	.384
1940	Meridian/Pens	SEastern	1B	148	572	74	184	30	11	1	88	1	.322
1941	Pensacola	SEastern	1B	143	535	76	158	29	7	3	84	6	.295
1942	Pensacola	SEastern	1B	104	410	52	138	33	6	0	50	6	.337
	Little Rock	South A	1B	45	161	20	54	9	0	1	27	0	.335
1943	Little Rock	South A	1B	139	572	99	204	26	7	0	74	9	.357
1944	Little Rock	South A	1B	44	177	44	79	16	4	0	34	4	.446
	Philadelphia	American	1B	77	287	27	83	12	0	1	19	2	.289
1945	Philadelphia	American	OF-1B	93	250	24	63	6	1	0	19	3	.252
1946	Pensacola	SEastern	1B	135	502	89	175	35	2	6	96	11	.349*
1947	Gadsden	SEastern	1B	113	436	64	131	24	4	7	72	6	.300
1948	Gadsden	SEastern	1B	15	55	19	19	2	2	0	9	1	.345
	Brewton	Ala St	1B	101	365	45	130	25	5	0	73	9	.356*
1949	Pensacola	SEastern	1B	67	251	34	72	15	1	1	39	4	.287
1950	Gadsden	SEastern	1B	94	367	62	122	33	1	2	69	4	.332
	Columbia	Sally	1B	37	147	26	50	9	0	1	31	1	.340
1951	El Dorado	Cot St	1B	135	494	79	164	28	2	5	94	5	.332
1957	Pensacola	Ala-Fla	1B	22	73	8	16	0	0	0	11	2	.219
Majors				**170**	**537**	**51**	**146**	**18**	**1**	**1**	**38**	**5**	**.272**
Minors				2292	8698	1289	2791	503	111	45	1346	157	.321

HOWARD BELL (POLLY) McLARRY
Born March 25, 1891 at Leonard, TX. Died November 4, 1971 at Bonham, TX.
Batted left. Threw right. Height 6.00. Weight 185.

Year	Club	League	Pos	G	AB	R	H	2B	3B	HR	RBI	SB	BA
1911	Beeville	SW Texas	OF-1B	98	357	52	101	27	1	5	-	13	.283
	Austin	Texas	OF	6	24	3	8	0	0	0	3	0	.333
1912	Austin	Texas	1B	125	452	46	133	24	5	5	-	21	.294
	Lincoln	Western	2B-OF	20	61	17	22	5	4	1	-	3	.361
	Chicago	American	PH	2	2	0	0	0	0	0	0	0	.000
1913	Topeka	Western	2B-OF	159	598	106	183	48	14	5	-	33	.306
1914	Louisville	A A	2B	157	529	93	167	36	9	11	70	21	.316
1915	Chicago	National	1B-2B	68	127	16	25	3	0	1	12	2	.197
1916	Los Angeles	P C	2B	168	553	73	162	22	5	7	-	22	.293
1917	Vernon	P C	2B	62	210	31	60	17	2	5	-	17	.286
	Shreveport	Texas	2B	80	278	39	74	12	5	3	-	11	.266
1918	Shreveport	Texas	1B	29	84	12	24	3	1	1	-	6	.286
	Binghamton	Int	1B	103	335	51	129	26*	7	4	-	15	.385
1919	Binghamton	Int	1B	140	478	85	156	26	13	3	-	21	.326
1920	Memphis	South A	1B	148	510	90	172	24	10	11	-	26	.337
1921	Memphis	South A	1B	156	556	120	196	36	19	15	135*	21	.353
1922	Memphis	South A	1B	151	530	83	154	32	11	3	-	10	.291
1923	Des Moines	Western	1B	169	656	149	238	57	2	16	-	12	.363
1924	Des Moines	Western	1B	56	211	21	65	11	1	2	-	1	.308
	Reading	Int	1B	88	332	64	111	25	3	5	63	10	.334
1925	Reading	Int	1B	166	600	103	185	46*	3	14	95	10	.308
1926	Nashville	South A	1B	144	500	115	167	32	7	12	100	18	.334
1927	Nash/Atlanta	South A	1B	126	437	65	137	21	4	12	71	9	.314
1928	Selma	SEastern	1B	51	168	20	42	11	3	0	25	7	.250
	Meridian	Cot St	1B	38	135	19	37	9	3	0	-	8	.274
Majors				**70**	**129**	**16**	**25**	**3**	**0**	**1**	**12**	**2**	**.194**
Minors				2440	8594	1457	2723	550	132	140	562	315	.317

ALBERT ERNEST (DUTCH) MELE

Born January 11, 1915 at New York, NY. Died February 12, 1975 at Hollywood, FL.
Batted left. Threw left. Height 6.01. Weight 195.

Year	Club	League	Pos	G	AB	R	H	2B	3B	HR	RBI	SB	BA
1934	Washington	Pa St A	OF	101	380	77	118	27	10	5	68	4	.311
	Wheeling	Mid Atl	OF	3	14	2	2	0	0	0	0	0	.143
1935	Joplin/Musk	West A	OF	128	497	81	141	20	15	5	75	17	.284
1936	Muskogee	West A	OF	130	519	115	183	31	14	23	132	12	.353
	Milwaukee	A A	OF	4	17	1	2	1	0	0	2	0	.118
1937	Muskogee	West A	OF	140	503	128	178	49*	5	30*	110	21	.354*
	Cincinnati	National	OF	6	14	1	2	1	0	0	1	0	.143
1938	Durham	Piedmont	OF	89	324	72	105	27	7	12	77	3	.324
1939	Durham	Piedmont	OF	87	318	38	108	21	6	10	67	8	.340
	Baltimore	Int	OF	27	96	14	25	5	0	0	15	0	.260
1940	Birmingham	South A	OF	133	468	93	159	33	7	19	116	5	.340
1941	Birmingham	South A	OF	152	537	104	169	28	10	27	113	6	.315
1942	Syracuse	Int	OF	137	466	67	123	21	6	13	73	3	.264
1943	Syracuse	Int	OF	132	449	49	113	19	2	8	67	6	.252
1944	Syracuse	Int	OF	150	522	80	153	32	5	11	86	6	.293
1945	Syracuse	Int	OF	138	498	96	149	28	8	19	108	12	.299
1946	Syracuse	Int	OF	117	420	63	122	14	3	15	74	6	.290
1947	Syracuse	Int	OF	149	534	90	168	27	5	20	100	12	.315
1948	(Not in O.B.)												
1949	Syracuse	Int	OF	136	494	68	141	30	3	15	86	7	.285
1950	Syracuse/JC	Int	OF	128	412	59	113	22	3	10	77	1	.274
1951	Ottawa	Int	OF	66	141	10	37	6	2	2	24	0	.262
	Majors			6	14	1	2	1	0	0	1	0	.143
	Minors			2147	7609	1307	2309	441	111	244	1470	129	.304

STEPHAN MATHIAS MESNER

Born January 13, 1918 at Los Angeles, CA. Died April 6, 1981 at San Diego, CA.
Batted right. Threw right. Height 5.09. Weight 178.

Year	Club	League	Pos	G	AB	R	H	2B	3B	HR	RBI	SB	BA
1934	Ponca City	West A	3B	135*	549	111	197*	44	13	6	106	1	.359
	Los Angeles	P C	3B	5	12	0	3	0	0	0	0	0	.250
1935	Los Angeles	P C	3B-SS	151	534	78	177	33	5	13	99	6	.331
1936	Los Angeles	P C	SS	176*	703	110	229	55*	9	17	132	3	.326
1937	Los Angeles	P C	3B-SS	133	505	79	166	38	8	10	91	4	.329
1938	Indianapolis	A A	SS-3B	127	441	79	146	37	9	7	91	2	.331
	Chicago	National	SS	2	4	2	1	0	0	0	0	0	.250
1939	Chicago	National	SS	17	43	7	12	4	0	0	6	0	.279
	Milwaukee	A A	SS-2B	85	309	47	100	21	4	5	54	4	.324
1940	San Diego	P C	SS	179*	680	114	232	40	12	0	97	6	.341
1941	St. Louis	National	3B	24	69	8	10	1	0	0	10	0	.145
	Rochester	Int	SS	19	59	9	16	6	1	0	9	2	.271
1942	Sacramento	P C	3B-2B	178	680	83	205	24	6	1	74	3	.301
1943	Cincinnati	National	3B	137	504	53	137	26	1	0	52	6	.272
1944	Cincinnati	National	3B	121	414	31	100	17	4	1	47	1	.242
1945	Cincinnati	National	3B-2B	150	540	52	137	19	1	1	52	4	.254
1946	Sacramento	P C	3B	188*	698	88	204	49*	2	4	85	5	.292
1947	Sacramento	P C	3B	176	636	84	162	30	5	2	71	0	.255
1948	Sacramen/SD	P C	2B-3B	172	586	75	174	35	1	8	76	3	.297
1949	San Diego	P C	SS-3B	114	343	49	102	17	1	0	40	1	.297
1950	Portland	P C	3B	69	194	24	44	7	1	0	16	0	.227
1951	Spokane	West Int	SS	132	492	97	156	25	5	3	94	16	.317
1952	Ogden	Pioneer	3-S-2	132*	469	100	161*	26	0	0	81	3	.343*
1953	Beaumont	Texas	3B-2B	63	128	11	35	4	0	0	16	1	.273
1954	Victoria	West Int	3B-2B	73	243	41	59	11	0	1	23	2	.243
	Majors			451	1574	153	397	67	6	2	167	11	.252
	Minors			2307	8261	1279	2568	502	82	77	1255	62	.311

ROBERT HUGH (ROXY) MIDDLETON
Born August 15, 1888 at Servia, IN. Died November 8, 1966 at Ft. Worth ,TX.
Batted left. Threw right. Height 5.10. Weight 150.

Year	Club	League	Pos	G	AB	R	H	2B	3B	HR	SB	BA
1907	Leavenworth	West A	OF	108	405	25	94	-	-	-	-	.232
1908	Wichita	West A	OF	126	482	55	134	26	5	1	15	.278
1909	Wichita	Western	OF	126	449	68	133	23	2	1	13	.296
1910	Wichita	Western	OF	164	678	89	189	22	7	3	30	.279
1911	Wichita/Pueb	Western	OF	145	579	104	183	22	9	4	40	.316
1912	Wichita	Western	OF	121	476	67	158	15	6	7	33	.332
	Toledo	A A	OF	8	33	3	7	0	0	0	1	.212
1913	Wichita	Western	OF	150	573	100	212	20	10	1	46	.370*
1914	Oakland	P C	OF	195	767	89	221	18	6	1	40	.288
1915	Oakland	P C	OF	199	750	81	216	22	6	3	29	.288
1916	Oakland	P C	OF	185	713	83	195	19	2	2	34	.273
1917	Oakland	P C	OF	187	696	89	183	33	6	0	26	.263
1918	Oakland	P C	OF	94	377	47	114	12	3	3	15	.302
1919	Sacramento	P C	OF	166	644	88	188	14	5	5	29	.292
1920	Sac/Seattle	P C	OF	179	718	96	206	25	4	2	27	.287
1921	Seattle	P C	OF	116	384	61	106	13	3	2	25	.276
1922	Oklahoma City	Western	OF	77	316	53	104	14	2	1	7	.329
1923	Columbia/Gast	Sally	OF	120	453	60	140	26	4	4	15	.309
1924	Albany	Eastern	OF	14	47		11	0	0	0		.234
	Syr/Read/Roch	Int	OF	105	355	52	119	13	4	2	9	.335
Minors				**2585**	**9895**	**1310**	**2913**	**337**	**84**	**42**	**434**	**.294**

JOSEPH MARTIN NAPOLEON MUNSON
Real name: Joseph Martin Napoleon Carlson. Played under name Joe Martin in 1918 and 1919.
Born November 6, 1899 at Renovo, PA.
Batted left. Threw right. Height 5.10. Weight 184.

Year	Club	League	Pos	G	AB	R	H	2B	3B	HR	RBI	SB	BA
1918	Martinsburg	Blue Rdg	OF-1B	5	21	3	7	2	0	0	4	0	.333
1919	Suffolk	Virginia	OF	35	122	11	33	8	2	0	-	3	.270
1920	Raleigh	Piedmont	OF	120	434	88	132	17	5	8	-	38*	.304
1921	Dallas	Texas	OF	154	568	106	169	40	11	8	52	20	.298
1922	Galveston	Texas	OF	102	306	47	95	18	5	9	40	6	.310
1923	Galveston	Texas	OF	142	489	71	138	31	6	10	65	9	.282
1924	Galveston	Texas	OF	11	27	3	4	0	1	0	1	0	.148
	Marlin	Texas A	OF	115	408	96	141	24	11*	17	-	23	.346*
1925	Harrisburg	NY-Penn	OF	131	470	132*	188*	34	17*	33*	129*	29	.400*
	Chicago	National	OF	9	35	5	13	3	1	0	3	1	.371
1926	Chicago	National	OF	33	101	17	26	2	2	3	15	0	.257
	Indianapolis	A A	OF	25	72	11	23	8	0	1	10	0	.319
	Terre Haute	III	OF	48	168	32	49	4	4	3	-	3	.292
1927	Tulsa	Western	OF	154	583	146	223	48	9	32*	-	17	.383
1928	Tulsa	Western	OF	165	611	171*	235	46	10	39	-	9	.385*
1929	Tulsa	Western	OF	161*	569	167*	210	40	5	32	-	8	.369
1930	Waco	Texas	OF	150	584	111	196	45	2	10	89	5	.336
1931	Galveston	Texas	OF	18	63	6	17	4	1	0	3	0	.270
	Des M/Topeka	Western	OF	122	420	60	128	31	2	3	75	8	.305
1932	Clarksburg	Mid Atl	OF	60	203	34	62	17	1	3	29	7	.305
Majors				**42**	**136**	**22**	**39**	**5**	**3**	**3**	**18**	**1**	**.287**
Minors				**1718**	**6118**	**1295**	**2050**	**417**	**92**	**208**	**497**	**185**	**.335**

L

JAMES O. MURRAY

Born January 16, 1880 at Galveston, TX. Died April 25, 1945 at Galveston, TX.
Batted right. Threw left. Height 5.10. Weight 180.

Year	Club	League	Pos	G	AB	R	H	2B	3B	HR	SB	BA
1900	Portsmouth	Virginia	OF-P	96	374	66	126	20	14*	11*	28	.337
1901	Portsmouth	Va-NC	OF-P	62	262	43	82	12	13*	3	18	.313
	Charlotte	N Caro	OF-P	29	115	10	34	7	4	1	3	.296
1902	Manchester	NEastern	OF	106	460	91	133	28	9	12*	40	.289
	Chicago	National	OF	12	47	3	8	0	0	0	0	.170
1903	Manchester	NEastern	OF	99	393	58	98	21	8	3	24	.249
	Toronto	Eastern	OF	11	43	5	12	0	2	0	3	.279
1904	Toronto	Eastern	OF	135	494	75	125	19	14*	4	46	.253
1905	Toronto/Buff	Eastern	OF	83	321	57	81	14	8	9*	20	.252
1906	Buffalo	Eastern	OF	136	529	68	150	23	13	7	38	.284
1907	Buffalo	Eastern	OF	115	430	57	117	19	7	5	30	.272
1908	Buffalo	Eastern	OF	122	448	47	103	17	8	4	27	.230
1909	St. Paul	A A	OF	103	376	39	92	16	9	5	10	.245
1910	St. Paul	A A	OF	140	507	73	131	18	10	11	37	.258
1911	St. Louis	American	OF	31	102	8	19	5	0	3	0	.186
	Buffalo	Eastern	OF	81	302	47	99	14	12	5	17	.328
1912	Buffalo	Int	OF	138	518	88	161	20	24	15	21	.311
1913	Buffalo	Int	OF	119	436	53	131	21	16	6	19	.300
1914	Boston	National	OF	39	112	10	26	4	2	0	2	.232
	St. Paul	A A	OF	74	281	42	74	12	5	7	9	.263
1915	Little Rock	South A	OF	107	371	45	101	17	10	3	12	.272
1916	Galveston	Texas	OF	56	215		43	10	2	1	5	.200
	Oklahoma City	West A	OF	47	181	25	59	10	1	11	4	.326
1917	Oklahoma City	West A	OF	143	519	77	151	27	2	22	16	.291
1918-19	(Not in O.B.)											
1920	Galveston	Texas	OF	18	58	4	12	4	0	0	2	.207
	Majors			**82**	**261**	**21**	**53**	**9**	**2**	**3**	**2**	**.203**
	Minors			**2020**	**7633**	**1070**	**2115**	**349**	**191**	**145**	**429**	**.277**

PHILIP NADEAU

Born in 1876 at Montreal, Canada (No death data).
Batted right. Threw right. Height 5.08½. Weight 175.

Year	Club	League	Pos	G	AB	R	H	2B	3B	HR	SB	BA
1894	Springfield	Eastern	2B	110	469	128	162	24	21	7	30	.345
1895	Brockton	New Eng	OF-SS	93	372	84	130	14	5	4	40	.349
1896	Brockton	New Eng	OF	106	453	110	152	40	3	9	37	.336
1897	Brockton	New Eng	OF	106	447	96	131	20	1	10	15	.293
1898	Brockton	New Eng	OF	48	189	41	53	13	1	4	12	.280
	Palmyra	NY St	OF	15	66	13	22	6	2	0	1	.333
1899	New Castle	InterSt	OF	135	517	83	134	24	6	7	28	.259
1900	Cortland	NY St	OF	108	433	81	130				25	.300
1901	Waverly	NY St	OF	105	424	57	143				20	.337
1902	Binghamton	NY St	OF	110	450	68	140				20	.311
1903	Portland	P C	OF	204	791	141	275				52	.348
1904	Portland	P C	OF		774	104	201	31	3	0	42	.260
1905	New Orleans	South A	OF	126	462	70	115	12	1	0	23	.249
1906	NO/Memphis	South A	OF	140	522	65	146	19	3	4	29	.280
1907	NO/Montgomery	South A	OF	123	475	38	109	13	4	0	20	.229
1908	Ft. Way/Zanes	Central	OF	114	416	44	120	25	6	0	18	.288
1909	Charles/Knox	Sally	OF	125	446	37	107				36	.240
1910	Joliet	North A	OF	39	135	24	45	8	3	0	16	.333
	Davenport	III	OF	93	353	38	96				22	.272
1911	Cent/Chehalis	Wash St	OF	19	79	8	15	11	1	0	9	.190
1912	Pendelton	W Tri-St	OF	93	387	59	124	21	5	0	29	.320
1913	LaGrande/N Yak	W Tri-St	OF	95	363	51	115	17	3	4	25	.317
1914	Boise	Union A	OF	12	41	6	11	2	2	1	1	.268
	Baker	W Tri-St	OF	65	219	25	69	11	0	2	16	.315
	Minors			**2184**	**9283**	**1471**	**2745**	**311**	**70**	**52**	**566**	**.296**

LEONARDO NAJO (ALANIS)

Born February 17, 1899 at La Lajilla, Nuevo Leon, Mexico. Died April 25, 1978 at Mission, TX.
Batted right. Threw right. Height 5.10. Weight 170.

Year	Club	League	Pos	G	AB	R	H	2B	3B	HR	RBI	SB	BA
1924	Tyler	E Texas	OF	108	392	93	150	33	8	21	-	21	.383
	San Antonio	Texas	OF	26	96	13	20	4	1	1	13	1	.208
1925	Okmulgee	West A	OF	150	599	195*	213	46	10	34	131	41	.356
	San Antonio	Texas	OF	2	8	1	2	0	1	0	1	0	.250
1926	San Antonio	Texas	OF	82	290	60	90	18	1	3	24	21	.310
1927	San Antonio	Texas	OF	123	390	56	115	19	5	2	54	19	.295
1928	San Antonio	Texas	OF	158	581	106	161	35	10	4	60	17	.277
1929	Omaha	Western	OF	120	421	88	133	41	3	3	-	21	.316
1930	Omaha	Western	OF	129	471	98	158	41	8	6	92	29	.335
1931	Omaha	Western	OF	94	337	78	119	29	5	1	57	11	.353
	San Antonio	Texas	OF	39	124	17	33	5	0	1	15	1	.266
1932	San Antonio	Texas	OF	33	120	19	31	6	2	0	8	2	.258
	Tulsa	Western	OF	113	427	81	138	23	10	3	94	6	.323
1933-37 (Not in O.B.)													
1938	McAllen	Tex Val	OF		367	106	130	28	5	20*	91	19	.354
	Minors			**1177**	**4623**	**1011**	**1493**	**328**	**69**	**99**	**640**	**209**	**.323**

HENRY WILLIS PATRICK (BILL) NORMAN

Born July 16, 1910 at St. Louis, MO. Died April 21, 1962 at Milwaukee, WI.
Batted right. Threw left. Height 6.02. Weight 190.
Manager for Detroit, AL, 1958-59.

Year	Club	League	Pos	G	AB	R	H	2B	3B	HR	RBI	SB	BA
1929	Laurel	Cot St	2B-OF	48	168	31	51	8	0	9	-	1	.304
1930	Shawnee/Musk	West A	OF	129	482	123	174	28	7	15	75	21	.361
1931	Muskogee	West A	OF	107	424	89	158	29	14	29	69	20	.373
	Chicago	American	OF	24	55	7	10	2	0	0	6	0	.182
1932	Chicago	American	OF	13	48	6	11	3	1	0	2	0	.229
	St. Paul	A A	OF	139	496	85	154	29	3	23	93	5	.310
1933	Louisville	A A	OF	138	493	84	144	28	9	24	108	7	.292
1934	Dallas	Texas	OF-1B	88	298	59	90	15	3	12	55	12	.302
	St. Paul	A A	OF	65	237	44	71	12	5	18	51	4	.300
1935	St. Paul	A A	OF	137	463	80	146	27	7	14	81	2	.315
1936	St. Paul	A A	OF	108	317	83	95	19	3	17	62	4	.300
1937	St. Paul	A A	OF	116	380	73	115	29	4	21	81	2	.303
1938	Hollywood	P C	OF	82	242	47	71	17	1	12	47	2	.293
1939	Hollywood	P C	OF	75	231	38	60	13	1	10	45	4	.260
	Oklahoma City	Texas	OF	32	106	21	28	7	0	4	23	2	.264
1940	Syracuse/Mont	Int	OF	21	66	11	21	8	1	1	14	0	.318
	Knoxville	South A	OF	15	47	7	14	6	1	1	13	1	.298
	Elmira	Eastern	OF	91	277	60	83	23	2	6	40	2	.300
1941	Houston	Texas	OF	156	533	103	157	37	7	13	107	7	.295
1942	Milwaukee	A A	OF	129	418	80	126	22	3	24*	85	2	.301
1943	Milwaukee	A A	OF	132	396	72	109	18	0	18	83	1	.275
1944	Milwaukee	A A	OF	138	443	84	131	21	1	17	90	7	.296
1945	Milwaukee	A A	OF	53	148	20	35	7	1	0	12	6	.236
	Toronto	Int	OF	76	237	53	69	12	4	5	49	2	.291
1946	Toronto	Int	OF	17	27	4	3	0	0	2	4	0	.111
	Majors			**37**	**103**	**13**	**21**	**5**	**1**	**0**	**8**	**0**	**.204**
	Minors			**2092**	**6929**	**1351**	**2105**	**415**	**77**	**295**	**1287**	**114**	**.304**

HENRY KAUHANE (PRINCE) OANA

Born January 22, 1908 at Waipahu, Hawaii. Died June 19, 1976 at Austin, TX.
Batted right. Threw right. Height 6.02. Weight 193.
Became primarily a pitcher in the 1940s. See pitching record below. One of first Hawaiians to gain prominence in minor leagues.

Year	Club	League	Pos	G	AB	R	H	2B	3B	HR	RBI	SB	BA
1929	Globe	Ariz St	OF	85	340	81	127	26	13	18	-	18	.374
1930	Globe	Ariz St	OF	79	310	87	128	22	12	21	88	15	.413
	San Francisco	P C	OF	79	298	46	97	18	4	11	53	7	.326
1931	San Francisco	P C	OF	172	742	116	256	44	16	23	161	12	.345
1932	San Francisco	P C	OF-P	131	440	60	105	22	9	2	52	5	.239
1933	Portland	P C	OF	174	686	127	228	63*	11	29	163	11	.332
1934	Philadelphia	National	OF	6	21	3	5	1	0	0	3	0	.238
	Portland	P C	OF	11	43	6	10	0	0	1	5	0	.233
	Atlanta	South A	OF	127	480	65	143	21	8	17	102	11	.298
1935	Atlanta	South A	OF	57	218	35	63	7	3	5	34	8	.289
	Syracuse	Int	OF	87	320	46	96	21	8	12	52	4	.300
1936	Syracuse/Balt	Int	OF	115	418	53	117	23	4	7	66	5	.280
1937	Knoxville/LR	South A	OF	48	187	31	53	4	4	6	27	2	.283
1938	Jackson	SEastern	OF-P	143	513	104	164	39	7	26*	116*	10	.320
1939	Jackson	SEastern	OF-P	139	508	114	164	20	12	39*	127*	11	.323
1940	Ft. Worth	Texas	OF	159	594	80	157	28	6	14	75	13	.264
1941	Ft. Worth	Texas	O-1-P	140	478	50	121	23	4	5	76	18	.253
1942	Ft. Worth	Texas	OF-P	87	223	18	47	8	1	5	21	13	.211
1943	Detroit	American	P	20	26	5	10	2	1	1	7	0	.385
	Milwaukee	A A	P	20	34	8	14	1	1	0	4	0	.412
1944	Buffalo	Int	P	82	137	17	33	2	1	4	23	1	.241
1945	Detroit	American	P	4	5	0	1	0	0	0	0	0	.200
	Buffalo	Int	P	82	169	22	47	6	3	3	25	2	.278
1946	Dallas	Texas	P-OF	61	145	24	44	13	2	7	34	3	.303
1947	Dallas	Texas	P	38	48	5	18	4	1	1	16	0	.375
1948	Austin	Big St	O-P-1	60	149	16	40	10	0	2	29	2	.268
1949	Austin	Big St	P	24	46	7	16	3	0	3	18	0	.348
1950	Austin	Big St	P-1B	3	5	0	0	0	0	0	0	0	.000
1951	Texarkana	Big St	P	11	14	1	4	0	0	0	1	0	.286
Majors				30	52	8	16	3	1	1	10	0	.308
Minors				2214	7545	1219	2292	428	130	261	1368	171	.304

Pitching Record

Year	Club	League	G	IP	W	L	H	R	ER	BB	SO	ERA
1932	San Francisco	P C	3	6	0	0	-	-	-	-	1	0.00
1938	Jackson	SEastern	1	1	0	0	0	0	0	0	0	0.00
1939	Jackson	SEastern	1	2	0	0	2	2	2	2	2	9.00
1941	Ft. Worth	Texas	7	14	0	0	7	9	6	9	9	3.86
1942	Ft. Worth	Texas	25	199	16	5	156	54	38	58	105	1.72
1943	Detroit	American	10	34	3	2	34	21	17	19	15	4.50
	Milwaukee	A A	14	64	3	5	59	35	29	29	32	4.08
1944	Buffalo	Int	38	211	13	13	199	100	85	103	112	3.63
1945	Detroit	American	3	11	0	0	3	2	2	7	3	1.64
	Buffalo	Int	31	242	15	14	260	134	113	117	138	4.20
1946	Dallas	Texas	38	284*	24*	10	253*	101	80	72	123	2.54
1947	Dallas	Texas	11	43	2	2	56	29	25	31	21	5.23
1948	Austin	Big St.	15	87	4	4	97	45	39	22	8	4.03
1949	Austin	Big St.	10	45	2	1	34	15	12	19	6	2.40
1950	Austin	Big St.	3	8	1	0	9	3	3	3	1	3.38
1951	Texarkana	Big St.	7	20	0	0	18	9	7	14	5	3.15
Majors			13	45	3	2	37	23	19	26	18	3.80
Minors			204	1226	80	54	1150	536	439	479	563	3.24

JAMES DORN OGLESBY

Born August 10, 1905 at Schofield, MO. Died September 1, 1955 at Tulsa, OK.
Batted left. Threw left. Height 6.00. Weight 190.

Year Club	League	Pos	G	AB	R	H	2B	3B	HR	RBI	SB	BA
1926 Paris	E Texas		(No record available)									
Okmulgee	West A	1B	13	59	15	19	2	0	2	-	0	.322
1927 Burlington	Miss Val	1B	119	437	73	141	28	10	5	-	11	.323
1928 Nashville	South A	1B	80	293	51	91	18	2	10	57	1	.311
Dallas	Texas	1B	65	243	25	82	15	2	1	36	2	.337
Minneapolis	A A	1B	5	2	0	0	0	0	0	0	0	.000
1929 Minneapolis	A A	1B	3	8	0	0	0	0	0	0	0	.000
Des Moines	Western	1B	153	605	96	189	39	14	10	-	15	.312
1930 Des Moines	Western	1B	142	572	118	176	32	7	9	100	12	.308
1931 Des Moines	Western	1B	144	587	119	200	30	15	6	106	10	.341
1932 Des Moines	Western	1B	99	405	84	156	28	19	9	86	5	.385
Los Angeles	P C	1B	64	263	46	85	16	0	5	61	5	.323
1933 Los Angeles	P C	1B	186	723	122	226	49	6	20	137	14	.313
1934 Los Angeles	P C	1B	188*	725	102	226	44	4	15	139	11	.312
1935 Los Angeles	P C	1B	173	678	133	237	56*	5	24	132	18	.350
1936 Philadelphia	American	1B	3	11	0	2	0	0	0	2	0	.182
1937 Kansas City	A A	1B	150	595	97	182	38	11	9	106	8	.306
1938 Buffalo	Int	1B	153	599	109	191	31	2	13	90	8	.319
1939 Buffalo	Int	1B	144	526	92	172	32	4	16	91	5	.327
1940 Albany	Eastern	1B	141	509	72	147	23	4	9	67	1	.289
1941 Albany	Eastern	1B	137	476	69	127	18	8	7	77	8	.267
1942 Memphis/LR	South A	1B	145	493	60	135	18	10	8	65	8	.274
Majors			3	11	0	2	0	0	0	2	0	.182
Minors			2304	8798	1483	2782	517	123	178	1350	142	.316

Jim Oglesby takes a giant stride for Los Angeles in 1935.

EDWARD JOSEPH ONSLOW

Born February 17, 1893 at Meadville, PA. Died May 8, 1981 at Dennison, OH.
Batted left. Threw left. Height 6.00. Weight 170.
Brother of Jack Onslow, former Major League catcher and manager. Holds International League career records for years played (17), games (2109), hits (2445), and triples (128).

Year	Club	League	Pos	G	AB	R	H	2B	3B	HR	RBI	SB	BA
1911	Lansing	S Mich	1B	127	469	72	142	34	6	1	-	27	.303
1912	Lansing	S Mich	1B	85	325	61	125	25	6	2	-	26	.385
	Detroit	American	1B	35	128	11	29	1	2	1	13	3	.227
1913	Providence	Int	1B	101	391	51	104	10	6	0	-	19	.266
	Detroit	American	1B	17	55	7	14	1	0	0	8	1	.255
1914	Providence	Int	1B	154	569	88	183	16	18	6	-	28	.322
1915	Providence	Int	1B	124	455	73	134	8	13	0	-	32	.295
1916	Providence	Int	1B	108	414	59	129	12	4	1	-	34	.312
1917	Providence	Int	OF-1B	144	543	81	146	15	9	2	-	29	.269
1918	Toronto	Int	1B	100	358	61	114	9	6	2	-	33	.318
	Cleveland	American	OF	2	6	4	1	0	0	0	0	0	.167
1919	Toronto	Int	1B	141	488	69	148	28	6	0	-	36	.303
1920	Toronto	Int	1B	135	511	87	173	23	12	7	-	31	.339
1921	Toronto	Int	1B	140	524	92	176	32	5	12	-	25	.336
1922	Toronto	Int	1B	155	554	91	180	30	13	7	105	22	.325
1923	Toronto	Int	1B	127	455	63	158	29	7	11	93	10	.347
1924	Toronto	Int	1B	146	489	96	162	25	9	12	88	21	.331
1925	Roch/Prov	Int	1B	131	475	73	149	36	5	9	83	7	.314
1926	Rochester	Int	1B	86	332	64	114	15	3	1	59	11	.343
1927	Rochester	Int	1B	95	354	50	110	15	6	0	57	11	.311
	Washington	American	1B	9	18	1	4	1	0	0	1	0	.222
1928	Indianapolis	A A	1B	4	3	0	0	0	0	0	0	0	.000
	Baltimore	Int	1B	155	570	85	197	36	5	7	114	21	.346
1929	Balt/Newark	Int	1B	67	221	37	68	10	1	4	34	1	.308
1930					(Did not play)								
1931	Harrisburg	NY-Penn	PH	1	1	0	0	0	0	0	0	0	.000
	Majors			**63**	**207**	**23**	**48**	**3**	**2**	**1**	**22**	**4**	**.232**
	Minors			**2326**	**8501**	**1353**	**2712**	**408**	**140**	**84**	**633**	**424**	**.319**

WILLIAM AUSTIN (CHINK) OUTEN

Born June 17, 1905 at Mt. Holly, NC. Died September 11, 1961 at Durham, NC.
Batted left. Threw right. Height 6.00. Weight 195.

Year	Club	League	Pos	G	AB	R	H	2B	3B	HR	RBI	SB	BA
1929	Asheville	Sally	C-3B	119	418	105	143	27	12	10	74	9	.342
1930	Greenville	Sally	OF	69	256	61	92	23	5	11	73	9	.359
	Albany	Eastern	OF	27	79	13	26	10	0	1	11	0	.329
	Jersey City	Int	OF	35	90	13	22	0	0	5	15	1	.244
1931	Scranton	NY-Penn	OF-C	136	520	108	169	33	11	11	77	3	.325
	Jersey City	Int	OF	11	19	3	7	1	1	1	6	1	.368
1932	Jersey City	Int	C-OF	128	344	66	116	17	5	15	86	5	.337
1933	Brooklyn	National	C	93	153	20	38	10	0	4	17	1	.248
1934	Buff/Mont	Int	C	94	201	36	56	8	1	5	38	2	.279
1935	SF Missions	P C	C	132	428	80	157	32	7	7	62	1	.367
1936	SF Missions	P C	C	122	344	39	115	22	0	2	59	1	.334
1937	SF Missions	P C	C-OF	115	282	33	89	16	3	3	44	1	.316
1938	Hollywood	P C	C-OF	52	103	17	33	6	0	0	13	0	.320
1939	Spartanburg	Sally	C	32	97	15	31	7	0	3	20	0	.320
	Lexington	N Caro	OF	14	41	9	11	4	0	0	4	0	.268
	Mayodan	Bi-St	C-OF	39	107	26	44	7	1	7	33	0	.411
	Majors			**93**	**153**	**20**	**38**	**10**	**0**	**4**	**17**	**1**	**.248**
	Minors			**1125**	**3329**	**624**	**1111**	**213**	**46**	**81**	**615**	**33**	**.334**

ISAAC BENJAMIN PALMER

Born June 11, 1925 at Conway, AK.
Batted left. Threw right. Height 6.00. Weight 185.

Year	Club	League	Pos	G	AB	R	H	2B	3B	HR	RBI	SB	BA
1946	Lamesa	WTNM	1-C-3	130	490	69	138	26	4	16	94	5	.282
1947	Lamesa	WTNM	3B	139	556	101	192	40	6	16	135	5	.345
1948	Lamesa	WTNM	3B	123	509	110	175	37	6	6	109	5	.344
1949	Clovis	WTNM	C-3B	139	574	119	212	53	6	18	148*	9	.369
1950	Macon	Sally	C	95	346	53	96	24	4	9	59	4	.277
1951	Macon	Sally	C	37	123	13	27	6	2	1	14	1	.220
	Lubbock	WTNM	C-OF	96	374	64	125	26	4	9	86	1	.334
1952	Lubbock	WTNM	C-OF	141	569	110	200	62	2	12	118	10	.351
1953	Abilene	WTNM	C-1-3	138	547	114	201	56	7	23	110	18	.367
1954	Borger/Pampa	WTNM	C-3B	139	546	132	199	52	3	28	132*	9	.364
1955	Plainview	WTNM	C	140	562	130	228*	46	4	39	138	9	.406*
1956	Carlsbad	SWestern	C	124	506	108	193	55	11	21	124	0	.381
1957	Danville	Carolina	PH	1	0	0	0	0	0	0	0	0	.000
	Minors			1442	5702	1123	1986	483	59	198	1267	76	.348

ROY PARKER

Born April 7, 1926 at Mansfield, LA.
Batted left. Threw left. Height 5.07. Weight 170.
Played an iron-man role in 1949-50 as pitcher-outfielder. (See pitching record below).

Year	Club	League	Pos	G	AB	R	H	2B	3B	HR	RBI	SB	BA
1946	Milford	E Shore	OF-P	77	215	45	63	8	3	2	27	10	.293
	Durham	Carolina	P	14	15	2	5	0	0	0	4	0	.333
1947	Oneonta	Can-Amer	P	3	-	-	0	0	0	0	0	0	.000
1948	Pampa	WTNM	P-OF	72	135	41	46	12	2	6	19	1	.341
1949	Pampa	WTNM	OF-P	120	385	96	114	22	8	24	91	11	.296
1950	Pampa	WTNM	P-OF	100	266	80	92	22	5	21	83	7	.346
1951	Sherman-Den	Big St	OF-P	129	481	100	166	19	15	18	92	7	.345
1952	Paris	Big St	OF-P	146	548	119	173	37	12	23	109	15	.316
1953	Clovis	WTNM	OF-P	140	549	177*	194	38	12	41	160	18	.353
1954	Del Rio	Big St	OF-P	81	333	83	106	26	9	17	62	6	.318
	Greater Miami	Fla Int	OF	20	70	11	16	4	1	1	12	4	.229
1955	Mex City Reds	Mexican	OF-P	88	340	90	110	16	9	16	80	6	.324
1956	Clovis	SWestern	OF-P	134	508	123	180	39	6	36	133	4	.354
1957	Clovis	SWestern	OF-P	28	113	29	36	9	1	5	28	1	.319
	Savannah	SWestern	OF	22	72	13	16	0	1	2	14	2	.222
	Wenatchee	NWestern	OF-P	79	269	36	64	13	2	5	36	4	.238
1958	Salem	NWestern	OF-P	72	256	47	71	19	2	5	44	3	.277
	Minors			1325	4555	1092	1452	284	88	222	994	99	.319

Pitching Record

Year	Club	League	G	IP	W	L	H	R	ER	BB	SO	ERA
1946	Milford	E Shore	13	97	7	4	69	33	27	62	82	2.51
	Durham	Carolina	6	17	0	1	25	20	-	15	15	
1947	Oneonta	Can-Amer	1	-	0	0	-	-	-	-	-	
1948	Pampa	WTNM	35	186	9	13	205	155	106	155	119	5.13
1949	Pampa	WTNM	36	263*	23*	10	269	192	142*	184*	235*	4.86
1950	Pampa	WTNM	49	297*	27*	12	307	198	150*	188*	256*	4.55
1951	Sherman-Den	Big St	25	156	10	11	151	100	79	125	110	4.56
1952	Paris	Big St	7	21	0	1	-	-	20	-	-	8.57
1953	Clovis	WTNM	35	182	12	11	187	140	100	112	102	4.95
1954	Del Rio	Big St	14	84	2	7	101	73	56	57	37	6.00
1955	Mex City Reds	Mexican	6	20	1	2	-	-	-	-	-	
1956	Clovis	SWestern	37	106	5	9	143	103	73	58	80	6.20
1957	Clovis	SWestern	1	4	0	0	2	1	1	1	3	2.25
	Wenatchee	NWestern	2	8	1	0	6	-	3	6	7	3.38
1958	Salem	NWestern	1	1	0	0	4	3	3	1	0	27.00
			268	1442	97	81	1469	1018	760	964	1046	4.87

FLOYD L. PATTERSON
Born October 13, 1904 at Quenemo, KS. Died August 9, 1978 at Quenemo, KS.
Batted left. Threw right. Height 5.10. Weight 170.

Year Club	League	Pos	G	AB	R	H	2B	3B	HR	RBI	SB	BA
1922 Kansas City	A A	OF	1	3	0	0	0	0	0	0	0	.000
1923-24 (Not in O.B.)												
1925 Tulsa	Western	OF	35	133	25	46	14	3	1	-	5	.346
Texarkana	E Texas	OF	25	103	21	31	3	0	2	-	3	.301
Shawnee	SWestern	OF	90	373	73	127	-	-	-	-	-	.340
1926 Tulsa	Western	OF	165	678	147	239	38	9	4	-	14	.353
1927 Tulsa	Western	OF	124	505	111	166	24	6	2	-	4	.329
1928 Decatur	III	OF	130	536	86	181	32	12	5	55	12	.338
1929 Decatur	III	OF	133	512	97	178	28	12	5	85	13	.348
Toledo	A A	OF	17	42	8	15	2	0	0	6	1	.357
1930 Decatur	III	OF	109	412	85	137	22	14	1	50	10	.333
1931 Decatur	III	OF	117	419	75	123	14	6	1	52	8	.294
1932 York	NY-Penn	OF	5	17		2	0	0	0		0	.118
Allentown	Eastern	OF	62	230	32	68	12	8	1	36	10	.296
1933 Rock Island	Miss Val	OF	109	398	94	135	33	8	2	76	28	.339
1934 Rock Island	Western	OF	122	445	90	163	32	9	2	74	14	.366
1935 Dayton	Mid Atl	OF	117	392	72	123	24	7	1	51	20	.314
1936 Canton	Mid Atl	OF	105	335	88	119	21	5	8	56	15	.355
1937 Canton	Mid Atl	OF	120	424	102	152	30	4	13	107	17	.358
1938 Canton	Mid Atl	OF	17	22	2	2	1	0	0	5	0	.091
1939-40 Canton	Mid Atl		(Manager; did not play)									
1941 Canton	Mid Atl	OF	20	54	2	16	2	0	0	6	0	.296
1942 Canton	Mid Atl	OF	3	4	0	0	0	0	0	0	0	.000
1943-44 (Not in O.B.)												
1945 Durham	Carolina	OF	10	18	5	4	0	0	0	3	1	.222
Minors			**1636**	**6055**	**1215**	**2027**	**332**	**103**	**48**	**662**	**175**	**.335**

JAMES CECIL (ZIP) PAYNE
Born April 9, 1909 at Swepsonville, NC.
Batted right. Threw right. Height 5.11. Weight 160.

Year Club	League	Pos	G	AB	R	H	2B	3B	HR	RBI	SB	BA
1929 Goldsboro	E Caro	OF	94	347	54	97	20	2	0	30	14	.280
1930 Columbia	Sally	OF	117	546	93	151	19	18	1	37	9	.277
1931 Wichita	Western	OF	19	73	10	17	5	2	1	5	0	.233
Henderson	Piedmont	OF	41	150	19	36	8	2	0	9	0	.240
1932-33 (Not in O.B.)												
1934 Mayodan	Bi-St	OF	79	333	64	125*	32*	6	14	-	2	.375
1935 Mayodan	Bi-St	OF	110	458	95	177	30	9	14	-	0	.386
1936 Mayo/Bassett	Bi-St	OF-3B	102	432	86	153	29	12	12	75	1	.354
1937 Mayodan	Bi-St	OF	115	476*	102	167*	44*	9	18	-	2	.351
1938 Mayodan	Bi-St	OF	108	439	80	155	46	12*	4	97	4	.353
1939 Leaksville	Bi-St	OF	114	455	110	177	38	12*	12	126	8	.389
1940 Portsmouth	Piedmont	OF	5	19	4	5	0	0	0	2		.263
Leaksville	Bi-St	OF	110	455	81	144	38	9	10	100	1	.316
1941 Leaksville	Bi-St	OF	100	412	89	147	33	5	6	75	1	.357
1942 Leaksville	Bi-St	OF	125	478	61	144	34	2	5	64	5	.301
1943 (Not in O.B.)												
1944 Lynchburg	Piedmont	OF	133	532	81	181*	29	10	0	99	4	.340
1945 Rochester	Int	OF	51	182	26	55	5	3	1	34	3	.302
Lynchburg	Piedmont	OF	42	143	19	44	6	1	0	21	0	.308
1946 Winston-Salem	Carolina	OF	93	334	52	115	23	4	4	53	1	.344
1947 Winston-Salem	Carolina	OF	63	221	35	81	17	1	0	33	5	.367
1948 Winston-Salem	Carolina		(Manager; did not play)									
1949 Fayetteville	Tob St	OF	14	37	3	8	1	1	0	9	0	.216
Minors			**1635**	**6522**	**1164**	**2179**	**457**	**120**	**102**	**869**	**60**	**.334**

HOMER HEFNER PEEL

Born October 10, 1902 at Port Sullivan, TX.
Batted right. Threw right. Height 5.09½. Weight 170.

Year	Club	League	Pos	G	AB	R	H	2B	3B	HR	RBI	SB	BA
1923	Marshall	E Texas	OF-C	117	454	79	146	25	2	17	-	12	.322
1924	Winston-Salem	Piedmont	OF	12	46	5	11	1	0	0	4	1	.239
	Texarkana	E Texas	OF	107	416	79	153	40	4	14	-	22	.368
	Houston	Texas	OF	19	69	10	20	3	4	1	11	0	.290
1925	Houston	Texas	OF	146	546	120	194	46	16	19	114	6	.355
1926	Houston	Texas	OF	154	605	120	198	42	11	18	99	21	.327
1927	Syracuse	Int	OF	140	539	114	177	39	8	16	107	14	.328
	St. Louis	National	OF	2	2	0	0	0	0	0	0	0	.000
1928	Houston	Texas	OF	79	238	28	67	10	1	4	35	5	.282
1929	Philadelphia	National	OF	53	156	16	42	12	1	0	19	1	.269
1930	St. Louis	National	OF	26	73	9	12	2	0	0	10	0	.164
	Houston	Texas	OF	58	211	41	81	22	6	5	40	4	.384
1931	Houston	Texas	OF	146	533	76	174	32	3	7	95	15	.326
1932	Houston	Texas	OF	155*	591	98	199*	52*	7	16	100	19	.337
1933	New York	National	OF	84	148	16	38	1	1	1	12	0	.257
1934	New York	National	OF	21	41	7	8	0	0	1	3	0	.195
	Minneapolis	A A	OF	31	122	14	36	7	0	1	14	0	.295
	Nashville	South A	OF	34	132	17	38	11	2	0	20	2	.288
1935	Rochester	Int	OF	88	275	35	80	17	1	3	36	0	.291
1936	Fort Worth	Texas	OF	120	411	57	127	24	2	7	47	15	.309
1937	Fort Worth	Texas	OF	147	525	108	194	48*	7	15	118*	25	.370*
1938	Fort Worth	Texas	OF	86	316	36	90	13	2	6	47	10	.285
	Toledo	A A	OF	59	162	31	53	9	2	1	21	0	.327
1939	Shreveport	Texas	OF	137	423	71	122	29	1	5	67	12	.288
1940	Shreveport	Texas	OF	64	169	24	55	12	0	2	31	4	.325
1941	Oakland/SD	P C	OF	29	71	8	17	1	0	0	9	0	.239
	Oklahoma City	Texas	OF	43	113	11	23	4	0	0	14	1	.204
1942	Oklahoma City	Texas	OF	16	21	4	5	0	0	0	4	0	.238
1943-45				(Did not play)									
1946	Paris	E Texas	1B-OF	55	115	19	37	8	0	4	29	2	.322
	Majors			**186**	**420**	**48**	**100**	**15**	**2**	**2**	**44**	**1**	**.238**
	Minors			**2042**	**7103**	**1205**	**2297**	**495**	**79**	**161**	**1062**	**190**	**.323**

RICHARD TWILLEY PORTER

Born December 30, 1901 at Princess Anne, MD. Died September 24, 1974 at Philadelphia, PA.
Batted left. Threw right. Height 5.10. Weight 170.

Year	Club	League	Pos	G	AB	R	H	2B	3B	HR	RBI	SB	BA
1921	Baltimore	Int	OF	16	56	5	18	0	0	0		1	.321
1922	Baltimore	Int	2-3-S	136	480	73	134	16	7	8	70	6	.279
1923	Baltimore	Int	2-3-S	155	617	117	195	27	12	18	111	9	.316
1924	Baltimore	Int	2B	129	509	116	185	36	14	23	125	13	.363
1925	Baltimore	Int	2-S-O	142	548	107	184	33	10	13	103	11	.336
1926	Baltimore	Int	SS-OF	95	361	82	116	23	3	8	54	9	.321
1927	Baltimore	Int	OF	155	599	128	225	43	18	25	152	8	.376*
1928	Baltimore	Int	2-3-S	165	618	126	216	34	15	12	97	15	.350
1929	Cleveland	American	OF-2B	71	192	26	63	16	5	1	24	3	.328
1930	Cleveland	American	OF	119	480	100	168	43	8	4	57	3	.350
1931	Cleveland	American	OF	114	414	82	129	24	3	1	38	6	.312
1932	Cleveland	American	OF	146	621	106	191	42	8	4	62	2	.308
1933	Cleveland	American	OF	132	499	73	133	19	6	0	41	4	.267
1934	Cleveland/Bos	American	OF	93	309	40	90	15	7	1	62	5	.291
1935	Newark	Int	OF	133	458	74	153	18	2	8	74	6	.334
1936	Newark	Int	OF	106	343	48	98	15	5	4	43	6	.286
1937	Syracuse	Int	OF	126	436	61	137	21	6	3	57	3	.314
1938	Syracuse	Int	OF	68	148	17	45	7	0	1	23	1	.304
1939	Syracuse	Int	OF	25	35	7	9	1	0	0	6	0	.257
1940	Syracuse	Int	OF	15	32	7	7	2	1	0	2	0	.219
1941	Anniston	SEastern	OF	6	9		1	0	0	0		0	.111
	Majors			**675**	**2515**	**427**	**774**	**159**	**37**	**11**	**284**	**23**	**.308**
	Minors			**1472**	**5249**	**968**	**1723**	**276**	**93**	**123**	**917**	**88**	**.328**

RAYMOND REATH (RABBIT) POWELL
Born November 20, 1888 at Siloam Springs, AK. Died October 16, 1962 at Chillicothe, MO.
Batted left. Threw right. Height 5.09. Weight 160.

Year	Club	League	Pos	G	AB	R	H	2B	3B	HR	RBI	SB	BA
1909	Bartlesville	West A	OF	121	477	74	117	15	5	1	-	47	.245
1910	St. Joseph	Western	OF	152	611	113	167	25	20*	9	-	43	.273
1911	St. Joseph	Western	OF	166	580	101	165	13	10	7	35	69	.284
1912	St. Jospeh	Western	OF	171*	669	139*	207	26	17	7	-	49	.309
1913	Detroit	American	OF	2	0	0	0	0	0	0	0	0	.000
	Providence	Int	OF	124	467	55	125	10	14	2	-	23	.268
1914	Providence	Int	OF	142	496	78	137	8	15	2	-	34	.276
1915	Providence	Int	OF	130	453	67	113	17	14	3	-	16	.249
1916	Providence	Int	OF	57	228	46	71	12	9	2	-	6	.311
1917	Providence	Int	OF	77	307	55	84	7	14	1	-	12	.274
	Boston	National	OF	88	357	42	97	10	4	4	30	12	.272
1918	Boston	National	OF	53	188	31	40	7	5	0	20	2	.213
1919	Boston	National	OF	123	470	51	111	12	12	2	33	16	.236
1920	Boston	National	OF	147	609	69	137	12	12	6	29	10	.225
1921	Boston	National	OF	149	624	114	191	25	18*	12	74	6	.306
1922	Boston	National	OF	142	550	82	163	22	11	6	37	3	.296
1923	Boston	National	OF	97	338	57	102	20	4	4	38	1	.302
1924	Boston	National	OF	74	188	21	49	9	1	1	15	1	.261
1925	Houston	Texas	OF	123	474	81	154	36	4	6	61	2	.325
1926	Houston	Texas	OF	152	584	94	179	42	7	10	84	10	.307
1927	Houston	Texas	OF	128	468	76	151	25	8	5	65	12	.323
1928	Houston	Texas	OF	112	354	58	107	11	7	5	40	4	.302
1929	Shawnee	West A	OF	137	519	121	173	35	21	8	72	15	.333
1930	Shawnee	West A	OF	126	432	101	149	36	13	7	92	24	.345
1931	Quincy	III	OF	69	272	57	73	11	4	0	27	2	.268
1932-34				(Did not play)									
1935	Siloam Spgs	Ark St	OF	36	69	14	21	5	1	0	5	3	.304
1936	Siloam Spgs	Ark-Mo	PH	12	10	0	1	0	0	0	0	0	.100
	Majors			**875**	**3324**	**467**	**890**	**117**	**67**	**35**	**276**	**51**	**.268**
	Minors			**2107**	**7470**	**1330**	**2194**	**334**	**183**	**75**	**481**	**371**	**.294**

ELLIS FOREE (MIKE) POWERS
Born March 2, 1906 at Crestwood, KY. Died December 2, 1983 at Louisville, KY.
Batted left. Threw left. Height 6.01. Weight 185.

Year	Club	League	Pos	G	AB	R	H	2B	3B	HR	RBI	SB	BA
1928	Jack/Gulf	Cot St	OF	123	454	95	174*	26	19*	8		30	.383*
1929	New Orleans	South A	OF	139	513	96	161	30	13	7	49	19	.314
1930	New Orleans	South A	OF	157	616	142	200	41	11	13	90	23	.325
1931	New Orleans	South A	OF	48	161	30	51	5	2	2	12	7	.317
	Oakland	P C	OF	55	207	30	62	9	5	0	19	7	.300
1932	Cleveland	American	OF	14	33	4	6	4	0	0	5	0	.182
	Toledo	A A	OF	121	482	104	179	34	11	10	72	4	.371
1933	Cleveland	American	OF	24	47	6	13	2	1	0	2	2	.277
	Toledo	A A	OF	84	352	60	113	20	9	6	60	5	.321
1934	Toledo	A A	OF	121	459	74	154	27	10	5	58	14	.336
1935	Toledo	A A	OF	131	489	81	166	19	5	14	90	3	.339
1936	Toledo	A A	OF	127	480	83	144	32	9	11	69	5	.300
1937	Toledo/Louis	A A	OF	76	196	28	60	10	4	3	40	2	.306
1938	Shreveport	Texas	OF	6	20	4	5	1	0	0	2	0	.250
	Knoxville	South A	OF	123	436	56	130	25	5	5	60	3	.298
1939	Huntington	Mtn St	1B	119	414	97	148	31	5	16	96	13	.357
1940	Bowling Green	Kitty	1B	124	492	112	187	60*	8	11	155*	21	.380
1941	Hot Springs	Cot St	1B	138	542	119	193	47*	1	16	137*	12	.356
1942	Bowling Green	Kitty	1B	45	175	40	60	16	0	2	34	5	.343
	Hartford	Eastern	1B	58	187	14	41	7	0	1	13	3	.219
	Majors			**38**	**80**	**10**	**19**	**6**	**1**	**0**	**7**	**2**	**.238**
	Minors			**1795**	**6675**	**1265**	**2228**	**440**	**117**	**130**	**1056**	**176**	**.334**

111

MURL ARGUS (DUTCH) PRATHER

Born July 7, 1909 at Branch, AK. Died March 13, 1967 at Ada, OK.
Batted left. Threw left. Height 6.00. Weight 200.

Year	Club	League	Pos	G	AB	R	H	2B	3B	HR	RBI	SB	BA
1927	Kinston	Virginia	1B	14	48	3	13	2	0	0	8	0	.271
1928	Independence	West A	1B	79	264	36	75	19	3	5	32	7	.284
1929	Independence	West A	1B	148	517	88	143	33	20	4	78	8	.277
1930	Independence	West A	1B	126	472	100	159	31	16	18	77	15	.337
1931	Kansas City	A A	1B	8	25	4	6	0	0	1	6	0	.240
	St. Joseph	Western	1B	137	491	93	149	26	12	19	112	5	.303
1932	Hazleton	NY-Penn	1B	129	482	89	145	36	13	17	104*	10	.301
1933	Nashville	South A	1B	145	519	84	145	34	8	23	96	5	.279
1934	Nashville	South A	1B	85	315	45	93	21	6	7	70	4	.295
	Dallas	Texas	1B	20	68	2	12	3	0	0	5	0	.176
1935	Longview	W. Dixie	1B	6									
	Albany	Int	1B	44	149	33	43	8	1	2	21	1	.289
	Dallas	Texas	1B	12	34	4	6	1	0	1	4	0	.176
	Williamsport	NY-Penn	1B	54	179	36	61	14	5	2	36	3	.341
1936	Rock Island	Western	1B	126	435	102*	140	20	6	22*	101	8	.322
1937	Sacramento	P C	1B	103	347	53	89	29	5	6	69	2	.256
1938-39					(Not in O.B.)								
1940	Pampa	WTNM	1B	125	461	132	177	47	5	27	167	9	.384
1941	Pampa/Amar	WTNM	1B	131	474	106	175	55	4	17	142*	4	.369
1942	Amarillo	WTNM	1B	66	242	55	75	15	2	10	65	4	.310
1943					(U.S. Army Air Corps)								
1944	Norfolk	Piedmont	1B	65	192	30	51	12	2	2	27	1	.266
	LR/Atlanta	South A	1B	18	65	14	17	3	0	1	13	0	.262
1945	Little Rock	South A	1B	29	81	19	25	4	0	2	13	3	.309
1946	El Paso	Mex Nat	1B	13	51	9	19	4	0	2	12		.373
	Tyler	E Texas	1B	106	354	59	122	31	1	8	83	2	.345
1947	Ardmore	Soon St	1B	82	200	48	75	20	2	3	64	11	.375
1948	Chick/Pauls Va	Soon St	1B	34	45	6	15	6	0	0	13	0	.333
1949	Ardmore	Soon St	1B	55	140	28	38	6	1	8	38	3	.271
1950	Duncan-Shawn	Soon St			(Manager; did not play)								
1951	Seminole	Soon St	1B	22	29	5	12	1	0	4	9	1	.414
	Minors			**1982**	**6679**	**1283**	**2080**	**481**	**112**	**211**	**1465**	**106**	**.311**

DERRILL BURNHAM PRATT

Born January 10, 1888 at Walhalla, SC. Died September 30, 1977 at Texas City, TX.
Batted right. Threw right. Height 5.11. Weight 175.

Year	Club	League	Pos	G	AB	R	H	2B	3B	HR	RBI	SB	BA
1910	Hattiesburg	Cot St	2B	20	79	16	29	6	1	0	13	8	.367
	Montgomery	South A	2B	51	181	20	42	5	2	0	12	8	.232
1911	Montgomery	South A	2B-3B	139	528	96	167	32	10	8	84	36	.316
1912	St. Louis	American	2-S-O	151	570	76	172	26	15	5	69	24	.302
1913	St. Louis	American	2B-1B	155*	592	60	175	31	13	2	87	37	.296
1914	St. Louis	American	2B	158*	584	85	165	34	13	5	65	37	.283
1915	St. Louis	American	2B	159*	602	61	175	31	11	3	78	32	.291
1916	St. Louis	American	2B	158*	596	64	159	35	12	5	103*	26	.267
1917	St. Louis	American	2B-1B	123	450	40	111	22	8	1	53	18	.247
1918	New York	American	2B	126	477	65	131	19	7	2	55	12	.275
1919	New York	American	2B	140	527	69	154	27	7	4	56	22	.292
1920	New York	American	2B	154*	574	84	180	37	8	4	97	12	.314
1921	Boston	American	2B	135	521	80	169	36	10	5	100	4	.324
1922	Boston	American	2B	154	607	73	183	44	7	6	86	7	.301
1923	Detroit	American	2-1-3	101	297	43	92	18	3	0	40	5	.310
1924	Detroit	American	2-1-3	121	429	56	130	32	3	1	77	6	.303
1925	Waco	Texas	2B	120	462	96	170	32	1	28	116	4	.368
1926	Waco	Texas	2B	151	546	96	168	39	4	25	102	4	.308
1927	Waco	Texas	2B	155	562	126	217	45	1	32*	140*	16	.386*
1928	Waco	Texas	2B-1B	120	418	62	120	19	2	14	61	6	.287

Year	Club	League	Pos	G	AB	R	H	2B	3B	HR	RBI	SB	BA
1929	Waco	Texas	SS-3B	91	194	22	58	12	1	2	32	1	.299
1930	Waco	Texas	3B	60	91	17	34	6	1	2	20	1	.374
1931	Galveston	Texas	3B-1B	70	159	13	37	5	2	1	24	1	.233
1932	Galveston	Texas	1B	15	41	1	12	3	0	0	4	3	.293
	Majors			1835	6826	856	1996	392	117	43	966	246	.292
	Minors			992	3261	565	1054	204	25	112	608	88	.323

EVERETT VIRGIL (PID) PURDY
Born June 15, 1904 at Beatrice, NE. Died January 16, 1951 at Beatrice, NE. Batted left. Threw right. Height 5.06. Weight 150.

Year	Club	League	Pos	G	AB	R	H	2B	3B	HR	RBI	SB	BA
1923	Lincoln	Neb. St.	OF	130	479	83	142	24	9	10	-	16	.296
1924	Beatrice	Tri St	OF	51*	205*	39*	65*	-	-	-	-	-	.317
	Lincoln	Western	OF-2B	72	276	45	97	19	4	6	-	2	.351
1925	Lincoln	Western	OF	145	554	96	160	37	7	5	-	18	.289
1926	Lincoln	Western	OF	111	457	81	170	39	21*	5	-	8	.372
	Chicago	American	OF	11	33	5	6	2	1	0	6	0	.182
1927	Seattle	P C	OF	150	603	122	221	38	8	8	76	22	.367
	Cincinnati	National	OF	18	62	15	22	2	4	1	12	0	.355
1928	Cincinnati	National	OF	70	223	32	69	11	1	0	25	1	.309
1929	Cincinnati	National	OF	82	181	22	49	7	5	1	16	2	.271
1930	Columbus	A A	OF	137	537	116	189	31	11	15	106	15	.352
1931	Columbus	A A	OF	111	371	80	122	27	3	5	61	8	.329
1932	Indianapolis	A A	OF	61	172	22	47	8	5	1	30	1	.273
	Dallas	Texas	OF	35	126	17	44	10	1	0	23	7	.349
1933	San Antonio	Texas	OF	114	427	86	153	27	9	1	65	9	.358
1934	San Antonio	Texas	OF	142	531	89	157	35	5	1	61	7	.296
1935	Oklahoma City	Texas	OF	27	87	16	23	1	2	0	14	5	.264
	Nashville	South A	OF	24	77	7	24	9	0	0	10	0	.312
1936	Lincoln	Neb St	OF	27	66	13	22	5	1	2	10	3	.333
	Rock Island	Western	OF	46	169	32	46	10	1	2	16	1	.272
1937	Beatrice	Neb St	OF	50	198	57	72	10	6	1	24	1	.364
1938	Beatrice	Neb St	OF	4	12	4	2	0	0	0	1	0	.167
	Majors			181	499	74	146	22	11	2	59	3	.293
	Minors			1437	5347	1005	1756	330	93	62	497	123	.328

TOM L. (JUDGE) PYLE
Born November 20, 1896 at Alto, TX. Batted left. Threw right. Height 6.02. Weight 200.

Year	Club	League	Pos	G	AB	R	H	2B	3B	HR	RBI	SB	BA
1922	Ranger	W Texas		(No averages issued)									
1923	Sherman	Texas A	OF	141*	554*	94*	199*	34*	8	14	-	8	.359*
1924	Ardmore	Okla St	OF	41	170	33	58	15	1	2	32	3	.341
1924	Greenville	E Texas	OF	43	166	37	73	15	1	13	-	5	.440
1925	Greenville	E Texas	OF	114	464	91	180	41*	6	22	-	15	.388*
1926	Green/Texar	E Texas	OF	112	454	91	169	40*	3	22	-	17	.372
1927	Tyler	LoneStar	OF	119	489*	77	164	37*	2	26*	-	13	.335
1927	Pensacola	SEastern	OF	17	70	18	31	5	1	1	-	3	.443
1928	Pensacola	SEastern	OF	147	547	110*	197*	36	18*	8	88	10	.360
1929	Pensacola	SEastern	OF	137	538*	83	190*	29	17*	5	100	13	.353
1930	Pensacola	SEastern	OF	136	524	73	169	30	18	9	99	9	.323
1931	Asheville	Piedmont	OF	57	235	46	65	15	3	2	34	8	.277
1931	Monroe	Cot St	OF	48	194	36	73	15	2	8	44	7	.376
1932	Monroe/DeQuin	Cot St	OF	44	177	30	65	15	2	7	-	6	.367
1932	Ft. Worth	Texas	OF	12	45	5	13	4	0	0	9	0	.289
1933	Tyler	Dixie	OF	33	129	14	32	8	1	0	13	5	.248
1934	Jacksonville	W Dixie	OF	123	485	88	174	38	9	17	107	3	.359
1935	Tyler	W Dixie	OF	124	466	61	175	41*	1	9	106*	3	.376*
1936	Tyler	E Texas	OF	77	300	49	97	26	0	6	49	4	.323
1938	Pensacola	SEastern	OF	1	1	0	0	0	0	0	0	0	.000
	Minors			1526	6008	1036	2124	444	93	171	681	132	.354

113

GEORGE BENNET RHINEHARDT
Born May 4, 1900 at Union, SC.
Batted left. Threw left. Height 6.00. Weight 185.

Year	Club	League	Pos	G	AB	R	H	2B	3B	HR	RBI	SB	BA
1923	Greenville	Sally	OF	143	573*	101	212*	44*	28*	3	101	22	.370
	Atlanta	South A	OF	10	33	3	11	1	1	0	8	0	.333
1924	Greenville	Sally	OF	120	495	110*	200*	45*	18	4	92	32*	.404*
	Memphis	South A	OF	9	22	1	7	4	0	0	1	0	.318
1925	Memphis	South A	OF	142	548	104	166	26	24	10	76	8	.303
1926	Knox/Mac/Spar	Sally	OF	136	520	75	159	28	10	9	89	5	.306
1927	Kinston	Virginia	OF	92	331	49	110	18	6	7	57	12	.332
	Waco	Texas	PF	2	2	0	0	0	0	0	0	0	.000
1928	Wilkes-Barre	NY-Penn	OF	68	245	27	72	15	2	0	24	7	.294
	Greenville	Sally	OF	20	66	16	20	1	0	5	9	1	.303
1929	Fayetteville	E Caro	OF	14	54	10	17	5	0	1	6	2	.315
1930	Greenville	Sally	OF	130	541	97	191	42*	6	11	88	19	.353
1931	Greenville	Palmetto	OF	39	132	28	47	8	1	5	37	4	.356
	Charlotte	Piedmont	OF	84	348	60	113	13	8	6	71	16	.325
1932	Charl/W-S	Piedmont	OF	12	51	7	16	4	0	0	9	0	.314
1938	Greenville	Sally	OF	5	11	0	1	0	0	0	1	0	.091
	Minors			1026	3972	688	1342	254	104	65	669	128	.338

LANCE CLAYTON RICHBOURG
Born December 18, 1897 at DeFuniak Springs, FL. Died September 10, 1975 at Crestview, FL.
Batted left. Threw right. Height 5.10½. Weight 160.

Year	Club	League	Pos	G	AB	R	H	2B	3B	HR	RBI	SB	BA
1916	Dothan	Dixie	OF	55	205	21	45	6	0	0	–	9	.220
1917	Dothan	Dixie	OF				(No averages issued)						
1918	Newport News	Virginia	OF-2B	48	169	22	48	8	2	0	–	6	.284
1919	Newark	Int	3B	1	4	0	0	0	0	0	0	0	.000
1920	Grand Rapids	Central	1-2-S	87	311	63	129	12	9*	2	–	13	.415
	Toledo	A A	1B	12	22	5	7	0	1	0	5	0	.318
1921	Philadelphia	National	2B	10	5	2	1	1	0	0	0	1	.200
	Dallas	Texas	1B	4	10	1	2	0	0	0	1	1	.200
1922	Charleston	Sally	1B	90	322	65	92	15	11	1	–	17	.286
1923	Nashville	South A	OF	46	188	36	71	7	4	3	29	11	.378
1924	Washington	American	OF	15	32	3	9	2	1	0	1	0	.281
	Milwaukee	A A	OF	123	502	82	161	33	15	6	56	10	.321
1925	Milwaukee	A A	OF	124	468	86	146	17	15	7	56	24	.312
1926	Milwaukee	A A	OF	164*	714*	151*	247*	38	28*	3	84	48*	.346
1927	Boston	National	OF	115	450	57	139	12	9	2	34	24	.309
1928	Boston	National	OF	148	612	105	206	26	12	2	52	11	.337
1929	Boston	National	OF	139	557	76	170	24	13	3	56	7	.305
1930	Boston	National	OF	130	529	81	161	23	8	3	54	13	.304
1931	Boston	National	OF	97	286	32	82	11	6	2	29	9	.287
1932	Chicago	National	OF	44	148	22	38	2	2	1	21	0	.257
	Albany	Int	OF	75	272	50	101	19	9	3	44	9	.371
1933	Nashville	South A	OF	140	580	120	208	46*	11	8	85	30*	.359
1934	Nashville	South A	OF	82	339	72	105	16	6	9	54	13	.310
1935	Nashville	South A	OF	121	480	74	146	24	4	3	46	23	.304
1936	Nashville	South A	OF	67	180	38	60	15	2	3	33	5	.333
1937	Nashville	South A	OF	6	8	0	1	0	0	0	0	1	.125
1938	Richmond	Piedmont	OF	70	254	46	80	22	7	2	34	6	.315
	Majors			698	2619	378	806	101	51	13	247	65	.308
	Minors			1315	5028	932	1649	278	120	50	527	226	.328

LINNEL PERRY ROBERTS

Born July 15, 1924 at Jonesboro, GA.
Batted left. Threw left. Height 6.00. Weight 185.
Won 42 games and lost 25 while pitching from 1945 to 1955. Led Florida State League with 15-2 won-lost mark and 1.94 ERA in 1952.

Year	Club	League	Pos	G	AB	R	H	2B	3B	HR	RBI	SB	BA
1943	Durham	Piedmont	1B	11	28	4	8	1	0	0	1	0	.286
	Kingsport	Appal	1B	88	354	58	119	14	2	2	59	7	.336
1944	Kingsport	Appal	1B	89	356	59	105	8	4	4	57	11	.295
	Chattanooga	South A	1B	9	26	-	6	-	-	-	-	-	.231
1945	Kingsport	Appal	1B-P	107	438	77	153	19	5	8	100*	38	.349
1946	Montgomery	SEastern	1B	2	8	0	0	0	0	0	0	0	.000
	Burlington	Carolina	1B-OF	66	243	34	72	13	1	2	30	7	.296
	Kingsport	Appal	OF-P	40	168	35	57	5	1	2	21	4	.339
1947	Greenville	Ala St	1B	135	586*	115	228*	49*	6	15	152*	19	.389*
1948	Dayt B/Deland	Fla St	1B-P	139	572*	101	173	38*	12	1	88	21	.302
1949	Deland	Fla St	1B-P	126	515	70	151	21	11	2	69	12	.293
1950	Deland/Gainsv	Fla St	OF-P	123	504	74	174	38	11	3	115	3	.345
1951	Gainsv/Deland	Fla St	OF-P	131	539	73	173	30	5	2	87	3	.321
1952	Deland	Fla St	1B-P	132	548	112	195	33	16*	5	129	8	.356
1953	Wichita Falls	Big St	1B-P	127	499	88	173	48*	5	9	84	3	.347
1954	Crps Christi	Big St	1B	50	215	38	66	13	5	2	44	0	.307
1955	W Palm Beach	Fla St	1B-P	72	285	53	102	13	10	11	64	3	.358
	Minors			**1447**	**5884**	**991**	**1955**	**343**	**94**	**68**	**1100**	**139**	**.332**

FRANCISCO RODRIGUEZ (ITUARTE)

Born October 4, 1943 at Cananea, Sonora, Mexico.
Batted right. Threw right. Height 5.09. Weight 160.
Brother of Aurelio Rodriguez, former major league third baseman.

Year	Club	League	Pos	G	AB	R	H	2B	3B	HR	RBI	SB	BA
1964	Salamanca	Mex Cent	SS	119	505	114	169	38	4	13	74	14	.335
1965	Tabasco	Mex SE	SS	91	376	70	98	13	4	1	28	10	.261
	Mex C Tigers	Mexican	SS	5	11	2	7	0	1	0	2	0	.636
1966	Campeche	Mex SE	SS	35	139	16	39	4	0	2	19	6	.281
	St. Petersburg	Fla St	SS	98	303	24	75	7	4	1	39	5	.248
1967	MC Tig/Aguila	Mexican	SS	129	442	43	108	16	6	1	40	6	.244
1968	Aguila	Mexican	SS	115	404	37	91	9	1	1	29	3	.225
1969	Aguila	Mexican	SS	149	561	73	152	20	9	5	41	10	.271
1970	Aguila	Mexican	SS	149	570	69	159	27	4	4	57	8	.279
1971	Aguila	Mexican	SS	147	565	72	165	19	0	3	45	7	.292
1972	Aguila	Mexican	SS	139	452	47	99	13	1	4	19	9	.219
1973	Aguila	Mexican	SS	116	439	59	117	35	1	5	37	6	.267
1974	Aguila	Mexican	SS	136	541	58	140	17	8	4	46	5	.259
1975	Aguascalient	Mexican	SS	137	533	68	158	20	5	10	69	2	.296
1976	Aguascalient	Mexican	SS	130	468	66	126	19	5	5	84	7	.269
1977	Aguascalient	Mexican	SS	136	456	53	115	12	5	5	42	2	.252
1978	Aguascalient	Mexican	SS	131	445	53	126	31	2	3	72	2	.283
1979	Aguascalient	Mexican	SS	125	457	48	125	22	5	3	58	2	.274
1980	Aguascalient	Mexican	SS	87	317	37	87	12	3	2	37	0	.274
1981	Aguascalient	Mexican	SS	129	504	69	151	21	4	3	40	10	.300
1982	Aguascalient	Mexican	SS	126	470	55	141	25	0	3	56	2	.300
1983	Aguascalient	Mexican	3B-SS	115	432	60	118	12	1	0	33	0	.273
1984	Aguascalient	Mexican	3B	7	19	1	0	0	0	0	0	0	.000
	Minors			**2551**	**9409**	**1194**	**2566**	**392**	**73**	**78**	**967**	**116**	**.273**

EDWARD ROSE
Born February 8, 1904 at Oakland, CA.
Batted left. Threw right. Height 6.00. Weight 185.
Holds Southern Association career records for runs scored (858) and RBIs (866).

Year	Club	League	Pos	G	AB	R	H	2B	3B	HR	RBI	SB	BA
1926	Idaho Falls	Utah-Ida	OF	110	451	122	177*	36	20*	10	-	4	.392
	SF Missions	P C	OF	21	61	14	21	4	0	1	15	0	.344
1927	SF Missions	P C	OF	182	677	115	226	54*	3	15	102	5	.334
1928	Des Moines	Western	OF	36	129	21	40	10	6	2	-	2	.310
	SF Miss/Port	P C	OF	131	457	62	127	24	4	4	40	7	.278
1929	Little Rock	South A	OF	151	557	65	171	29	15	10	74	8	.307
1930	Little Rock	South A	OF	147	536	105	176	35	6	16	110	15	.328
1931	Kansas City	A A	OF	12	38	7	10	1	0	1	8	1	.263
	New Orleans	South A	OF	126	491	74	143	19	10	5	90	9	.291
1932	New Orleans	South A	OF	131	496	93	159	20	6	3	72	7	.321
1933	New Orleans	South A	OF	154	558	97	173	35	7	15	110*	10	.310
1934	New Orleans	South A	OF	153	557	99	168	34	9	9	80	6	.302
1935	New Orleans	South A	OF	158*	574	90	162	45*	3	14	102	5	.282
1936	New Orleans	South A	OF	127	436	62	116	20	3	3	49	3	.266
1937	NO/Atlanta	South A	OF	150	557	101	164	39	4	11	112*	4	.294
1938	Atlanta	South A	OF	131	479	68	146	21	9	3	63	7	.305
1939	Chattanooga	South A	OF	10	22	4	6	2	0	1	4	0	.273
	Savannah	Sally	OF	116	450	79	159	28	5	8	94	7	.353
1940	Savannah	Sally	OF	147	571	98	173	33	7	13	98	7	.303
	Minors			**2193**	**8097**	**1376**	**2517**	**489**	**117**	**144**	**1223**	**107**	**.311**

SIMON ROSENTHAL
Born November 13, 1903 at Boston, MA. Died April 7, 1969 at Boston, MA.
Batted left. Threw left. Height 5.09. Weight 165.

Year	Club	League	Pos	G	AB	R	H	2B	3B	HR	RBI	SB	BA
1922	Hartford	Eastern	OF	134	451	56	126	21	5	10	-	4	.279
1923	Albany/Pitts	Eastern	OF	149	568	104	192	34	9	15	-	10	.338
1924	San Antonio	Texas	OF	44	178	28	67	11	7	4	38	1	.376
1925	San Antonio	Texas	OF	131	507	108	168	40	5	21	115	9	.331
	Boston	American	OF	19	72	6	19	5	2	0	8	1	.264
1926	Boston	American	OF	104	285	34	76	12	3	4	34	4	.267
1927	Louisville	A A	OF	76	246	36	68	12	5	6	36	5	.276
1928	Chattanooga	South A	OF	39	118	20	39	9	3	0	27	0	.331
	Dallas	Texas	OF	84	296	60	108	22	5	1	41	5	.365
1929	Dallas	Texas	OF	145	516	94	175	45	5	5	78	7	.339
1930	Atlanta	South A	OF	148	552	106	196	43	15	2	109	19	.355
1931	Galveston	Texas	OF	9	28	1	7	0	0	0	1	0	.250
	Mobile/Knox	South A	OF	86	311	42	108	17	8	3	55	2	.347
1932	Atlanta	South A	OF	78	298	51	88	16	8	3	49	4	.295
1933	Quincy	Miss Val	OF	108	428	99	166	39	8	7	98	23	.388
1934	Dayton/Beck	Mid Atl	OF	89	340	63	110	21	4	1	55	3	.324
1935	Peoria	Ill	OF	37	129	27	36	8	4	2	22	4	.279
	Majors			**123**	**357**	**40**	**95**	**17**	**5**	**4**	**42**	**5**	**.266**
	Minors			**1357**	**4966**	**895**	**1654**	**338**	**91**	**80**	**724**	**96**	**.333**

ANGEL SCULL
Born October 2, 1930 at Mantanzas, Cuba.
Batted right. Threw right. Height 5.06. Weight 162.

Year	Club	League	Pos	G	AB	R	H	2B	3B	HR	RBI	SB	BA
1951	Wellsville	Pony	OF	124	520	113	171	23	12	3	45	60*	.329
1952	Key West/Hav	Fla Int	OF	137	544	74	149	15	14*	1	39	54*	.274
1953	Charleston	A A	OF	150	545	66	156	18	5	2	48	29	.286
1954	Havana	Int	OF	119	435	64	117	13	5	1	20	31	.269
1955	Havana	Int	OF	108	403	53	102	15	4	2	40	10	.253

Year	Club	League	Pos	G	AB	R	H	2B	3B	HR	RBI	SB	BA
1956	Havana	Int	OF	123	445	56	121	13	7	5	42	17	.272
1957	Havana	Int	OF	145	540	73	142	28	8	21	77	14	.263
1958	Toronto	Int	OF	64	237	34	67	11	4	2	19	7	.283
1959	Toronto/Mont	Int	OF	140	559	81	151	27	7	4	49	25	.270
1960	Montreal	Int	OF	151	578	83	168	24	7	6	44	7	.291
1961	Syracuse	Int	OF	133	456	77	129	22	4	5	42	11	.283
1962	Vancouver	P C	OF	50	135	12	33	0	1	0	8	3	.244
	Atlanta	Int	OF	70	259	46	84	9	2	5	27	5	.324
1963	Poza Rica	Mexican	OF	102	385	78	132	17	9	12	53	10	.343
1964	Poza Rica	Mexican	OF	136	526	109	174	24	10	22	108	14	.331
1965	Poza Rica	Mexican	OF	131	498	73	155	31	9	4	70	14	.311
1966	Poza Rica	Mexican	OF	139	462	75	136	27	5	3	52	6	.294
1967	Poza Rica	Mexican	OF	105	350	55	108	10	7	6	42	13	.309
1968	Poza Rica	Mexican	OF	44	130	21	34	8	4	2	16	3	.262
	Minatit/Cam	Mex SE	OF	44	163	26	54	6	4	4	17	2	.331
1969	Campeche	Mex SE	OF	120	458	72	149	17	4	5	49	10	.325
	Minors			2335	8628	1341	2532	358	132	115	907	345	.293

WALTER ANTHONY SESSI

Born July 23, 1918 at Finleyville, PA.
Batted left. Threw left. Height 6.03. Weight 225.

Year	Club	League	Pos	G	AB	R	H	2B	3B	HR	RBI	SB	BA
1937	Kinston	Coast Pl	OF	22	84	10	21	4	0	0	5	1	.250
	Shelby/Thomas	N Car St	OF	24	75	18	22	1	1	3	12	0	.293
	Williamson	Mt St	OF	32	109	18	36	9	4	0	18	0	.330
1938	Williamson	Mt St	OF	118	456	104	143	41	7	25	126*	3	.314
1939	Williamson	Mt St	OF	126	465	104	173	32	10	21	125	7	.372
	Columbus	Sally	OF	2	5	1	1	0	0	0	0	1	.200
1940	Mobile	SEastern	OF	148	528	92	151	32	6	11	96	5	.286
1941	Houston	Texas	OF	154	561	93	169	28	16	14	98	4	.301
	St. Louis	National	OF	5	13	2	0	0	0	0	0	0	.000
1942-45	(Military Service)												
1946	St. Louis	National	PH	15	14	2	2	0	0	1	2	0	.143
1947	Montreal	Int	OF	130	386	69	101	16	3	20	80	0	.262
1948	Montreal	Int	OF	22	75	13	21	0	0	5	11	0	.280
	Mobile	South A	OF	109	375	58	105	21	7	10	86	7	.280
1949	Ft. Worth	Texas	OF	88	208	35	53	10	0	3	27	8	.255
1950	Abilene	WTNM	OF	136	483	121	152	34	2	23	103	3	.315
1951	Abilene	WTNM	OF-1B	132	481	106	149	28	2	18	121	7	.310
1952	Brownsville	Gulf Cst	1B-OF	153	552	148	207	34	2	45*	179*	2	.375
1953	Brownsville	Gulf Cst	OF-1B	137	505	74	119	14	0	14	76	1	.236
1954	Lake Charles	Evang	OF-1B	141	520	105	173	43	6	25	124	0	.333
1955	Lake Charles	Evang	OF	104	384	61	104	20	0	16	83	4	.271
	Majors			20	27	4	2	0	0	1	2	0	.074
	Minors			1778	6252	1230	1900	367	66	253	1370	53	.304

WILLIAM WALTON (BILL) SHARMAN

Born May 25, 1926 at Abilene, TX.
Batted right. Threw right. Height 6.01. Weight 190.
All-American basketball player at USC, 1949 and 1950, and a star guard in the NBA, 1950-61. Elected to the National Basketball Hall of Fame in 1975.

Year	Club	League	Pos	G	AB	R	H	2B	3B	HR	RBI	SB	BA
1950	Elmira	Eastern	OF	10	38	5	11	2	0	1	11	0	.289
	Pueblo	Western	OF	111	427	65	123	22	8	11	70	11	.288
1951	Ft. Worth	Texas	OF	157	570	84	163	18	5	8	53	23	.286
1952	St. Paul	A A	OF	137	411	63	121	16	4	16	77	2	.294
1953	Mobile	South A	OF	90	228	21	48	8	1	5	17	0	.211
1954	(Not in O.B.)												
1955	St. Paul	A A	OF-3B	133	424	59	124	15	0	11	58	3	.292
	Minors			638	2098	297	590	81	18	52	286	39	.281

EDWARD JOSEPH SICKING
Born March 30, 1897 at St. Bernard, OH. Died August 30, 1978 at Cincinnati, OH.
Batted both. Threw right. Height 5.09½. Weight 165.

Year	Club	League	Pos	G	AB	R	H	2B	3B	HR	RBI	SB	BA
1916	Norfolk	Virginia	3B	96	349	38	93	15	2	3		15	.266
	Chicago	National	PH	1	1	0	0	0	0	0	0	0	.000
1917	San Antonio	Texas	SS	160	542	69	150	17	12	3		20	.277
1918	San Antonio	Texas	SS	63	221	36	68	10	5	2		12	.308
	New York	National	3-2-S	46	132	9	33	4	0	0	12	2	.250
1919	NY/Phila	National	SS-2B	67	200	18	45	2	1	0	18	4	.225
1920	NY/Cincin	National	2-3-S	83	257	23	56	6	1	0	26	8	.218
1921	Indianapolis	A A	2B	167	590	82	168	29	3	2	82	22	.285
1922	Indianapolis	A A	2B	169*	656	110	190	14	4	4	87	14	.290
1923	Indianapolis	A A	2B-SS	162	638	101	185	20	12	3	61	28	.290
1924	Indianapolis	A A	2B-SS	167	653	115	209	32	10	1	63	12	.320
1925	Indianapolis	A A	2B	120	469	73	148	27	4	1	43	16	.316
1926	Indianapolis	A A	2B-SS	162	617	97	185	27	7	1	50	17	.300
1927	Ind/Louis	A A	2B-SS	118	459	81	139	25	5	1	41	12	.303
	Pittsburgh	National	2B	6	7	1	1	1	0	0	3	0	.143
1928	Louisville	A A	2B	168	658	114	242	38	4	1	72	14	.368
1929	Louisville	A A	2B	148	593	108	184	22	8	2	62	16	.310
1930	Ind/Minn	A A	2B	148	609	129	190	36	5	4	69	17	.312
1931	Minneapolis	A A	2B	142	523	118	169	28	2	5	59	14	.323
1932	Minneapolis	A A	2B	84	262	50	72	4	2	0	15	8	.275
1933	Keokuk	Miss Val	2B	115	442	85	142	33	8	1	52	24	.321
	Majors			203	597	51	135	13	2	0	59	14	.226
	Minors			2189	8281	1406	2534	377	93	34	756	261	.306

FRANCIS LEONARD SIGAFOOS
Born March 21, 1904 at Easton, PA. Died April 12, 1968 at Indianapolis, IN.
Batted right. Threw right. Height 5.09. Weight 170.
Hit in 39 consecutive games for Indianapolis in 1933, an American Association record since broken.

Year	Club	League	Pos	G	AB	R	H	2B	3B	HR	RBI	SB	BA
1925	Providence	Int	3B-2B	119	380	46	108	13	8	3	55	2	.284
1926	Reading	Int	S-3-2	134	507	62	163	35	9	8	74	10	.321
	Philadelphia	American	SS	13	43	4	11	0	0	0	2	0	.256
1927	Portland	P C	2-0-S	147	559	97	187	31	2	10	76	-11	.335
1928	Portland	P C	2-S-3	178	695	109	206	62	7	8	76	32	.296
1929	Portland	P C	3B	56	204	32	55	5	2	3	28	5	.270
	Detroit/Chi	American	3-2-S	21	26	4	5	1	0	0	3	0	.192
1930	Los Angeles	P C	2B	165	702	129	214	46	9	19	103	25	.305
1931	Cincinnati	National	3B-SS	21	65	6	11	2	0	0	8	0	.169
	Indianapolis	A A	2B	107	420	59	137	30	4	6	70	14	.326
1932	Indianapolis	A A	2B	163	635	105	199	29	11	10	77	14	.313
1933	Indianapolis	A A	2B	152	635	108	235	53*	11	6	126	24	.370*
1934	Indianapolis	A A	2B	109	394	57	111	19	1	1	36	10	.282
1935	Memphis	South A	2B-3B	44	175	26	47	9	0	1	28	6	.269
	Louisville	A A	3B	98	398	51	125	18	5	3	52	6	.314
1936	Louisville	A A	3S	114	434	79	148	24	7	5	61	10	.341
1937	Louisville	A A	3B-2B	76	182	19	46	9	4	0	23	2	.253
1938	Monett	Ark-Mo	3B	15	39	5	11	1	2	2	10	0	.282
	Decatur	III	2B	12	40	1	10	2	0	0	0	0	.250
	Oklahoma City	Texas	2B	2	3	1	1	0	0	0	0	0	.333
	Majors			55	134	14	27	3	0	0	13	0	.201
	Minors			1691	6402	986	2003	386	82	85	895	164	.313

FREDERICK WILLIAM SINGTON

Born February 24, 1910 at Birmingham, AL.
Batted right. Threw right. Height 6.02. Weight 215.
All-American football player at the University of Alabama in 1929 and 1930. Elected to Football Hall of Fame in 1955.

Year	Club	League	Pos	G	AB	R	H	2B	3B	HR	RBI	SB	BA
1931	High Point	Piedmont	OF	12	47	9	16	2	1	2	8	2	.340
	Jackson	Cot St	OF	50	185	24	51	12	5	4	33	4	.276
1932	Columbus	SEastern	OF	33	124	29	46	9	6	6*	37	1	.371
	Beckley	Mid Atl	OF	102	400	110*	147	30	12*	29*	110*	3	.368*
1933	Atlanta	South A	OF	106	363	58	95	22	7	12	69	4	.262
1934	Albany	Int	OF	155	562	123	184	32	10	29	147*	4	.327
	Washington	American	OF	9	35	2	10	2	0	0	6	0	.286
1935	Washington	American	OF	20	22	1	4	0	0	0	3	0	.182
	Chattanooga	South A	OF	73	261	48	83	20	4	6	50	19	.318
1936	Chattanooga	South A	OF	142	526	97	202	46	22*	6	107	3	.384*
	Washington	American	OF	25	94	13	30	8	0	1	28	0	.319
1937	Washington	American	OF	78	228	27	54	15	4	3	36	1	.237
1938	Chattanooga	South A	OF	153	533	109	165	47*	11	10	84	3	.310
	Brooklyn	National	OF	17	53	10	19	6	1	2	5	1	.358
1939	Brooklyn	National	OF	32	84	13	23	5	0	1	7	0	.274
	Louisville	A A	OF	83	264	48	67	17	3	13	55	1	.254
1940	Louisville	A A	OF	123	425	55	115	19	7	10	76	1	.271
	Majors			**181**	**516**	**66**	**140**	**36**	**5**	**7**	**85**	**2**	**.271**
	Minors			**1032**	**3690**	**710**	**1171**	**256**	**88**	**127**	**776**	**45**	**.317**

EARL LEONARD SMITH

Born January 20, 1891 at Oak Hill, OH. Died March 14, 1943 at Portsmouth, OH.
Batted both. Threw right. Height 5.11. Weight 170.

Year	Club	League	Pos	G	AB	R	H	2B	3B	HR	RBI	SB	BA
1911	Green Bay	Wis-Ill	OF	116	453	56	104	-	-	-	-	22	.230
1912	Green Bay	Wis-Ill	OF-1B	98	384	61	116	21	7	12	-	15	.302
	Milwaukee	A A	1B-OF	7	18	5	5	1	0	0	-	0	.278
1913	Fond du Lac	Wis-Ill	OF	68	256	41	54	10	1	3	-	16	.211
	Manistee	Mich St	OF	51	197	34	51	14	1	0	-	13	.259
1914	Twin Cities	Wis-Ill	OF	104	384	40	108	11	4	3	-	24	.281
1915	Omaha	Western	OF	139	571	87	143	21	3	4	-	18	.250
1916	Omaha	Western	OF	121	510	89	152	27	8	2	-	21	.298
	Chicago	National	OF	14	27	2	7	1	1	0	4	1	.259
1917	Omaha	Western	OF	88	341	62	113	21	11	9	-	13	.331
	St. Louis	American	OF	52	199	31	56	7	7	0	10	5	.281
1918	St. Louis	American	OF	89	286	28	77	10	5	0	32	13	.269
1919	St. Louis	American	OF	88	252	21	63	12	5	1	36	1	.250
1920	St. Louis	American	3B-OF	103	353	45	108	21	8	3	55	11	.306
1921	St. Louis/Wash	American	OF-3B	84	258	27	65	9	4	4	26	1	.252
1922	Washington	American	OF-3B	65	205	22	53	12	2	1	23	4	.259
	Minneapolis	A A	OF	48	196	44	62	10	3	6	25	1	.316
1923	Minneapolis	A A	OF	139	487	86	154	34	9	11	82	12	.316
1924	Minneapolis	A A	OF	158	641	139	226	64*	4	23	127	25	.353
1925	Minneapolis	A A	OF	164	665*	132	208	54	11	31	156	11	.313
1926	Minneapolis	A A	OF	159	642	103	194	47	8	15	94	17	.302
1927	Minneapolis	A A	OF	161	658	132	225	49	11	25	135	16	.342
1928	Minneapolis	A A	OF	163	604	81	169	31	4	16	103	10	.280
1929	Minneapolis	A A	OF	151	580	111	188	27	10	20	124	14	.324
1930	Minn/Columb	A A	OF	150	603	103	198	43	4	16	130	11	.328
1931	Columbus	A A	OF	56	200	42	63	14	2	8	50	7	.315
	Houston	Texas	OF	67	257	34	70	20	3	1	19	3	.272
1932	Denver	Western	OF	112	456	63	126	30	9	1	72	13	.276
1933	Huntington	Mid Atl	OF	20	79	10	25	4	0	0	12	0	.316
1934	(Not in O.B.)												
1935	Charleroi	Pa St A	OF	59	202	28	61	5	3	5	35	2	.302
	Majors			**495**	**1580**	**176**	**429**	**72**	**32**	**9**	**186**	**36**	**.272**
	Minors			**2399**	**9384**	**1583**	**2815**	**558**	**116**	**211**	**1164**	**284**	**.300**

FRANK HERSHEL (PAT) STASEY
Born March 11, 1918 at Stephensville, TX.
Batted left. Threw right. Height 5.10. Weight 173.

Year	Club	League	Pos	G	AB	R	H	2B	3B	HR	RBI	SB	BA
1938	Big Spring	WTNM	OF-P	78	239	51	77	17	4	6	55	11	.322
1939	Big Spring	WTNM	OF	138	561	131	193	34	13	25	134	27	.344
1940	Moline	III	OF	108	430	79	134	19	14	1	30	9	.312
1941	Moline	III	OF	121	502	78	139	26	12	8	56	5	.277
1942	Minneapolis	A A	OF	52	120	18	37	7	4	1	17	0	.308
	Jersey City	Int	OF	14	43	3	10	0	0	0	3	0	.233
	Knoxville	South A	OF	19	79	14	20	1	2	1	12	0	.253
1943-46	(Military Service)												
1947	Big Spring	Longhorn	OF	123	502	145	209*	45*	6	19	153	22	.416
1948	Big Spring	Longhorn	OF	110	404	100	157	38	5	9	102	5	.389*
1949	Big Spring	Longhorn	OF	125	441	108	166	30	4	11	109	4	.376*
1950	Big Spring	Longhorn	OF	130	434	85	150	36	2	8	101	2	.346
1951	Big Spring	Longhorn	OF	128	483	107	187	48	5	14	118	2	.387*
1952	Big Spring	Longhorn	OF	136	512	102	176	34	3	13	120	2	.344
1953	Roswell	Longhorn	OF	80	290	59	99	17	3	4	69	2	.341
1954	Roswell	Longhorn	OF	105	414	75	122	25	2	8	80	3	.295
1955	Hobbs	Longhorn	OF	12	48	9	19	7	0	2	18	0	.396
	Minors			**1479**	**5502**	**1164**	**1895**	**384**	**79**	**130**	**1177**	**94**	**.344**

WILLIAM ROBERT STEINECKE
Born February 7, 1907 at Cincinnati, OH.
Batted right. Threw right. Height 5.08. Weight 175.

Year	Club	League	Pos	G	AB	R	H	2B	3B	HR	RBI	SB	BA
1927	Lawrence	New Eng	C	16	56	7	13	1	0	1	7	1	.232
	Waterloo	Miss Val	C	48	158	27	52	11	5	2	-	4	.329
1928	Waterloo	Miss Val	C	109	411	75	128	31	11	7	-	7	.311
	Seattle	P C	C	9	25	1	6	0	0	0	-	0	.240
1929	Seattle	P C	C	94	240	36	76	11	2	5	32	3	.317
1930	Beaumont	Texas	C	17	54	4	8	1	0	0	4	0	.148
	Binghamton	NY-Penn	C-OF	83	290	44	89	16	4	7	51	9	.307
1931	Binghamton	NY-Penn	C-OF	137	496	78	179	41	7	7	84	19	.361
	Pittsburgh	National	PH-C	4	4	0	0	0	0	0	0	0	.000
1932	Binghamton	NY-Penn	OF	46	165	27	55	6	3	3	26	10	.333
	Ft. Worth	Texas	C	31	79	12	15	3	0	1	4	0	.190
	Davenport	Miss Val	C	36	132	23	33	7	2	2	24	13	.250
	Omaha	Western	C	17	65	14	22	6	2	0	5	2	.338
1933	Scranton	NY-Penn	C	118	405	54	125	18	11	4	56	12	.309
1934	Scranton	NY-Penn	C-OF	83	314	50	100	28	7	0	52	7	.318
	Dayton	Mid Atl	C	48	197	38	73	13	7	2	44	4	.371
1935	(Not in O.B.)												
1936	Williamsport	NY-Penn	C	132	501	95	175	33	9	6	110	12	.349
1937	Savannah/Jack	Sally	C	69	239	32	67	8	3	2	43	5	.280
1938	(Not in O.B.)												
1939	Jacksonville	Sally	C	2	7	1	1	0	0	0	0	0	.143
	Portsmouth	Piedmont	C	36	106	9	21	3	0	2	15	1	.198
1940	Jacksonville	Sally	C	25	84	8	27	2	1	1	14	0	.321
	Portsmouth	Piedmont	C	40	129	9	33	7	1	0	11	0	.256
	Tarboro	Coast Pl	C	23	83	14	30	5	1	0	12	8	.361
1941	Portsmouth	Piedmont	C	113	389	35	97	21	6	0	49	9	.249
1942	Portsmouth	Piedmont	C	66	210	21	47	4	0	0	18	1	.224
1943	Portsmouth	Piedmont	C	81	253	24	57	12	3	0	25	1	.225
1944	Portsmouth	Piedmont	C	86	238	35	70	15	4	1	45	8	.294
1945	Kansas City	A A	C	60	181	21	51	7	2	0	28	0	.282
	Newark	Int	C	28	79	9	25	2	0	0	14	5	.316
1946	St. Augustine	Fla St	C-OF	90	253	38	77	12	2	0	35	10	.304
1947	DeLand	Fla St	C	84	268	31	69	12	2	2	14	9	.257

Year Club	League	Pos	G	AB	R	H	2B	3B	HR	RBI	SB	BA
1948 Suffolk	Virginia	C	53	128	21	39	8	2	2	26	2	.305
1949 Suffolk	Virginia		(Manager, did not play)									
1950 Leesburg	Fla St	C	27	84	3	14	2	0	0	7	0	.167
Majors			4	4	0	0	0	0	0	0	0	.000
Minors			1907	6319	896	1874	346	97	57	855	162	.297

LINDO IVAN STORTI
Born December 5, 1906 at Santa Monica, CA. Died July 24, 1982 at Ontario, CA.
Batted both. Threw right. Height 5.10. Weight 165.

Year Club	League	Pos	G	AB	R	H	2B	3B	HR	RBI	SB	BA
1927 Portland	P C	3-2-S	27	35	3	8	0	0	1	4	0	.229
DM/Amarillo	West	3B	41	131	13	37	8	2	0	-	0	.282
1928 Muskogee	West A	SS	14	57	8	13	3	0	1	6	0	.228
Amarillo	West	3-2-S	83	233	19	67	12	4	1	-	2	.288
1929 Tulsa	West	2B	161*	675	146	230*	61*	7	28	-	10	.341
1930 Wichita Falls	Texas	2B	154	659	127	204	50	7	30	114	5	.310
St. Louis	American	2B	7	28	6	9	1	1	0	2	0	.321
1931 St. Louis	American	3B	86	273	32	60	15	4	3	26	0	.220
1932 St. Louis	American	3B	53	193	19	50	11	2	3	26	1	.259
1933 St. Louis	American	3B-2B	70	210	26	41	7	4	3	21	2	.195
1934 Milwaukee	A A	2B	147	567	98	187	32	2	35	145	2	.330
1935 Milwaukee	A A	2B-3B	152	605	123	178	31	10	29	87	6	.294
1936 Milwaukee	A A	3B-2B	157	600	98	184	25	10	31	108	5	.307
1937 Milwaukee	A A	2B-3B	155	603	107	186	45	6	25	125	7	.308
1938 Milwaukee	A A	2B-3B	112	362	59	96	9	2	21	79	6	.265
1939 Minneapolis	A A	2B	147	502	88	141	28	5	30	105	5	.281
1940 Minneapolis	A A	2B-3B	120	384	50	120	10	1	20	80	2	.313
1941 Minn/Toledo	A A	2B-3B	86	299	40	78	17	2	5	48	0	.261
Syracuse	Int	3B	56	173	19	41	7	0	9	32	0	.237
1942 Toledo	A A	2B-3B	83	239	21	48	7	1	3	23	0	.201
1943 Toledo	A A	3B	99	301	26	72	16	0	3	40	3	.239
1944 Toledo	A A	3B	5	9	0	0	0	0	0	0	0	.000
Oakland	P C	2B-3B	53	135	11	26	6	0	0	12	1	.193
1945 Oakland/Holly	P C	2B-3B	13	28	0	2	0	0	0	0	0	.071
Majors			216	704	83	160	34	11	9	75	3	.227
Minors			1865	6597	1056	1918	367	59	272	1008	54	.291

KENNETH ELMER STRONG
Born August 6, 1906 at West Haven, CT. Died October 5, 1979 at New York, NY.
Batted right. Threw right. Height 6.01. Weight 210.
All-American football player at New York University in 1928. Had long career in NFL as halfback and kicker.
Named to Professional Football Hall of Fame in 1967. Hit four homers in one game for Hazleton in 1930.

Year Club	League	Pos	G	AB	R	H	2B	3B	HR	RBI	SB	BA
1929 New Haven	Eastern	OF	104	378	62	107	19	3	21	80	4	.283
1930 New Haven	Eastern	OF	27	92	17	25	4	2	4	26	5	.272
Hazleton	NY-Penn	OF	117	450	114	168	31	16	41*	130*	10	.373
1931 Toronto	Int	OF	118	438	70	149	30	14	9	80	12	.340
Minors			366	1358	263	449	84	35	75	316	31	.331

Phil Cavarretta caused quite a stir when be broke in with the Chicago Cubs in late 1934. He hit .381 in seven games and contributed a dramatic 1-0 game-winning homer on September 25. His O.B. debut several months earlier also was newsworthy. Breaking in with Peoria in the Central League on May 15, 1934 the 17-year-old high school star collected four hits, including a home run in his first at bat and a double.

Ken Strong with Toronto in 1931 when an injury ended his baseball career.

Jimmy Walsh played two years with Buffalo and won two batting titles.

GUY R. STURDY
Born August 7, 1899 at Sherman, TX. Died May 4, 1965 at Marshall, TX.
Batted left. Threw left. Height 6.00½. Weight 180.

Year	Club	League	Pos	G	AB	R	H	2B	3B	HR	RBI	SB	BA
1920	Sweetwater	W Texas	1B	89	323	55	98	28	7	2	-	15	.303
1921	Chickasha	West A	1B	148	581	95	182	32	16	8	-	30	.313
1922	Joplin	West A	1B	132	496	99	166	18	8	6	-	67*	.335
1923	Little Rock	South A	1B	36	136	14	37	2	2	2	14	1	.272
	Joplin	West A	1B	104	410	84	136	22	9	8	-	25	.332
1924	Muskogee	West A	1B	159	654	147	218	45	7	25	119	45	.333
1925	Muskogee	West A	1B	44	190	45	69	13	2	11	41	13	.363
	Tulsa	Western	1B	65	263	62	91	23	5	12	-	6	.346
1926	Tulsa	Western	1B	165	660	163*	233	54	9	49*	-	22	.353
1927	Tulsa	Western	1B	148	605	144	226	44	14	23	-	17	.374
	St. Louis	American	1B	5	21	5	9	1	0	0	5	1	.429
1928	St. Louis	American	1B	54	45	3	10	1	0	1	8	1	.222
	Milwaukee	A A	1B	36	125	16	37	8	2	0	10	8	.296
1929	Birmingham	South A	1B	156	603	116	179	19	21*	14	74	33	.297
1930	Birmingham	South A	1B	152	556	116	176	24	7	9	108	33	.317
1931	Houston	Texas	1B	159	552	76	163	27	11	3	69	15	.295
1932	New Orleans	South A	1B	134	487	82	158	24	9	10	91	14	.324
1933	San Antonio	Texas	1B	24	75	9	14	2	0	0	8	2	.187
	Little Rock	South A	1B	107	374	73	123	17	6	5	55	12	.329
1934	Johnstown	Mid Atl	1B	55	204	44	61	8	5	2	39	12	.299
	Baltimore	Int	1B	72	229	37	49	14	0	2	26	10	.214
1935	Baltimore	Int	1B	51	63	6	14	3	0	0	9	0	.222
1936-37	Baltimore	Int		(Manager; did not play)									
1938	Marshall	E Texas	1B	88	312	63	112	22	0	12	82	4	.359
1939	Marshall	E Texas	1B	(Less than 10 games)									
1940	El Dorado	Cot St	1B	17	17	0	3	0	0	0	0	0	.176
	Majors			**59**	**66**	**8**	**19**	**2**	**0**	**1**	**13**	**2**	**.288**
	Minors			**2141**	**7915**	**1546**	**2545**	**449**	**140**	**203**	**745**	**384**	**.322**

MIGUEL SUAREZ (LOPEZ)
Born September 29, 1952 at Guasave, Sinaloa, Mexico.
Batted left. Threw left.

Year	Club	League	Pos	G	AB	R	H	2B	3B	HR	RBI	SB	BA
1969	Tampico	Mex Cent	OF	107	414	83	130	13	9	12	72	1	.314
1970	Tampico	Mex Cent	OF	126*	460*	105	181	37	4	14	101	15	.393*
1971	Mex City Reds	Mexican	OF	141	505	84	188*	28	8	3	53	6	.372
1972	Mex City Reds	Mexican	OF	140*	537*	84	181	25	5	3	57	10	.337
1973	Mex City Reds	Mexican	OF	133	524*	84	169	20	13*	1	59	4	.323
1974	Mex City Reds	Mexican	OF	128	494	62	167	21	10	0	56	5	.338
1975	Mex City Reds	Mexican	OF	134	514	74	185	18	3	2	59	4	.360
1976	Mex City Reds	Mexican	OF	132	492	62	171*	18	5	1	53	2	.348
1977	Mex City Reds	Mexican	OF	152	614*	91	227*	22	9	1	80	4	.370
1978	Mex City Reds	Mexican	OF	140	544	72	170	20	10	2	69	2	.313
1979	Cordoba	Mexican	OF	131	531	77	167	12	12	2	52	1	.315
1980	Rey/MC Tigers	Mexican	OF	77	293	22	84	8	3	1	20	3	.287
	Mex City Tig	Mex #2	OF	36	131	16	42	4	2	0	8	0	.321
1981	Mex City Tig	Mexican	OF	123	502	67	152	17	2	0	34	7	.303
1982	MC Tig/Aguila	Mexican	OF	110	413	42	112	11	2	2	29	3	.271
1983	Tabasco	Mexican	OF	113	438	39	140	9	2	0	20	3	.320
1984	Tabasco/Vera	Mexican	OF	96	370	59	123	14	0	1	36	4	.332
	Minors			**2019**	**7776**	**1123**	**2589**	**297**	**99**	**45**	**858**	**74**	**.333**

ANTONIO V. THEBO

Played under name of Henderson for Denison in 1912, Ardmore in 1913, Muskogee in 1915-16, and Paris-Ardmore in 1917. Was a weak hitter but an outstanding fielder and base runner. Batted both. Threw right.

Year	Club	League	Pos	G	AB	R	H	2B	3B	HR	SB	BA
1902	Paris	Texas	OF	89	364	62	112	19	4	3	31	.308
1903	Natchez	Cot St	OF	17	57	10	14	0	3	0	3	.246
	Corsicana	Texas	OF	79	292	40	62	8	7	4	24	.212
1904	Corsicana	Texas	OF	41	160	26	31	6	2	0	26	.194
	Beaumont	S Texas	OF	55	194	43	32	-	-	-	29	.165
1905	Beau/S Anton	S Texas	OF	104	382	61	94	-	-	-	45	.246
1906	San Antonio	S Texas	OF	108	437	56	82	-	-	-	21	.188
1907	Temple	Texas	OF	134	484	73	123	-	-	-	35	.254
1908	Shreveport	Texas	OF	135	470	79	105	12	-	2	90*	.223
1909	Waco	Texas	OF	132	504	73	113	18	8	3	63*	.224
1910	Waco/Dallas	Texas	OF	134	451	52	79	9	3	4	39	.175
1911	Dallas/Galv	Texas	OF	139	473	58	107	10	6	4	19	.226
1912	Gal/Bea/S Ant	Texas	OF	72	222	30	51	11	1	3	8	.230
	Denison	Tex-Okla	OF	40	128	28	38	-	-	-	20	.297
1913	Ardmore	Tex-Okla	OF	99	348	50	83	-	-	-	32	.239
1914	Flint	S Mich	OF	147	505	75	121	20	7	2	30	.240
1915	Muskogee	West A	OF	120	465	85	113	33	1	4	17	.243
1916	Muskogee	West A	OF	137	517	96	127	26	0	15	34	.246
1917	Paris-Ardmore	West A	O-P-1	144	560	80	133	21	3	19	27	.238
1918-20	(Not in O.B.)											
1921	Clarksdale	Miss St	OF	14	50	7	12	3	1	0	0	.240
	Minors			**1940**	**7063**	**1084**	**1632**	**196**	**46**	**63**	**593**	**.231**

JAMES CHARLES WALSH

Born September 22, 1885 at Kallila, Ireland. Died July 3, 1962 at Syracuse, NY. Batted right. Threw right. Height 5.10½. Weight 170. In 1926 he led IL in batting with .388 mark when he was 40 years old.

Year	Club	League	Pos	G	AB	R	H	2B	3B	HR	RBI	SB	BA
1907	Syracuse	NY St	OF	1	3	0	1	0	0	0	0	1	.333
1908	Albany	NY St	OF	94	302	41	61	11	5	5	-	20	.202
1909	Northampton	Conn	OF	96	331	61	96	17	9	3	-	29	.290
1910	Baltimore	Eastern	OF	140	481	70	129	17	7	5	-	18	.268
1911	Baltimore	Eastern	OF	151	529	88	140	15	15	5	-	29	.265
1912	Baltimore	Int	OF	117	438	96	155	22	20	2	-	35	.354
	Philadelphia	American	OF	31	107	11	27	8	2	0	15	7	.252
1913	Philadelphia	American	OF	94	303	56	77	16	5	0	27	15	.254
1914	Phil/New York	American	OF	110	352	48	77	12	9	4	47	12	.219
1915	Philadelphia	American	OF	117	417	48	86	15	6	1	20	22	.206
1916	Phil/Boston	American	OF	127	406	47	93	13	6	1	29	30	.229
1917	Boston	American	OF	57	185	25	49	6	3	0	12	6	.265
1918	(Military Service)												
1919	Seattle	P C	OF	162	586	72	155	25	3	1	-	24	.265
1920	Akron	Int	OF	150	589	102	189	36	13	15	-	13	.321
1921	Newark	Int	OF	153	581	106	209	39	16	2	-	29	.360
1922	Baltimore	Int	OF	164	636	131	208	47	9	5	106	10	.327
1923	Baltimore	Int	OF	151	564	107	188	41	5	15	134	14	.333
1924	Jersey City	Int	OF	143	536	89	163	37	4	9	78	18	.304
1925	Buffalo	Int	OF	154	544	120	194	34	3	22	122	8	.357*
1926	Buffalo	Int	OF	147	526	122	204	43	3	17	131	4	.388*
1927	Indianapolis	A A	OF	16	38	6	11	1	0	1	6	0	.289
	Toronto	Int	OF	69	248	41	80	9	2	1	38	8	.323
1928	Jersey City	Int	OF	157	543	71	176	39	9	3	90	6	.324
1929	Jersey City	Int	OF	128	421	55	123	26	2	4	61	5	.292
1930	Hartford	Eastern	OF	66	192	37	59	11	1	4	21	5	.307
	Fairmont	Mid Atl	OF	58	196	35	70	9	2	2	32	5	.359
1931	Fairmont	Mid Atl	OF	68	253	33	85	20	4	1	48	3	.336
	Majors			**536**	**1770**	**235**	**409**	**70**	**31**	**6**	**150**	**92**	**.231**
	Minors			**2385**	**8537**	**1483**	**2696**	**499**	**132**	**122**	**867**	**284**	**.316**

WILLIAM EARL WEBB

Born September 17, 1898 at Bon Air, TN. Died May 23, 1965 at Jamestown, TN.
Batted left. Threw right. Height 6.01. Weight 185.
Compiled 37-47 won-lost record in 118 games as hurler. Holds major league record for most doubles in a season with 67 in 1931.

Year Club	League	Pos	G	AB	R	H	2B	3B	HR	RBI	SB	BA
1921 Clarksdale	Miss St	OF-P	92	309	41	87	8	13	7	49	5	.282
1922 Memphis	South A	P	32	67	8	19	2	1	0	-	0	.284
1923 Pittsfield	Eastern	P-OF	62	133	20	43	12	3	1	-	0	.323
1924 Pittsfield	Eastern	OF-P	119	408	68	140	42*	5	14	-	15	.343
Toledo	A A	OF	17	69	11	23	3	3	0	10	0	.333
1925 Toledo	A A	OF	114	422	77	139	22	9	11	66	3	.329
New York	National	OF	4	3	0	0	0	0	0	0	0	.000
1926 Louisville	A A	OF	130	474	96	158	32	8	18	111	8	.333
1927 Chicago	National	OF	102	332	58	100	18	4	14	52	3	.301
1928 Chicago	National	OF	62	140	22	35	7	3	3	23	0	.250
1929 Los Angeles	P C	OF	188	658	163	235	56	6	37	164	14	.357
1930 Boston	American	OF	127	449	61	145	30	6	16	66	2	.323
1931 Boston	American	OF	151	589	96	196	67*	3	14	103	2	.333
1932 Boston/Det	American	OF	139	530	72	151	28	9	8	78	1	.285
1933 Detroit/Chi	American	OF	64	118	17	34	5	0	1	11	0	.288
1934 Milwaukee	A A	OF	106	424	72	156	27	4	11	84	1	.368*
1935 Milwaukee	A A	OF	144	533	98	180	33	6	6	98	0	.338
1936 Knoxville	South A	OF	133	466	83	162	24	7	20*	102	1	.348
1937 Knoxville	South A	OF	106	385	55	107	26	1	7	56	3	.278
Majors			**649**	**2161**	**326**	**661**	**155**	**25**	**56**	**333**	**8**	**.306**
Minors			**1243**	**4348**	**792**	**1449**	**287**	**66**	**132**	**740**	**50**	**.333**

FRANK HOXIE (KID) WILLSON

Born November 3, 1895 at Bloomington, NE. Died April 17, 1964 at Union Gap, WA.
Batted left. Threw left. Height 6.01. Weight 190.

Year Club	League	Pos	G	AB	R	H	2B	3B	HR	RBI	SB	BA
1918 Tacoma/Vanc	P C Int	OF	47	195	32	68	10	11	0		23	.349
Chicago	American	PH	4	1	2	0	0	0	0	0	0	.000
1919 Regina	West Can	OF	13	43		10	2	0	0		2	.233
1920 Vancouver	P C Int	OF	106	403	70	123	17	7	7		25	.305
1921 Vancouver	P C Int	OF	112	450	74	162	32	3	5		27	.360
1922 Vancouver	P C Int	OF	46	179	34	55	12	2	2		8	.307
Greenville	Sally	OF	18	59	11	14	5	1	0	2	1	.237
1923 Greenville	Sally	OF	23	79	21	34	5	4	2	8	3	.430
1924 Hutchinson	West A	OF	100	486	116	190	32	11	28	117	15	.391
1925 Waco	Texas	OF	78	299	56	105	22	3	9	49	9	.351
1926 Waco	Texas	OF	25	100	25	40	8	0	2	21	5	.400
1927 Waco	Texas	OF	28	109	31	48	6	3	3	16	4	.440
Chicago	American	OF	7	10	1	1	0	0	0	1	0	.100
1928 Shrev/Dallas	Texas	OF	97	353	61	121	28	3	2	56	10	.343
1929			(Voluntarily Retired)									
1930 Toledo	AA	OF	48	128	30	44	11	2	3	28	0	.344
1931 Seattle	P C	OF	32	85	13	19	6	1	3	20	0	.224
Majors			**11**	**11**	**3**	**1**	**0**	**0**	**0**	**1**	**0**	**.091**
Minors			**773**	**2968**	**574**	**1033**	**196**	**51**	**66**	**317**	**132**	**.348**

Pete Schneider may have had the biggest one-game batting splurge in Pacific Coast League history, but his minor league career was not very significant. Playing for Vernon at Salt Lake City on May 11, 1923, he hit five home runs and a double and knocked in 14 runs. Although he played the full season and had a good year, the former Cincinnati hurler still hit only 19 homers. He hit only 88 in his 11 seasons in the minors.

NESBIT CLARENCE WILSON
Born October 11, 1922 at East Spencer, NC.
Batted right. Threw right. Height 6.00. Weight 200.

Year	Club	League	Pos	G	AB	R	H	2B	3B	HR	RBI	SB	BA
1940	Mooresville	N Car St	1B	40	137	14	29	3	0	3	17	1	.212
1941	Moor/Conc/Lan	N Car St	OF	57	220	16	59	7	0	1	33	3	.268
1942	Landis	N Car St	OF	93	375	74	117	40*	3	7	49	5	.312
1943-45	(Military Service)												
1946	Tallassee	Ga-Ala	OF	34	125	23	40	11	3	2	17	0	.320
	Anniston	SEastern	OF	91	344	66	118	27	3	18	88	3	.343
1947	Pensacola	SEastern	OF	140	527	104	171	45	6	25	129*	9	.324
1948	Pensacola	SEastern	OF	106	389	75	128	25	6	19	79	2	.329
	Atlanta	South A	OF	19	61	8	19	3	0	0	14	0	.311
1949	Pensacola	SEastern	OF	138*	509	93	165*	34	3	16	95	13	.324
1950	Pensacola	SEastern	OF	134	507	121	180	37	1	35*	163*	8	.355*
1951	Denver	Western	OF	43	139	19	41	8	0	3	23	0	.295
	Shreveport	Texas	OF	82	263	33	74	9	2	11	47	2	.281
1952	St. Petersburg	Fla Int	OF	152	558	92	151	23	4	15	82	5	.271
1953	Keokuk	III	OF	65	240	53	80	17	2	17	70	4	.333
	Macon	Sally	OF	75	256	37	64	17	2	10	37	1	.250
1954	St. Petersburg	Fla Int	OF	103	389*	96*	128	32*	4	20	109*	7	.329
	Montgomery	Sally	OF	35	119	28	45	9	2	7	25	0	.378
1955	Crestview	Ala-Fla	1B-OF	117	402	124	162	23	6	32	108	5	.403*
1956	Donalsonville	Ala-Fla	1B	117	410	133*	143	25	1	40*	125*	15	.349
	Birmingham	South A	OF	14	51	5	18	3	0	2	14	0	.353
1957	St. Petersburg	Fla St	1B-OF	139	515	108	192*	47*	8	9	104	10	.373*
1958	Ft. Wal B/Pen	Ala-Fla	OF-1B	119	409	102*	162	38*	3	24*	106*	3	.396*
1959	Mobile	South A	OF	46	149	19	38	7	0	5	18	0	.255
	Pensacola	Ala-Fla	OF	43	137	32	32	5	0	8	23	0	.234
1960	Tampa	Fla St	1B	16	45	8	13	5	0	0	9	0	.289
	Minors			**2018**	**7276**	**1483**	**2369**	**500**	**59**	**329**	**1584**	**96**	**.326**

RICHARD CLYDE WILSON
Born October 4, 1922 at Salina, KS.
Batted right. Threw right. Height 6.00. Weight 185.

Year	Club	League	Pos	G	AB	R	H	2B	3B	HR	RBI	SB	BA
1944	Holly/S Fran	P C		12	23	3	9	1	1	0	1	0	.391
	Little Rock	South A	3B	16	52	10	14	0	2	0	8	2	.269
	Portsmouth	Piedmont		3	8	0	0	0	0	0	0	0	.000
1945	San Francisco	P C	PH	2	2	0	0	0	0	0	0	0	.000
	Little Rock	South A		11	39	7	11	4	0	0	6	1	.282
1946	(Military Service)												
1947	Idaho Falls	Pioneer	C	19	67	12	13	1	1	3	12	3	.194
	Ontario	Sunset	3B-C	59	205	52	78	22	2	9	47	1	.380
1948	Mexicali	Sunset	C-O-1	137	507	146	176	28	12	42*	188*	41	.347
1949	Los Angeles	P C		24	72	13	23	5	0	0	11	1	.319
	Visalia	Calif	C-OF	101	340	70	102	22	2	26	93	22	.300
1950	Modesto	Calif	1B	140	521	120	166	31	6	30*	154*	26	.319
1951	Modesto	Calif	1-3-0	146	552	144	205*	55*	2	40*	151	16	.371*
1952	Hollywood	P C	OF-1B	48	120	24	28	8	1	3	16	1	.233
	Modesto	Calif	1B	60	216	47	67	12	1	10	52	1	.310
1953	Modesto	Calif	1B	140	510	108	162	37	3	24	125	8	.318
1954	Boise	Pioneer	1B	14	50	9	13	1	1	1	11	1	.260
	San Jose	Calif	OF-C	47	165	35	51	7	2	5	32	0	.309
1955	(Voluntarily Retired)												
1956	Bakersfield	Calif	1-0-3	137	520	108	182	35	3	33	132	10	.350
1957	Bakersfield	Calif	1B	138	479	88	144	20	2	27*	110	24	.301
1958	Magic Valley	Pioneer	1B-3B	101	288	56	105	23	1	17	78	5	.365
1959	Wenatchee	NWest	1B	133	453	80	130	30	1	9	81	6	.287
1960	Wenat/Salem	NWest	1B	35	104	14	26	7	0	1	10	2	.250
	Bakersfield	Calif	3B	22	69	13	24	3	0	5	18	0	.348
	Minors			**1545**	**5362**	**1159**	**1729**	**352**	**43**	**285**	**1336**	**171**	**.322**

WILLIAM SMITH (RASTY) WRIGHT
Born January 31, 1863 at Birmingham, MI. Died October 14, 1922 at Duluth, MN.
Height 6.01.
Probably first player to collect 2000 hits in minor leagues. Scored 217 runs in 1894.

Year	Club	League	Pos	G	AB	R	H	2B	3B	HR	SB	BA
1884	Muskegon	NWestern	OF	52	209	43	41	6	1	0	-	.196
1885	Toledo	Western	OF	27	101	20	23	1	1	0	-	.228
1886	Hamilton	Int	OF	93	378	78	103	15	6	1	23	.272
1887	Hamilton	Int	OF	100	464	93	198	16	4	2	73	.427
1888	Syracuse	Int A	OF	107	454	143	162	11	20	4	40	.357
1889	Syracuse	Int A	OF	107	423	107	131	11	9	1	29	.310
1890	Syracuse	A A	OF	88	348	82	106	10	6	0	30	.305
	Cleveland	National	OF	13	45	7	5	1	0	0	3	.111
	Bradford	NY-Penn	OF	16	64	19	19	4	3	0	5	.297
1891	Detroit	NWestern	OF	25	91	19	27	11	1	1	1	.297
	Duluth/Omaha	West A	OF	68	272	61	96	15	7	2	12	.353
1892	Los Angeles	Calif	OF	172	726	166	205	28	12	0	49	.282
1893	Los Angeles	Calif	OF	92	400	121	140	24	11	3	9	.350
1894	Grand Rapids	Western	OF	133	551	217*	233	54	19	8	38	.423
1895	Grand Rapids	Western	OF	124	549	172	224	35	16	3	29	.408
1896	Newark	Atlantic	OF	119	491	163	189	44	12	12	45	.385
	Grand Rapids	Western	OF	9	35	13	15	4	0	2	1	.429
1897	Newark	Atlantic	OF	130	519	144	193	43	12	1	20	.372
1898	Wilkes-Barre	Eastern	OF	58	210	57	78	11	2	2	13	.371
1899	Buffalo	Western	OF	8	32	3	9	1	0	0	0	.281
	Paterson	Atlantic	OF	14	53	16	25	2	1	0	1	.472
	Majors			**101**	**393**	**89**	**111**	**11**	**6**	**0**	**33**	**.282**
	Minors			**1454**	**6022**	**1655**	**2111**	**336**	**137**	**42**	**388**	**.351**

ANTHONY BATTON (TONY) YORK
Born November 27, 1912 at Irene, TX. Died April 18, 1970 at Hillsboro, TX.
Batted right. Threw right. Height 5.10. Weight 165.

Year	Club	League	Pos	G	AB	R	H	2B	3B	HR	RBI	SB	BA
1933	Baton Rouge	Dixie	SS	125	485	61	141	31	9	2	64	8	.291
1934	Dallas	Texas	SS-2B	121	447	47	115	31	1	4	49	6	.257
1935	Dallas	Texas	SS	149	524	59	133	17	6	4	54	11	.254
1936	Dallas/Tulsa	Texas	SS	107	373	45	99	15	2	4	46	6	.265
1937	Tulsa	Texas	SS	151	559	70	163	46*	4	6	81	12	.292
1938	St. Paul	A A	SS	145	597	77	144	26	7	12	58	9	.241
1939	St. Paul	A A	SS	141	515	63	127	18	5	9	54	7	.247
1940	Shreveport	Texas	SS	162	628	84	149	37	6	15	86	9	.237
1941	Shreveport	Texas	SS	141	490	53	119	26	2	4	52	5	.243
1942	Shreveport	Texas	SS	138	514	65	131	18	3	16	62	5	.255
1943	Milwaukee	A A	SS	150	651*	109	187*	28	8	10	55	2	.287
1944	Chicago	National	SS-3B	28	85	4	20	1	0	0	7	0	.235
	Los Angeles	P C	SS	32	39	3	9	4	0	0	9	0	.231
1945	(Military Service)												
1946	Seattle	P C	2B-SS	158	546	53	137	23	5	2	51	11	.251
1947	Seattle	P C	2B	150	506	73	143	21	2	7	41	5	.283
1948	Seattle	P C	2B-SS	166	547	52	140	28	1	8	60	3	.256
1949	Seattle	P C	2B-SS	140	414	46	123	14	6	4	47	1	.297
1950	Seattle	P C	2-3-S	98	215	23	47	6	0	3	18	3	.219
1951	San Diego	P C	3B	68	89	7	23	7	1	1	7	0	.258
1952	Texarkana	Big St	3B	83	289	47	91	20	0	14	58	1	.315
1953	Crowley	Evang	3B	98	321	64	104	19	0	11	53	1	.324
1954	Crowley	Evang	3B	125	450	66	131	20	0	10	73	4	.291
1955	Odessa	Longhorn	3B	99	304	44	93	18	2	10	50	4	.306
1956	Ballinger	SWestern	3B	33	42	7	14	3	0	2	7	0	.333
	Majors			**28**	**85**	**4**	**20**	**1**	**0**	**0**	**7**	**0**	**.235**
	Minors			**2780**	**9545**	**1218**	**2563**	**476**	**70**	**158**	**1135**	**113**	**.269**

Prince Oana, outfielder-pitcher

Jimmy Zinn, pitcher-outfielder

Aurelio Monteagudo

"Jittery Joe" Berry

Pitchers

HARRY TERRELL ABLES

Born October 4, 1884 at Terrell, TX. Died February 8, 1951 at San Antonio, TX.
Threw left. Batted left. Height 6.02½. Weight 200.
Pitched two 9-inning shutout games over Ft. Worth, July 4, 1905, allowing a total of five hits. Pitched 23-inning 1-1 tie against Waco, July 5, 1910. On August 8, 1910, Ables fanned the first 10 Dallas batters he faced. He struck out 325 batters that season, a Texas League record.

Year	Club	League	G	IP	W	L	H	R	ER	BB	SO	ERA
1904	Memp/Shrev	South A	7	55	3	2	55	34	28	26	21	4.58
1905	Dallas	Texas	30	261	17	13	189	79	56	71	169	1.93
	St. Louis	American	6	31	0	3	37	15	13	13	11	3.77
1906	Dallas	Texas	1	9	1	0	11	6	3	2	4	3.00
1907	Dallas	Texas	18	158	12	5	102	44	31	35	126	1.77
1908	Birmingham	South A	2	11	1	1	14	6	4	6	9	3.27
	Dallas/San Ant	Texas	24	185	15	6	119	59	42	47	142	2.04
1909	San Antonio	Texas	36	293	19	12	207	79	-	80	259	
	Cleveland	American	5	30	0	2	26	14	7	10	24	2.10
1910	San Antonio	Texas	34	320	12	12	200	86	-	96	325*	
1911	New York	American	3	11	0	1	16	15	12	7	6	9.82
	Oakland	P C	38	324	22	11	-	76	-	88	218	
1912	Oakland	P C	45	363*	25*	18	-	131	-	134*	303*	
1913	Oakland	P C	37	229	9	15	-	95	-	73	130	
1914	Oakland	P C	34	223	13	17	203	98	50	82	95	2.02
1915	Oakland	P C	36	229	8	16	237	120	88	78	99	3.46
1925	San Antonio	Texas	1	5	0	1	5	3	2	4	1	3.60
1926	San Antonio	Texas	1	4	1	0	1	0	0	0	0	0.00
	Majors		**14**	**72**	**0**	**6**	**79**	**44**	**32**	**30**	**41**	**4.00**
	Minors		**344**	**2669**	**158**	**129**	**1343**	**916**	**304**	**822**	**1901**	**2.40**

RAMON ARANO (BRAVO)

Born July 24, 1939 at Tierra Blanca, Veracruz, Mexico.
Throws right. Bats right. Height 5.08. Weight 160.
Only hurler to win 300 games in one minor league. Mexican League career leader in games pitched, innings, wins, losses, hits, runs, earned runs, and strikeouts.

Year	Club	League	G	IP	W	L	H	R	ER	BB	SO	ERA
1957	Aguascalient	Cent Mex	5	-	0	1	-	-	-	-	-	
1958				(Did not play)								
1959	Poza Rica/Ver	Mexican	26	129	8	9	130	75	64	47	63	4.47
1960	Veracruz	Mexican	33	80	0	5	104	73	58	53	50	6.53
1961	Veracruz	Mexican	34	172	11	3	198	78	71	48	124	3.72
1962	Veracruz	Mexican	28	197	17	6	180	76	57	46	121	2.60*
	Oklahoma City	A A	3	11	1	1	17	12	12	10	3	9.82
1963	Mex City Reds	Mexican	24	137	13	4	146	55	51	33	73	3.35
1964	Mex City Reds	Mexican	32	204	16	9	234	103	92	62	120	4.06
1965	Mex City Reds	Mexican	26	148	9	8	199	95	79	49	84	4.80
1966	Mex City Reds	Mexican	39	207	16	11	210	92	68	72	130	2.96
1967	Mex City Reds	Mexican	40	249*	15	11	265*	101	77	53	153	2.78
1968	Mex City Reds	Mexican	37	223	17	10	191	73	50	50	117	2.02
1969	Mex City Reds	Mexican	14	82	5	7	90	37	29	26	36	3.18
1970	Mex City Reds	Mexican	36	198	15	14	242	108	87	47	114	3.95
1971	MC Reds/Salt	Mexican	33	180	12	15	193	74	59	41	109	2.95
1972	Cordoba	Mexican	34	185	13	13	203	95	75	39	112	3.65
1973	Cordoba	Mexican	10	76	6	4	68	24	14	22	43	1.66
1974	Cordoba	Mexican	32	197	12	10	197	78	56	44	96	2.56

Year	Club	League	G	IP	W	L	H	R	ER	BB	SO	ERA
1975	Cordoba	Mexican	26	175	15	8	187	74	61	38	66	3.14
1976	Cordoba	Mexican	29	184	14	9	197	72	59	39	75	2.89
1977	Cordoba	Mexican	35	218	15	14	227	89	69	62	100	2.85
1978	Cordoba	Mexican	31	215	19	10	186	68	60	37	96	2.51
1979	Cordoba	Mexican	36	269	19	13	249	89	70	53	131	2.34
1980	Reynosa	Mexican	21	164	12	9	169	58	54	36	89	2.96
	Reynosa	Mex #2	9	49	2	6*	73*	33*	24	11	21	4.41
1981	Mex City Reds	Mexican	26	181	14	5	180	66	59	29	50	2.93
1982	Mex City Reds	Mexican	29	156	9	9	194	80	67	33	38	3.87
1983	Coatzacoalcos	Mexican	27	163	8	14	173	74	63	27	66	3.48
1984	Veracruz	Mexican	22	143	11	9	161	64	55	45	47	3.46
	Minors		**777**	**4592**	**324**	**247**	**4863**	**2016**	**1640**	**1152**	**2327**	**3.21**

JONAS ARTHUR (JITTERY JOE) BERRY
Born December 16, 1904 at Huntsville, AK. Died September 27, 1958 at Anaheim, CA.
Threw right. Batted right. Height 5.10½. Weight 145.

Year	Club	League	G	IP	W	L	H	R	ER	BB	SO	ERA
1927	Laurel/Gulf	Cot St	30	180	8	13	184	84	-	53	59	
1928	Gulfport/Vick	Cot St	33	245	16	10	250	92	-	56	73	
1929	Vicksburg	Cot St	45*	297*	21*	13	287*	126	88	58	81	2.67*
1930	Vick/Pine Bl	Cot St	32	195	14	12	234	143	106	56	78	4.89
1931	Pine Bluff	Cot St	35	243	16	12	224	97	74	68	122	2.74
1932	Macon	SEastern	7	23	1	2	32	30	21	17	9	8.22
	Pine Bluff	Cot St	18	151	10	3	140	63	43	42	84	2.56
	Muskogee	West A	19	100	2	10	114	65	57	27	60	5.13
1933	Joplin	Western	49*	280*	20	15	291*	131	-	82	124	
1934	Joplin	West A	47	332*	21	17	339*	180	131	64	233*	3.55
1935	Ponca City	West A	13	102	7	5	105	44	30	25	66	2.65
1936	Los Angeles	P C	32	125	7	7	135	67	52	28	70	3.74
1937	Los Angeles	P C	34	266	13	13	224	94	82	48	91	2.77
1938	Los Angeles	P C	40	187	16	11	179	94	71	51	90	3.42
1939	Los Angeles	P C	47	122	8	7	153	94	60	48	62	4.43
1940	Los Angeles	P C	53*	143	9	5	118	67	38	41	69	2.39
1941	Los Angeles	P C	52	125	6	10	145	105	73	51	48	5.26
1942	Tulsa	Texas	48	239	18	8	168	62	50	47	133	1.88
	Chicago	National	2	2	0	0	7	4	4	2	1	18.00
1943	Milwaukee	A A	37	236	18	10	224	99	73	63	98	2.78
1944	Philadelphia	American	53	111	10	8	78	32	24	23	44	1.95
1945	Philadelphia	American	52*	130	8	7	114	40	34	38	51	2.35
1946	Phil/Cleve	American	26	50	3	7	47	23	18	24	21	3.24
	Toronto	Int	16	37	0	2	37	18	11	16	28	2.68
1947	OC/Shreveport	Texas	49	109	6	7	88	36	29	29	60	2.39
1948	Tulsa	Texas	31	47	4	2	44	22	11	19	27	2.11
1949	(Not in O.B.)											
1950	Vernon	Longhorn	16	35	3	0	42	19	15	7	25	3.86
1951	Vernon	Longhorn	8	24	2	1	17	7	2	7	17	0.75
	Corp Christi	Gulf Cst	12	26	2	3	23	7	5	13	10	1.73
	Majors		**133**	**293**	**21**	**22**	**246**	**99**	**80**	**87**	**117**	**2.46**
	Minors		**803**	**3869**	**248**	**198**	**3797**	**1846**	**1122**	**1016**	**1817**	**3.19**

KARL LEONARD BLACK (LAUTENSCHLAGER)
Born in 1891 at Newark, OH.
Threw left. Batted both. Height 5.11. Weight 195.
Appeared in 70 games as a Western League pitcher in 1928.

Year	Club	League	G	IP	W	L	H	R	ER	BB	SO	ERA
1911	Iron/Charles	Mtn St	46*	-	16	23*	-	-	-	53	84	
1912	Charleston	Mtn St	10	72	3	4	-	-	-	-	-	
	Mansfield	Ohio St	12	99	5	6	-	-	-	-	-	
1913	Huntington	Ohio St	37	288	15	16	-	-	-	89	127	
1914	Montgomery	South A	45	310	10	29*	338	175	-	89	127	

Year	Club	League	G	IP	W	L	H	R	ER	BB	SO	ERA
1915	Birmingham	South A	42	276	17	10	262	127	-	85	106	
1916	Birmingham	South A	34	234	11	13	211	85	-	58	71	
1917	Birmingham	South A	40	216	13	10	192	91	67	56	62	2.79
1918	Birmingham	South A	13	57	5	5	82	-	-	21	11	
1919	Shreveport	Texas	36	242	15	10	238	89	72	69	98	2.68
1920	Shreveport	Texas	17	115	8	4	88	36	23	24	52	1.80
1921	Des Moines	Western	52	320	16	23*	380	195	-	68	146	
1922	DM/Tulsa	Western	46	243	11	11	326	162	-	32	93	
1923	Tulsa	Western	58	345	29*	13	429	180	-	63	118	
1924	Tulsa	Western	59	300	20	15	394	201	-	70	108	
1925	Tulsa	Western	56	307	18	20	349	146	-	53	156	
1926	Tulsa	Western	45	236	15	15	303	236	-	50	78	
1927	Tulsa	Western	25	150	12	2	201	108	-	34	52	
1928	Tulsa/OC	Western	70*	274	15	10	305	142	-	36	88	
1929	Selma	SEastern	34	205	13	9	201	81	60	29	37	2.63
1930	Selma	SEastern	10	34	1	5	43	28	22	11	10	5.82
	Baton Rouge	Cot St	10	55	3	4	73	39	36	4	15	5.89
	Mobile	South A	6	20	0	3	25	19	16	7	5	7.20
	Wheeling	Mid Atl	11	62	4	3	71	47	39	14	21	5.66
	Minors		**814**	**4460**	**275**	**263**	**4511**	**2187**	**335**	**926**	**1538**	

CLARENCE WALDO BLETHEN

Born July 11, 1893 at Dover-Foxcroft, ME. Died April 11, 1973 at Frederick, MD.
Threw right. Batted left. Height 5.11. Weight 175.

Year	Club	League	G	IP	W	L	H	R	ER	BB	SO	ERA
1920	Frederick	Blue Rdg	16	119	9	7	121	59	-	33	74	
1921	Frederick	Blue Rdg	20	133	9	3	128	75	-	29	62	
1922	Frederick	Blue Rdg	22	156	13	7	140	63	-	27	65	
1923	Frederick	Blue Rdg	18	142	8	9	126	64	-	39	78	
	Boston	American	5	18	0	0	29	18	14	7	2	7.00
1924	San Antonio	Texas	15	50	3	1	46	38	25	19	20	4.50
	Little Rock	South A	2	3	0	1	13	10	9	1	0	27.00
	Greenville	Sally	17	112	7	8	124	67	60	33	69	4.82
1925	Mobile	South A	5	21	1	3	34	24	21	9	5	9.00
	Macon	Sally	32	170	16	5	223	96	84	37	82	4.45
1926	Macon	Sally	42	270	19	13	288	144	122	57	76	4.07
1927	Macon	Sally	45	288	25	11	235	139	146	61	72	4.56
1928	Atlanta	South A	40	175	14	10	204	96	87	33	45	4.47
1929	Atlanta	South A	43	313	22	11	307	120	108	65	51	3.11
	Brooklyn	National	2	2	0	0	4	3	2	3	0	9.00
1930	Atlanta	South A	42	228	16	9	248	121	92	60	48	3.63
1931	Atlanta	South A	40	240	20	11	293	119	87	41	53	3.26
1932	Atlanta	South A	33	241	13	15	288	141	112	47	37	4.18
1933	Atlanta/Knox	South A	43	263	17	12	309	139	121	44	52	4.14
1934	Knoxville	South A	27	194	8	14	228	111	95	29	32	4.41
1935	Knoxville	South A	34	216	8	13	265	113	93	35	41	3.88
1936	Wilkes-Barre	NY-Penn	22	113	8	10	174	87	74	22	29	5.89
1937	Leaksville	Bi-State	3	15	0	0	15	5	4	2	6	2.40
	Savannah	Sally	24	173	10	10	186	60	44	25	51	2.29
1938	Savannah	Sally	37	183	11	10	209	82	65	16	54	3.20
	Majors		**7**	**20**	**0**	**0**	**33**	**21**	**16**	**10**	**2**	**7.20**
	Minors		**622**	**3818**	**257**	**193**	**4204**	**1973**	**1449**	**764**	**1102**	**3.99**

GEORGE STUART BRUNET

Born June 8, 1935 at Houghton, MI.
Throws left. Bats right. Height 6.00. Weight 200.
Holds Minor League career record with 3175 strikeouts. Also holds Mexican League career record with 55 shutouts. Active hurler in O.B. for 32 consecutive years.

Year	Club	League	G	IP	W	L	H	R	ER	BB	SO	ERA
1953	Shelby	Tar Heel	7	19	1	0	22	19	17	15	17	8.05
	Alexandria	Evang	3	16	1	2	17	13	8	13	9	4.50
1954	Seminole	Soon St	33	171	6	12	198	152	121	132	123	6.37
1955	Hot Springs	Cot St	9	37	3	2	45	30	23	25	13	5.59
	Seminole	Soon St	25	157	8	9	182	111	80	102	141	4.59
1956	Abilene	Big St	10	29	2	3	27	25	18	20	26	5.59
	Crowley	Evang	11	87	7	2	53	23	21	44	114	2.17
	Columbia	Sally	10	56	0	6	44	26	24	54	59	3.86
	Kansas City	American	6	9	0	0	10	8	7	11	5	7.00
1957	Little Rock	South A	33	213	14	15	162	92	81	127	235*	3.42
	Kansas City	American	4	11	0	1	13	7	7	4	3	5.73
1958	Buffalo	Int	22	94	3	8	92	62	54	48	76	5.17
	Little Rock	South A	13	97	6	5	73	47	38	63	80	3.53
1959	Portland	P C	28	138	5	13	139	73	58	41	116	10.80
	Kansas City	American	2	5	0	0	10	9	6	7	7	3.78
1960	Kansas City	American	3	10	0	2	12	6	5	10	4	4.50
	Louisville	A A	7	46	4	1	31	10	4	13	53	0.78
	Milwaukee	National	17	50	2	0	53	31	28	22	39	5.04
1961	Milwaukee	National	5	5	0	0	7	3	3	2	0	5.40
	Vancouver	P C	20	104	5	4	108	50	44	67	86	3.81
1962	Hawaii	P C	7	34	2	3	23	16	12	22	35	3.18
	Oklahoma City	A A	20	109	7	6	91	47	39	59	98	3.22
	Houston	National	17	54	2	4	62	31	27	21	36	4.50
1963	Houston	National	5	13	0	3	24	11	10	6	11	6.92
	Oklahoma City	A A	13	87	8	3	69	23	20	25	96	2.07
	Baltimore	American	16	20	0	1	25	15	12	9	13	5.40
1964	Rochester	Int	3	2	0	1	3	2	2	2	0	9.00
	Oklahoma City	P C	21	123	10	6	112	53	41	48	121	3.00
	Los Angeles	American	10	42	2	2	38	17	17	25	36	3.64
1965	California	American	41	197	9	11	149	64	56	69	141	2.56
1966	California	American	41	212	13	13	183	88	78	106	148	3.31
1967	California	American	40	250	11	19*	203	99	92	90	165	3.31
1968	California	American	39	245	13	17*	191	83	78	68	132	2.87
1969	Calif/Seattle	American	35	164	8	12	168	92	81	67	93	4.45
1970	Washington	American	24	118	8	6	124	64	58	48	67	4.42
	Pittsburgh	National	12	17	1	1	19	5	5	9	17	2.65
1971	St. Louis	National	7	9	0	1	12	6	6	7	4	6.00
	Hawaii	P C	14	66	4	4	67	33	30	21	54	4.09
1972	Hawaii	P C	28	169	14	9	160	85	75	75	119	3.99
1973	Eugene	P C	5	36	2	1	37	21	20	16	21	5.00
	Poza Rica	Mexican	4	26	1	2	19	7	4	8	16	1.38
1974	Poza Rica	Mexican	41	218	13	13	199	75	60	60	166	2.48
1975	Poza Rica	Mexican	34	230	17	9	190	82	67	71	147	2.62
1976	Poza Rica	Mexican	30	172	10	12	193	89	63	74	132	3.30
1977	Poza Rica	Mexican	15	100	6	5	77	21	14	25	62	1.26
1978	Poza Rica	Mexican	35	246	15	14	228	100	73	79	208	2.67
1979	Coat/MC Tigers	Mexican	36	227	14	17	221	93	79	82	165	3.13
1980	Aguila	Mexican	24	179	11	10	166	69	52	56	125	2.61
	Coatzacoalcos	Mex #2	7	60	3	3	37	11	9	12	39	1.35
1981	Aguila	Mexican	29	216	13	12	206	75	62	77	126	2.58
1982	Veracruz	Mexican	25	169	14	9	163	62	50	67	108	2.66
1983	Aguila	Mexican	23	186	9	12	160	56	40	61	124	1.94
1984	Salt/Monterrey	Mexican	21	122	6	9	147	79	63	50	65	4.65
	Majors		324	1431	69	93	1303	639	576	581	921	3.62
	Minors		666	4041	244	242	3761	1832	1466	1754	3175	3.27

WILLIAM EDWIN BURWELL

Born March 27, 1895 at Jarbalo, KS. Died June 11, 1973 at Ormond Beach, FL.
Threw right. Batted left. Height 5.11. Weight 175.
Won 193 games in American Association. Served there 22 years as player, coach, and manager (Louisville 1940-43 and Indianapolis 1945-46). Also served as coach, Boston AL 1944, and Pittsburgh 1947-48 and 1958-62.

Year	Club	League	G	IP	W	L	H	R	ER	BB	SO	ERA
1915	Elgin	B-State	16	107	6	7	98	47	-	30	44	
	Rockford	III		(Less than 10 games)								
1916	Topeka	Western	23	131	6	8	137	-	41	33	57	2.82
1917	Joplin	Western	6	33	1	3	45	25	17	8	12	4.72
	Clinton/MC	Cent A	15	87	9	1	-	-	14	-	-	1.45
1918				(Military Service)								
1919	Joplin	Western	29	224	12	12	251	127		67	61	
1920	St. Louis	American	33	113	6	4	133	55	46	42	30	3.66
1921	St. Louis	American	33	84	2	4	102	62	48	29	17	5.14
1922	Columbus	A A	48	304	14	23*	364*	196*	151*	66	55	4.47
1923	Indianapolis	A A	46	342*	18	21	411*	179	136	77	64	3.58
1924	Indianapolis	A A	33	237	17	10	275	122	108	52	47	4.10
1925	Indianapolis	A A	41	303	24*	9	282	116	92	40	92	2.73*
1926	Indianapolis	A A	43	294	21	14	311	128	107	63	75	3.28
1927	Indianapolis	A A	37	254	14	20	296	170	144	55	56	5.10
1928	Indianapolis	A A	30	219	13	10	230	90	77	50	47	3.16
	Pittsburgh	National	4	21	1	0	18	11	11	8	2	4.71
1929	Indianapolis	A A	38	271	15	20*	284	138	111	48	68	3.69
1930	Indianapolis	A A	40	237	17	12	271	132	106	55	56	4.03
1931	Indianapolis	A A	36	239	17	10	311	144	120	59	46	4.52
1932	Indianapolis	A A	24	141	5	8	170	92	-	39	31	
1933	Indianapolis	A A	13	102	6	5	107	42	34	23	18	3.00
1934	Ft. Wayne	Central	3	14	1	0	16	6	-	2	7	
	Indianapolis	A A	14	107	8	4	132	61	44	15	35	3.70
1935	Terre Haute	III	18	84	5	4	89	43	-	20	39	
1936	Minneapolis	A A		(Coach, did not pitch)								
1937	Minneapolis	A A	10	30	4	0	36	17	10	5	4	3.00
	Rock Island	Western	13	64	5	2	72	25	23	21	41	3.23
1938	Crookston	Northern	14	53	1	3	55	29		12	23	
	Majors		**70**	**218**	**9**	**8**	**253**	**128**	**105**	**79**	**49**	**4.33**
	Minors		**590**	**3877**	**239**	**206**	**4243**	**1929**	**1335**	**840**	**978**	**3.68**

TILLER H. (PUG) CAVET

Born December 26, 1889 at McGregor, TX. Died August 4, 1966 at San Luis Obispo, CA.
Threw left. Batted left. Height 6.03. Weight 176.

Year	Club	League	G	IP	W	L	H	R	ER	BB	SO	ERA
1908	Dallas	Texas	1	-	0	1	-	-	-	-	-	
1909	Muskogee	West A	36		13	16	-	-	-	65	232	
1910	Rock Island	III	40	316*	18	15	259	113	-	99	248*	
1911	Minneapolis	A A	34	158	14	6	182	86	-	64	59	
	Detroit	American	1	4	0	0	6	4	3	1	1	6.75
1912	Providence	Int	3	8	0	2	17	13	11	3	1	12.38
	Mobile	South A	26	190	14	7	155	66	-	56	105	
1913	Mobile	South A	38	313	23	12	221	94	-	97	128	
1914	Detroit	American	31	151	9	7	129	61	41	44	51	2.44
1915	Detroit	American	17	71	4	2	83	39	32	22	26	4.06
	San Francisco	P C	18	94	5	6	90	62	45	35	28	4.31
1916	Mobile	South A	43	299	14	23	265	124	-	87	104	
1917	Nashville	South A	37	286	21	13	268*	112	85	59	70	2.67

Year	Club	League	G	IP	W	L	H	R	ER	BB	SO	ERA
1918	Mobile	South A	19	152*	7	9	147*	-	-	32	41	
	Indianapolis	A A	7	54	4	2	41	20	12	9	24	2.00
1919	Indianapolis	A A	60*	359	28*	16	357	125	90	50	127	2.26
1920	Indianapolis	A A	50	317	14	17	348	137	109	65	82	3.09
1921	Indianapolis	A A	48	331*	23	16	363	154	121	69	93	3.29
1922	Indianapolis	A A	47	256	14	11	308	111	90	41	66	3.16
1923	Indianapolis	A A	40	180	7	15	265	126	107	44	44	5.35
1924	New Orleans	South A	41	268	19	14	286	102	79	58	77	2.65*
1925	Atlanta	South A	36	208	16	10	249	101	89	47	54	3.85
1926	Atlanta	South A	35	223	15	8	230	100	76	53	40	3.07
1927	Atlanta	South A	27	154	6	9	187	94	86	73	31	5.03
	Peoria	III	5	31	3	1	37	16	12	5	8	3.48
1928	Macon	Sally	18	88	4	6	130	71	62	16	17	6.34
	Columbus	SEastern	11	87	5	4	88	36	31	35	28	3.21
1929	Hollywood	P C	3	5	0	1	12	7	6	1	0	10.80
	Tucson	Ariz St	7	49	2	0	58	32	17	9	16	3.12
1930	Tucson	Ariz St	8	53	2	3	74	43		8	12	
Majors			49	226	13	9	218	104	76	67	78	3.03
Minors			738	4479	291	243	4637	1945	1128	1180	1735	3.39

CHESTER ROGERS COVINGTON

Born November 6, 1910 at Cairo, IL. Died June 11, 1976 at Pembroke Park, FL.
Threw left. Batted left. Height 6.02. Weight 195.
Minor League Player of the Year in 1943. Compiled one of lowest career ERAs in minor league history (2.57). On May 23, 1943, he pitched a perfect game against Springfield. On May 23, 1950, he hurled a 16-inning two-hitter over Lakeland, winning 1-0.

Year	Club	League	G	IP	W	L	H	R	ER	BB	SO	ERA
1939	Portsmouth	Piedmont	2	4	0	0	2	0	0	1	5	0.00
	Gold/Tarboro	Coast Pl	25	113	7	9	144	71	68	51	69	5.42
1940	Hollywood	Fla E C	32	266*	21*	10	254	91	62	72	212*	2.10
1941	Ft. Pierce	Fla E C	37	241	22	7	198	79	51	64	197	1.90*
	Jacksonville	Sally	12	67	2	5	73	37	31	28	40	4.16
1942	Louisville	A A	10	32	3	2	43	21	19	11	19	5.34
	Birmingham	South A	4	13	1	1	24	20	17	6	8	11.77
	Springfield	Eastern	25	131	8	8	122	60	47	50	89	3.23
1943	Louisville	A A	1	5	0	1	9	5	5	3	2	9.00
	Scranton	Eastern	37	251	21*	7	174	51	42	61	187*	1.51*
1944	Philadelphia	National	19	39	1	1	46	22	20	8	13	4.62
	Utica	Eastern	23	166	10	11	155	73	60	53	115	3.25
1945	Chattanooga	South A	9	56	4	3	57	29	24	17	32	3.86
1946	Tampa	Fla Int	45*	303*	28*	8	250*	83	56	55	260*	1.66*
1947	Tampa	Fla Int	17	129	12	2	113	39	30	26	108	2.09
	Montgomery	SEastern	28	187	13	6	180	90	67	42	126	3.22
1948	Miami	Fla Int	18	109	9	6	96	42	36	47	56	2.97
	Portsmouth	Piedmont	30	83	10	5	79	36	21	25	55	2.28
1949	Tampa	Fla Int	22	167	11	9	138	41	27	58	91	1.46*
	Palatka	Fla St	14	105	11	2	77	31	20	27	94	1.71
1950	Ft. Lauderdale	Fla Int	36	260	18	11	231	85	65	82	105	2.25
1951	Ft. Lauderdale	Fla Int	5	14	0	1	27	22	12	12	8	7.71
1952	Greensboro	Carolina	4	25	2	1	26	10	10	7	21	3.60
	Tampa/Lakeland	Fla Int	34	172	6	10	178	81	58	73	71	3.03
1953	Ft. Lauderdale	Fla Int	3	13	1	1	14	6	4	7	4	2.77
Majors			19	39	1	1	46	22	20	8	13	4.62
Minors			473	2912	220	126	2664	1103	832	878	1974	2.57

JAMES OTIS (DOC) CRANDALL

Born October 8, 1887 at Wadena, IN. Died August 17, 1951 at Bell, CA.
Threw right. Batted right. Height 5.10½. Weight 180.
A good hitter, particularly in majors where he also played in the infield. He hit .285 in 500 major league games, and .263 in 622 minor league games.

Year	Club	League	G	IP	W	L	H	R	ER	BB	SO	ERA
1906	Cedar Rapids	III	11	-	8	3	-	-	-	24	61	
1907	Cedar Rapids	III	17	-	6	7	92	44	-	19	50	
1908	New York	National	32	215	12	12	198	83	70	59	77	2.93
1909	New York	National	30	122	6	4	117	59	39	33	55	2.88
1910	New York	National	42	208	17	4	194	86	59	43	73	2.55
1911	New York	National	41	199	15	5	199	82	58	51	94	2.62
1912	New York	National	37	162	13	7	181	85	65	35	60	3.61
1913	New York	National	35	98	4	4	102	45	31	24	42	2.85
1914	St. Louis	Federal	27	196	12	9	194	94	77	52	84	3.54
1915	St. Louis	Federal	51	313	21	15	307	118	90	77	117	2.59
1916	St. Louis	American	2	1	0	0	7	9	4	1	0	36.00
	Oakland/LA	P C	33	234	11	17	234	111	77	80	70	2.96
1917	Los Angeles	P C	49	364	26	15	343	134	112	83	91	2.77
1918	Los Angeles	P C	27	222	16	9	193	69	51	35	69	2.07
	Boston	National	5	34	1	2	39	11	9	4	4	2.38
1919	Los Angeles	P C	47	355	28	10	328	122	95	43	99	2.41
1920	Los Angeles	P C	38	277	15	13	296	111	90	51	90	2.92
1921	Los Angeles	P C	40	328	24	13	311	141	114	53	106	3.13
1922	Los Angeles	P C	37	269	17	19	318	139	109	34	95	3.65
1923	Los Angeles	P C	30	258	17	12	265	105	89	28	84	3.10
1924	Los Angeles	P C	34	256	19	11	256	108	77	32	72	2.71
1925	Los Angeles	P C	39	239	20	7	250	113	92	40	89	3.46
1926	Los Angeles	P C	33	245	20	8	238	66	60	48	86	2.20
1927	Wichita	Western	9	64	4	2	64	33	-	16	20	
1928	Wichita	Western	8	33	1	0	53	30	-	5	14	
	Sacramento	P C	13	81	6	4	87	43	35	19	22	3.89
1929	Sac/LA	P C	34	202	11	13	252	125	94	58	50	4.19
	Majors		302	1548	101	62	1538	672	502	379	606	2.92
	Minors		499	3427	249	163	3580	1494	1095	668	1168	2.96

FRANCIS JOSEPH NICHOLAS DASSO

Born August 31, 1917 at Chicago, IL.
Threw right. Batted right. Height 5.11½. Weight 185.

Year	Club	League	G	IP	W	L	H	R	ER	BB	SO	ERA
1936	Canton	Mid Atl	16	105	4	7	100	60	45	78	72	3.86
1937	Rocky Mount	Piedmont	40	197	10	12	187	122	-	120	126	
1938	Hazleton	Eastern	38	243	13	14	231	125	105	124*	179*	3.89
1939	Scranton	Eastern	15	68	4	3	54	34	22	32	59	2.91
	Little Rock	South A	27	111	4	7	119	69	60	70	90	4.86
1940	San Francisco	P C	37	212	10	15	205	113	78	121*	126	3.31
1941	Hollywood	P C	43	230	15	15	232	106	100	116*	147	3.91
1942	San Diego	P C	42	284	15	18	280	110	91	127*	155	2.88
1943	San Diego	P C	27	177	12	8	170	60	54	93	154*	2.75
1944	San Diego	P C	40	298	20	19	252	112	93	131*	253*	2.81
1945	Cincinnati	National	16	96	4	5	89	50	39	53	39	3.66
1946	Cincinnati	National	2	1	0	0	2	3	3	2	1	27.00
	Hollywood	P C	26	146	12	5	127	68	53	71	88	3.27
1947	Hollywood/Sac	P C	43	194	9	18	225	110	101	108	117	4.69
1948	Sacramento	P C	6	18	0	1	24	15	14	10	15	7.00
1949	Sacramento	P C	34	214	17	10	205	95	89	93	108	3.74
1950	Sacramento	P C	31	100	4	9	107	66	61	65	48	5.49
1951	Modesto	Calif	36	244	17	13	251	135	103	111	210*	3.80
1952	Wenatchee	West Int	39	256	8	25*	288	162	126	129	169	4.43
1953	Wenatchee	West Int	3	19	1	1	25	16	12	14	13	5.68
	Majors		18	97	4	5	91	53	42	55	40	3.90
	Minors		543	3116	175	200	3082	1578	1207	1613	2129	3.72

VALLIE ENNIS (CHIEF) EAVES

Born September 6, 1911 at Allen, OK. Died April 19, 1960 at Norman, OK.
Threw right. Batted right. Height 6.02½. Weight 180.
Father of Jerry Eaves, who also pitched in O.B. They were teammates at Hobbs in 1957.

Year	Club	League	G	IP	W	L	H	R	ER	BB	SO	ERA
1935	Philadelphia	American	3	14	1	2	12	9	8	15	6	5.14
1936	Galveston	Texas	3	6	0	0	2	2	2	9	1	3.00
	Bartlesville	West A	7	19	0	2	22		22	27	18	10.42
1937	(Not in O.B.)											
1938	Texarkana	E Texas	23	174	15	4	137	79	67	66	209	3.47
	Shreveport	Texas	19	123	6	8	106	69	56	54	75	4.10
1939	Shreveport	Texas	42	263	21	10	214	105	81	119	165*	2.77
	Chicago	American	2	12	0	1	11	7	6	8	5	4.50
1940	Chicago	American	5	19	0	2	22	16	14	24	11	6.63
	Toronto	Int	29	148	5	14	155	90	78	68	90	4.74
1941	Toronto	Int	21	119	2	12	141	90	73	52	55	5.52
	Milwaukee	A A	11	58	4	6	46	21	19	28	35	2.95
	Chicago	National	12	59	3	3	56	27	23	21	24	3.51
1942	Chicago	National	2	3	0	0	4	3	3	2	0	9.00
	Milwaukee	A A	12	61	4	5	69	38	37	34	26	5.46
	Nashville	South A	19	95	6	6	111	64	53	51	45	5.02
1943	Montgomery	South A	3	20	1	1	16	3	3	10	16	1.35
	Minneapolis	A A	4	21	0	3	21	12	11	13	16	4.71
1944	Minneapolis	A A	(Broke leg. Did not play.)									
1945	San Diego	P C	52	312	21	15	290	136	104	127*	187*	3.00
1946	San Diego	P C	4	29	1	3	31	13		16	21	
	Oklahoma City	Texas	12	55	2	4	56	33	19	20	30	3.11
	Texarkana	E Texas	17	127	13	4	114	45	38	30	88	2.69
1947	Texarkana	Big St	34	261	25*	5	262	152	129	77	172	4.45
1948	Texarkana	Big St	17	109	7	5	137	73	55	39	69	4.54
	Gladewater	LoneStar	20	133	9	7	204	85	60	56	74	4.06
1949	Borg/Abilene	WTNM	32	108	7	11	142	101	78	66	56	6.50
1950	Lufkin-Leesv	Gulf Cst	43	297	26	10	288	141	104	89	217	3.15
1951	Lake Charles	Gulf Cst	1	1	0	1	6	4	4	0	0	36.00
	Greenville	Cot St	5	30	0	3						
	Texarkana	Big St	2	14	0	2	26	16	5	3	5	3.21
1952	Port Arthur	Gulf Cst	26	138	13	6	151	67	54	50	65	3.52
	Meridian	Cot St	7	57	6	1	48	22	19	16	27	3.00
1953	Brownsville	Gulf Cst	32	272	19	11	247	104	79	68	115	2.61
1954	Gal/Del Rio	Big St	33	180	12	11	221	130	108	78	90	5.40
	Roswell/Sweet	Longhorn	3	24	1	2	43	28	26	7	12	9.75
1955-56	(Not in O.B.)											
1957	Hobbs	SWestern	4	4	1	0	3	2	2	0	4	4.50
	Majors		24	107	4	8	105	62	54	70	46	4.54
	Minors		537	3258	227	172	3309	1725	1386	1273	1983	3.90

JESSE MORGAN (RUBE) ELDRIDGE

Born July 20, 1888 at Speiro, NC. Died 1968 at Glenola, NC.
Threw left. Batted right. Height 5.11. Weight 165.
One of best control pitchers in minors, allowing only 1.26 walks per 9-inning game for his career.

Year	Club	League	G	IP	W	L	H	R	ER	BB	SO	ERA
1909	Greensboro	Caro A	8	52	3	1	47	17	11	7	24	1.90
1910	Greensboro	Caro A	27	234	11	16	-	-	-	39	115	
1911	Greensboro	Caro A	38*	333	25	13	-	-	-	45	191	
1912	Greensboro	Caro A	33	288	13	19*	-	-	-	44	153	
1913	Columbus/Charl	Sally	34	265	10	16	264	111	-	43	121	
1914	Charleston	Sally	34	255	20	9	201	61	-	41	92	
1915	Charleston	Sally	25	206	14	8	167	61	-	28	79	
	Frederick	Blue Rdg	7	61	2	3	62	28	19	7	22	2.80
	Portsmouth	Virginia	5	34	4	0	31	6	5	5	15	1.32

Year Club	League	G	IP	W	L	H	R	ER	BB	SO	ERA
1916 Portsmouth	Virginia	24	161	6	10	158	78	–	15	53	
Raleigh	N Caro	22	99	4	8	93	37	33	8	40	3.00
1917 Raleigh/Durham	N Caro	15	105	6	5	104	–	–	10	37	
Columbia	Sally	7	61	5	2	63	17	–	6	19	
Hagerstown	Blue Rdg	7	43	4	1	27	7	–	6	15	
1918 (Not in O.B.)											
1919 Charlotte	Sally	38*	295*	20*	12	277*	107	–	32	80	
1920 Charlotte	Sally	12	77	5	4	90	45	34	7	27	3.97
High Point	Piedmont	22	159	13	6	122	33	24	11	41	1.36
Columbus	A A	7	45	4	2	50	31	24	16	13	4.80
1921 High Point	Piedmont	43	286	15	19*	284	112	–	22	89	
1922 High Point	Piedmont	37	297	26*	9	286	108	–	40	81	
1923 High Point	Piedmont	35	254	20	10	281	127	–	38	59	
1924 High Point	Piedmont	30	199	8	12	236	125	106	35	44	4.79
1925 Danville	Piedmont	27	215	14	9	234	108	90	40	67	3.77
1926 Greensboro	Piedmont	31	195	13	11	233	125	106	37	63	4.89
1927 High Point	Piedmont	37	226	15	12	266	124	102	38	54	4.06
1928-32 (Not in O.B.)											
1933 Greens/Wilm	Piedmont	4	35	4	0	33	12	9	7	10	2.31
1934 Greensboro	Piedmont	1	9	1	0	9	3	3	1	5	3.00
Minors		**610**	**4489**	**285**	**217**	**3618**	**1483**	**566**	**628**	**1609**	**3.62**

PAUL CLARENCE FITTERY
**Born October 10, 1887 at Lebanon, PA. Died January 28, 1974 at Cartersville, GA.
Threw left. Batted both. Height 5.08½. Weight 156.
Compiled 48-8 won-lost record after age 40.**

Year Club	League	G	IP	W	L	H	R	ER	BB	SO	ERA
1910 Harrisburg	Tri-St	5	36	2	2	44	22	15	11	12	3.75
1911 Harrisburg	Tri-St	31	217	7	19*	171	112	78	83	156	3.24
1912 Harrisburg	Tri-St	6	40	1	4	46	26	14	9	27	3.15
Anderson	Caro A	29	–	19	8	–	–	–	84	191*	
1913 Birmingham	South A	5	37	1	4	36	17	–	16	20	
Evansville	Central	34	237	13	12	221	112	–	74	187	
1914 Evansville	Central	36	281	22	7	198	88	–	103	249*	
Cincinnati	National	8	44	0	2	41	22	15	12	21	3.07
1915 Salt Lake	P C	58	312	22	17	312	159	105	111	177	3.03
1916 Salt Lake	P C	65*	448*	29	19	407*	191*	148*	158*	203*	2.97
1917 Philadelphia	National	17	56	1	1	69	36	28	27	13	4.50
1918 Los Angeles	P C	25	210	11	13*	187	77	62	86*	85	2.66
1919 Los Angeles	P C	47	301	18	20	286	132	101	121	102	3.02
1920 Sacramento	P C	46	331	19	21	326	144	113	110	153	3.07
1921 Sacramento	P C	49	361*	25	14	370	137	116	82	164*	2.89
1922 Sacramento	P C	49	334	16	26*	346	167	123	107	152	3.31
1923 Sacramento	P C	40	225	15	14	265	136	96	71	83	3.84
1924 St. Paul	A A	41	214	16	10	246	133	104	97	64	4.37
1925 Asheville	Sally	15	112	8	5	116	60	46	29	49	3.70
Atlanta	South A	14	65	2	5	100	51	42	27	14	5.82
1926-27 (Not in O.B.)											
1928 Carroltown	Ga-Ala	28	225*	21*	2	194	64	40	29	137	1.60*
1929 Carroltown	Ga-Ala	23	174	16	2	165	56	–	30	89	
1930 Anniston	Ga-Ala	17	128	11	4	154	62	50	17	45	3.52
Majors		**25**	**100**	**1**	**3**	**110**	**58**	**43**	**39**	**34**	**3.87**
Minors		**663**	**4288**	**294**	**228**	**4190**	**1946**	**1253**	**1455**	**2359**	**3.17**

GUY FLETCHER
Born August 23, 1913 at East Bend, NC.
Threw right. Batted right. Height 6.01. Weight 190.

Year	Club	League	G	IP	W	L	H	R	ER	BB	SO	ERA
1933	Winston-Salem	Piedmont	2	4	1	0	6	5	4	4	4	9.00
1934	(Not in O.B.)											
1935	Beaumont	Texas	19	106	5	8	104	74	56	42	37	4.75
	Springfield	Ill	10	60	4	3	48	26	-	14	33	
1936	San Antonio	Texas	33	118	4	8	137	75	60	51	38	4.58
	Palestine	E Texas	7	44	2	4	53	31	30	17	23	6.14
1937	Hazleton	NY-Penn	32	207	10	12	226	101	89	61	54	3.87
1938	Hazleton	Eastern	23	155	11	8	163	66	59	56	53	3.43
	Minneapolis	A A	1	5	0	0	9	5	5	0	2	9.00
	Baltimore	Int	6	19	1	2	21	-	-	15	6	
1939	Scranton/W-B	Eastern	27	130	8	10	147	93	73	61	65	5.05
1940	Wilkes-Barre	Eastern	30	158	6	9	175	98	87	65	58	4.96
1941	Springfield	Eastern	4	9	1	0	17	9	7	6	5	7.00
1942	Knoxville	Sally	7	18	0	1	16	13	13	16	6	6.50
	Richmond	Piedmont	27	196	13	9	174	76	52	68	133	2.39
1943	Richmond	Piedmont	5	39	5	0	37	18	-	11	28	
1944	Sacramento	P C	38	268	12	19	249	111	84	94	126	2.82
1945	Sacramento	P C	45	335	24	14	292	104	87	92	144	2.34
1946	Sacramento	P C	36	225	19	12	230	86	84	74	92	3.36
1947	Sac/Seattle	P C	43	284	18	13	279	118	114	87	121	3.61
1948	Seattle	P C	37	249	16	15	269	110	102	82	114	3.69
1949	Seattle	P C	42	318	23*	12	317	116	116	113	162	3.28
1950	Seattle	P C	35	217	11	12	249	115	105	83	88	4.35
1951	San Fran/SD	P C	28	170	9	12	181	76	65	62	91	3.44
1952	San Diego	P C	36	232	14	16	236	121	97	87	108	3.76
1953	Modesto	Calif	31	217	13	10	180	76	57	50	139	2.36
1954	Lewiston	W.Int	25	199	11	12	221	107	83	57	86	3.75
	Sacramento	P C	5	9	1	1	9	6	4	5	4	4.00
	Minors		**634**	**3991**	**242**	**222**	**4045**	**1836**	**1533**	**1373**	**1820**	**3.56**

WILLIAM MILTON HARRIS
Born July 23, 1900 at Wylie, TX. Died August 21, 1965 at Indian Trail, NC.
Threw right. Batted right. Height 6.01½. Weight 180.

Year	Club	League	G	IP	W	L	H	R	ER	BB	SO	ERA
1921	Charlotte	Sally	11	69	3	4	60	30	17	26	31	2.22
1922	Winston-Salem	Piedmont	40	321	24	15	276	125	-	101	124	
1923	Cincinnati	National	22	70	3	2	79	42	40	18	18	5.14
1924	Cincinnati	National	3	7	0	0	10	7	7	2	5	9.00
	Minneapolis	A A	47	219	10	13	286	151	123	92	118	5.05
1925	Minneapolis	A A	54	263	18	15	279	159	130	101	140	4.45
1926	Minneapolis	A A	9	26	0	1	34	19	-	22	6	
	Asheville	Sally	34	195	12	7	188	100	81	76	65	3.74
1927	Portsmouth	Virginia	17	120	8	5	140	66	44	36	39	3.30
	Asheville	Sally	13	82	3	5	97	63	48	28	26	5.27
1928	Asheville	Sally	37	257	25	9	247	123	96	88	116	3.36
1929	Dallas/Waco	Texas	34	219	8	20	268	163	138	96	61	5.67
1930	Waco	Texas	32	248	15	13	264	131	114	70	127	4.14
1931	Gal/Ft. Worth	Texas	33	270	11	21	227	107	86	70	132	2.87
	Pittsburgh	National	4	31	2	2	21	6	3	9	10	0.87
1932	Pittsburgh	National	34	168	10	9	178	84	68	38	63	3.64
1933	Pittsburgh	National	31	59	4	4	68	28	21	14	19	3.20

Year	Club	League	G	IP	W	L	H	R	ER	BB	SO	ERA
1934	Pittsburgh	National	11	19	0	0	28	15	14	7	8	6.63
	Albany	Int	14	108	9	2	81	34	27	33	65	2.25
1935	Buffalo	Int	38	242	19	11	244	116	101	75	137	3.76
1936	Buffalo	Int	35	201	15	10	223	135	128	52	110	5.73
1937	Buffalo	Int	36	257	16	16	262	120	100	46	140	3.50
1938	Buffalo	Int	26	147	10	6	161	97	90	45	81	5.51
	Boston	American	13	80	5	5	83	39	36	21	26	4.05
1939	Jersey City	Int	30	209	18	10	196	79	65	31	115	2.80
1940	Jersey City	Int	36	164	10	9	142	59	49	42	85	2.69
1941	Jersey City	Int	23	151	10	5	134	51	44	26	52	2.62
1942	Jersey City	Int	11	42	4	3	41	19	18	10	12	3.86
1943	Jersey City	Int	4	6	1	0	9	-	-	4	0	
1944	Erie	Pony	25	66	8	4	73	26	20	10	31	2.73
1945	Erie	Pony	-	-	0	0	-	-	-	-	-	
	Majors		**118**	**434**	**24**	**22**	**467**	**221**	**189**	**109**	**149**	**3.92**
	Minors		**639**	**3882**	**257**	**204**	**3932**	**1973**	**1519**	**1217**	**1833**	**3.87**

WILLIAM FRANKLIN HART

Born July 19, 1865 at Louisville, KY. Died September 19, 1936 at Cincinnati, OH. Height 6.00. Weight 165.

Year	Club	League	G	IP	W	L	H	R	ER	BB	SO	ERA
1885	Memphis/Chatt	Southern	42	342	13	25	312	226	52	57	196	1.37
1886	Chattanooga	Southern	27	241	11	16	251	158	56	48	122	2.09
	Philadelphia	A A	22	186	9	13	183	144	66	66	78	3.19
1887	Philadelphia	A A	3	26	1	2	28	22	13	17	4	4.50
	Lincoln	Western	33	275	26	6	356	265	124	96	115	4.06
1888	Buffalo	Int A	18	163	7	11	200	171	65	43	75	3.59
	Jackson	Tri St	5	38	1	4	42	32	16	7	23	3.79
1889	Des Moines	West A	40	360	16	19	370	269	102	152	257	2.55
1890	DM/Lincoln	West A	42	349	14	26	326	227	102	183	157	2.63
1891	Sioux City	West A	49	397	25	20	352	224	65	199	148	1.47
1892	Brooklyn	National	28	195	9	12	188	109	71	96	65	3.28
1893				(No record available)								
1894	Sioux City	Western	50	398	28	15	504	347	164	194	135	3.71
1895	Pittsburgh	National	36	262	14	17	293	186	138	135	85	4.74
1896	St. Louis	National	42	336	12	29*	411	271	191	141	65	5.12
1897	St. Louis	National	39	295	9	27	395	292	205	148	67	6.25
1898	Pittsburgh	National	16	125	5	9	141	81	67	44	19	4.82
1899	Milwaukee	Western	-	-	9	16	-	-	-	-	-	
1900	Chicago	American	34	294	18	15	260	125	-	101	86	
1901	Cleveland	American	20	158	7	11	180	109	66	57	48	3.76
1902	Peoria	Western	28	-	8	19	-	-	-	-	-	
1903	Peoria	Western	29	-	15	13	-	-	-	-	-	
1904				(Did not play; American Association umpire)								
1905	Columbus	A A	17	157	12	4	143	49	38	45	48	2.18
1906	Indianapolis	A A	5	36	2	3	42	34	23	17	11	5.75
1907	Little Rock	South A	23	-	13	10	-	-	-	-	-	
1908	Little Rock	South A	30	-	13	16	-	-	-	-	-	
1909	Little Rock	South A	26	-	15	11	-	-	-	-	-	
1910	Chattanooga	South A	10	-	5	4	-	-	-	-	-	
	Majors		**206**	**1583**	**66**	**120**	**1819**	**1214**	**817**	**704**	**431**	**4.64**
	Minors		**508**	**3050**	**251**	**253**	**3158**	**2127**	**807**	**1142**	**1373**	**2.64**

CHESTER LILLIS JOHNSON

Born August 1, 1917 at Redmond, WA. Died April 10, 1983 at Seattle, WA. Threw left. Batted left. Height 6.00. Weight 175. Brother of Earl Johnson, pitcher with Boston and Detroit in the American League, 1940-51. Chet Johnson was a colorful baseball comedian in the PCL.

Year	Club	League	G	IP	W	L	H	R	ER	BB	SO	ERA
1939	El Paso	Ariz-Tex	5	29	3	0	30	23	17	19	22	5.28

Year Club	League	G	IP	W	L	H	R	ER	BB	SO	ERA
1940 El Paso	Ariz-Tex	26	158	10	8	175	92	69	51	112	3.93
Tacoma	West Int	2	4	0	1	10	6	4	3	1	10.00
1941 Bakersfield	Calif	40	268	18	12	257	117	87	103	213	2.92
San Francisco	P C	1	1	0	0	6	4	-	1	0	
1942 Tacoma	West Int	33	270	15	15	276	147	110	122	177	3.67
1943 San Diego	P C	35	242	14	16	256	108	88	97	106	3.27
1944 San Diego	P C	29	186	12	11	167	85	73	94	138	3.53
1945 Seattle	P C	27	178	14	12	178	74	68	82	117	3.44
1946 St. Louis	American	5	18	0	0	20	12	10	13	8	5.00
Toledo	A A	36	199	12	12	224	98	81	104	151	3.66
1947 Toledo	A A	35	211	8	20	241	130	119	108	133	5.08
1948 Toledo/Indian	A A	34	215	16	12	218	112	97	134	148	4.06
1949 Indianapolis	A A	37	193	11	9	207	109	98	99	112	4.57
1950 San Francisco	P C	45	310	22	13	316	141	121	132	164	3.51
1951 SF/Oakland	P C	40	181	7	18	223	126	114	98	91	5.67
1952 Sacramento	P C	37	206	10	17	224	111	93	90	99	4.06
1953 Sacramento	P C	39	195	12	14	199	98	78	55	81	3.60
1954 Sacramento	P C	33	201	8	15	211	99	88	82	80	3.94
1955 Sacramento	P C	36	176	10	9	187	85	78	64	49	3.99
1956 Sacramento	P C	12	39	2	1	48	20	16	13	14	3.69
Majors		5	18	0	0	20	12	10	13	8	5.00
Minors		582	3462	204	215	3653	1785	1499	1551	2008	3.89

FREDERICK EDWARD (CACTUS) JOHNSON
Born March 5, 1897 at Hanley, TX. Died June 14, 1973 at Kerrville, TX.
Threw right. Batted right. Height 6.00. Weight 185.

Year Club	League	G	IP	W	L	H	R	ER	BB	SO	ERA
1920 Cisco	W Texas		164	8	9	181	107	-	58	72	
1921 Abilene/Cisco	W Texas	27	218	12	11	183	84	-	37	37	
1922 Mexia	Tex-Okla	17	130	9	7	113	46	-	26	63	
San Antonio	Texas	8	72	5	2	53	22	21	18	34	2.63
New York	National	2	18	0	2	20	8	8	1	8	4.00
1923 San Antonio	Texas	14	81	6	7	119	75	63	36	15	7.00
Waco	Texas A	5	32	1	3	35	16	-	6	22	
Toledo	A A	19	117	4	11	140	81	74	37	26	5.69
New York	National	3	17	2	0	11	8	8	7	5	4.24
1924 Toledo	A A	21	79	4	5	89	66	42	31	20	4.78
1925 Toledo	A A	57	168	7	8	197	97	88	57	47	4.71
1926 Toledo	A A	16	40	3	2	53	26	21	13	6	4.73
Nashville	South A	22	121	9	6	135	75	56	39	36	4.17
1927 Nashville	South A	44	267	17	16	307	140	128	85	70	4.31
1928 Memphis	South A	41	250	18	13	263	113	97	63	56	3.49
1929 Mobile/NO	South A	35	234	13	11	262	106	92	58	62	3.54
1930 New Orleans	South A	38	262	16	8	269	113	99	82	52	3.40
1931 New Orleans	South A	38	287	21*	12	306	125	106	71	76	3.32
1932 New Orleans	South A	37	299*	16	16	348*	159*	139*	89	62	4.18
1933 New Orleans	South A	38	288	21*	9	301	135	97	48	84	3.03*
1934 New Orleans	South A	34	252	20	5	287	123	109	45	56	2.87
1935 Ft. Worth	Texas	28	210	9	14	223	89	67	43	62	4.64
1936 Ft. Worth	Texas	38	231	8	18	278	142	119	47	68	3.57
1937 Toledo	A A	31	169	9	7	192	93	67	26	56	4.56
1938 Toledo	A A	23	140	12	4	155	75	71	27	24	5.61
St. Louis	American	17	69	3	7	91	50	43	9	2	6.43
1939 St. Louis	American	5	14	0	1	23	12	10	14	25	4.27
Toledo	A A	19	59	1	6	59	31	28	9	2	5.50
1940 Toledo	A A	9	18	1	1	20	12	11	3	7	3.75
Shreveport	Texas	6	24	0	2	27	11	10	2	0	7.50
Memphis	South A	4	6	1	0	8	5	5	16	12	9.35
1941 Vick/Mon/Mar	Cot St	9	51	1	4	97	60	53	3	0	3.00
Little Rock	South A	1	3	0	1	3	1	1	44	39	5.26
Majors		27	118	5	10	145	78	69	1104	1183	4.02
Minors		679	4272	252	218	4703	2228	1664			

141

RUDOLPH KALLIO

Born December 14, 1892 at Portland, OR. Died April 6, 1979 at Newport, OR.
Threw right. Batted right. Height 5.10. Weight 160.

Year	Club	League	G	IP	W	L	H	R	ER	BB	SO	ERA
1913	Butte	Union A	43	280	13	17	308	209	-	130	155	
1914	Saskatoon	West Can	37	251	15	12	234	108	-	107	190	
1915	Las Cr/El Paso	RG Val A	19	139	7	7	154	86	-	57	81	
1916	Great Falls	NWestern	36	275	20	14	246	114	-	108	190*	
	San Francisco	P C	8	40	3	1	38	21	19	33	25	4.28
1917	San Francisco	P C	7	48	2	3	36	16	15	30	19	2.81
	Des Moines	Western	38	306	25	9	219	-	60	107	179	1.76
1918	Detroit	American	30	181	8	14	178	91	73	76	70	3.63
1919	Detroit	American	12	22	0	0	28	15	14	8	3	5.73
1920	Portland	P C	33	211	9	10	202	96	79	62	66	3.37
1921	Port/Salt Lake	P C	49	277	9	21	351	161	138	82	107	4.48
1922	Salt Lake	P C	46	264	17	12	275	140	102	92	118	3.48
1923	Salt Lake	P C	41	234	14	9	305	145	123	96	106	4.73
1924	Salt Lake	P C	37	244	18	14	269	131	105	93	102	3.87
1925	Boston	American	7	19	1	4	28	17	16	9	2	7.58
	Salt Lake	P C	16	109	8	5	119	53	44	34	46	3.63
1926	Sacramento	P C	44	326	18	16	323	138	117	85	123	3.23
1927	Sacramento	P C	40	239	12	16	273	131	111	85	69	4.18
1928	Sacramento	P C	33	179	12	11	187	101	86	58	65	4.32
1929	Seattle	P C	44	278	15	19	349	157	125	91	85	4.05
1930	Seattle	P C	38	267	18	16	281	140	109	92	140	3.67
1931	Seattle/Port	P C	31	194	12	13	238	140	123	81	78	5.71
1932	Seattle	P C	39	285	11	20	338	147	120	105	121	3.79
1933	Portland	P C	27	211	17	7	248	99	80	58	97	3.41
1934	Portland/Sea	P C	39	207	13	18	238	128	97	93	74	4.22
1935-39 (Not in O.B.)												
1940	Portland	P C	2	3	0	0	11	9	8	5	1	24.00
	Majors		**49**	**222**	**9**	**18**	**234**	**123**	**103**	**93**	**75**	**4.18**
	Minors		**747**	**4867**	**288**	**270**	**5242**	**2470**	**1661**	**1784**	**2237**	**3.81**

WALTER FRED LEVERENZ

Born July 21, 1888 at Chicago, IL. Died March 19, 1973 at Atascadero, CA.
Threw left. Batted left. Height 5.10. Weight 175.

Year	Club	League	G	IP	W	L	H	R	ER	BB	SO	ERA
1908	Worcester	NEastern	35	-	24	8	-	-	-	-	-	-
1909	Hartford	Conn	29	-	13	12	-	-	-	91	110	
1910	Hartford	Conn	27	-	10	10	191	72	-	69	140	
1911	Hartford	Conn	10	-	5	2	46	19	-	23	43	
	Los Angeles	P C	30	194	10	12	-	89	-	58	61	
1912	Los Angeles	P C	52	334	23	13	-	135	-	111	173	
1913	St. Louis	American	30	203	6	17	159	81	58	89	87	2.57
1914	St. Louis	American	27	111	1	12	107	67	47	63	41	3.81
1915	St. Louis	American	5	9	1	2	11	9	8	8	3	8.00
	Indianapolis	A A	7	54	3	3	41	26	14	35	20	2.33
	Oakland	P C	7	27	0	6	33	23	16	16	21	5.33
1916	Rochester	Int	25	187	9	13	172	-	55	94	103	2.65
1917	Salt Lake	P C	45	349	22	18	333	140	106	147	126	2.73
1918	Salt Lake	P C	22	192	16*	5	189	60	48	74	74	2.25
1919	Salt Lake	P C	28	216	13	11	243	124	90	96	94	3.75
1920	Salt Lake	P C	41	277	18	13	302	146	115	110	111	3.74
1921	Salt Lake	P C	40	246	11	19	324	197	149	113	119	5.45
1922	Portland	P C	37	266	15	18	297	140	94	86	103	3.18
1923	Portland	P C	34	245	17	11	274	118	95	62	98	3.49
1924	Portland	P C	29	218	14	14	268	137	106	75	84	4.38
1925	Portland	P C	26	193	11	11	224	108	80	61	77	3.73
1926	Buffalo	Int	28	146	9	7	144	73	62	61	81	3.82
1927	Buffalo	Int	23	143	9	7	147	69	55	43	50	3.46
1928	Toronto	Int	22	136	7	9	149	59	54	55	68	3.57

Year	Club	League	G	IP	W	L	H	R	ER	BB	SO	ERA
1929	Toronto	Int	19	136	10	5	133	58	52	60	46	3.44
1930	Reading	Int	3	14	0	1	20	15	14	9	4	9.00
	Majors		62	323	8	31	277	157	113	160	131	3.15
	Minors		619	3573	269	228	3530	1808	1205	1549	1806	3.56

JOSE RAMON LOPEZ

Born May 26, 1937 in Central Hormiguero, Las Villas, Cuba. Died September 4, 1982 at Miami, FL. Threw right. Batted right. Height 6.00. Weight 175.

Year	Club	League	G	IP	W	L	H	R	ER	BB	SO	ERA
1958	North Platte	Neb St	14	52	4	3	40	26	19	46	46	3.29
	Cocoa	Fla St	3		1	1						
1959	Minot	Northern	32	76	9	6	88	56	48	61	54	5.68
1960	Minot	Northern	15	92	4	7	78	54	35	45	72	3.42
	Burlington	Carolina	15	64	2	4	69	52	43	35	48	6.05
	Reading	Eastern	5	10	0	1	9		6	11	9	5.40
1961	Reading	Eastern	37	194	10	16	198	103	85	87	141	3.94
1962	Charleston	Eastern	57	111	9	9	100	60	53	50	82	4.30
1963	Monterrey	Mexican	22	119	8	6	108	67	51	52	108	3.86
1964	Monterrey	Mexican	37	245	13	13	224	110	94	101	213*	3.45
1965	Monterrey	Mexican	38	242*	14	16	229	116	91	91	201*	3.38
1966	Monterrey	Mexican	47	266*	17	18*	195	86	74	96	309*	2.50
	California	American	4	7	0	1	4	5	4	4	2	5.14
1967	Seattle	P C	3	11	0	1	10	10	10	5	6	8.18
1968	Monterrey	Mexican	34	197	16	9	194	87	57	58	162	2.60
1969	Monterrey	Mexican	31	189	11	14	200	96	85	74	143	4.05
1970	Monterrey	Mexican	33	205	16	13	204	74	64	51	152	2.81
1971	Reynosa	Mexican	35	219	9	19	210	110	92	71	178	3.78
1972	Yucatan	Mexican	31	173	8	15	182	90	78	65	114	4.06
1973	Tampico	Mexican	9	45	3	2	40	24	24	21	23	4.80
1974	Aguila	Mexican	32	202	15	13	195	86	70	66	98	3.12
	Majors		4	7	0	1	4	5	4	4	2	5.14
	Minors		530	2712	169	186	2573	1307	1079	1086	2159	3.58

WILLARD EBEN (GRASSHOPPER) MAINS

Born July 7, 1868 at North Windham, ME. Died May 23, 1923, at Bridgton, ME. Threw right. Height 6.02. Weight 190.
A good hitter, he also played the outfield. He batted .377 in 1893 and .364 in 1895. First minor league hurler to win 300 games.

Year	Club	League	G	IP	W	L	H	R	ER	BB	SO	ERA
1887	Portland	New Eng	7	60	4	2	67	48	21	20	14	3.15
1888	Chicago	National	2	11	1	1	8	10	6	6	5	4.91
	Davenport	C Int-St	23	204	18	5	168	100	-	221	214	
1889	St. Paul	West A	49		38	11	419	341	159	196	193	2.88
1890	St. Paul	West A	46	384	16	26	421	305	123	117	78	3.07
1891	Cin/Milw	A A	32	214	12	14	210	146	73	74	73	1.63
1892	Portland	Pac NW	28	182	11	9	173	132	33	32	68	3.81
1893	Portland	New Eng	18	118	10	5	131	87	50	39	67	2.31
1894	Portland	New Eng	18	148	8	9	160	87	38	77	169	
1895	Lewiston	New Eng	42	353	24	14	366	206	-			
1896	Boston	National	8	43	3	2	43	35	26	31	13	5.44
	Bangor	New Eng	19	154	14	4	143	64	-	39	76	
1897	Spring/Toron	Eastern	40	293	20	13	294	152	-	85	92	
1898	Augusta	Southern	7	71	5	2	65	34	-	11	17	
	Taunton	New Eng	6	48	2	3	48	35	-	14	25	
1899	Rome	NY St	32	247	20	8	248	113	-	62	81	
1900	Rome	NY St	34	296	27	5	328	147	-	67	82	
1901	Rome	NY St	36	274	19	10	278	108	-	52	57	
1902	Syracuse	NY St	34	292	17	14	283	140	-	82	89	
1903	Syracuse	NY St	35	304	23	11	226	96	-	56	110	
1904	Syracuse	NY St	32	287	21	11	252	86	-	63	108	
1905	Syracuse	NY St	30	270	18	11	256	102	-	67	117	
1906	Syracuse	NY St	9	79	3	6	73	34	-	23	17	
	Majors		42	268	16	17	261	191	105	154	96	3.53
	Minors		545	4014	318	179	4399	2417	424	1280	1669	

HARRY DUQUESNE (DUKE) MARKELL
(Played under family name of Makowsky in 1945-47).
Born August 17, 1923 at Paris, France. Died June 14, 1984 at Ft. Lauderdale, FL.
Threw right. Batted right. Height 6.01½. Weight 209.

Year	Club	League	G	IP	W	L	H	R	ER	BB	SO	ERA
1945	Hickory	NCar St	15	82	5	2	46	28	24	40	82	2.63
1946	Manchester	New Eng	4	19	1	0	27	13	9	8	15	4.26
	Danville	Carolina	17	84	3	9	110	76	-	46	52	
	Seaford	E Shore	13	85	5	5	56	29	15	36	88	1.59
1947	Seaford	E Shore	37	249	19	9	246	117	97	110	274	3.51
1948	Schenectady	Can-Am	39	250	14	10	208	103	88	144	280*	3.17
	Utica	Eastern	1	4	0	1	4	6	6	6	2	13.50
1949	Utica	Eastern	23	114	5	7	101	62	49	72	111	3.87
	Seaford	E Shore	14	108	10	1	89	34	26	54	118*	2.17*
1950	Portsmouth	Piedmont	43	260	19	12	218	102	90	101	219*	3.12
1951	Oklahoma City	Texas	45	273*	13	19	218	114	84	129	211	2.77
	St. Louis	American	5	21	1	1	25	16	15	20	10	6.43
1952	Toronto	Int	40	191	14	8	178	91	74	74	120	3.49
1953	Syracuse	Int	52	247	11	17	258	136	106	98	155	3.86
1954	Syracuse/Roch	Int	43	169	8	12	150	72	57	91	87	3.04
1955	Rochester	Int	41	191	13	13	163	107	94	79	105	4.43
1956	Rochester	Int	53	167	10	10	145	61	57	67	101	3.07
1957	Rochester	Int	16	63	3	4	67	40	37	22	35	5.29
	Indian/Charl	A A	21	74	1	3	96	45	38	33	36	4.62
	Majors		**5**	**21**	**1**	**1**	**25**	**16**	**15**	**20**	**10**	**6.43**
	Minors		**517**	**2630**	**154**	**142**	**2380**	**1236**	**951**	**1210**	**2091**	**3.36**

CLIFFORD MONROE MARKLE
Born May 3, 1894 at Pittsburgh, PA. Died May 24, 1974 at Temple City, CA.
Threw right. Batted right. Height 5.09. Weight 163.

Year	Club	League	G	IP	W	L	H	R	ER	BB	SO	ERA
1913	Galveston	Texas	2	4	0	1	5	5	4	4	6	9.00
	Morristown	Appal	33	274	18	10	183	77	-	46	214*	
1914	Norfolk	Virginia	47*	345*	31*	9	206	90	-	133	265*	
1915	Waco	Texas	45	284	19	11	194	83	-	118	228*	
	New York	American	3	23	2	0	15	3	1	6	12	0.39
1916	New York	American	11	46	4	3	41	26	23	31	14	4.50
	Toronto	Int	11	83	4	6	93		35	46	65	3.80
1917	Toronto	Int	(Suspended)									
1918	(Military Service)											
1919	Salt Lake City	P C	44	320	18	15	351	166	135*	123	162	3.80
1920	Atlanta	South A	26	183	17	6	142	60		52	98	
1921	Atlanta	South A	37	243	19	12	228	96	86	90	140	3.19
	Cincinnati	National	10	67	2	6	75	36	28	20	23	3.76
1922	Cincinnati	National	25	76	4	5	75	41	32	33	34	3.79
1923	St. Paul	A A	54*	319	25	12	302	142	119	117	184*	3.36
1924	St. Paul	A A	40	254	19	9	233	115	85	110	128	3.01
	New York	American	7	23	0	3	29	27	23	20	7	9.00
1925	St. Paul	A A	40	262	13	18	282	169	141	111	121	4.84
1926	Atlanta	South A	40	261	14	12	287	114	96	84	72	3.31
1927	Atlanta	South A	39	239	12	19	257	133	116	86	55	4.37
1928	Omaha	Western	4	25	1	2	44	22	-	10	13	
	Dallas	Texas	4	12	1	2	-	-	-	-	-	
	Majors		**56**	**235**	**12**	**17**	**235**	**133**	**107**	**110**	**90**	**4.10**
	Minors		**466**	**3108**	**211**	**144**	**2807**	**1272**	**817**	**1130**	**1751**	**3.69**

RICHARD JAMES McCABE

Born February 21, 1896 at Mamaroneck, NY. Died April 11, 1950 at Buffalo, NY.
Threw right. Batted right. Height 5.10½. Weight 159.

Year	Club	League	G	IP	W	L	H	R	ER	BB	SO	ERA
1914	Bridgeport	East A	8	41	5	1	44	8	-	11	30	
1915	Lewiston/Lynn	New Eng	27	-	13	9	-	-	-	-	-	
1916	Lynn/Hartford	Eastern	9	49	2	3	48	-	-	19	31	
1917	Buffalo	Int	38	259	15	13	264	-	88	83	94	3.06
1918	Boston	American	3	10	0	1	13	4	3	2	3	2.70
	Jersey City	Int	10	85	2	8	80	32	27	19	42	2.86
1919	Bing/Newark	Int	35	270	15	16	268	115	79	49	108	2.63
1920	Buffalo	Int	37	232	22	6	221	94	66	40	103	2.56
1921	Buffalo	Int	41	283	17	17	310	133	76	54	114	2.42
1922	Buffalo	Int	19	104	4	7	136	68	58	19	35	5.02
	Chicago	American	3	3	1	0	4	3	2	0	1	6.00
	Salt Lake	P C	14	75	6	4	79	37	28	10	22	3.36
1923	Salt Lake	P C	57	261	14	16	321	168	144	44	112	4.97
1924	Salt Lake	P C	48	260	18	15	335	193	163	87	95	5.64
1925	Salt Lake	P C	46	266	17	15	320	161	137	56	86	4.64
1926	Hollywood	P C	35	239	15	19	249	101	87	45	62	3.28
1927	Hollywood	P C	42	196	11	16	218	109	79	35	53	3.63
1928	Hollywood	P C	37	224	16	10	260	112	98	45	59	3.94
1929	Hollywood	P C	19	62	1	4	83	46	40	13	20	5.81
	Ft. Worth	Texas	17	95	8	3	108	51	44	24	33	4.17
1930	Ft. Worth	Texas	44	245	20	7	261	117	104	34	82	3.82
1931	Ft. Worth	Texas	36	310	23	7	263	86	68	36	111	1.97
1932	Ft. W/Dallas	Texas	35	241	15	15	277	140	103	34	59	3.85
1933	Montreal	Int	1	2	0	0	4	4	4	1	0	18.00
	Birmingham	South A	6	15	0	1	26	20	15	8	4	9.00
	Majors		**6**	**13**	**1**	**1**	**17**	**7**	**5**	**2**	**4**	**3.46**
	Minors		661	3814	259	212	4175	1795	1508	766	1355	3.64

ULYSSES SIMPSON GRANT (STONEY) McGLYNN

Born May 26, 1872 at Lancaster, PA. Died August 26, 1941 at Manitowoc, WI.
Threw right. Batted right. Height 6.01. Weight 200.
Won 41 games for York and Steubenville in 1906. Pitched 14 shutouts for Milwaukee in 1909.

Year	Club	League	G	IP	W	L	H	R	ER	BB	SO	ERA
1902	Lancaster	Penn St	5	36	5	0	33	21	11	4	32	2.75
1903	(Played semipro ball)											
1904	York	Tri-St	46	385*	30*	11	316*	124	-	71	188	
1905	York	Tri-St	47	387*	28	16	359*	163*	-	84	195	
1906	York	Tri-St	52*	412*	36*	10	327*	138*	-	77	206*	
	Steubenville	POM	6	51	5	1	29	5	4	9	69	0.71
	St. Louis	National	6	48	2	2	43	16	13	15	25	2.44
1907	St. Louis	National	45	352*	14	25*	329	157	114	112*	109	2.91
1908	St. Louis	National	16	76	1	6	76	39	29	17	23	3.43
1909	Milwaukee	A A	64*	446*	27*	21*	304*	127*	-	114	183*	
1910	Milwaukee	A A	63*	392*	16	21	337*	178	-	129*	166	
1911	Milwaukee	A A	55	287	22	15	281	138	-	81	115	
1912	Milwaukee	A A		(Suspended)								
1913	Salt Lake	Union A	16	96	4	5	85	55	-	22	52	
1914				(Not in O.B.)								
1915	Las Cr/EIP	RG Val	19	129	9	9	150	88	-	47	57	2.95
	Majors		**67**	**476**	**17**	**33**	**448**	**212**	**156**	**144**	**157**	
	Minors		373	2621	182	109	2221	1037	15	638	1263	

JAMES BLAINE MIDDLETON

Born May 28, 1889 at Argos, IN. Died January 12, 1974 at Argos, IN.
Threw right. Batted right. Height 5.11½. Weight 165.

Year	Club	League	G	IP	W	L	H	R	ER	BB	SO	ERA
1910	Decatur	North A	16	108	8	7						
	Springfield	III	18		13	4	107	43		51	56	
1911	Decatur	III	34	244	13	16	222	90		82	98	
1912	Springfield	III	35	265	20	10	239	92		50	127	
1913	Springfield	III	51*	367*	21	19	351*	167*		109	194	
1914	Davenport	III	37	297	26*	10	221	71	41	76	188	1.24*
1915	Louisville	A A	44	258	12	14	265	124	89	76	99	3.10
1916	Louisville	A A	38	278	21	9	221	84	62	66	137	2.01
1917	Louisville	A A	13	45	2	4	42	16	13	15	24	2.60
	New York	National	13	36	1	1	35	18	11	8	9	2.75
1918	Kansas City	A A	(Suspended)									
1919	Toledo	A A	(Voluntarily retired)									
1920	Toledo	A A	46	332	26	14	337	135	108	66	123	2.93
1921	Detroit	American	38	122	6	11	149	83	68	44	31	5.02
1922	Portland	P C	46	277	15	16	319	158	124	103	72	4.03
1923	Portland	P C	47	230	12	10	259	120	90	54	74	3.52
1924	Ft. Worth	Texas	40	154	14	7	143	76	57	44	63	3.33
1925	Minneapolis	A A	49	193	12	7	211	110	85	80	73	3.96
1926	Minneapolis	A A	53*	273	20	15	315	163	127	100	87	4.19
1927	Minneapolis	A A	41	207	12	7	238	123	100	73	64	4.35
1928	Seattle	P C	10	44	2	4	51	27	19	15	4	3.89
1929	Minneapolis	A A	41	197	10	9	249	143	112	77	38	5.12
	Majors		**51**	**158**	**7**	**12**	**184**	**101**	**79**	**52**	**40**	**4.50**
	Minors		**659**	**3769**	**259**	**182**	**3790**	**1742**	**1027**	**1137**	**1521**	**3.32**

AURELIO FAUTINO MONTEAGUDO

Born November 19, 1943 at Caibarien, Las Villas, Cuba.
Threw right. Batted right. Height 5.11. Weight 185.

Year	Club	League	G	IP	W	L	H	R	ER	BB	SO	ERA
1961	Albuquerque	Soph	23	154	11	4	160	86	69	45	160	4.03
1962	Binghamton	Eastern	11	56	1	3	62	43	33	25	54	5.30
	Albuquerque	Texas	6	18	0	1	30	21	17	12	19	8.50
	Lewiston	NWestern	11	66	5	2	72	33	26	31	62	3.55
1963	Portland	P C	31	173	10	13	157	83	73	49	205	3.80
	Kansas City	American	4	7	0	0	4	2	2	3	3	2.57
1964	Kansas City	American	11	31	0	4	40	32	31	10	14	9.00
	Dallas	P C	19	116	10	5	101	41	36	48	108	2.79
1965	Vancouver	P C	27	171	11	10	150	69	63	78	128	3.32
	Kansas City	American	4	7	0	0	5	4	3	4	5	3.86
1966	Kansas City	American	6	13	0	0	12	4	4	7	3	2.77
	Houston	National	10	15	0	0	14	8	8	11	7	4.80
	Oklahoma City	P C	8	59	4	2	50	20	15	22	59	2.29
1967	Indianapolis	P C	24	137	4	8	139	61	54	34	88	3.55
	Chicago	American	1	1	0	1	4	3	3	2	0	27.00
1968	Asheville	Southern	17	94	8	2	77	31	29	19	89	2.78
	Hawaii/Indian	P C	17	59	3	5	58	23	20	9	48	3.05
1969	Indian/Tulsa	A A	37	99	5	4	124	69	52	29	54	4.73
1970	Omaha	A A	14	28	3	1	22	9	8	8	28	2.57
	Kansas City	American	21	27	1	1	20	11	9	9	18	3.00
1971	Omaha	A A	46	83	12	4	80	26	24	37	66	2.60
1972	Hawaii	P C	58	95	8	6	75	29	25	37	83	2.37
1973	Haw/Salt Lake	P C	39	70	6	3	89	43	32	37	58	4.11
	California	American	15	30	2	1	23	18	14	16	8	4.20
1974	Pueblo	Mexican	20	120	12	0	109	49	46	31	103	3.45
1975	Puebla	Mexican	27	185	15	9	171	73	62	43	115	3.02
1976	Puebla	Mexican	31	193	15	8	186	70	55	37	133	2.56

Year Club	League	G	IP	W	L	H	R	ER	BB	SO	ERA
1977 Coahuila	Mexican	37	264	16	18	235	106	81	77	168	2.76
1978 Coahuila	Mexican	42	275	17	12	236	89	69	58	222*	2.26
1979 Coahuila	Mexican	38	276	21	12	280	95	75	73	159	2.45
1980 Monclova/Tol	Mexican	23	151	5	12	196	100	80	51	75	4.77
1981 Nu Lar/Aguila	Mexican	22	139	5	14	125	58	54	45	50	3.50
Majors		72	131	3	7	122	82	74	62	58	5.08
Minors		628	3081	207	158	2984	1327	1098	935	2334	3.21

OTHO JAMES NITCHOLAS
Born September 13, 1908 at McKinney, TX.
Threw right. Batted right. Height 6.00. Weight 190.

Year Club	League	G	IP	W	L	H	R	ER	BB	SO	ERA
1930 Ft. Wayne	Central	1	-	0	0	-	-	-	-	-	-
1931 (Not in O.B.)											
1932 Baton Rouge	Cot St	18	127	12	2	131	52	42	21	65	2.98
Tyler	Texas	14	79	3	3	86	39	33	16	46	3.76
1933 Oklahoma City	Texas	36	221	13	15	237	83	68	55	90	2.77
1934 Sacramento	P C	34	223	11	13	284	127	110	50	68	4.44
1935 Missions	P C	42	243	12	17	332	184	137	85	91	5.07
1936 Missions	P C	36	248	16	14	282	106	100	36	65	3.63
1937 Missions	P C	39	207	11	17	266	119	102	40	53	4.43
1938 Hollywood	P C	39	217	14	13	257	119	100	46	59	4.15
1939 Hollywood	P C	(Did not play)									
1940 Ft. Worth/OC	Texas	35	193	13	10	214	91	68	18	59	3.17
1941 Dallas	Texas	41	213	12	12	263	121	94	33	60	3.97
1942 Dallas	Texas	32	217	12	12	236	98	69	40	65	2.86
1943 St. Paul	A A	36	226	13	14	218	86	75	47	59	2.99
1944 St. Paul	A A	29	218	14	11	231	80	70	40	75	2.89
1945 Brooklyn	National	7	19	1	0	19	14	11	1	4	5.21
St. Paul	A A	22	143	11	6	139	49	46	36	49	2.90
1946 St. Paul	A A	32	181	12	10	190	86	72	38	77	3.58
1947 St. Paul	A A	19	87	6	5	111	62	51	20	29	5.28
1948 Tyler	LoneStar	26	219	18	7	174	58	48	27	120	1.97*
1949 Dallas	Texas	21	61	3	3	73	42	22	19	20	3.25
Gladewater	E Texas	15	132	11	1	129	59	49	15	55	3.34
1950 Tyler	E Texas	11	91	6	5	106	51	46	10	22	4.55
1951 Alexandria	Evang	28	218	17	5	246	100	83	25	94	3.43
1952 Abilene	WTNM	19	158	14	5	177	87	66	24	65	3.76
1953 Brownsville	Gulf Cst	(Record not available)									
Majors		7	19	1	0	19	14	11	1	4	5.21
Minors		625	3922	254	200	4382	1899	1551	741	1386	3.56

ALFREDO ORTIZ (UZCANGA)
Born January 12, 1944 at Medellin de Bravo, Veracruz, Mexico.
Throws left. Bats right. Height 5.08. Weight 150.

Year Club	League	G	IP	W	L	H	R	ER	BB	SO	ERA
1960 Leon	Mex Cent	23	118	8	8	101	52	42	68	36	3.20
1961 Leon	Mex Cent	31	198	8	13	205	102	82	96	100	3.73
1962 Fresnillo	Mex Cent	42	235*	19*	10	264	141	131	102	145*	5.02
1963 Mex City Reds	Mexican	13	28	2	1	33	14	12	9	21	3.86
1964 Mex City Reds	Mexican	31	187	15	6	194	91	77	61	108	3.71
1965 Mex City Reds	Mexican	26	123	5	10	161	79	70	40	52	5.12
1966 Mex City Reds	Mexican	33	207	17	12	202	84	69	46	134	3.00
1967 Mex City Reds	Mexican	31	194	16	9	206	75	54	33	128	2.51
1968 Mex City Reds	Mexican	31	175	11	12	203	87	65	41	87	3.34
1969 Mex City Reds	Mexican	33	255	23*	9	257	76	64	44	129	2.26
1970 Mex City Reds	Mexican	21	115	10	3	138	56	46	22	69	3.60
1971 Mex City Reds	Mexican	33	228	18	12	227	79	69	36	90	2.72
1972 Mex City Reds	Mexican	32	213	15	13	224	95	88	37	113	3.72

Year	Club	League	G	IP	W	L	H	R	ER	BB	SO	ERA
1973	Mex City Reds	Mexican	28	175	12	8	202	84	58	37	103	2.98
1974	Mex City Reds	Mexican	30	218	17	9	224	76	64	44	104	2.64
1975	Mex City Reds	Mexican	30	211	15	11	240	98	80	53	94	3.41
1976	Mex City Reds	Mexican	23	141	6	11	168	73	55	33	60	3.51
1977	Mex City Reds	Mexican	20	135	9	7	147	56	37	27	72	2.47
1978	Tabasco	Mexican	22	130	2	13	150	56	40	39	55	2.77
1979	Nuevo Laredo	Mexican	28	221	16	10	209	75	60	39	105	2.44
1980	Tabasco	Mexican	19	121	3	10	148	67	47	29	43	3.50
1981	Tabasco	Mexican	28	182	12	11	180	56	42	41	65	2.08
1982	Tabasco	Mexican	27	178	9	11	186	74	56	37	49	2.83
1983	Mex City Reds	Mexican	26	147	9	7	178	65	53	29	48	3.24
1984	MC Reds/Vera	Mexican	25	139	10	7	176	72	57	20	54	3.69
	Minors		**686**	**4274**	**287**	**233**	**4623**	**1883**	**1518**	**1063**	**2064**	**3.20**

JOSE PENA (GUTIERREZ)
Born December 3, 1942 at Ciudad Juarez, Chihuahua, Mexico.
Throws right. Bats right. Height 6.02. Weight 190.

Year	Club	League	G	IP	W	L	H	R	ER	BB	SO	ERA
1961	Aguascalientes	Mex Cen	22	112	4	6	81	49	37	75	65	2.97
1962	MC Tigers	Mexican	38	124	4	5	116	79	63	55	52	4.57
1963	MC Tigers	Mexican	40	123	6	10	. 130	85	76	76	84	5.56
1964	MC Tigers	Mexican	38	175	10	11	177	92	76	104*	127	3.91
1965	MC Tigers	Mexican	44	226	16	13	191	98	83	101*	137	3.31
1966	MC Tigers	Mexican	37	235	19	7	209	88	73	96	161	2.80
1967	Buffalo	Int	43	86	4	3	88	34	29	34	63	3.03
1968	Indianapolis	P C	42	194	11	14	163	86	68	88	178	3.15
1969	Indianapolis	A A	9	32	0	2	38	22	16	11	26	4.50
	Reynosa	Mexican	22	93	11	5	61	23	14	28	68	1.35
	Cincinnati	National	6	5	1	1	10	10	10	5	3	18.00
1970	Los Angeles	National	29	57	4	3	51	32	28	29	31	4.42
	Spokane	P C	10	25	2	2	24	12	9	9	20	3.24
1971	Spokane	P C	9	21	1	2	32	15	13	11	10	5.57
	Los Angeles	National	21	43	2	0	32	18	17	18	44	3.56
1972	Los Angeles	National	5	7	0	0	13	8	7	6	4	9.00
	Albuquerque	P C	46	116	10	9	105	65	55	53	96	4.27
1973	Puebla	Mexican	47	201	11	15	178	81	61	67	195*	2.73
1974	Puebla/Coah	Mexican	30	138	9	12	134	74	64	68	81	4.17
1975	Villahermosa	Mexican	42	287*	21*	12	216	76	59	102	199*	1.85
1976	Cordoba	Mexican	34	222	18	7	186	73	56	77	135	2.27
1977	Cordoba	Mexican	41	241	21	10	227	89	57	80	150	2.13
1978	Cordoba	Mexican	32	247	22*	9	210	78	60	86	164	2.19
1979	Cordoba	Mexican	9	29	0	2	37	22	22	21	4	6.83
1980	Reynosa/Coatz	Mexican	20	115	6	10	133	74	61	47	58	4.77
	Coatzacoalcos	Mex #2	7	51	4	3	46	16	11	16	23	1.94
1981	Yucatan	Mexican	28	159	12	10	167	76	64	66	75	3.62
1982	Ciudad Juarez	Mexican	22	118	10	1	134	57	42	49	54	3.20
1983	MC Tigers	Mexican	26	155	12	8	161	66	57	48	52	3.31
1984	Leon	Mexican	8	37	2	4	45	27	24	11	13	5.84
	Majors		**61**	**112**	**7**	**4**	**106**	**68**	**62**	**58**	**82**	**4.98**
	Minors		**746**	**3562**	**246**	**192**	**3289**	**1557**	**1250**	**1479**	**2290**	**3.16**

LOUIS AMERICO POLLI

Born July 9, 1901 at Barre, VT.
Threw right. Batted right. Height 5.10½. Weight 165.

Year Club	League	G	IP	W	L	H	R	ER	BB	SO	ERA
1922 Montreal	E Canada	5	-	3	1	-	-	-	-	-	
1923-25 (Not in O.B.)											
1926 Nashua	New Eng	5	-	1	2	-	-	-	-	109*	2.25
1927 Harrisburg	NY-Penn	35	228	18*	10	187	79	57	65	70	3.53
1928 St. Paul	A A	40	232	13	15	263	110	91	67	85	3.75
1929 St. Paul	A A	41	288*	22*	9	310	154	120	88	47	5.82
1930 Louisville	A A	37	167	8	13	221	136	108	80	102	4.90
1931 Milwaukee	A A	42	281	21	15	337*	185*	153*	80	59	
1932 Milwaukee	A A	27	168	14	6	181	96	-	52	59	
St. Louis	American	5	7	0	0	13	8	4	3	5	5.14
1933 Milwaukee	A A	41	248	15	14	303	151	136	72	87	4.94
1934 Milwaukee	A A	34	241	16	15	279	143	124	87	108	4.63
1935 Milwaukee	A A	32	209	13	12	219	130	109	62	93	4.69
1936 Montreal	Int	33	211	12	14	225	109	93	64	74	3.97
1937 Montreal	Int	27	157	11	8	170	85	76	69	54	4.36
1938 Montreal	Int	7	28	2	1	42	31	-	17	15	
Chattanooga	South A	29	182	9	11	201	99	77	55	72	3.81
1939 Chattanooga	South A	35	204	17	11	223	109	91	67	69	4.01
1940 Chattanooga	South A	39	270*	16	17	300*	121	90	53	104	3.00*
1941 Chattanooga	South A	35	199	10	16	259	137	115	65	71	5.20
1942 Knoxville	South A	6	24	1	3	41	34	31	17	10	11.63
Jacksonville	Sally	32	210	16	10	221	81	58	44	92	2.49
1943 Jersey City	Int	35	220	14	12	183	62	45	59	68	1.84*
1944 Jersey City	Int	13	50	4	3	52	20	16	12	20	2.88
New York	National	19	36	0	2	42	25	18	20	6	4.50
1945 Jersey City	Int	25	101	7	8	116	63	53	50	37	4.72
Majors		**24**	**43**	**0**	**2**	**55**	**33**	**22**	**23**	**11**	**4.60**
Minors		**655**	**3918**	**263**	**226**	**4333**	**2135**	**1643**	**1225**	**1446**	**3.97**

HERSCHEL CLINTON (BILL) PROUGH

Born November 25, 1888 at Martle, IN. Died November 29, 1936 at Richmond, IN.
Threw right. Batted right. Height 6.03. Weight 185.

Year Club	League	G	IP	W	L	H	R	ER	BB	SO	ERA
1908 Keokuk	Cent A	10	-	-	-	-	-	-	-	-	
1909 Keokuk	Cent A	38	292	20	11	178	71	-	54	198	
1910 Keokuk	Cent A	29	268	14	13	181	58	-	50	184	
1911 Birmingham	South A	39	270	21	13	215	90	-	84	147	
1912 Cincinnati	National	1	3	0	0	7	5	2	1	1	6.00
Birmingham	South A	28	182	14	10	140	72	-	43	101	
1913 Birmingham	South A	34	274	23	6	227	69	-	51	117	
1914 Oakland	P C	45	328	14	23	342	152	104	75	175	2.85
1915 Oakland	P C	52	357	15	25	371	164	122	72	194	3.08
1916 Oakland	P C	48	389	18	23	373	141	116	57	142	2.68
1917 Oakland	P C	50	374	22	22	391	139	98	54	108	2.36
1918 Oakland	P C	25	226*	13	12	218	65	49	33	68	1.95
1919 Sacramento	P C	32	185	12	13	182	85	52	22	69	2.53
1920 Sacramento	P C	48	348	20	20	361	143	124	40	105	3.21
1921 Sacramento	P C	44	320	20	12	326	122	107	61	118	3.01
1922 Sacramento	P C	29	243	11	14	268	110	93	42	77	3.44
1923 Sacramento	P C	39	285	20	11	326	123	114	38	81	3.60
1924 Sacramento	P C	35	242	10	17	294	150	133	50	75	4.95
1925 Shreveport	Texas	17	94	2	7	118	53	49	28	44	4.69
Majors		**1**	**3**	**0**	**0**	**7**	**5**	**2**	**1**	**1**	**6.00**
Minors		**642**	**4677**	**269**	**252**	**4511**	**1807**	**1161**	**854**	**2003**	**3.08**

WOODROW EARL RICH
Born March 9, 1917 at Morganton, NC. Died April 18, 1983 at Morganton, NC.
Threw right. Batted left. Height 6.02. Weight 185.

Year	Club	League	G	IP	W	L	H	R	ER	BB	SO	ERA
1937	Clarksdale	Cot St	32	240	12	15	255	127	118	53	159	4.43
1938	Little Rock	South A	33	229	19	10	194	81	63	100	122	2.48
1939	Louisville	A A	8	30	2	2	40	19	17	17	17	5.10
	Boston	American	21	77	4	3	78	46	42	35	24	4.91
1940	Boston	American	3	12	1	0	9	3	1	1	8	0.75
	Louisville	A A	12	26	1	2	33	21	19	14	11	6.58
	Scranton	Eastern	13	90	6	4	66	32	26	37	41	2.60
1941	Boston	American	2	4	0	0	8	7	7	2	4	15.75
	Louisville	A A	9	27	2	2	35	17	10	15	28	3.33
	San Diego	P C	23	139	9	9	137	66	54	60	66	3.50
1942	Indianapolis	A A	40	201	10	10	198	101	79	102	114	3.54
1943	Indianapolis	A A	26	138	6	10	142	83	61	74	83	3.98
1944	Boston	National	7	25	1	1	32	17	16	12	6	5.76
	Indianapolis	A A	26	168	4	14	204	105	84	94	103	4.50
1945	Indianapolis	A A	18	73	6	4	82	42	37	38	47	4.56
1946	Indianapolis	A A	2	3	0	0	5	1	1	0	1	3.00
1947	Anniston	SEastern	35	236	19	10	233	123	87	81	197*	3.32
1948	Anniston	SEastern	41	247	17	10	183	91	68	101	196*	2.48*
	Shreveport	Texas	3	3	0	1	9	6	6	2	0	18.00
1949	Anniston	SEastern	25	176	10	11	129	73	55	95	155	2.81
1950	Greensboro	Carolina	34	209	16	9	182	79	56	69	140	2.41*
1951	St. Petersberg	Fla Int	36	269	25*	6	223	85	70	87	173	2.34
1952	Memphis	South A	31	205	13	10	194	111	78	83	104	3.42
1953	Memphis	South A	3	8	1	0	10	7	6	1	3	6.75
	Ruth County	Tar Heel	18	136	11	2	119	47	40	48	126	2.65
1954	Ruth County	Tar Heel	5	34	3	2	23	9	7	4	38	1.85
	HP-Thomas	Carolina	20	143	13	6	137	76	57	50	94	3.59
1955	HP-Thomas	Carolina	26	212	19	4	189	77	67	88	129	2.84
1956	HP-Thomas	Carolina	33	258	17	12	207	108	84	95	165	2.93
1957	Savannah	Sally	29	40	2	0	26	14	11	15	22	2.48
1958	Charlotte	Sally	16	24	1	5	24	12	11	12	12	4.13
	Boise	Pioneer	30	65	6	4	59	29	24	36	59	3.32
	Majors		**33**	**118**	**6**	**4**	**127**	**73**	**66**	**50**	**42**	**5.03**
	Minors		**627**	**3629**	**250**	**174**	**3338**	**1642**	**1296**	**1471**	**2405**	**3.21**

JOHN THEODORE SALVESON
Born January 5, 1914 at Fullerton, CA. Died December 28, 1974 at Norwalk, CA.
Threw right. Batted right. Height 6.00½. Weight 180.

Year	Club	League	G	IP	W	L	H	R	ER	BB	SO	ERA
1932	Winston-Salem	Piedmont	26	156	7	12	196	97	80	35	58	4.62
1933	Dallas	Texas	7	50	2	3	30	9	8	17	19	1.44
	New York	National	8	31	0	2	30	17	13	14	8	3.77
1934	New York	National	12	38	3	1	43	16	15	13	18	3.55
	Montreal	Int	19	121	11	4	126	58	51	34	24	3.79
1935	Pittsburgh	National	5	7	0	1	11	12	7	5	2	9.00
	Chicago	American	20	67	1	2	79	39	36	23	22	4.84
1936	Los Angeles	P C	35	251	21	7	249	85	77	70	127	2.76
1937	Los Angeles	P C	16	73	5	5	76	32	25	10	24	3.08
1938	Los Angeles	P C	32	205	11	10	237	100	94	44	91	4.13
1939	Oakland	P C	46	233	12	15	290	116	99	42	75	3.82
1940	Oakland	P C	38	286	19	13	278	100	73	43	71	2.30
1941	Oakland	P C	42	288	15	20	321	142	120	63	100	3.75
1942	Oakland	P C	39	310	24	12	297	106	89	60	93	2.58
1943	Cleveland	American	23	86	5	3	87	36	32	26	24	3.35
1944	(Not in O.B.)											
1945	Cleveland	American	19	44	0	0	52	23	18	6	11	3.68

Year	Club	League	G	IP	W	L	H	R	ER	BB	SO	ERA
1946	Portland	P C	35	261	15	14	248	91	72	41	119	2.48
1947	Portland	P C	37	287	17	14	334	141	116	52	96	3.64
1948	Sac/Oakland	P C	41	245	13	18	300	155	129	55	95	4.74
1949	Hollywood	P C	42	148	11	7	150	68	49	35	59	2.98
1950	Hollywood	P C	30	165	15	4	155	56	52	37	62	2.84
1951	Hollywood	P C	36	219	15	10	224	86	77	55	74	3.16
1952	San Diego	P C	26	168	10	10	196	74	71	34	57	3.80
1953	San Diego/Oak	P C	12	60	1	7	75	42	39	22	16	5.85
	Majors		**87**	**273**	**9**	**9**	**302**	**143**	**121**	**87**	**85**	**3.99**
	Minors		**559**	**3526**	**224**	**185**	**3782**	**1558**	**1321**	**749**	**1260**	**3.37**

CHARLES M. (BUD) SHANEY
Born January 9, 1900 at New Albany, IN.
Threw right. Batted right. Height 5.11½. Weight 177.

Year	Club	League	G	IP	W	L	H	R	ER	BB	SO	ERA
1922	Independence	SWestern	32	233	19	8	195	90	67	61	152	2.59
1923	Independence	SWestern	42	312	18	18	317	150	-	60	168	
	Milwaukee	A A	8	47	4	2	63	26	22	11	9	4.21
1924	Milwaukee	A A	24	85	2	6	113	60	52	26	25	5.51
	Mobile	South A	12	65	2	6	100	52	41	17	23	5.68
1925	Mobile	South A	4	4	0	1	16	13		5	0	
	Asheville	Sally	38	233	13	10	271	126	100	54	86	3.86
1926	Asheville	Sally	40	262	19	14	315	156	126	56	90	4.33
1927	Asheville	Sally	41	273	15	14	271	110	83	46	95	2.74
1928	Asheville	Sally	42	257	21	11	270	104	74	55	93	2.59
1929	Asheville	Sally	37	255	17	12	295	128	104	62	92	3.67
1930	Williamsport	NY-Penn	35	224	14	14	219	92	84	49	72	3.38
1931	Charlotte	Piedmont	39*	280*	24*	10	258	126		67	161	
1932	Charlotte	Piedmont	37	235	14	13	288	146	125	52	129	4.79
1933	W-B/Scranton	NY-Penn	38	199	7	15	238	112	99	47	60	4.48
1934	Columbia	Piedmont	12	44	3	3	59	44		17	16	
1935	Portsmouth	Piedmont	19	98	6	5	127	70	59	35	28	5.42
1936	(Played independent ball)											
1937	Trenton	NY-Penn	17	100	5	5	105	49	35	15	36	3.15
	Sydney	Cp Bret	5	31	3	1	19	4	1	5	23	0.29
1938	Spartanburg	Sally	15	84	3	6	100	54	40	8	42	4.29
1939	(Not in O.B.)											
1940	Hickory	Tarheel	33	194	12	10	202	98	80	25	111	3.71
1941	Asheville	Piedmont	1	8	0	1	9	4	4	0	0	4.50
1942	Hickory	N Car St	30	179	8	9	199	94	58	16	88	2.92
1943-52	(Not in O.B.)											
1953	Asheville	Tri-St	1	5	0	0	9	3	3	0	2	5.40
1954	Asheville	Tri-St	1	5	1	0	4	0	0	1	0	0.00
1955	Asheville	Tri-St	1	2	0	1	7	7	7	2	2	31.50
	Minors		**604**	**3714**	**230**	**195**	**4069**	**1918**	**1263**	**792**	**1603**	**3.70**

WILLIAM HENRY (HARRY) SMYTHE
Born October 24, 1904 at Augusta, GA. Died August 28, 1980 at Augusta, GA.
Threw left. Batted left. Height 5.10. Weight 179.

Year	Club	League	G	IP	W	L	H	R	ER	BB	SO	ERA
1922	Lakeland	Fla St	35	241	16	14	214	92		59	108	
1923	Augusta	Sally	37	247	12	13	265	112	84	80	99	3.06
1924	Aug/Macon	Sally	39	273	12	15	300	159	114	84	101	3.76
1925	Augusta	Sally	39	261	16	9	266	111	82	65	88	2.83
1926	Asheville	Sally	42	292	19	12	325	140	110	65	100	3.39
1927	Winston-Salem	Piedmont	10	89	7	3	85	35	20	26	37	2.02
	Asheville	Sally	26	175	10	10	217	92	73	53	62	3.75

Year Club	League	G	IP	W	L	H	R	ER	BB	SO	ERA
1928 Asheville	Sally	37	228	16	11	260	94	74	44	72	2.92
1929 Asheville	Sally	22	166	15	5	177	83	68	41	64	3.69
Philadelphia	National	19	69	4	6	94	47	40	15	12	5.22
1930 Philadelphia	National	25	50	0	3	84	60	43	31	9	7.74
Baltimore	Int	6	26	2	1	29	14	13	5	9	4.50
1931 Baltimore	Int	52	155	12	10	178	74	62	58	39	3.60
1932 Baltimore	Int	53	214	17	12	251	136	116	72	70	4.88
1933 Baltimore	Int	54	213	21	8	227	108	94	60	92	3.97
1934 New York	American	8	15	0	2	24	13	13	8	7	7.80
Brooklyn	National	8	21	1	1	30	24	14	8	5	6.00
Montreal	Int	26	115	8	6	121	63	58	49	38	4.54
1935 Montreal	Int	45	259	22	11	280	118	95	54	109	3.30
1936 Montreal	Int	43	189	12	13	217	86	75	52	79	3.57
1937 Montreal	Int	35	229	16	13	248	108	88	53	81	3.46
1938 Montreal	Int	40	215	16	12	247	98	78	61	86	3.27
1939 Minneapolis	A A	41	208	12	12	261	126	113	58	102	4.89
1940 Minneapolis	A A	38	173	13	9	196	88	73	43	76	3.80
1941 Minneapolis	A A	2	4	0	1	7	5	4	2	0	9.00
Knoxville	South A	27	181	14	9	207	108	91	31	58	4.52
1942 Charlotte	Piedmont	21	151	10	9	133	50	35	28	53	2.09
1943-45 (Not in O.B.)											
1946 Augusta	Sally	14	51	3	3	63	25	22	11	25	3.88
Majors		**60**	**155**	**5**	**12**	**232**	**144**	**110**	**62**	**33**	**6.39**
Minors		**784**	**4355**	**301**	**221**	**4774**	**2125**	**1642**	**1154**	**1648**	**3.59**

BYRON FRANKLIN SPEECE
Born January 6, 1897 at West Baden, IN. Died September 29, 1974 at Elgin, OR.
Threw right. Batted right. Height 5.11. Weight 170.

Year Club	League	G	IP	W	L	H	R	ER	BB	SO	ERA
1922 Norfolk	Neb St	28	201	14	9	192	80		31	145	
1923 Omaha	Western	49	314	26	14	344	177		82	129	
1924 Washington	American	21	54	2	1	60	30	16	27	15	2.67
1925 Cleveland	American	28	90	3	5	106	44	43	28	26	4.30
1926 Cleveland	American	2	3	0	0	1	1	0	2	1	0.00
Indianapolis	A A	36	204	17	10	234	103	92	47	93	4.06
1927 Indian/Toledo	A A	41	174	12	10	185	96	80	60	59	4.14
1928 Indianapolis	A A	28	83	1	4	109	59	48	26	37	5.20
1929 Indianapolis	A A	36	109	9	2	109	55	46	35	44	3.80
1930 Philadelphia	National	11	20	0	0	41	30	29	4	9	13.05
Newark	Int	19	48	3	4	36	19	18	13	29	3.38
1931 Newark	Int	50	95	12	6	93	36	30	37	34	2.84
1932 Newark	Int	13	19	1	1	28	17	17	10	4	8.05
Nashville	South A	19	96	9	6	101	47	41	35	48	3.84
1933 Nashville	South A	38	216	17	10	222	100	88	64	95	3.67
1934 Nashville	South A	38	247	22	8	242	98	82	61	112	2.99
1935 Nashville	South A	38	207	15	12	219	89	76	41	105	3.30
1936 Nashville	South A	42	240	22*	9	244	126	103	57	118	3.86
1937 Nashville	South A	40	144	10	15	184	103	92	42	46	5.75
1938 Nashville	South A	2	9	0	0	10	4	4	0	1	4.00
1939 (Played semipro ball)											
1940 Portland	P C	36	173	7	9	182	101	76	43	62	3.95
1941 Portland	P C	26	148	9	12	163	72	58	30	42	3.53
1942 Portland	P C	19	124	9	6	127	65	54	36	48	3.92
1943 Seattle	P C	27	175	13	9	167	66	55	41	54	2.83
1944 Seattle	P C	31	180	10	13	181	68	56	30	67	2.80
1945 Seattle	P C	17	54	3	3	61	31	26	17	17	4.33
Majors		**62**	**167**	**5**	**6**	**208**	**105**	**88**	**61**	**51**	**4.74**
Minors		**673**	**3260**	**241**	**172**	**3433**	**1612**	**1142**	**838**	**1389**	**3.74**

GEORGE W. STOVEY

No demographic data available on Stovey, a top black hurler of the 19th century, other than that he threw lefthanded. In 1889 he pitched for both the Cuban Giants, home-based at Trenton, and the NY Gorhams, home-based in Philadelphia. In 1891 he played for the Cuban Giants at Ansonia. These were all-black teams playing in O.B. in those two seasons. He also played some in the outfield, batting .256 in a total of 122 games.

Year	Club	League	G	IP	W	L	H	R	ER	BB	SO	ERA
1886	Jersey City	Eastern	31	270	16	15	189	113	34	43	203	1.13
1887	Newark	Int	48	424	34	14	419	244	116	119	107	2.46
1888	Worcester	New Eng	11	98	6	5	112	72	25	26	43	2.30
1889	Tren/Phil	Mid St	7	45	1	4	58	40	22	28	20	4.40
1890	Troy	NY St	2	18	1	1	12	5	4	5	6	2.00
1891	Ansonia	Conn St	3	27	2	1	24	21	12	7	8	4.00
	Minors		102	882	60	40	814	495	213	228	387	2.17

MONTY FRANKLIN PIERCE STRATTON

Born May 21, 1912 at Celeste, TX. Died September 29, 1982 at Greenville, TX.
Threw right. Batted right. Height 6.05. Weight 180.
Lost leg in hunting accident in November 1938. Coach for Chicago White Sox, 1939-41. Won 18 games in pitching comeback in 1946; pitched complete-game shutout in 1949; and won all four starts for four teams in 1950.

Year	Club	League	G	IP	W	L	H	R	ER	BB	SO	ERA
1934	Galveston	Texas	9	40	1	4	39	26	19	11	12	4.28
	Chicago	American	1	3	0	0	4	2	2	1	0	6.00
	Omaha	Western	23	160	8	10	170	85	-	47	108	
1935	St. Paul	A A	33	226	17	9	261	115	101	63	120	4.02
	Chicago	American	5	38	1	2	40	17	17	9	8	4.03
1936	Chicago	American	16	95	5	7	117	66	55	46	37	5.21
1937	Chicago	American	22	165	15	5	142	55	44	37	69	2.40
1938	Chicago	American	26	186	15	9	186	95	83	56	82	4.02
1942	Lubbock	WTNM	5	9	0	0	19	17	-	-	-	
1946	Sherman	E Texas	27	218	18	8	271	125	101	43	108	4.17
1947	Waco	Big St	15	103	7	7	155	89	75	30	46	6.55
1949	Temple	Big St	1	4	0	1	8	4	-	-	-	0.00
	Vernon	Longhorn	1	9	1	0	-	0	0	-	-	4.50
1950	Green/Sher-Den	Big State	2	18	2	0	25	12	9	1	6	
	CC/Brownsville	RG Val	2	18	2	0	-	7	-	-	-	
1953	Greenville	Big St	1	1	0	1	5	-	-	2	-	
	Sherman-Den	Soon St	1	8	0	1	-	7	-	-	-	
	Majors		70	487	36	23	489	235	201	149	196	3.71
	Minors		120	814	56	41	953	487	305	197	400	4.47

AUSTIN BEN TINCUP

Born December 14, 1890 at Adair, OK. Died July 5, 1980 at Claremore, OK.
Threw right. Batted left. Height 6.01. Weight 180.
Full-blooded Cherokee Indian. Pitched perfect game against Birmingham, June 18, 1917. Batted .271 in 1203 minor league games.

Year	Club	League	G	IP	W	L	H	R	ER	BB	SO	ERA
1912	Muskogee	Okla St	22	162	7	13	157	84	47	47	163*	2.61
	Sherman	Tex-Ok	5	35	2	3	23	6	5	9	27	1.29
1913	Sherman	Tex-Ok	41	247	17	11	202	93	62	45	233*	2.26
1914	Philadelphia	National	28	155	8	10	165	71	45	62	108	2.61
1915	Philadelphia	National	10	31	0	0	26	8	7	9	10	2.03
1916	Philadelphia	National	(One game as pinch hitter; did not pitch)									
1916	Providence	Int	33	222	16	11	225	82	63	90	112	2.55
1917	Little Rock	South A	33	202	11	10	176	77	56	35	90	2.50
1918	Philadelphia	National	8	17	0	1	24	18	14	6	6	7.41

Year Club	League	G	IP	W	L	H	R	ER	BB	SO	ERA
1919 Louisville	A A	24	183	11	8	183	74	58	46	72	2.85
1920 Louisville	A A	34	238	15	12	222	93	75	67	71	2.84
1921 Louisville	A A	26	105	9	0	101	40	33	31	43	2.83
1922 Louisville	A A	46	279	20	14	297	166	130	111	91	4.19
1923 Louisville	A A	43	252	17	16	260	124	113	81	98	4.04
1924 Louisville	A A	49	293	24	17	338	154	129	98	109	3.96
1925 Louisville	A A	37	243	14	15	261	133	110	99	108	4.07
1926 Louisville	A A	34	242	18	7	246	96	83	57	95	3.09
1927 Louisville	A A	38	265	16	15	289	148	126	89	121	4.28
1928 Louisville	A A	38	208	14	10	229	97	79	55	87	3.42
Chicago	National	2	9	0	0	14	7	7	1	3	7.00
1929 Louisville	A A	33	172	7	16	219	133	104	61	70	5.44
1930 Louisville	A A	43	123	14	3	119	50	48	42	66	3.51
1931 Louis/Minn	A A	14	28	1	4	53	33	27	19	9	8.68
1932 Sacramento	P C	28	168	9	12	180	104	81	62	66	4.34
1933-35 (Not in O.B.)											
1936 Paducah	Kitty	11	58	6	0	67	28	19	8	35	2.95
1937 Peoria	III	2	3	1	0	4	0	0	0	2	0.00
1938 Muskogee	West A	7	23	0	0	21	14	11	10	18	4.30
1939 Paducah	Kitty	4	21	2	0	16	1	1	3	13	0.43
1940 (Did not play)											
1941 Paducah	Kitty	2	9	0	1	7	3	3	2	5	3.00
1942 Fargo-Mhd.	Northern	1	3	0	0	6	4	4	1	0	12.00
Majors		**48**	**212**	**8**	**11**	**229**	**104**	**73**	**78**	**127**	**3.10**
Minors		**648**	**3784**	**251**	**198**	**3901**	**1837**	**1467**	**1168**	**1804**	**3.49**

CLAYTON MAFFITT TOUCHSTONE

Born January 24, 1904 at Moore, PA. Died April 28, 1949 at Beaumont, TX.
Threw right. Batted right. Height 5.09. Weight 175.

Year Club	League	G	IP	W	L	H	R	ER	BB	SO	ERA
1925 Waterbury	Eastern	46	217	10	11	209	115	90	95	89	3.73
1926 (Not in O.B.)											
1927 Providence	Eastern	44	270	17	17	280	142	112	128*	99	3.73
1928 Providence	Eastern	31	220	16	13	201	101	80	77	100	3.27
Boston	National	5	8	0	0	15	8	4	2	1	4.50
1929 Boston	National	1	3	0	0	6	5	5	0	1	15.00
Providence	Eastern	40	292*	22	12	290	124	110	90	132*	3.39
1930 Newark	Int	7	20	1	2	22	14	-	4	3	
Birmingham	South A	26	191	15	6	195˙	91	81	48	54	3.82
1931 Birmingham	South A	29	223	15	11	255	126	118	60	68	4.76
1932 Birmingham	South A	36	225	16	15	265	151	139	73	84	5.56
1933 Birmingham	South A	37	283	21*	13	281	119	101	56	90	3.21
1934 Memphis	South A	42	275	16	18	290	122	85	62	102	2.78
1935 Memphis	South A	36	283	22	11	316	144	126	44	79	4.01
1936 Memphis	South A	39	223	12	18	255	139	113	56	81	4.56
1937 Oklahoma City	Texas	43	277	19	11	218	105	78	97	181	2.53
1938 Oklahoma City	Texas	37	242	16	11	184	75	65	57	123	2.42
1939 Dallas	Texas	40	253	20	12	204	93	76	77	163	2.70
1940 Dallas	Texas	34	218	11	14	228	109	89	46	104	3.67
1941 Oklahoma City	Texas	44	241	13	18	238	108	80	58	112	2.99
1942 Oklahoma City	Texas	56	223	10	17	207	103	77	68	102	3.11
1943-44 (Not in O.B.)											
1945 Chicago	American	6	10	0	0	14	10	6	6	4	5.40
Majors		**12**	**21**	**0**	**0**	**35**	**23**	**15**	**8**	**6**	**6.43**
Minors		**667**	**4176**	**272**	**230**	**4138**	**1981**	**1620**	**1196**	**1766**	**3.51**

OSCAR TUERO (MONZON)

Born December 17, 1892 at Havana, Cuba. Died October 21, 1960 at Houston, TX.
Threw right. Batted right. Height 5.08. Weight 158.

Year Club	League	G	IP	W	L	H	R	ER	BB	SO	ERA
1913 Jersey City	Int	4	25	2	0	20	12	-	12	13	
1914 Portland	New Eng	33	-	16	6	-	-	-	-	-	

Year Club	League	G	IP	W	L	H	R	ER	BB	SO	ERA
1915 Lewiston	New Eng	34	-	17	10	-	-	-		87	141
1916 Lynn	Eastern	42*	301	22*	13	-	-	-	43	156*	1.34
1917 Wilkes-Barre	NY St	33	-	24	7	193	54				
1918 Binghamton	Int	8	62	5	2		15	13	15	40	1.89
Little Rock	South A	17	44	6	6	85	-	-	35	50	
St. Louis	National	11	44	1	2	32	12	5	10	13	1.02
1919 St. Louis	National	45*	155	5	7	137	71	55	42	45	3.19
1920 St. Louis	National	2	1	0	0	5	4	4	1	0	36.00
Memphis	South A	18	140	8	8	126	57		39	52	
Kansas City	A A	19	103	2	8	111	72	59	38	41	5.16
1921 Memphis	South A	43	325	27*	8	312	114	97	84	101	2.69
1922 Memphis/Atl	South A	44	237	15	13	257	146	120	83	61	4.56
1923 Atlanta	South A	37	224	8	10	238	106	87	69	48	3.50
1924 Reading	Int	28	150	5	11	196	114	94	64	38	5.64
1925 Birmingham	South A	1	2	0	0	5	7	7	1	0	31.50
Waco	Texas	28	186	11	9	214	107	87	71	43	4.21
1926 Waco	Texas	38	278	10	21*	321*	166	134	97	75	4.34
1927 Waco	Texas	35	203	15	10	215	99	86	59	42	3.81
1928 Waco	Texas	27	191	10	14	224	123	93	61	49	4.38
1929 Shreveport	Texas	35	204	16	5	237	116	95	80	43	4.19
1930 Shreveport	Texas	37	204	17	6	202	93	77	60	52	3.40
1931 Shreveport	Texas	32	193	7	16	227	129	85	68	48	3.96
1932 Shreveport	Texas	4	9	0	2	18	9	9	6	4	9.00
Jackson	SEastern	1	9	1	0	4	1	0	8	1	0.00
1933 (Not in O.B.)											
1934 Tyler	W Dixie	26	173	12	9	255	130	106	58	91	5.51
1935 (Not in O.B.)											
1936 Marshall	E Texas	10	52	3	3	60	30	23	19	6	3.98
1937 Newt-Conover	N Car St	11	72	3	5	62	37	26	16	33	3.25
1938 Longview	E Texas	20	42	4	4	47	36	27	11	29	5.79
Alexandria	Evang	3	25	2	0	23	12	9	5	10	3.24
Shreveport	Texas	1	3	0	0	3	2	2	1	1	6.00
1939 Midland	WTNM	3	10	-	-	-	-	-	-	-	
1941 Shreveport	Texas	4	6	1	1	11	6	3	2	4	4.50
Marshall	Cot St	1	8	0	1	9	3	3	2	4	3.38
Majors		**58**	**200**	**6**	**9**	**174**	**87**	**64**	**53**	**58**	**2.88**
Minors		**677**	**3481**	**269**	**208**	**3729**	**1796**	**1342**	**1194**	**1276**	**4.09**

HARRY PORTER (RUBE) VICKERS

Born May 17, 1878 at Pittsford, MI. Died December 9, 1958 at Belleville, MI.
Threw right. Batted left. Height 6.02. Weight 225.
Pitched 517 innings in 1906, an O.B. record. Pitched for Burlington in Vermont League (outlaw) in 1904-05.

Year Club	League	G	IP	W	L	H	R	ER	BB	SO	ERA
1902 Rock Is./T.H.	III	36	321	19	17	288	154	-	102	168	
Cincinnati	National	3	21	0	3	31	20	14	8	6	6.00
1903 Brooklyn	National	4	14	0	1	27	22	17	9	5	10.93
Holyoke	Conn	34	287	22	10	188	97	-	67	202	
1904 Holyoke	Conn	29	239	17	10	172	71	-	51	171	
1905 Holyoke	Conn	21	171	11	7	138	63	-	53	140	
Seattle	P C	19	162	12	6	121	51	-	31	103	
1906 Seattle	P C	64*	517*	39*	20	395	167	-	139	409*	
1907 Williamsport	Tri-St	37	301	25*	9	228	85	-	63	173	
Philadelphia	American	10	50	2	2	44	26	19	12	21	3.42
1908 Philadelphia	American	53	300	18	19	264	140	78	71	156	2.34
1909 Philadelphia	American	18	56	3	3	60	32	21	19	25	3.38
1910 Baltimore	Eastern	55	364	25	24*	333*	126	-	112	214	
1911 Baltimore	Eastern	57*	369*	32*	14	313	116	-	105	169	
1912 Baltimore	Int	43	215	13	14	244	131	-	101	95	
1913 Baltimore	Int	1	1	0	1	5	4	-	0	0	
1914 Jersey City	Int	5	23	2	2	40	23	-	11	8	
Majors		**88**	**441**	**23**	**28**	**426**	**240**	**149**	**119**	**213**	**3.04**
Minors		**401**	**2970**	**217**	**134**	**2465**	**1088**		**835**	**1852**	

JAMES HUEY WALKUP

Born November 3, 1895 at Havana, AK.
Threw left. Batted right. Height 5.08. Weight 150.
Cousin of James Elton Walkup, pitcher for St. Louis Browns, 1934-39. Was top control pitcher in Texas League six seasons, 1925-26; 1928-30; and 1934.

Year	Club	League	G	IP	W	L	H	R	ER	BB	SO	ERA
1915	Muskogee	West A	26	197	14	9	177	80	57	47	98	2.60
1916	Musk/Tulsa	West A	13	79	4	3	91	42	25	25	34	2.85
	Ennis	Cent Tex	4	-	2	1	-	-	-	-	-	-
1917	Clinton	Cent A	22	177	10	7	-	-	44	-	-	2.24
	Oklahoma City	Western	11	82	4	5	89	44		18	39	
1918-20		(No record available)										
1921	Joplin	Western	2	10	1	0	10	5	-	3	6	
	Okmulgee	West A	31	239	12	16	244	97	-	30	130	
1922	Okmulgee	West A	31	206	11	9	197	89	-	49	98	
1923	Okmulgee	West A	39	266	25*	8	250	86	-	56	174	
1924	Okmulgee	West A	32	242	23	3	214	94	70	37	165	2.60
	Ft. Worth	Texas	6	48	4	1	43	24	19	9	31	3.56
1925	Ft. Worth	Texas	36	196	19	7	193	83	72	57	97	3.31
1926	Ft. Worth	Texas	38	268	22*	11	243	89	71	47	73	2.38*
1927	Newark	Int	4	16	0	1	19	16	16	7	7	9.00
	Detroit	American	2	2	0	0	3	1	1	0	0	4.50
	Ft. Worth	Texas	23	137	11	8	146	62	47	34	30	3.09
1928	Ft. Worth	Texas	31	224	14	12	219	88	69	27	77	2.77
1929	Ft. Worth	Texas	34	273	18	11	294	131	100	35	78	3.30
1930	Ft. W/Beau	Texas	37	226	12	14	249	110	88	45	96	3.50
1931	Birmingham	South A	30	249	20	5	255	95	79	30	49	2.86
1932	Birmingham	South A	32	247	15	15	293	133	114	35	43	4.15
1933	Birmingham	South A	29	173	8	13	221	100	82	27	33	4.27
1934	Tulsa/Galv	Texas	25	162	10	5	204	84	70	22	63	3.89
	Majors		**2**	**2**	**0**	**0**	**3**	**1**	**1**	**0**	**0**	**4.50**
	Minors		534	3717	259	164	3651	1552	1023	640	1421	3.20

JAMES EDWARD ZINN

Born January 31, 1895 at Benton, AK.
Threw right. Batted both. Height 6.00½. Weight 195.
Also pinch hit and played outfield and first (see batting record below). While pitching a victory over Columbus on July 20, 1926, he collected six hits in six trips and batted in six runs.

Year	Club	League	G	IP	W	L	H	R	ER	BB	SO	ERA
1915	Ft. Smith	West A	20	190	12	3	140	47	34	48	119	1.61
1916	Waco	Texas	18	129	11	5	87	-	28	33	74	1.95
1917	Waco	Texas	32	208	14	8	165	82	58	72	85	2.51
1918	Waco	Texas	4	34	2	2	32	17	17	9	21	4.50
1919	Waco	Texas	9	62	1	7	47	24	11	27	19	1.60
	Philadelphia	American	5	26	1	3	38	20	18	10	9	6.23
1920	Wichita Falls	Texas	34	262	18	10	216	94	64	74	138	2.20
	Pittsburgh	National	6	31	1	1	32	14	12	5	18	3.48
1921	Pittsburgh	National	32	127	7	6	159	63	52	30	49	3.69
1922	Pittsburgh	National	5	10	0	0	11	4	2	2	3	1.80
	Kansas City	A A	27	217	18	5	250	120	96	71	82	3.98
1923	Kansas City	A A	43	297	27	6	342	139	130	60	99	3.94
1924	Kansas City	A A	37	255	14	16	296	135	105	70	78	3.71
1925	Kansas City	A A	39	274	16	16	326	173	146	69	122	4.80
1926	Kansas City	A A	35	258	16	13	286	134	108	65	67	3.77
1927	Kansas City	A A	45	330	24	12	250	143	113	55	83	3.08*
1928	Kansas City	A A	45	323*	23	13	334	137	125	84	90	3.48
1929	Cleveland	American	18	105	4	6	150	75	59	33	29	5.06
1930	San Francisco	P C	39	316	26*	12	336	158	143	80	132	4.07
1931	San Francisco	P C	20	146	9	7	167	73	54	31	49	3.33
1932	San Francisco	P C	37	258	18	15	301	148	128	53	95	4.47

Year Club	League	Pos	G	AB	R	H	2B	3B	HR	RBI	SB	BA
1933 San Francisco	P C		42	317	20	19	337	191	145	69	99	4.12
1934 San Francisco	P C		36	320	14	17	328	160	124	64	71	3.49
1935 SF/Sacramento	P C		26	134	7	7	187	96	66	29	42	4.43
1936 (Not in O.B.)												
1937 El Paso	Ariz-Tex		9	41	5	2	40	10	8	2	31	1.76
1938 El Paso	Ariz-Tex		4	12	0	1	20	13	7	4	4	5.25
1939 Sioux City	Western		3	11	0	2	19	11	8	1	1	6.55
Majors			66	299	13	16	390	176	143	80	108	4.30
Minors			604	4394	295	198	4506	2105	1718	1070	1601	3.52

Batting Record

Year Club	League	Pos	G	AB	R	H	2B	3B	HR	RBI	SB	BA
1915 Ft. Smith	West A	P	34	100	7	15	4	1	0	-	0	.150
1916 Waco	Texas	P	19	44	3	11	0	0	0	-	0	.250
1917 Waco	Texas	P	43	91	12	21	4	1	2	-.	2	.231
1918 Waco	Texas	P	4	13	3	4	0	0	1	-	0	.308
1919 Waco	Texas	P	9	25	1	6	1	0	0	1	0	.240
Philadelphia	American	P	10	13	2	4	0	0	1	3	1	.308
1920 Wichita Falls	Texas	P-OF	64	158	23	54	13	5	2	29	1	.342
Pittsburgh	National	P-OF	8	15	2	3	0	1	0	1	0	.200
1921 Pittsburgh	National	P-OF	33	49	6	11	2	0	0	3	1	.224
1922 Pittsburgh	National	P	5	1	0	0	0	0	0	0	0	.000
Kansas City	A A	P	29	86	11	27	7	1	1	12	0	.314
1923 Kansas City	A A	P	52	130	29	46	8	1	3	22	2	.354
1924 Kansas City	A A	P-OF	87	197	22	64	19	2	4	27	2	.325
1925 Kansas City	A A	P-OF	60	122	20	40	8	4	2	20	1	.328
1926 Kansas City	A A	P-OF	54	112	15	41	8	4	1	19	1	.366
1927 Kansas City	A A	P-OF	81	152	28	47	11	5	4	32	1	.309
1928 Kansas City	A A	P-OF	77	151	19	41	6	4	0	20	1	.272
1929 Cleveland	American	P	20	42	7	16	4	1	1	8	0	.381
1930 San Francisco	P C	P-OF	105	193	41	63	11	1	5	36	0	.326
1931 San Francisco	P C	P	42	74	16	24	5	3	2	10	0	.324
1932 San Francisco	P C	P-OF	86	145	21	39	9	1	2	25	2	.269
1933 San Francisco	P C	P-OF	98	178	20	49	10	1	4	22	0	.275
1934 San Francisco	P C	P-OF	77	135	15	40	5	2	1	22	0	.296
1935 SF/Sacramento	P C	P-OF	83	101	10	24	3	1	1	11	0	.238
1936 (Not in O.B.)												
1937 El Paso	Ariz-Tex	P-OF	34	72	11	30	4	0	4	22	0	.417
1938 El Paso	Ariz-Tex	O-1-P	47	116	22	40	8	3	2	29	5	.345
1939 Jacksonville	E Texas	OF	12	30	3	6	1	0	0	0	0	.200
Sioux City	Western	OF-P	24	57	8	15	2	1	3	14	2	.263
Majors			76	120	17	34	6	2	2	15	2	.283
Minors			1221	2482	360	747	147	41	44	373	20	.301

What pitcher holds the season record for shutouts in the minor leagues? That particular record is not fully documented because some leagues did not publish that information in the final averages until after World War II. *The Story of Minor League Baseball,* published in 1952, credits little known hurler Jack Halla with 16 shutouts for Topeka in the Western Association in 1907. However, game-by-game research shows that Halla, who also played first base, pitched only eight shutouts. It is possible that he was in the Topeka lineup during 16 team shutouts, but not always on the mound. It is probable that the minor league season record is shared by three hurlers at 14. We do know that Grover Alexander hurled that number for Syracuse (NY State) in 1910, and Vean Gregg duplicated the total the same year with Portland (P C). In 1909, Stoney McGlynn pitched 14 shutouts for Milwaukee (AA).

A 1907 shutout record which has been documented occurred in September of that year in the Southern Association. Irvin (Kaiser) Wilhelm, no relation to the recent Hall of Fame relief pitcher, hurled six consecutive shutout games for Birmingham in the last two weeks of the season. He would up the season with a flourish, blanking Shreveport in a doubleheader on September 14, the last day. Wilhelm actually pitched 56 consecutive scoreless innings as he started the string with two runless frames in relief on August 31. He won 22 and lost 13 for Birmingham, a fifth-place club, and moved up to the Brooklyn Dodgers in 1908.

At The Crossroads

Minor league games sometimes provide the crossroads for name players of different generations. One such game was the opening contest of the 1931 Dixie Series between Birmingham of the Southern Association and Houston of the Texas League. The opposing hurlers were Ray Caldwell, still a star hurler for the Barons at age 43, and Jerome (Dizzy) Dean, the 20-year-old sensation of the Buffs, who was obviously on his way up. Both were colorful characters, but one had a career likened to a comet flashing across the sky. The other was like a star that flickers but doesn't quite go out.

After one season with Williamsport, Caldwell started with the Yankees in 1910, a year before Dean was born. He had several unusual experiences — being flattened by a lightning bolt while pitching; being inserted as a pinch runner and stealing home; hitting pinch homers in consecutive games; jumping the Yankees and going to Panama; pitching a no-hitter against the New Yorkers after they got rid of him; and winning 20 games for the champion Indians in 1920. By 1921 he appeared washed-up and shortly returned to the minors. He had some big seasons in the American and Southern Associations, one of which was a 19-7 mark in 1931.

Dean had an even better record in 1931, winning 26 games for Houston and being named the league's MVP. He went up to the Cardinals in 1932 and was one of the best hurlers in the game for several seasons. However, he developed arm trouble after an injury in the 1937 All-Star game and by 1940 was sent down to Tulsa. At age 29 his career was essentially at an end. In 1940, Caldwell was still in the minors, managing Fremont in the Ohio State League. He pitched in several games and worked one inning in the league all-star game that season. He was 52.

Oh yes, what happened in the Dixie League opener in 1931? Caldwell bested Dean in a thriller, 1-0.